FOR INFORMATION SPECIALISTS

Interpretations of Reference and Bibliographic Work

INFORMATION MANAGEMENT, POLICY, AND SERVICES
Charles R. McClure and Peter Hernon, Editors

FOR INFORMATION SPECIALISTS

Interpretations of Reference and Bibliographic Work

Howard D. White

College of Information Studies
Drexel University

Marcia J. Bates

Graduate School of Library and Information Science
University of California at Los Angeles

Patrick Wilson

School of Library and Information Studies
University of California at Berkeley

ABLEX PUBLISHING CORPORATION
NORWOOD, NEW JERSEY

Printed in the United States of America

Library of Congress Cataloging-in-Publication Data

For information specialists : interpretations of reference and bibliographic work /
  Howard D. White, Marcia J. Bates, Patrick Wilson.
      p.   cm.
    Includes bibliographical references and index.
    ISBN 0-89391-810-5 (cl). -- ISBN 0-89391-983-7 (ppb)
    1.   Reference services (Libraries)   2.   Information services.
    I.   White, Howard D.   II.   Bates, Marcia J.   III.   Wilson, Patrick,
    1927-
Z711.F64   1992   92-25017
025.5'—dc20   CIP

Ablex Publishing Corporation
355 Chestnut St.
Norwood, NJ 07648

Table of Contents

1

A First Note

Howard D. White

INTRODUCTION

As instigator and editor of a book made up of separate contributions, I feel bound to offer a word of intent. These are interrelated essays on fundamental and permanent concerns of information specialists: the tools of reference work (both printed and electronic), fact-finding, bibliographic writing, and literature searching. The retrieval of writings (in whole or in part) and the creation of bibliographic products are the essence of information work. Since such work is usually done on behalf of others, mediation between writings and customers is also part of our subject, and we are at some pains to describe the distinctive skills of information specialists vis-à-vis those they serve.

The three authors, all experienced teachers, are accustomed to introducing concepts to students, and in a sense these essays can be read as lectures. But they are also free interpretations and critiques that go beyond the introductory. We think they may appeal to persons who already know a good bit about the subject matter but have perhaps not made our connections— that is, to practicing librarians and information specialists. Although many aspects of information work (for example, its management) are not covered, enough of substance is present, we hope, to merit these professionals' attention. We offer, for example, insights into human aspects of the profession that are seldom treated elsewhere.

Reference librarians are our archetypes, but other kinds of information specialists will recognize themselves as well. While there are many books for this audience, none, we think, is quite like this—at once committed to the exposition of mainstream ideas and idiosyncratically personal, with more than a few passages that display old notions in new lights, or that sound notes not heard before. It is more tutorial than most professional reading, but less predictable than a textbook. It is also conceptually rich without being mathematical. Despite its novelties, we think it could serve as a set of readings for aspiring professionals in schools of library and information science, and we particularly recommend it to their teachers as an "idea book." Some parts, we hope, are provocative enough to interest general readers as well.

We have not included annotated lists of reference sources. There are already more than enough of these (for example, Sheehy, 1986, or Walford, 1980–1987), and they date quickly. Our goal instead has been to arrive at a general understanding of the tools, processes, and social contexts of information work. We are interested in why the tools function as they do, the choices typically associated with them, and the ways in which people use (or fail to use) them in seeking answers.

The book's organization is somewhat looser than what a single author might achieve, since it conjoins writings produced at different times and with different motives. The reader may notice certain variations in style—for example, in preference for "I" or "we" as the author's viewpoint, or in propensity to cite (Bates and I cite other writings; Wilson, whose texts are closer to talks, does not). Despite the inconsistencies and an implicit debate or two, I think the book achieves coherence. While the organization is not linear, there is a great deal of theme-passing from author to author. The essays, sequenced with some care, echo and amplify each other in numerous ways.

The reasons for coherence are biographical as well as editorial. One of the authors, Patrick Wilson, taught the other two at the University of California, Berkeley, in the late 1960s and early 1970s, and he and his writings have influenced our ideas, as will be seen. That influence appears as well in our preference for presenting technical matter in a conversational style. The readable exposition of complex thought is Wilson's hallmark, and it has been Bates's and my intention to follow his example here.

Bates's essays may be known to some readers through their previous appearances in journals. They have been extensively rewritten for this volume, which also sets them in a fresh context. The other contributions are either new or not likely to have been seen by most readers.

Since the three of us wrote in a time of swift advances in computing and telecommunications, our continuing emphasis on specimens of print may seem misguided. We would reply that, far from being on its way out, print is still a very successful technology—one with over 500 years of inertia to carry it into the 21st century. While in many cases we would *welcome* computerization of reference and bibliographic capabilities, print remains an effective and efficient storage medium, and, as non-utopians, we do not expect it soon to disappear. On the other hand, it would be merely inane to pretend that information work has not been transformed by computerization and telecommunication of large textual stores—broadly, by database technology. Throughout the book, readers will see us striving to accommodate both the older and the newer realities. Thus, for example, Wilson's "Searching: Strategies and Evaluation," Bates's "Search and Idea Tactics," and my own "Reference Books, Databases, and the Reportoire" apply to *both* printed and computerized sources. We hope that our attempts at unification result in new clarities, rather than a blur.

PREVIEW

Insofar as printed or computerized sources yield relatively quick answers to routine sorts of questions, they may be said to work rather like human memory—they are, in McLuhan's (1964) sense, extensions of it—except that, being non-human, they can produce answers only through artifice, notably indexing. In a way they can be seen as low-grade robots, programmed to mimic a few of the question-answering responses of which their creators are capable. A non-fiction book with an index, for example, is not merely an account by an author, it is a device prepared by an indexer to respond with one or more answers to questions readers presumably will put to it. (Since the book in no way understands the questions, what is evoked may, of course, be simply passages rather than answers.) The indexer's art is to create the responses this non-androidal "robot" can make. Superior present-day "robots" replace human scanning ability (which printed tools require) with the computer's ability to scan vast amounts of indexing at high speeds and with complex criteria for what constitutes a hit. But again, since human understanding has not been externalized (only human scanning ability), they, too, may produce not answers but simply passages.

Whether printed or computerized, these answering devices are numerous, and their interrelationships are complex. Taken together, they constitute an important segment of what we may call *external memory*. However, external memory works only if it is heavily complemented, in the overall system, with human memory and intelligence. (The externalization of the latter in machines—the goal of the field called artificial intelligence—lags considerably behind the externalization of memory.) Information specialists, we take it, are expert users of external memory: they are better at interrogating it, in all its obtuseness, than most. They may not, of course, interrogate a particular source better than anyone else, but they know more of the population and more about how one source can lead them to another.

The first section of the book comprises two essays on the nature of these answering devices, better known as bibliographic and factual reference works. There is, as well, a good deal on what might be called the interface between them and their users, since reference works are all exercises in applied human psychology. Bates's "What Is a Reference Book?" identifies printed reference sources with the ordered *field–record–file* structure used in describing databases and relates this to a particular function, minimization of human scanning. My "Reference Books, Databases, and the Repertoire" builds directly on the Bates essay to develop a general account of how printed and machine-readable sources and their human interlocutors combine in an overall retrieval system. Toward the end are notes on the mindset and aptitudes that define information specialists as a type.

The second section attempts to enliven the study of bibliography, which is the object of information specialists' most reliable expertise and the *rohstoff* of library and information science. It starts with my description of the publication process and the different kinds of bibliographic statements made in its support. (Information specialists, among others, both produce and use these statements.) I conclude by describing a status system to which the different kinds of statements give rise. Bates then defines the specifications by which systematic bibliographies are produced and explains why they should be made explicit. In the section's last piece, I compare the more complex kinds of bibliographic writing to arrive at reasons for preferring a review of a literature or even an annotated bibliography to the so-called bibliographic essay.

The third section enlarges on a fundamental matter in the other two: the search through large-scale bibliographies for publications. Wilson introduces various broad strategies that might be adopted, focusing at last on the search by subject—the most problematical kind. He lucidly explains how indexing affects searching and how a successful outcome is judged. Next, Bates codifies a variety of search tactics, several of them discussed by Wilson, under short, memorable names, including names for means of fostering creativity ("idea tactics"). In effect, she provides information specialists with a new vocabulary for conceptualizing their tasks. These tactics are then specifically illustrated in her essay on online searching, which also elaborates on themes from Wilson, such as search evaluation, ending a search, and the effects of various kinds of subject indexing. Finally, in "Pragmatic Bibliography," Wilson shows how persons with different goals search to different depths, and draws inferences for information specialists in the bibliographic instruction movement (which is also touched on in section two).

All of these essays describe interplays between human beings and the enormous stocks of imperfectly retrievable records outside their heads—which is to invoke, once again, the systems of external memory. The last piece offers my notion of external memory as a unifying concept, both for the book and for the field of professional information work—particularly the disciplines, now called "information studies" by some, that constitute its academic base. Readers will here find answers to such questions as: what is the difference between information systems (as a field) and library and information science? Between library science and information science? Between library science and librarianship? Where does archival science fit in? What do they all have in common? What is their relation to mass communications and to cognitive psychology? How do they all differ from computer science, artificial intelligence, and other fields? Such questions often arise, particularly among students and outsiders, but it is hard to find good answers in the literature. I attempt here to give accounts the reader can actually use. Interwoven are statements about the distinctive skills of information specialists and the problems they face in helping customers deal with the chief burden of external memory, information overload.

There is a remark on information overload by W. H. Auden, as quoted in Charles Osborne's (1979) biography: "The annual tonnage of publications is terrifying if I think about it, but I don't have to think about it. That is one of the wonderful things about the written word: it cannot speak until it is spoken to" (p. 330). The present book is about (a) the annual tonnage of publications, (b) those who do not have to think about it, and (c) those who do. Among the latter are information specialists, who, by various devices, allow the written word to be spoken to, and speak on its behalf.

ACKNOWLEDGMENTS

The authors gratefully acknowledge permission to use materials that appeared in other forms in the *Drexel Library Quarterly, Journal of the American Society for Information Science, Online, RQ,* and the papers of the Bibliographic Instruction Section, Association of College and Research Libraries, American Library Association.

The editor wishes to thank his wife, Maryellen McDonald, for her generosity and skill in preparing the manuscript for publication.

Section I

Reference Work

2

What Is a Reference Book*

Marcia J. Bates

INTRODUCTION

The answer to the question in the title would seem obvious. We all know what a reference book is, do we not? Here I will argue that the standard definitions in our field are useful in some respects and quite inadequate in others, particularly as a basis for research or analytical thinking on topics relating to reference books in reference service. When we use the term, we are relying much more on our intuitive sense of what a reference book is than on the limited definitions to be found in print.

After reviewing some existing definitions of the term, I will propose a new one to improve our understanding of this core concept. The new definition will be based on structural contrasts between reference books and "regular" books, thus illuminating forms of information organization common to both types. Much work has been done in computer science and in library and information science to develop models of databases using the terminology *file, record,* and *field.* Manual information sources share many of the characteristics of computer databases, but generally have not been viewed in relation to them. The use of such terminology in the analysis of manual sources should contribute to a broader understanding of information organization, and to a future in which all databases, both manual and automated, are viewed within a common context.

---

* This chapter first appeared, in another form, as Bates (1986), © American Library Association, used by permission.

After the new definition is developed, I present some empirical data relating to it. Reference and stack collections in three different libraries were randomly sampled to see whether the definition was borne out by the character and placement of materials in them, and whether unanticipated cases arose. The study identified an interesting range of materials appearing in both reference and stack collections. While it produced a few exceptions, in general it strongly supported the position taken here.

CURRENT DEFINITIONS

Standard definitions of "reference book" are provided by the *ALA Glossary* (H. Young, 1983, p. 188):

> 1. A book designed by the arrangement and treatment of its subject matter to be consulted for definite items of information rather than to be read consecutively.

> 2. A book whose use is restricted to the library building.

The British *Librarians' Glossary* (Prytherch, 1984, p. 647) contains a very similar pair. These pairs in fact are used throughout the field, appearing in source after source. The first is what Stiffler (1972) calls a "functional" definition. The second is what he calls an "administrative" definition. The latter has obvious practical uses in the administration of a library. Books may be put into the reference section that are not really reference books in any intuitive sense—for example, a book may be put there to prevent it from being stolen or defaced. But at bottom the administrative definition says that *a reference book is what we call a reference book*— not very illuminating when one is trying to identify the distinctive character of this type of material.

The functional definition is helpful as far as it goes. It is useful to know that a reference book is one that is consulted and not read through, as opposed to, say, a binder of letters of reference that a domestic servant takes around to show prospective employers. But a functional definition does not identify the essential features of a reference book; it does not tell us what it is about reference books that leads us to *want* to use them for reference. Is our inclination merely arbitrary?

Stiffler identifies a third type of definition, the "descriptive," which defines the reference book "by virtue of the intrinsic characteristics of the book itself." This is lacking in the widely-used definitions. The first, from the *ALA Glossary* (1983), hints at a descriptive definition when it says "designed by their arrangement and treatment..." but we are not told what the distinctive arrangement and treatment is. The corresponding British definition in the *Librarians' Glossary* enumerates some classes of books that are well suited for reference—"dictionaries, encyclopedias, gazetteers, yearbooks, directories, concordances, indexes, bibliographies and atlases"—but it, too, fails to say what it is about these types that makes them suitable.

The lack of a descriptive definition is puzzling when we come to think of it. If the definitions state only how a reference book is supposed to be used, then how is one to identify one in the first place? The introductions to some books convey that they are to be used for reference, but many comparable books have no introductions at all. Certain classes of books, such as those mentioned by the *Librarians' Glossary,* are associated with reference use, but not all books used for reference have one of those names.

Some writers have concluded that it is impossible to provide a descriptive definition. Davinson (1980, p. 12) states:

> To say there are a class of books and other materials which can unequivocally be recognized, fundamentally and distinctively, as reference material is misleading. To library users reference material is likely to be anything which is useful to them in finding the solution to any information problems they have.

Similarly, in his introductory text, Katz (1978, p. 14) says, "A reference source is any source, regardless of form or location, which provides the necessary answer or answers." Rugh (1975) says that reference books serve the convenience of the user; convenience is relative; therefore the reference book must be defined in relative rather than absolute terms.

Such arguments are valuable in that they remind us that information may be gotten from any of the resources in the library (and many outside it). Since instruction in library schools so strongly emphasizes what are conventionally called reference books, it is easy to forget the other resources. But in making this point, it is not necessary, I believe, to make the further claim that reference books exhibit nothing distinctive.

The International Organization for Standardization (1983, p. 9) tells us that a reference work is a "document providing rapid access to information or sources of information on a given subject." But this still does not enable one to *identify* one: how rapid is rapid enough for a book to qualify?

Of all the writers reviewed, Ranganathan (1961, p. 257) comes closest to a true descriptive definition. First he describes an "ordinary book":

> It is made of continuous exposition. Sentences mount into a paragraph. Paragraphs mount into a chapter. Chapters get woven into a single swelling exposition, in the continuous pursuit of a single idea, simple or complex.

A reference book is not like this. Rather:

> It is characterized internally by an ensemble of disjointed entries of short, though varying lengths. The sequence of the entries is not determined strictly

by intimate thought-sequence. It is determined by the scheme of arrangement chosen. It is often alphabetical in the main. It is occasionally systematic [i.e., *classified*]. Even then, the connection between consecutive entries is not as compelling and continuous or as free from jerks as between the paragraphs of an ordinary book.

So at last we have some articulation of what distinguishes ordinary books from reference books. Ordinary books contain a continuous, developing exposition, while reference books have disjointed entries; movement from one entry to the next is in "jerks." This definition is indeed descriptive, in Stiffler's (1972) terms. But it is also vague and hard to operationalize. How could one determine whether the text was more or less free from "jerks"? In the succeeding sections, I will develop a fully descriptive definition— unambiguous, easy to operationalize—that can be added to the administrative and functional definitions used now.

ANTICIPATING CRITICS

Before getting into the discussion proper, I should say that I have shown preliminary versions of this essay to at least a dozen people in the field, both practitioners and library school faculty. A reaction has run through their responses that is so paradoxical as to require comment. The same respondent in the same conversation will say, on the one hand, that the ideas are obvious ("I knew that all along") and, on the other, that they are flat wrong. One individual cycled through these alternate positions three times in one conversation!

Although I do not know the full reasons behind this response, I have some suggestions that may help the reader better analyze his or her own. The ideas may seem obvious because they use familiar terms—"files," "records," and the like. There is a traditional bias against the term "file" in librarianship because of its association with lower-level positions in libraries such as "file clerk." For librarians and information specialists to discuss files is seen in some quarters as lowering our professional standing. A moment's reflection, however, reminds us that computer scientists use the term all the time without reducing their professional standing. Questions of file organization and database design, as discussed here, need to be approached at quite a sophisticated level—well beyond the expertise of a file clerk. To analyze books in terms of their file structure is *to add another level* to the conceptual analysis of information resources and their retrieval—not to substitute for the existing levels of analysis, such as subject content or quality and reliability of information. Adapting these terms to the description of manual sources in a reasonably parsimonious way is not at all obvious; it takes considerable thought.

Secondly, the ideas may seem obvious because we have an *intuitive* awareness of the structural and organizational characteristics of reference books, even though we do not discuss them in analyses of reference work and searching techniques. We know it but we do not. Here, too, the process of bringing subliminal awareness to conscious analysis is not as straightforward as my results may make it appear.

As to why the analysis is "wrong," a common reaction goes something like this: "When I buy books I select them on the basis of all sorts of criteria. It is ridiculous to say I select a reference book on the basis of its file structure." True, we seldom *select* a book on the basis of its file structure. We bring many criteria to bear on our selection of both reference and stack materials. But what makes us *assign* a book to the reference collection—whether at the time of selection or later—is, I will argue, primarily file structure. Something in its intellectual organization makes it good for reference look-ups as opposed to consecutive reading.

NEEDED TERMINOLOGY

Let us now see if we can find out what that something is. Some common terms must first be defined in ways suitable for our needs:

> *Manual File:* A set of two or more records ordered by a rule or principle, and existing in printed form (i.e., not machine-readable).
> *Record:* A unitary or internally related body of information; an "information individual."
> *Field:* A unit of information within a record.

The definition on which the others logically depend is that of "record." A *record* is any body of information which its creators or organizers wish to treat *as a unit.* The information in a record is descriptive of some other object and gains its unity because all items of information in it describe that object. For example, an entry in a catalog is a record, and its unity consists in the fact that all the information relates in some way to a single book. Alternatively, the information in a record may itself have an internally related, unitary character. James Herriot's book *All Creatures Great and Small* has unity as a body of discourse, and so we find it convenient to treat this body as an "information individual."

Fields are distinguishable segments of information within a record. *All Creatures Great and Small* may be considered to have several fields—the usual bibliographic elements, appearing mostly on the title page, and one very large field, the body of discourse that constitutes the actual text of Herriot's work. Librarians typically label certain items of information in a book as distinct fields, with names like author, title, etc., because they have important uses for each of those elements in catalogs and bibliographies. Other people, with different uses for a book, might divide and label the segments of information in different ways.

A *manual file* is a set of two or more records that have been arranged according to some "ordering principle." Common principles are alphabetical, numerical, and classified (such as arrangement according to the biological classification scheme). Even a random collection of records has *some* order, but chances are there is no rule by which their sequence could be described. I will not use here the very general definition of "file"—as simply any collection of data—that is often employed in the computer science literature. Manual files are characteristically *ordered,* and for good reason, as we shall see.

Even when the arrangement of a file can be described by a rule, that ordering principle must be one that is readily recognizable within the user's cultural context. The sounds of the Thai alphabet, for example, are arranged in a completely different order from that found in Western languages. Though it may be said that tens of millions of Thais would recognize an alphabetizing scheme that begins with the sound "K" (the first letter of their alphabet), such a scheme would not be readily recognizable for Western users. Similar arguments can be made about intellectual cultures. Biologists may immediately recognize files arranged by biological classification, and know where to look for a certain taxon. For the lay person, however, such a scheme would be as mysterious as one arranged by the Thai alphabet.

There must be at least two records to constitute a manual file (hereafter "file," for short). Ordering, or sorting, implies a relationship, and there must be at least two things to be related. By this definition, a set with only one record, or a set of unordered records, is not a file.

The field by which a record is ordered in a file is the *access field.* (There may be more than one.) The phrase "Alphabetical by author's name," for example, contains both the ordering principle and the access field. One finds a record in a manual file by searching on the access field(s) according to the ordering principle. If one lacks a search term of the same kind as those in the access field, the record is virtually unretrievable. For example, in the typical manual catalog, one has almost instant access to information on a book if one has the author's name and the title, but knowing only the publisher is worthless—even though the records contain this field—because the entries are not arranged by publisher.

The most efficient searching in manual files is done when the information in the access field can be searched directly rather than indirectly, through an index. For example, if we know an author's name, it is possible to go to a file arranged by author and search directly. In contrast, when we know an author's name but the entries are arranged by abstract number, we must first consult an author index file to find this arbitrary number; only then can we proceed to the entry.

FILES AND REFERENCE BOOKS

We can apply these concepts to reference books as soon as we are clear on usage. In librarianship, "reference books" has two senses. In the narrower, it means works that contain the information sought, in contrast to bibliographic sources, which contain only citations to other works—books, articles, reports, etc.—presumably containing the information. However, the term is also used to cover both reference books in the narrow sense and bibliographic sources. The "reference department" in a library, for instance, provides both types. Here, unless noted, the term will be used in this broader sense.

Does that mean that a card catalog is a reference book? It is certainly a bibliographic source and a manual file, and it certainly serves a reference function. Only its format prevents calling it a "book." But if, as sometimes happens, it is printed out in book form—for example, so that it may be sold to other libraries—it indeed becomes one. What about an auto parts dealer's catalog? It may be that no library in the world holds that particular document. Is it a reference book? Yes; items do not have to be held by libraries to qualify.

With this background, we pass to the main point: reference books, of whatever kind, tend to be full of files. Consider a famous bibliographic source, the *Readers' Guide to Periodical Literature*. It has five sections: "Abbreviations of Periodicals Indexed," "Periodicals Indexed," "Abbreviations," the main body of listings, and "Book Reviews." Each of these is a file of records arranged by some ordering principle. For example, records in the periodical abbreviations file have two fields, the abbreviated title and the full title of each periodical, alphabetized by the former. Records in the main file are citations entered under author and subject; authors and subjects are interfiled in alphabetical order. And so on. *Readers' Guide* as a whole can be considered a manual database, with its five files serving the common purpose of providing access to articles and other writings in the general periodical literature.

When there are many citations under a given author or subject, the editors of *Readers' Guide* have, for brevity's sake, avoided repetition of the author or subject name at the beginning of each citation. For example, "Video games," the access term for, say, 20 citations in a given volume, appears only once at the beginning of the list. But it is the *implicit* access term for each of the 20 items. So it is each individual citation that is an independent record, not the term "Video games" plus the 20.

Reflection will suggest that this kind of file organization is found throughout bibliographic sources. Bibliographies, periodical indexes, abstracting and indexing services, and catalogs invariably contain records arranged by some access field (or fields) into files. A variety of access fields are used—author, title, subject, publication date, classification categories—but they are ordered by *some* principle. For most conceivable purposes, randomly arranged sets of citations in manual sources would be worthless.

NON-BIBLIOGRAPHIC SOURCES

What of non-bibliographic reference books? Dictionaries, biographical indexes, directories, gazetteers, encyclopedias, atlases, handbooks, and almanacs can also be seen as organized into files. The entries may be highly structured, with specified fields consistently in the same order (as in most dictionaries, directories, and gazetteers); or they may be more flexible and variable (as in handbooks and encyclopedias).

Each word in a dictionary, each person or organization in a directory, and each place or geographic feature in a gazetteer constitutes the access field for the records in these sources, and the basis for arrangement. The information provided *about* each word, person, and so on, constitutes the remainder of the record, which may be more or less highly structured into further fields.

Some notes on complexities in other types of reference books follow.

Encyclopedias. In most, the main file consists of entries arranged alphabetically by subject. After the access field , which is usually in boldface, the other important field of the entry, the text, may be quite variable in length and format.

Atlases. An index to location may be an important subsidiary file, while in the main file the maps are records arranged alphabetically, geographically, or (in a historical atlas) chronologically. The title of the map is the access field; a second field is the map as drawn. Thus it can be seen that, while information in files is generally linguistic, it need not be: drawings, diagrams, photographs, etc., can also be fields in records.

Handbooks and almanacs. These consist of a great many files (which may be harder to visualize than the examples above). A table such as handbooks contain can be viewed as a two-way or two-dimensional file. Consider a table which lists the names of countries down the left side, and decade years (1900, 1910, etc.) across the top. The information in each cell (where year and country intersect) consists of that country's population that year. The same information could be presented in one dimension. If this were done, under "1900" the file would list all the country names, followed by their populations that year; "1910" would be followed by all the countries and their populations a decade later; and so on, through all the years. Such a file would be arranged chronologically by date and subarranged alphabetically by country. This arrangement, while clear, would be very lengthy and wasteful of space, since the set of countries would be listed repeatedly. Instead, the table lists the data for each decade in parallel. The country names need not be repeated, which saves space, but the populations are still easily found.

Two-dimensional files, or tables, are even more quickly accessed than those with one dimension. Works like the *World Almanac and Book of Facts* contain a very large number of these tabular files. Small and compact, they have internal order but need not be arranged relative to each other (except by page number). That is because the user gains access to them through yet another file in the almanac or handbook, the alphabetical subject index.

To sum up thus far, reference books vary on an enormous range of characteristics. Their blooming, buzzing variety is one of the things, I believe, that has heretofore stopped efforts to define them descriptively. But a first cut on a descriptive definition is now possible: *Reference books are books substantially or entirely composed of files.* File structure explains the "jerks" Ranganathan (1961) referred to; movement from one record to another produces the jerks that distinguish files from the continuous flow of normal printed discourse. In succeeding sections the definition will be refined and potential exceptions considered.

STRUCTURE RELATED TO FUNCTION

If reference books have a characteristic file structure and are to be used for look-up, while "regular" books contain running discourse and are to be read through, then probably there is a causal connection: the two structures lend themselves to these two functions, and if we understand the structures better, we can see why the functions so often follow.

The searcher can use a book for look-up when it is possible to find a desired datum or segment of information without having to search through the whole text linearly (from the beginning to the point of encounter) or, in desperation, randomly. With look-up there is a leap from the whole body of information to the specific information desired, or at least to a significantly smaller segment of the information than the whole body. The leap from the whole to the part is the crucial idea.

What makes the leap possible? For manual sources, the answer is file structure. By glancing at a small portion of the file, the searcher discerns the ordering principle and access field. The searcher then selects a specific value of the access field. If, for example, the access field is "country," the searcher mentally summons a specific country name. Then, using the ordering principle, the searcher homes in on the desired entry, needing only a glance at the occasional record along the way to determine location in the file. Since the records in the file are in certain positions relative to each other, it is no longer necessary to examine every record to find the desired one.

A question may be raised here: *must* function follow structure? Ranganathan (1961) has commented that some people like to read dictionaries and encyclopedias rather than use them strictly for look-up. On the other hand, every reference librarian can remember occasions when he or she has had to look for an answer in a book with no contents list or files of any kind. Do structure and function not go together then?

It is possible to read through, rather than refer to, the information in files, but this use of information sources is exceptional and idiosyncratic—rare enough that we comment on it when it occurs. And it is possible to search for definite items of information in a body of discourse not organized for that purpose, but those who have tried it would not recommend it. To put the matter differently, we can use a potato masher as a hammer, and a hammer as a potato masher, but we still know which we would prefer to use for what. Let us return to how book structure relates to function *as a rule*.

One category, already implied, is that of books containing *only* discourse. These books contain no files whatever—no ordered records. Such books are often fiction or popular non-fiction.

A second, opposite category is books composed entirely of files. All would be considered reference books.

A third category is that of books which are mostly running discourse but which also contain files, such as a contents list, a back-of-the-book index, or both. Here, structure and function are more complicated. A back-of-the-book index file provides look-up access into the main text through page number access. While the main text itself does not consist of ordered records, the index nonetheless makes it possible to leap to a segment of text in true look-up fashion. This is made possible by designating artificial "records" that are numbered pages.

A contents list, while superficially similar, speeds access in a way that is fundamentally different from that of a back-of-the-book index. A contents list reproduces the order of discourse found in the main text of the book. That order is unique and idiosyncratic to the author's own sequence of thought, and therefore does not generally follow a recognizable ordering principle. Thus the searcher does not have look-up access within a contents list; there is no way to leap from the whole directly to a desired term or number according to an ordering principle, the way one can with a back-of-the-book index. Instead, it is necessary to scan the list from the beginning to find the promising segment of text and its associated page number.

Figure 2.1.   Search Patterns in Common Book Structures

Book Structure	Search Pattern
1. Discourse only	Lengthy scan only
2. Contents list plus discourse	Scan—look-up—moderate scan
3. Discourse plus back-of-the-book index	Look-up—look-up—moderately brief scan
4. File(s) only	One or several look-ups, or look-up—brief scan

For example, a textbook on library cataloging may devote a section to problems of *retrospective conversion.* The searcher can look up that term directly in an alphabetical back-of-the-book index but would have to scan the contents list from the beginning to find the same section listed there. The contents list speeds access only because it is much shorter than the full text itself, containing only the latter's headings.

We now have a strong sense of what distinguishes reference books from the "ordinary" kind: the different methods of access are summarized in Figure 2.1.

Books in its first category contain discourse only; the user can find information only by scanning, browsing, or reading. One must scan them from front to back to find a specific piece of information, or randomly riffle through pages in hopes of finding a promising passage. (Once a book has been read, a person may use remembered context to locate something quickly; but "ready reference" should not require prior reading of a source.)

Books in the second category are mostly discourse but also have a table of contents. The searcher must scan the table of contents to find the desired section, and then do a look-up by means of the page number. Since sections listed in the contents are often large, the searcher may have to scan through several (or many) pages of text to find the specific information desired. The search pattern here is *scan* (table of contents), *look up* (from table to text), *scan* (text).

In the third category—books with indexes—the pattern is *look up* (of the desired term), *look up* (from index to text), and then *scan* (of the designated page or pages). Since entries in indexes are often more specific than entries in contents lists, the searcher will probably not have to scan as many pages as otherwise, but the access is still not as fast as direct look-up.

The final case involves books containing a single large file, or several files, and no discourse at all except that which is contained within fields of records. Where the information in the fields is relatively brief, the desired information may be found with little or no scanning, in contrast to the multi-page scanning required with the other structures above. The searcher may do a single look-up, as in a dictionary, or several quick look-ups, as when moving among several files in a complex bibliographical source like *Granger's Index to Poetry* or *Biological Abstracts*. If one of the fields contains large amounts of discourse, as in encyclopedias and manuals, some brief scanning or reading will be necessary.

Scanning almost always takes longer than look-ups, so this sequence of book structures can be seen to go from least to most efficient for reference purposes. The differences are even greater than the *scan/look-up* contrast implies, however, because the characteristic amount of scanning decreases enormously as we move from the first category to the last.

We can now, incidentally, begin to operationalize the ISO definition above, which gave "rapid access" as the distinctive characteristic of reference books. Such books are designed so as to permit relatively more look-up than scan access.

This brings us to a dividing line between reference and non-reference books. Files-only books clearly serve the look-up function best and are definitely reference books. Discourse-only books serve the read-through function best and are definitely not reference books. Books containing discourse plus contents lists and/or indexes serve both functions. Most of the text of this latter kind of books is devoted to discourse, and the lists and indexes combined usually add up to less than 10% of each book's length. These are the books that Davinson (1980), Katz (1978), and others allude to when they say that the whole library can serve as the reference collection. However, given the efficiency of files-only books for reference purposes, it makes sense not to overcrowd them by interfiling them with the much larger number of less efficient "mixed" books, which are usually put in the stacks.

PROBLEM CASES

Some problem cases in book structure may occur to critical readers. Here are examples, with commentary.

Books with tables. How shall we view books of discourse that have occasional tables scattered through them? Since the tables are a type of file, are books containing them reference books? No, because the tables are embedded in text, and are not easily found in look-up mode. Books mainly of running text may provide contents lists of tables, but these lists have the same idiosyncratic order of presentation as the author's discourse. The books thus fit into the middle categories of Figure 2.1 (discourse plus contents list or index).

But suppose there are *many* tables and not much discourse? If a book contains whole chapters of files or tables, for example, then segments this large may be substantial enough to stand alone and serve as "mini-reference" sources. In an empirical study of book structure (reported below) I considered this possibility: the pages of such segments were treated as files and counted as such. However, these middle cases were less of a worry than might be expected—they are actually quite rare.

Numbered pages and chapters. A book, such as a novel, usually has its text segmented into numbered pages. The numbers constitute a field arranged by a readily recognized ordering principle. Are the pages therefore records, and the novel therefore a file? Similarly, suppose the book is divided into chapters numerically arranged. Are the chapters records, the records a file, and the book a reference book?

There is a simple and direct argument again viewing these two cases as files. In both, the pieces of text identified by the numbers are not records in any but the *physical* sense, because the segments are not "information individuals." An operational test of information individuals is that they can be arranged in different orders with respect to each other without harming their meaning or use; they are "stand-alone." For example, records in a typical bibliography could be ordered by several different ordering principles and still be of value, no matter where they appeared with respect to other records in the file. On the other hand, reordering the pages or chapters of a book would produce a jumble. Therefore, pages or chapters are only *segments of discourse,* not records, and the novel (or whatever) is not a file or a reference book.

Collections. A collection of poems or short stories contains information individuals rather than segments of text. Are all such collections therefore files? Not unless the file contains *ordered* information individuals (or records), and the principle of arrangement is readily recognizable. The poems in a book of British poetry arranged alphabetically by poet *do* constitute a file; those in a collection arranged "thematically" or by the poet's or anthologist's idiosyncratic choice do not. If we wanted to find a popular poem by Pope, we could use the former in look-up mode. The latter we could not, and it is not a reference book.

The distinctions made in this section leave open what to do about books that fall between being files-only and discourse-mostly. Intuitively, a book that is mostly discourse but has noticeably more than 10% of its pages in files begins to feel like a reference book. Reference books were earlier defined as consisting substantially or entirely of files. How much is "substantially"? Can we provide a more precise descriptive definition of "reference book" and still preserve the claims made above that relate functions to structure? The empirical data reported in the next section will provide clues and solutions. We will return to these questions after the empirical study is described.

EMPIRICAL DATA FROM THREE LIBRARIES

Are there exceptions? Books with non-file structure that we still call reference books? Alternatively, are books with file structure stored in stack

Figure 2.2.   Library and Samples

Library	Samples	
	Ref. books	Stack books
University Research Library, UCLA (ca. 2.2 million vols.)	92	99
Los Angeles regional public library branch (ca. 50,000 vols.)	53	49
Special library in major aeronautics firm (ca. 60,000 vols.)	25	25
TOTALS	170	173
		Grand TOTAL: 343

collections, too? A sample of books in reference departments does not provide a perfect answer because, as noted earlier, books may be put in reference departments for reasons other than anticipated use in look-ups. A librarian, when asked, would admit that the book was "reference" only in an administrative sense—e.g., to protect it from theft. Similarly, some books are stored in the stacks because they are earlier issues of a reference book whose current copy is kept in the reference department. So a sample drawn from libraries cannot be expected to exhibit only "pure types" from reference and stack collections.

Nevertheless, if my thesis is correct, most of the types should exhibit the structures discussed here. Furthermore, a sample allows us to see what types of books actually appear in representative libraries, and possibly to uncover for analysis some types I did not anticipate.

Sample. I wanted to examine reference and stack books from several environments, and so selected a large academic research library, a medium-sized branch public library, and a medium-large industrial special library in a major aeronautics firm. Systematic samples were drawn from the reference and stack collections at each library, as shown in Figure 2.2. The books were examined, bibliographic data recorded, and number of pages in files, lists, and running text were counted for each item. I expected a university library to have more types of books from various cultures and periods in history, and so drew a larger sample there to expose the variety. Altogether, 343 books were analyzed.

The main variable measured in each book was *the percentage of total pages devoted to files and lists.* The lists were almost all lists of contents or tables of illustrations. They were rarely longer than two pages, and constituted a minor factor in the calculated totals. When "files" are mentioned below, these lists are included.

Percent of book
in files/lists

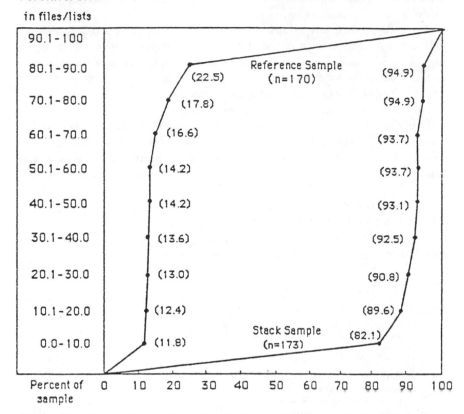

Figure 2.3   Percentage of Each Book Devoted to Files or Lists (Cumulative Distributions)

Results. Overall, 78% of the books in the reference sample contained *at least 90%* files. On the other hand, 82% of the books in the stack sample had *at most 10%* of their pages in files. Figure 2.3 illustrates this result vividly. The contrasting cumulative distributions show how different in structure the materials from the two parts of the libraries are. *Librarians, it appears, assign books to the reference or stack collections on the basis of book structure or a highly correlated factor.*

Some 82% of the reference items had *more than 80%* of their pages in files, while 90% of the stack items had *below 20%*—huge majorities. The single figure that provided the best discrimination between reference and stack books, leaving the fewest books in the "opposite" category, was *60% of pages in files:* 86% of the reference sample were above it, and 94% of the stack sample were below it. The 60% figure, although somewhat arbitrary, is used below as a discriminator.

Exceptions. Very few books of "mixed structure" occurred. These are defined as having *between 20% and 80%* of their pages in files. Of the entire sample of 343, only 18 fell in this intermediate range. Most of these seemed properly assigned: six books above 60% were from reference collections, and seven below 60% were from the stacks. Only five "mixed structure" books remained to be analyzed as genuine exceptions.

Other exceptions were 21 books of discourse (0% to 20% files) found in reference collections, and nine reference books (80%–100% files) found in stack collections. Thus a total of 35 books, only about one in 10 of the whole sample, were problematical. My analysis of the exceptions is shown in Figure 2.4.

The reference sample *did* produce an important exception to the rule that reference books are books with file structure. These are "canonical texts"— that is, texts considered authoritative in some way within the culture. There were 14 of them, subdivided by subject as in Figure 2.4.

Figure 2.4.   Exceptions Analysis

Reference Collection Exceptions
(books with less than 60% of pages in files or
lists housed in reference collections)

A. Canonical texts (14 total)

1. Treatises	5
2. Laws, regulations	5
3. Standards, specifications	2
4. Authoritative texts (literary, religious, etc.)	2
B. High-demand stack items protected in reference collections	3
C. Appearance	2
D. Other	5
Subtotal	24

Stack Collection Exceptions
(books with 60% or more of pages in files or
lists housed in reference collections)

A. Earlier dated editions	6
B. Comic material in reference book form	1
C. Other	4
Subtotal	11
GRAND TOTAL	35

While such texts are undoubtedly discourse, they nonetheless often have some file-like characteristics, and some may be considered borderline. For example, canonical texts often have arbitrary numbering imposed on them to make it easier to find particular segments, as with chapter and verse numbers in religious texts, section numbers of laws, or numbered regulations, standards, or specifications. In widely used texts these numbers themselves become known to educated persons, as in the case of famous Biblical passages, such as the 23rd Psalm. Such knowledge may hasten look-up in what is otherwise discourse.

In the stacks sample, the exceptions were books with file structure. Over half of those found were past editions of reference books, such as back files of statistical sources.

The reference and stack samples drawn at the research library contained a number of foreign language and pre-1900 books. These were broken out, and their file structure compared to that of modern English books. Patterns of organization were remarkably similar across cultural and language barriers and through time. The use of files and lists appears to be the prime means Western cultures have found to organize material for quick look-up.

Re-examining the definition. Now that we have seen how few books fall in the middle ranges of percent of length in files, it becomes less important to define "substantially" in the earlier statement that a reference book is composed substantially or entirely of files. Only about 5% of books are likely to have between 20% and 80% of their length in files anyway. If we pick a figure like 50% or 60%, we will get the best discrimination between reference and running-text books. At the same time, perhaps 5% to 10% of the books in reference collections will be canonical texts, which are exceptions to the "files rule."

Recall the earlier figures that 86% of reference books were *more* than 60% files, and that 94% of books in the stacks were *less.* If we were to instruct a clerk to note the percentage of length in files of all books coming into the library, and that clerk assigned all books with *over 60%* to the reference department and *under 60%* to the stacks, the clerk would make the correct assignment *about 90% of the time.* It would take a librarian, of course, evaluating the books on many criteria, to select them in the first place.

IMPLICATIONS FOR THEORY AND RESEARCH

This effort to define "reference book" descriptively has led to an extensive analysis of the organization of both reference and other books, and made it possible to see structural similarities within classes of books that would not be evident otherwise. A benefit of this view may be that we will be better able to see both manual and computerized sources in terms of the same vocabulary of file/record/field. Much of our literature still deals with the organization of the two kind of sources as if they were unrelated.

It can also be seen that the organizational possibilities with manual files appear limited compared to those in automated files. While many different forms of file organization have been developed for the latter, manual files seem to gain their look-up potential almost wholly through the mechanism of search on *ordered* records. Hence "file" here is not as broadly defined as in the vocabulary of computing.

Most materials in libraries, however, will remain as manual files for some time to come. I believe there is great potential in the present approach for the study of *search strategy through manual files*. Efforts to study search strategy to date have been limited to examination of fairly global behaviors on the part of searchers, because of the immense variety of search topics and resources available within which to search. How can one give a recommendation for how to search that is both general enough to apply to many potential searches and specific enough to help in a particular search?

Some light may be shed on that dilemma by examining the file organization of materials to be searched. Underneath the immense variety of materials in a library lies a limited range of organizational structures, most of which have been discussed here. Searching can be seen as a series of accesses to files and discourse, each having certain characteristic look-ups and scans. Look-up power can be measured as amount of search-time reduction due to organization into files. Average scan times needed for books of certain characteristics can be measured: for example, if a file has 400 pages, a certain degree of readability in the formatting on the page, and an average of 12 entries per page, the average searcher may be found to take 20 seconds to find a desired entry.

Searches involving a *series* of linked file look-ups can be studied on the basis of number of file accesses, time taken with each access, percentage of look-up vs. scanning needed in searching, and so on. For example, even a search as ostensibly simple as using the *Readers' Guide* involves several file look-ups—first in the main *RG* file to find articles on the desired subject, then at the journal title abbreviations file to find the correct full title, then in the library catalog to find the journal call number, then in the stacks— another file—to find the journal volumes, and so on. The culmination of such analyses would be to compare different routes to find optimal ones for various classes of search. This structural view of manual reference sources could thus contribute to a novel and potentially very precise study of human search strategy.

3

Reference Books, Databases, and the Repertoire

Howard D. White

INTRODUCTION

Many reference and bibliographic works long known in printed form have now been recast as machine-readable databases. The process is part of the computer revolution and is certain to continue. The reason these works can be recast is that their underlying structure is the same as that of newly created databases without print counterparts. I intend to examine that underlying structure using terms from writers on database organization. The goal is increased understanding of both printed and machine-readable resources, which will co-exist for a long time. While the computer revolution seems to me an unmixed blessing, I also think that large numbers of reference works will not be computerized, and that they will nonetheless continue to be taught and used.

In a sense, database service *is* traditional reference service, or a direct outgrowth: it simply automates and extends human powers to scan large numbers of records. The technology for minimizing scanning of print has a long history. Broadly, this would be the history of human-readable indexes. But outside librarianship, databases are seldom related to the technology of printed reference books. (Other roots lie in centuries of office forms and files.) With the possible exception of those who computerize bibliographies, the people who discuss databases in computer science textbooks seem unaware of any connection with library reference service, even when to some degree they are re-inventing it. A personal computer owner, creating a directory for his business with dBase, might be unaware that he is also *compiling a reference work,* just like those in libraries—to which his may stand as a toy to the real thing.

Writers such as James Martin tend to ignore not only printed reference books but also the large bibliographic and reference databases vended to libraries and other information agencies by external suppliers. They focus on databases created "in house" in business, industry, or government—for example, parts inventories or payroll files. Even so, they have evolved a vocabulary and a style of analysis that permits the study of reference works at a more fundamental level than that of most "library writers." The latter mainly annotate titles—item after separate item. While the "endless lists" approach has its value, it hides basic facts in a tangle of detail. Using language adapted from Martin and others, I will try to integrate the discussion of reference books and databases by seeking fundamental things to say about both.

The successful use of such works is artful practice rather than science, and, in using database terminology, I am not trying to make it more "scientific." Rather, I seek a concise description of the kinds of things users of reference works should know to be passably artful.

The most artful users of reference works are professional librarians and information specialists. The ultimate point of this essay is to characterize anew the competence that sets them apart from others. They possess, to a much greater degree than most, a *repertoire* of sources—reference books and databases—whose structure, uses, and whereabouts they know. This is distinctive. Many learned persons are walking treatises, and a few are walking encyclopedias: given questions in the subjects in which they specialize, they can supply answers from personal knowledge. In contrast, while information specialists may not know the answers personally, they know, or have means of discovering, where published answers to questions appear.

It may not be far-fetched to liken information specialists to professional actors. Many people have appeared in a play or two, but actors are distinguished by having large repertoires of parts at their command. Just so, many people have used a dictionary or an encyclopedia, but professional information specialists are distinguished by knowing *large numbers* of reference works. The actor says, "I have been Lear, Stanley Kowalski, Othello, Willy Loman, etc. I am a walking gallery." The information specialist says—granted, the parts are not as good—"I have been the *Oxford English Dictionary, Kane's Famous First Facts, Donnelley's Demographics, Who's Who,* etc. I am a walking index." The nature of the information specialist's "indexical repertoire" will be explored in a later section of this essay.

The initial sections were developed in conjunction with the previous chapter, "What Is a Reference Book?" They will be found to have points in common with it, although the emphasis is generally different. Allusions to "Bates" indicate that work throughout.

SCANNING, READING, AND LOOK-UP

Our goal when we are looking for anything in a printed source is to minimize what we have to scan. *Scanning* is glancing over, a way of finding or recognizing some feature in a body of information. It is faster than reading—too fast to permit the absorption of details of meaning in text. (As Woody Allen said, on speed-reading *War and Peace*, "It's about Russia.") Scanning is actually a different mental process from reading; it is rapid visual search. *Reading*, the more time-consuming process, permits details of meaning to be absorbed and retained in long-term memory. Both scanning and reading consume attention, one of our most precious commodities—we "pay" it; something is "worth" it—but they have greatly different values. Reading may be a source of pleasure and enlightenment—it is often intrinsically "worthwhile." Scanning is simply utilitarian, and may or may not have a payoff.

Reference works are designed to replace lengthy scanning with direct look-up. As Bates said, a person can do look-up when it is possible to find a desired statement or passage in a body of information without having to search through the information linearly. Another way of describing what we want in reference books, and what their compilers provide, is *power to partition*. We want to partition large blocks of text—too large to scan quickly, let alone read—into smaller, more scannable blocks, and then to spend as little time on scanning as possible. On our behalf, the compilers describe a set of entities in language that includes noun phrases (which could be single nouns or numerals). From these they choose a subset of noun phrases and arrange them in a certain order. To do look-up, we must correctly match a noun phrase we know with one or more in their arrangement.

They do not suppose that we will necessarily know the matching noun phrases in advance of use. (If not, we are supposed to be able to guess or learn them, with or without explicit help from the reference book. Help consists of things like "see" and "see also" references.) The compilers do, however, suppose that we will know how to use their ordering principle in advance. All reference books are predicated on this foreknowledge.

Ordering principles are systems of division. With them, it is possible to group items assigned the same or similar noun phrases into relatively small, scannable sets; everything else is "partitioned off." Further, they are always capable of subdividing text to the point where a unique address can be given to any item of language, thereby breaking out the smallest unit for scanning.

In look-up, we estimate the position of our noun phrase in the ordering (which is an abstract, verbal thing), and, like an analog computer, translate this into a *physical* position on the material that supports the language. (It may be remembered that *topic,* another name for my "noun phrase," comes ultimately from *topos,* the Greek for "place.") We may then manipulate the physical material to scan over successive positions—as few as possible—until we find the exact place where our noun phrase is supposed to match: its address. Either we find its match or we don't. If we do, we may still not find in the associated text the answer we seek, but we have, in Bates's phrase, made the leap from the whole to the correct part.

The ordering principle of ordinary books is also foreknown: start at the front of the text, and read to the back. ("Dipping here and there" may be the reader's ordering principle, but it is not the author's.) The ordering principles of reference books, in contrast, make front-to-back perusal unnecessary. They yield addresses over the pagination of the book, and these are discoverable at the level of individual pages, or even smaller segments of a page, which of course shortens scanning. In many cases these addresses are *independent* of the page-numbering scheme, which is a separate ordering principle.

A way of grasping this independence is to imagine the text of an ordinary book and that of a reference book floating in the air as long ribbons of language, not distributed over numbered pages. If we were then told that the reference book text was ordered *alphabetically by names of U.S. states* and told to find a discussion of *mining in Montana,* we could do so fairly quickly based on our knowledge of the alphabet. That would give us an ordinate—if we first encountered *Missouri* or *Nevada,* we would know which way to go—and we would not need any page numbering to steer us. Within the "Montana text" we would have to scan until we found the location of the discussion of mining, but our search would still be relatively limited. With the text of the ordinary book, on the other hand, we would have to scan from the beginning or haphazardly until we encountered the correct passage. By good luck, we might find the passage in the ordinary book immediately. Over repeated trials, however, there is no doubt our searches would be shorter in the reference book than the ordinary book, as long as all questions involved the correct kind of noun phrase—names of U.S. states. *Neither* book would *directly* answer a question like "In what states did the James and Younger Brothers rob banks?"—assuming they both discussed this—without additional indexing.

Ordering principles are few in practice because they must be foreknown to members of a culture in common. Those readily identifiable as "common knowledge" are:

- the order of the alphabet (for speakers of languages with alphabets);
- cardinal and ordinal numbering;

- decimal numbering (*not* the Dewey or Universal Decimal Schemes);
- chronological and calendrical orders.

Those identifiable as "uncommon knowledge" are:

- classified or systematic orders.

Alphabetizing of indexes is pre-eminent, because only it puts noun phrases—of the sort occurring in questions—in an order foreknown to everyone.

Classified orders of noun phrases may be foreknown to specialists or insiders, but cannot be assumed as common knowledge. For example, a zoologist might know where to find *nematodes* in a book ordered by the biosystematic classification scheme; a Dantean might know in which circle to find *the lustful* in a book ordered by the circles of Dante's hell. If so, these specialists could partition their books more or less directly to get to passages associated with these noun phrases. But the rest of us would need alphabetized indexes that mapped the topics onto page numbers. The exception would be classified orders with relatively few categories; signs of the zodiac, for example, would be easy to scan even if one did not know the sequence starting with Aries.

While commonly known, the various numerical orders are rarely useful *in the first step* of direct look-up. One would seldom say, "I know page 27 is between pages 26 and 28, and I will see what it contains." So, too, many people learn decimal numbering in school—they know that 30.2 comes before 301—but most do not remember, if they ever knew, what these stand for as codes within the Dewey Decimal Classification scheme. If they had a substantive question about a topic, it would do little good to present them with the main DDC schedule, which is in decimal order, because the numerals simply express topics in *classified* order. Unless the latter is known—some people learn it at least in broad outline—a front-to-back scan would be necessary. (Hence Dewey's Relative Index, which is supposed to map alphabetized noun phrases onto their decimal number codes and to bring together subject groupings that the classification scheme has scattered.) Almost all classification schemes with numeric or alphanumeric codes require alphabetical indexes. McArthur (1986) notes that Peter Mark Roget, compiler of the famous *Thesaurus,* thought that users would find their way to particular words through his very abstract, "largely Latinate" classification scheme, and provided a brief alphabetical index only as an afterthought. "The experience of users, however, evidently prompted the realization that some kind of fuller alphabetic support was needed. A much more elaborate index was provided, therefore, by Roget's son John in the 1879 edition, and from then on has quite clearly been the principal way in for the vast majority of Roget-users" (p. 121).

The only classified or numerical arrangements that may not need alphabetical indexes are those reflecting familiar conventions of the measurement of time. While these are culture-specific, in our culture most persons would have no trouble doing direct look-up of such items as June 15 or 9 a.m. or 450 B.C. or Wednesday in suitably arranged but non-alphabetical sequences.

MATRIX STRUCTURE

All reference books designed for direct look-up have the same underlying form—that of a *matrix*. This is the general form of field–record–file structure, as will be seen.

The matrix contains data on one or more properties of a set of things. Much of information retrieval, whether manual or computerized, involves operations on matrixes. It is the matrix that permits direct look-up and minimizes scanning, in contrast to the other major mode of displaying information—*discourse*—which does not permit direct look-up and thus necessitates scanning or reading. Both matrixes and discourse, as things made of written language, are species of *text*.

A matrix is a row-by-column structure. *Entities* (also called items, objects, cases, or units of analysis) are conventionally on the *rows*. An entity, according to Webster's Third, is "something that has objective reality and distinctness of being or character"—a *thing* in the most general sense. *Attributes* (also called properties, features, variables, characteristics, or measures) are on the *columns*. In the intersection of each row and column—called a *cell*—is a *value* for the attribute. This reflects an observation made on the entity. Attributes can be recorded as words or numerals or both. For example:

> Attribute: *Sex* of persons. Values: MALE or FEMALE. [words]
> Attribute: *Age* of persons. Values: 1 to 110. [numerals]
> Attribute: Person's *address*. Value: 150 Grail Rd., Devon, PA 19333
> [mixed]

The crucial distinction between entities and attributes is that entities are *invariable in kind,* whereas the attributes of these same entities *vary.* In other words, if we recorded in the matrix the kind of thing each entity is, there would be a constant down one of the columns, such as Person, Person, Person...or Book, Book, Book....There is not much point in recording a constant for every case. If all entities have the same value on some important attribute, that fact will usually be shown in a title outside the matrix; for example, *Books in Print*, if all entities are books; *Dictionary of American Biography,* if all entities are American persons. (Something similar happens

Primary key	Attribute 1	Attribute 2	Attribute 3	Attribute m
Entity 1	Value 11	Value 12	Value 13	Value 1m
Entity 2	Value 21	Value 22	Value 23	Value 2m
Entity 3	Value 31	Value 32	Value 33	Value 3m
Entity 4	Value 41	Value 42	Value 43	Value 4m
Entity n	Value n1	Value n2	Value n3	Value nm

Figure 3.1   Abstract Matrix

in mathematical expressions when a constant that applies to all terms is moved "outside the parentheses," leaving only variables inside.) An attribute, on the other hand, will vary over cases. That is, it will be capable of taking at least two values. (*Sex,* in the example above, can take two; *Age* can take 110.) It may have a different value for every entity or case in the matrix (as is possible with *Address* and required with such variables as *Social Security Number*).

Figure 3.1 illustrates general matrix structure. Examples of specific matrixes include a file of questionnaire data from a sample survey of persons, a library card catalog, lab sheets with times in which rats in experimental and control groups ran a maze, and reference books like *Who's Who, Books in Print*, and the *Encyclopedia of Associations*.

A matrix of the kind described here has two major uses:

1. It can be used to organize the raw data from which *summary statistics* are produced, such as counts, percentages, rankings, means, and correlations.
2. It can be used for *information retrieval*—of particular values in cells, whole groups of values, or passages of discourse. I will concentrate on this second use, but not to the exclusion of the first.

The essence of the matrix for information retrieval is that each cell has a unique row-by-column address. For example, the top left cell of Figure 3.1, labeled "Value 11," is the intersection of row 1 and column 1, the only such position in the entire grid. (Those who work with computerized spreadsheets will be familiar with the principle.) The whole point of matricizing texts is that it makes the scanning units addressable through known row-by-column coordinates, and thus quickly findable by human beings. (Other addressing systems are used in matrixes searched by computer, but the intent is the same.) Once found, the units are also small in relation to the total text. Within this small scanning area, presumably one will find, or at least have a chance of finding, the unknown answer one seeks.

MEASUREMENT AND DATA[1]

The filling in of matrix cells with values often represents acts of *measurement,* which is associating *numbers* with *cases* by observing the cases against scales. Observation of *N* entities on *M* different attributes creates an *N* by *M* matrix. The values in the cells may reflect scales at the nominal, ordinal, interval, or ratio levels, as discussed in elementary statistical textbooks.

In this view, the matrix has its beginning in a simple *list of like things.* Their names—the identifying tags by which they are listed—constitute one attribute or "dimension." If list order is preserved and values on another dimension are then recorded for each thing, we move from a one-dimensional list to a two-dimensional matrix—the simplest kind. A list of one's credit cards, together with the amount of money owed on each, would be a two-dimensional matrix. Suppose that one then added the monthly periodic interest rate and the annual percentage rate for each card. This addition of two new variables would create a *multidimensional* matrix—and, indeed, that is what we often see when data are organized for statistical summarization or retrieval.

Numeric matrixes of the sorts manipulated in matrix algebra would be included in this general formulation. (These "arrays" often presume ratio-level scales.) The formulation is broad enough, however, to include matrixes with "dimensions" at lower levels of measurement—the ordinal and the nominal—on which standard arithmetic operations (addition, multiplication, etc.) cannot be validly performed.

The lowest level of measurement—the nominal—is equivalent to classification and allows us to sort cases into categories having purely verbal values. The mutually exclusive and jointly exhaustive "numbers" of nominal-level measurement are literally *codes* for words and phrases, and the words and phrases are simply translations of the codes. A good example is Dewey

Decimal Classification, in which, for brevity among other reasons, one writes the codes "973" to mean "U.S. History" and "500" to mean "General Science." The numeric and verbal expressions are interchangeable. I make the point as a reminder that many reference books made up *primarily of words rather than numbers* can still be regarded as matrixes of nominal-level measurements reflecting attributes of cases. *Who's Who in America*, the U.S. *National Union Catalog*, and thousands of other reference works fit this description.

In science and social science, entities are observed against measurement scales, and variable values are recorded. These values are often called *data*. The word *data* is best used when its origin is remembered; it comes from a Latin verb meaning "to give" and can be understood as "what the world gives (or can be made to yield) to the senses." In the language of science the word usually has a more restricted meaning: "what the world yields to systematic observation," that is, to the same question or questions repeatedly put. *Theory*, of course, determines what these questions will be, and how they relate to what is already known or conjectured. Moreover, scientists seek *concise summarization of relationships* in data; I do not mean to imply that creation of "raw data matrixes" is their main end. However, the results of their summarization activities are themselves often put in matrix form. Much science and social science ends up in reference works, arranged so that specific facts or claims can be quickly found.

Some writers, incidentally, distinguish *information* from *data* on the ground that information is "more organized." In understanding this nuance, it may help to think of data as *that which is in the matrix before summarization or retrieval*, and information as *that which is summarized or retrieved from the matrix in response to a request*. Data, in other words, become information not through qualitative change but by being marshaled on behalf of a questioner.

Imagine that the following questions have never been answered, and that they are being investigated for the first time:

- What are the frequencies in cycles per second of atomic vibrations in vanadium? (Physics)
- What are the heart rates per minute in rats undergoing water deprivation? (Experimental psychology)
- What is the current incidence of gun ownership among American women? (Sociology or political science)
- What are the authors, titles, and imprints of all American trade books published in 1945? (Enumerative bibliography)

Suitably rephrased and operationalized, all of these questions could be put to appropriate segments of the world, and what the world gave back would be data. Note that all instances would involve focused observation across entities of one kind (atoms, rats, women, books) and not observers' unstructured perceptions of "anything and everything."

The systematic data gathering of science and social science, then, amounts to putting the same set of questions to, or carrying out the same acts of observation on, each of N entities of the same kind. Such activity is also found in commerce, business, government, information work—in all walks of life where "standard" questions recur. These are questions that can be anticipated and routinized for answer on forms. Systematic data gathering explicitly or implicitly involves *forms*— a number of named blanks in a fixed order to be filled in according to directions.

Matrixes generally are (or can be) *form-generated.* In each of the examples above, a form with labeled blanks could have been used to focus observations and to make sure the questions were completely and consistently asked. In data processing circles, an often-used name for the "blank" or "space" in which the values of a particular attribute are recorded is *field.* Fields are generally labeled with the name of the attribute or variable on which they contain data—for example, *Sex* or *Address* or *Temperature.* Values themselves may be called *data items* or *data elements.*

In any matrix the fields may hold a fixed or a variable number of characters. An attribute like *Year of Birth* requires a fixed-length field of four spaces for a value such as "1939"; an attribute like *Address* requires a field of variable length, since we cannot say in advance how many characters a home address will comprise. Variable-length fields can be made very extensive, to hold, for example, long passages of discourse. Whatever their length, fields in a matrix will generally be set in an arbitrary but fixed order, as they are on forms.

RECORDS AND FILES

An identically ordered set of fields for each entity constitutes a *record.* A record gains its unity from the fact that all its fields describe one thing—a person, a word, a country, a book, a credit card, and so on. When another thing is described, we move to a new record. (A sense of transition is unnecessary between records, unlike paragraphs in prose, and, as Bates noted, Ranganathan (1961) felt its absence as *jerks.*) Records are important because they are the unit retrieved in a look-up, although not all fields of the record are necessarily chosen for display or use. In a typical look-up, one uses a field whose value and position are *known* to locate a record (or records) with fields whose value is *unknown but desired* as the answer to a question.

Usually one or more fields serve to identify a record uniquely—that is, set it apart from all others. Often a serial number serves as the unique identifier—for example, a Social Security Number for records of persons; an International Standard Book Number (ISBN) for records of books. The object is always to "disambiguate" to the level where one record stands for one thing. Thus two persons might have the same name and address, but presumably their Social Security Numbers would be different, two copies of an edition of a book would have the same ISBN, but could be disambiguated in a library through different accession numbers.

Combinations of fields may also be used to disambiguate, as when an airline name, flight number, and date serve to distinguish a particular *flight* (all are necessary for this purpose). In database parlance the unique identifier is called the *primary key;* it is used by the computer to locate a particular record. *Secondary keys* are fields that can be searched but that do not identify a record uniquely.

Records of all entities in a population or sample of interest constitute a *file.* An entity–attribute matrix is a major kind of file. "File" now loosely covers many kinds of numerical, textual, and pictorial materials when they are placed in some kind of order to facilitate retrieval of records. Etymologically, the word comes from Latin *filum* for "thread" (cf. "filament"), and "threaded writings" is in fact an early sense.

The word is much used in computing to cover any work that is machine-readable. If, for example, one makes the text of *Paradise Lost* machine-readable to do computer-assisted stylistic analysis, it is common to call this a "file." In fact, *any* discourse—a letter, memo, poem, or term paper, and so on—created with word-processing software may be called a file, and so may artwork or graphs created with graphics software. However, the term is probably most often used in information work to denote an entity-attribute matrix with records built up from fields. That is its usual meaning in database management, statistical computing, and information retrieval. In discussing reference books I will use "file" in this sense and mean, as Bates did, a set of two or more records ordered by a rule or principle.

AN EXAMPLE: MATRIXES OF BOOKS AND PEOPLE

Although bibliographic and survey data files are usually thought of as unlike—MARC tapes are not commonly supposed to resemble Gallup Polls—it can be shown that in important respects they are structurally similar.

Consider what is meant by *identification* in bibliography: the provision of enough information about a work to set one group of copies, usually an edition, apart from any other. This setting apart, which asserts the unique-ness of the edition (or other unit), can be symbolized by assigning a unique number to the group of copies. The rule is a one-to-one mapping between the number and verbal statements such as author, title, and imprint that jointly identify the edition.

Setting the verbal statements equal to the unique number is measurement on a nominal scale. In this lowest kind of measurement, the number does not represent a count of equal dimensional units, such as pounds or inches. All it means is that we have been able to put the edition in a category that excludes all others. Numbers used as names (i.e., "on the nominal level") are a succinct way of designating categories. Nominal-level measurement (essentially classification) involves matching every unit of analysis against the numbered categories and stating whether the unit belongs to ("equals") the category or not. Arithmetically, the signs = and ≠ are meaningful with nominal-level numbers, but not the signs < or >, or the operators for addition, subtraction, multiplication, or division. (If "Random House" = 1 and "Knopf" = 2 in a survey of novels, the number codes are arbitrary and reversible. Therefore, it makes no sense in this case to say that 2 is *greater than* 1 or 1 *less than* 2; nor does it make sense to do arithmetic—e.g., compute a mean—with the codes.)

Now suppose we want to classify an edition by subject. In effect, we want to assert that such-and-such an edition has such-and-such a subject, and by searching a classification scheme and using our sense of likeness and unlikeness (our sense of = and ≠), we eventually make the assertion. Here again, we are setting the edition apart, now not from all other works and all other editions of the same work, but only from most other works; we want to bring out its similarity to the relatively few items that seem to be "identical" with it in subject. Our rule now is to permit a many-to-one mapping of all items identical in subject matter to one subject category. Again, we are measuring works on a nominal scale comprising all subject categories, but with a different sort of mapping permissible.

Thus one cay say: the hardcover edition of *Religions of America,* edited by Leo Rosten (New York: Simon and Schuster, 1975), can be distinguished from the paperback edition of the same work, but both have as subject matter, "Christian denominations and sects in the U.S." And both editions of Rosten can be distinguished from M. Thomas Starkes' *Confronting Popular Cults* (Nashville: Broadman Press, 1972), which, however, is identical to them in subject. All three items can be distinguished from Francis Huxley's *The Way of the Sacred* (Garden City: Doubleday, 1974), which also belongs to a different subject category—"Comparative religions." One can proceed to make verbal statements about hundreds and thousands of works in this vein; or one can use numeric codes to reflect the (not very exciting) nominal-level measurement, and arrange them in matrix form, as introduced above. Adopting the conventions of the ISBN and Dewey Decimal Classification notation, the matrix would appear as in Figure 3.2.

Figure 3.2.   Matrix of Books

Primary key ISBN	Attribute 1 Dewey No.
0-671-21970-7	280.0973
0-671-21971-5	280.0973
0-8054-1805-9	280.0973
0-385-04618-9	291

Note: From top down, the ISBNs stand for Rosten (hardcover and paperback), Starkes, and Huxley. Fuller information and a translation of the Dewey numbers appear in the text.

The meaning of the numbers can be recaptured as long as we have documentation to translate the codes back into plain English. Such documentation is a necessary part of any file that uses numeric values; in social science research, it is commonly called a *codebook*. A bibliographic tool that translates ISBNs back into "catalog entry language" would be a codebook. Seen in this light, the Dewey Decimal Classification schedule and the Library of Congress Classification schedule are also codebooks—very large ones for enormous nominal-level scales.

The bibliographic data shown in Figure 3.2 are no different in logical structure from much numeric social science data. This becomes clear in the matrix in Figure 3.3, in which *persons* are the unit of analysis, and the first measure performed on them involves matching their occupations to the categories of a nominal-level occupational scale. Here the unique identification of each person is represented by Social Security Number (which could be replaced by a temporary case number if personal anonymity were important). The SSN is mapped one-to-one with personal identity statements (name, address, etc.). This corresponds to the ISBN for books. The occupa-

Figure 3.3.   Matrix of Persons

Primary key SSN	Attribute 1 Occupation
168-42-1769	104
528-46-2359	002
396-42-8466	962
176-40-5778	170

Note: From top down, the U.S. census occupation codes stand for embalmer, actor, oysterman, and religious worker.

tions are represented by codes created by the U.S. Census Bureau, onto which SSN's are mapped many-to-one. These correspond with Dewey or Library of Congress class numbers showing subject.

Plainly, the data on persons in Figure 3.3 could be a fragment of a social survey in which a question on occupation was asked. But if this is so, it is possible to view the very similar Figure 3.2, and much of the record-keeping and file-building of librarianship, as a specialized kind of survey work directly relatable to what empirical social scientists do. In making bibliographic files, librarians have items of print or nonprint as their unit of analysis (instead of persons or groups). In cataloging, they are conducting a census (i.e., a complete enumeration) of a population (their holdings), to which they repeatedly put a fixed number of standard questions (just as in the decennial U.S. census of persons). The Library of Congress, and such firms as Bowker and H. W. Wilson, routinely conduct censuses of new print and nonprint titles on a national basis. Other organizations—for example, abstracting and indexing services and special libraries—periodically put standardized questions to judgmental (as opposed to random) samples of materials when they do selective subject bibliographies. These are comparable to sample surveys in which standardized questions are put to persons. It is true that, in surveying persons, many social scientists intend to produce statistical summaries, whereas in bibliography-making, the goal is almost always information retrieval. It is also true that social scientists are interested in *relationships* of variables, as specified by theory, and bibliographers generally are not. But otherwise their two kinds of surveys have much in common, as reflected in their common matrix structure.

MATRIXES, DISCOURSE, AND SORTING

The importance of the matrix in information retrieval can be shown by contrasting it with another major way of organizing information: as discourse. Discourse is not "form-generated" in the same sense as a matrix. It is much freer, governed only by the author's sense of exposition or argument or narrative. This is not to say that it lacks demonstrable structure, but its structure is not one in which questions are repeatedly put to entities of the same type and the answers recorded in some fixed order.[2]

The essence of discourse is that it is in "author's order," which is not a principle foreknown to everyone. It must be serially scanned—or even

---

[2] Discourse analysis, a relatively new area of linguistics, focuses on units of meaning larger than the sentence, such as how paragraphs cohere. It may have implications for the field of information retrieval, still largely matrix-based.

read!—from beginning to end if its contents are to be known. In information retrieval we would like to be able to sort discourse into an order we choose, so that what we wish to find is "broken out" from its context and made immediately available to our eyes. But print, as a medium, does not allow this, and if it did, to re-sort discourse out of "author's order" is to destroy it, at least as a work of expository or artistic intent. The best we can do is to create one or more separate indexes to the main file.

In contrast, a printed matrix can be sorted on the values in one or more of its fields without damage. (Fields containing discourse are the exception.) Far from destroying it as an information source, each new sort on a different field may generate a new and useful information product. The Bowker bibliographies of U.S. trade books, sold as separate products, are essentially the same data sorted and resorted by values in different fields. The telephone directory, which most of us own in the version alphabetized by customers' surnames, gives new powers when it is sorted by their addresses, grouping callable people by where they live, or by their phone numbers, enabling one to trace a known number to its unknown owner.

Matrixes are inherently rearrangeable because they have no theme—no underlying paraphrasable content for the work as a whole. They are reducible to a multitude of independent statements. Take some typical statements from Bowker's *Books in Print,* for example. Implicit terms are bracketed in the following:

- [There is an author named] Gay Talese.
- Gay Talese [wrote] *The Kingdom and the Power.*
- Gay Talese [wrote] *Honor Thy Father.*
- Gay Talese [wrote] *Thy Neighbor's Wife.*
- *Honor Thy Father* [was published by] World [in] 1971.
- *Honor Thy Father* [has as its subject] "Mafia."
- *Thy Neighbor's Wife* [has as its subjects] "Sex customs—United States," "United States—moral conditions," " Sexual ethics," and "Sex (Psychology)." Etc., etc.

These statements, in addition to being logically and rhetorically primitive, are all approximately equal in value. That is, there is no way of deciding that some are more important than others in conveying an overall meaning. Therefore there is no way to abridge or summarize them as writing; one can only extract some elements and leave others out. (Database managers might speak of presenting *views* of some fields and not others.) Moreover, while the statements are not incoherent, they cohere only through a rudimentary device—the repetition of noun phrases as subjects or objects. They develop neither a line of reasoning nor a narrative, two major goals of discourse. As a consequence, they do not invite reading—and are usually unread—except in brief segments.

Literally thousands of reference books and databases have this athematic structure. Their compilers have sacrificed the virtues of discourse for the matrix with its single, all-important end—quick retrieval of information.

To retrieve information quickly from a matrix, we need to know the name of the field(s) on which it is sorted and the ordering principle of the sort. The phrase "Alphabetical by subject," for example, contains both the ordering principle and the access field for a file. We also must be able to supply a likely value on which to search, such as a heading or "descriptor." Often it is no trivial task to turn one's likely value into one that was actually used in the indexing, particularly in subject searching. Nevertheless, given success in matching this value, one gains access to the data in the other fields for a relatively small subset of records—perhaps only one. The sort "breaks out," from the total set of possible values, the record or records with the value on which we searched. Our scanning or reading is limited to this subset. That is the essential structural principle of all works designed for look-up or "ready reference."

The commonest kinds of printed works in matrix form generally are sorted on a primary key (unique identifier) or some combination of keys (e.g., alphabetically by name of state, name of city, and then name of newspapers and magazines published there). One goes in with a noun or noun phrase of the kind permitted by the field(s) chosen to access the work. One then finds additional fields of data of more or less fixed types, designed to answer a limited number of questions.

As question-answering tools, matrixes obviously have much greater "predictability" than discourse. Once the fields of the matrix and the type of entities covered are known, one has a clear notion of what can be reasonably expected from the matrix as an information retrieval tool. One knows how it can be entered and with what kinds of data one may emerge. Figures 3.4 and 3.5 illustrate for two well known reference books—one bibliographic; the other, non-bibliographic.

Some works of reference have records with readily recognizable fields presented in more or less fixed order, and are easy to see as matrixes; others, because of layout, might have to be reconstituted for their structure to be clear. (More on this below.) Still others, such as encyclopedias and yearbooks, are combinations of matrix and discourse. The articles are alphabetical by subject—each article title would be a primary key value—but the variable-length field after the title holds a longish patch of discourse whose content is unpredictable. We know that certain facts are likely to be in certain articles—dates of persons, capitals of countries, etc.—but much or all of the text will have to be read, since with discourse one does not know what to expect from page to page.

(1) *4420*
(2) AMERICAN SOCIETY OF EARTH SCIENCES (3) (Geology) (4) (ASES)
(5) 123 Main St.   (6) Phone: (303) 472-1212
Denver, CO 80213   (7) John J. Doe, Exec. Sec.
(8) Founded: 1949. (9) Members: 3500. (10) Staff: 6. (11) State Groups. 15.
Local Groups: 62. (12) Professional society of geologists, geological
engineers and educators. Associate members: students and others with an
avocational interest in geology. Seeks to promote the study of geology and
allied sciences. Conducts special research program on depletion of mineral
resources. Sponsors summer courses in geology for high school and
college students, and awards 100 tuition scholarships for graduate study.
Maintains library of 5000 volumes on earth sciences. (13) Committees:
Career Counseling; Depletion Studies; History of Minerals. (14) Divisions: Education; Exploration. (15) Publications: (1) ASES News, monthly;
(2) Proceedings, annual; also publishes career pamphlets on geology and a
directory of mineral resources. (16) Affiliated with: Earth Sciences Institute
(research arm). (17) Formed by merger of: Earth Sciences Council founded
1929) and National Geology Society (founded 1935). (18) Convention/
Meeting: annual - 1981 Apr. 28-30, Chicago, IL; 1982 May 1-3, Dallas,
TX; 1983 Apr. 30-May 1, Denver, CO; 1984 Apr. 26-28, Detroit, MI.

This record is a "model listing" from the non-bibliographic *Encyclopedia of Associations*, which exists in both printed and online versions. In this file the *entities* are organizations, each identified by a unique number (field 1) and a name (field 2). The *attributes* begin with a "key word" denoting subject interest (field 3) and the organizational acronym (field 4); other attributes are labeled or self-explanatory. Such character-strings as 4420, (Geology), and (ASES) are *values*.

Figure 3.4.   A File of Organizations

A natural objection here is that, if discourse is considered a "value" in a variable-length field, the concept of a matrix becomes so broad as to cover any printed text at all. I would argue that the concept of the matrix can indeed be stretched quite far without losing meaning, as in the case of encyclopedias. Any underlying form that has a field for *Notes* or *Comments* is similar to that for encyclopedias, except that the latter allow this field to hold commentary that is often very long indeed. However, it is not the length of the commentary, nor the fact that different commentaries vary in length that makes a discourse field different from others. It is that discourse is inherently not sortable (without destruction), whereas many fields in matrixes are specifically intended to contain sortable values for look-up access.

Before leaving the matter, I should note that discourse, like any text, can be made self-indexing for look-up access if one is willing to decompose it into constituent words. With computers (or enormous labor) it is possible to "matricize" an entire body of discourse even though it is not originally in

SAMPLE ENTRY

DEWEY DECIMAL
CLASSIFICATION
              940   COUNTRY CODE
                                     FR   ISSN 1234-5679
MAIN ENTRY TITLE —— ASSOCIATION DES HISTORIENS EUROPEENS.
              JOURNAL/ASSOCIATION OF EUROPEAN —— PARALLEL LANGUAGE TITLE
FREQUENCY   HISTORIANS. JOURNAL; une revue d'histoire —— SUBTITLE
OF PUBLICATION   depuis la Renaissance jusqu'a present. (Text in —— PRICE
LANGUAGE NOTATION —— French and English) 1952. a. 200 F. (Institute of
PUBLISHER NAME   European Studies) Timsitt Publications, 55 rue —— CORPORATE AUTHOR
AND ADDRESS   Desaix, 7500-Paris, France. Ed. Richard Duprey. —— YEAR FIRST PUBLISHED
SPECIAL FEATURES —— bk.rev. bibl. illus. cum.index: 1952-1960 (vol. 9).
MICROPUBLISHER —— also avail. in microfiche from XUM. Indexed: Hist. —— EDITOR
INDEXED IN HISTORICAL —— Abstr. Key Title: Journal de l'Association des   INDEX INFORMATION
    ABSTRACTS   Historiens Europeens.
FORMER TITLE ———— Formerly: Review of Military History
              (ISSN 1232-5678)
ANNOTATION ———— Military History

This record is a "sample entry" from *Irregular Serials and Annuals*, a bibliography published by Bowker in both printed and online versions (now as part of *Ulrich's International Periodicals Directory*). In this file the *entities* are serial publications, each uniquely identified by an international standard serial number (ISSN, top right). The *attributes*, labeled in the margins, include a Dewey decimal classification, a country code, and a main entry title. Such character-strings as 940, FR, and 1234-5679 are *values*.

Figure 3.5.   A File of Serials

matrix form—for example, *Paradise Lost*. The most obvious reason to do this with a work of literature would be to re-sort it into a concordance. Thus any machine-readable text is potentially a reference work or "information source." After nonsignificant words like *of, the, and,* and so on, are deleted by a stop list, all significant words become secondary keys to the lines or passages in which they appear. It is as if a human indexer noted the occurrence of every significant word in the text and keyed it to a page or passage number, instead of merely lifting selected nouns and noun phrases as is common in back-of-the-book indexes now.

Matricized discourse appears in printed form as Keyword-in-Context (KWIC) or Keyword-out-of-Context (KWOC) indexes, which usually use terms from titles only. The improved online counterpart is full-text retrieval, in which one can search on words and phrases from natural language across entire bodies of discourse. Full-text retrieval is increasingly available for newspapers, magazines, abstracts, statutes, and case laws, and is foreseeable for other kinds of publications. Possible retrievals follow.

Example: Find me judicial precedents in cases involving personal injury from FALLING ICICLES.

Example: Find me recent news stories in which the words MONOCLO-NAL ANTIBODIES appear.

Figure 3.6.   Varieties of Text

Discourse	Matrixes
Not form-generated	Form-generated
Entities and attributes not fixed	Fixed entities; fixed attributes
Not sortable	Sortable within fields
Sorting order not foreknown	Sorting order foreknown (e.g., alphabetical)
Has theme or thesis or plot	No theme or thesis or plot
Relatively complex logic	Relatively simple logic
Some statements more important than others	All statements equally important
Direct look-up not possible; must be read or scanned	Direct look-up possible
Can be summarized	Cannot be summarized (except statistically)

By way of summary, I have placed some differences between discourse and matrixes in Figure 3.6.

A NOTE TO SKEPTICS

Persons who see all reference books as "unique particulars" may resist attempts at finding a common structure among them as reductionist. I hasten to state my belief that, in information work, knowledge of individual reference books is indispensable. The intent here is simply to lay a foundation, with as much implication as possible, for their study.

Other persons, while not ideologically opposed, may still have trouble envisioning what is meant. If one picks up a standard reference book—a dictionary or a handbook, say—one does not encounter a matrix in the sense of a small table of neatly ruled and labeled cells, like those found in textbooks on databases. The real world of reference books is much more complicated than the schematic in Figure 3.1.

There are at least four reasons why matrixes—rectangular matrixes with fields in fixed order—are not immediately apparent, though they are present.

First, the size of the matrix as an abstract piece of text may be enormous compared to the size of its support medium, the typical book (even oversized books). If the fields in each record could be printed side by side, one row per entity, the matrix structure would be visible, though one might need a billboard or football field tarpaulin to support it in that form. The (much more convenient) technology of the portable book forces the records to be reshaped from long rows into smallish, "vertical" blocks of type on pages; one record, in fact, may run over several pages. Page presentation, which is what we are used to, works against seeing large matrix structure, at least initially.

Second, in real reference books the neat "rectangularity" of the matrix may be obscured by the intentional omission of fields in which, for the entity in question, data values are missing or inapplicable. This is a tacit convention of print that we need not have explained. For example, in a printed bibliography, the underlying form actually has many fields to be used only when needed, such as a field for second and third authors, a field for series title, and a field for notes. Books and journal articles, if both are included in a bibliography, have mutually inapplicable fields. When the underlying form is made explicit, as it has been in the MARC formats for cataloging various kinds of materials, the real structure of the matrix is made plain. But we do not expect a given entry in a real bibliography to be printed out showing all the fields that were "not filled in." (Occasionally, this elision leads to ambiguity: if *price* is a field and nothing is shown, is the item free or do we simply have a missing value?) If all the "unfilled" fields were shown, the matrix would indeed be rectangular, but no one is that compulsive or wasteful of space.

Third, again because of space-saving conventions of print, matrixes are often only implicit, even if all values are "filled in." Understanding these conventions, we know that in the *Readers' Guide to Periodical Literature,* the term "Video games"—to use Bates's example—is a value in the Subject field, and that it applies to all of the citations below it, even though it appears only once. The implicit matrix can easily be made explicit, as in Figure 3.7a, which uses real data from the 1986 annual *Readers' Guide* (p.2034).

Figure 3.7.   Readers' Guide to Periodical Literature

3.7a: Entries in Matrix Form ('Flat File')

Subject	Title	Author	Illustrations	Journal	etc.
Video games	Armageddon under...	A. Gross	il	Technol Rev	
Video games	Bombs away...	–	–	Time	
Video games	Computer gaming	–	–	Futurist	
Video games	Eddie and the Cruisers	K. Vreeke	il pors	Cycle	
Video games	Entertainment	D. Caruso	il	Pers Comput	
:					
Video games— Design	'The medium of doing'	W. M. Hawkins	por	Pers Comput	
:					
Video games— Testing	ATC computer game	P. Reifsnyder	–	Flying	
:					
Video games and youth	Children and video...	–	il	Consum Res Mag	
:					
Video stores	Clash of the video...	S. Koepp	il	Time	

3.7b: 'See' and 'See also' References in Matrix Form ('Flat Files')

Subject	See
Video disc players	Video discplayers
Video equipment	Television equipment
:	:
Video games and children	Video games and youth

Subject	See also
Video games	Activision
Video games	Atari, Inc.
Video games	Computer novels
:	:
Video stores	National Video (Firm)
Video stores	New Video (Firm)
Video stores	Video Software Dealers Association

Likewise, a subject index in which *see* and *see also* references are interfiled with the substantive entries is actually three matrixes; parts of the latter two (also from p.2034) are disentangled and made explicit in Figure 3.7b. Data conforming to print conventions might have to be converted into explicit "flat files" like those in Figures 3.7a and 3.7b in the creation of computerized databases from printed data in reference books.[3]

Fourth, the matrixes seen in textbooks usually have fixed-length or very short variable-length fields, and cover only a few entities. (That way, they fit on textbook pages.) In real reference books, matrixes may be "rubbery" in the sense of having many variable-length fields (cf. Figures 3.4 and 3.5), one or more of which may have very long values. If the longest value in each variable-length field were known, the matrix could be made rectangular by "padding out" all shorter values with leading or trailing blanks. That would be very odd and unnecessary (computer technology exists to handle variable- as well as fixed-length fields). But if it were done, the matrix structure would be revealed.

---

[3] Flat files can have only one value per cell, and each value not a primary key must be associated with only one primary key. Their creation is part of the process of "normalization" of relational databases. A discussion of the various forms of normalization will be found in database textbooks, which explain why failure to observe these forms can lead to difficulties in inserting, updating, and deleting fields of records by computer. Normalization is of concern primarily to database designers, not reference book users. Its main use is with volatile databases—those with frequently updated values in fields. Many reference books, for example, bibliographies, do not require frequent updating in this sense, since values in fields like Author, Title, Subject, and so on, almost never change. Reference books such as bibliographies are frequently updated through the addition of whole new records (and the removal of old)—but that is very different from changing values in fields within records.

INDEXES

Printed matrixes and discourse can be indexed, of course, to permit quick look-ups not otherwise possible. In both cases, the index is a matrix imposed on the other file.

The familiar road map is a useful example. A map in one sense is simply a text—words and symbols—distributed over a durable surface such as a large paper sheet. The larger the map, the more difficult it is to find a particular word or symbol by scanning. The text of the map is ordered so as to correspond to physical and political terrain, which is not an order foreknown to everyone. (Few would need the map, if it were.) The established technique for reducing the scanning area is to complement the map with an alphabetized list of place names and to tie these to coordinates whose ordering is also foreknown—one dimension marked by alphabetized letters, the other by cardinal numbers. Actually we have two matrixes here—first the verbal index, consisting of names tied to coordinates (such as "Paint Rock, C6"), and then the abstract system of coordinates itself, which has no geographic reality but overlays the map as an information retrieval device. In effect, the coordinates "paginate" the map, as if cutting it into atlas pages. Thus, if I am scanning a map of Texas for the town Paint Rock, it helps greatly to be directed to scan no more than square (or "page") C6, a much smaller area than the whole map.

In a sense, *any* text is indexed merely by being distributed over numbered pages. One can think of a text as an entity that is physically realized in a certain way—in particular typefaces, with a particular line length, on a certain-sized page, and so on. (This is tantamount to saying that an *edition* of the text has been prepared.) In the process, blocks of text are created (of page size or less) and each is given a unique identifier—a page number, which is a primary key. The sort puts the primary key in numeric order. Unfortunately, while this allows us to find any page by direct look-up, it is useless for answering most questions, because they involve noun phrases that cannot be matched directly against page numbers. An alphabetized index of noun phrases must be created to mediate between those in our questions and those appearing on numbered pages. I shall examine the indexing of discourse first and of matrixes second.

A typical back-of-the-book index for non-fiction is a matrix in which the entities are *blocks of text*—the author's intellectual work segmented over a number of pages, which are *physical* records. The attribute *Subject* is noun phrases found in those blocks, the attribute *Page Number* gives each noun phrase a numerical address, and the sort puts the values of *Subject* in alphabetical order.

Usually the *Subject* noun phrases are lifted directly from the text, on the basis of assumptions about what questions readers will ask. What I can retrieve clearly depends on what an indexer has included in the list of noun

Fabian Society, founded (1884), 69,
124; *History* by E. R. Pease, 125;
first members never saw Marx,
123; origin of name, 124; difficulty
of admission to membership, 126;
growth of membership, 126; first
publication, 128; G.B.S. elected
member (1884), 128; other famous
members, 129; G.B.S. writes *A
Manifesto*, 128; Essex Hall meetings, 107, 128; Fabian Essays published (1889), 126, 129, 203-5;
G.B.S.'s unpaid work for, 129, 130,
183, 205, 240, 259, 313, 198; addressed by Annie Besant, 138;
women members, 152, 157; early
members and I.L.P., 217; Beatrice
Webb's idea for marriage of young
Fabians, 226-7; influence on contemporary political thought, 229;
G.B.S. writes tract for (1892), 243;
Charlotte becomes member (1896),
303, 304; G.B.S. regular attender
at meetings, 304; members' aloof-
ness, 305; Anatole France lectures,
307; and municipal trading, 354;
members among Liberals, 354,
360; attitude to the Empire and
Colonies, 353-9; attitude to China,
359-60; and international rights of
travel and trade, 359-60; and sec-
tarian schools, 370; summer
schools, 393, 496, the Labour Party
a product of, 125, 359, 413; H. G.
Wells's campaign for reform (1906),
412-421; demand for Rent of Ability, 442; attitude to G.B.S. (1914),
470; G.B.S. defines purpose, 472;
causes of decline in authority, 125-
126, 127; passing of early members,
581; G.B.S. on its failure, 590

Entry for "Fabian Society" from the index to St. John Ervine's *Bernard Shaw; His Life, Work and Friends* (New York: Morrow, 1956), p. 607. While most subheadings are in order of pagination, there are exceptions. This indexing is not very efficient for quick retrieval since it puts idiosyncratic natural language in non-alphabetical order.

Figure 3.8.   Non-Alphabetical Subheadings

phrases. Every feature not indexed is retrievable only by scanning or reading. It is relatively rare for indexers to paraphrase so as to bring out higher-level "themes," and so on, and they tend to include only nouns that are very easy to identify, such as proper names of persons or places. (Perfunctory indexes are much more common than artfully elaborated ones.)

Sometimes the noun phrases are further divided and one gets separately alphabetized values for, for example, a "Persons Index," "Subject Index," and "Geographic Index." There are different conventions for arranging *subheadings* under alphabetized subject headings. While subheadings themselves are often alphabetized, in some non-fiction books they are in page-number order (and that not always consistent—see Figure 3.8). Such complex sorts are made by human indexers, and it is doubtful that they could readily be delegated to a computer.

If the back-of-the-book index were sorted on the primary key—unique page identifiers in numerical order—one would get something like a very detailed table of contents for the book. Of course, conventional tables of contents reflect a page-number sort on the author's chapter and subchapter headings rather than on noun phrases drawn from the entire text.

Tables of contents reproduce the order of the author's thought and lack a foreknown ordering principle. Thus the searcher does not have look-up access with a table of contents; there is no way to leap from the whole list directly to a desired term and page number, the way one can with a back-of-the-book index. Instead, one must scan the list from the beginning to find a promising segment of text. The table of contents speeds access only because it is much shorter than the body of discourse it represents.

Printed matrixes (as opposed to discourse) are generally sorted on one or more fields of the main file and thus have "indexical arrangement" even if they lack detailed tables of contents or back-of-the-book indexes. If the latter are present, they generally represent alphabetical sorts on secondary fields within the matrix. Otherwise they have the same structure as those for discourse.

This structure often goes by the name of "inverted file." In the main (also called "linear") file, complete records are placed in alphabetical, classified, or numeric (perhaps page number) order. The indexes "invert" main file order by sorting on some other key and associating it with the field that physically locates the record(s) in the main file—a page number, serial or accession number, classification code, etc. Complete records (i.e., all fields) appear only once, in the main file. Each additional index gives a different kind of access to them.

In books and other publications, the presence of a *main file* and at least one *related index file* is print technology's equivalent of a *database*. As we shall see, databases have unique characteristics attributable to the computer, but *interrelatedness of files* is a characteristic they share with millions of printed items.

The creation of indexes incurs costs. In printed reference works, these costs are held to a minimum by deliberately restricting the kinds of questions users can ask. Each new index makes a certain kind of question relatively easy to answer through direct look-up. Each index not created (because a field is not sorted on) means that certain kinds of questions can only be answered through tedious scanning, if at all. In *Books in Print*, for example, one has almost instant access to further information on a book if one has the author or title, but knowing only the place of publication is worthless. The records contain *values* for the field *Place of Publication* but this field is not an access field—not sorted on. These constraints are largely lifted when reference works become databases (as *Books in Print* has), but even then some fields may be non-indexed and non-searchable. With road maps, it is assumed that map users will most often ask questions containing the names of settlements ("Are there any ski resorts near Laramie?") or streets and roads; hence these go into the index. Other kinds of questions ("What towns in Wyoming have ski resorts near them?") can be answered only by scanning the map, not by look-up.

Occasionally, one finds that an index has been created which requires uncommon foreknowledge to use. I have noted this with classified orderings. Another example occurs with the printed version of *Cumulative Book Index*. The back files of this current bibliography, widely held in libraries, are annual (or periodized) cumulations corresponding to *Year of Publication* of the English-language books they cover. The result of sorting first by *Year of Publication* is that one must know when a book was published in order to look up anything else about it, and a full citation with publication date is precisely what one often lacks. For ready-reference purposes, it makes sense to assume a book is still for sale and look it up by author or title in *Books in Print*, which is not arranged by publication date.

However the values of fields in matrixes are sorted, print technology *locks in* the sorts. Some searches become easy; others become impracticable if the file is of any size. The number of indexical sorts (or access fields) is usually much smaller than the total number of fields in a given record. The main file of the printed *Who's Who in America*, for example, is sorted only by persons' surnames. It readily permits one to learn what books, say, John Updike has published and where he went to school. But since it is not sorted on its *Writings* or *Education* fields, one cannot ask it "Who wrote *The Centaur*?" or "What famous people went to Harvard?" Nor can one ask it questions based on *combinations* of fields, such as "What authors born in 1945 went to Harvard?" Only with computer technology is it possible to use multiple values per field and to combine values from two or more fields in the search statement.

The essential boon of computers is that they replace, and vastly improve upon, human scanning ability. We have seen that printed reference works are designed to minimize scanning. But the limitations of print, and of people as scanners, are still such that only a small part of the text is truly available for searching, and even then searches fail because of human lapses or fatigue. While computers cannot, in any real sense, *read*, they *scan* accurately and indefatigably, and they scan the whole text, or complex subsets of it, in a way human beings never could.

For many reference questions, then, computer technology is inherently superior to print technology. That is why the number of reference and bibliographic works converted to databases is steadily growing. *(Who's Who in America,* for example, now appears as a database as well as in print.) When the data in the fields are volatile and have time-value (such as stock quotations that may mean a profit one hour, a loss the next), the ease with which computerized files can be updated and communicated gives them an advantage over print. Even when timeliness is unimportant, the ease with which files can be cumulated and searched makes computerization the technology of choice. For reasons of cost, however, thousands of files are likely to be available only as printed reference books in the foreseeable future. The question-answering powers they confer, while limited, are still worth knowing about.

FILES AND DATABASES

Some persons use the terms *file* and *database* synonymously. This blurs a useful distinction made by those who use "database" to mean *two or more interrelated files;* it is the highest level of aggregation in the fields–records–files hierarchy. According to James Martin (1977, p. 22), a database is marked by interrelatedness of files, minimization of redundant data elements from file to file, independence of the data from computer programs that employ them, and a common and controlled approach to adding, modifying, and retrieving data. "Interrelatedness" implies that the files *have one or more fields in common* so that operations such as computerized merging and matching on specified values are possible.

Files in reference books have some of the characteristics of files in databases but not others. For example, they may deal with the same entities and may be matchable on specified values, such as "France" or "Coca-Cola," yet lack the "common and controlled approach" to data management that the term "database" implies—probably because they come from different publishers and are in a precomputerized state. Thus, two articles on France might contain much that is redundant; two descriptions of Coca-Cola might both be out of date. (Publishers want autonomy and a competitive advantage in producing works; they are not economically motivated to join competitors in a "common and controlled approach" so as to make products that are *jointly* useful.)

Even so, with machine-readability and appropriate software, reference books can—and have—become computer databases. Conversely, databases sorted on particular fields and printed out are equivalent to reference books, and are sometimes bound and sold as such. These works can be converted back and forth because matrix structure is simply being adapted to the two technologies. We now can use a common language for describing information retrieval in both printed and computerized files.

ELEMENTARY QUERIES FOR SEARCHING DATABASES

James Martin (1977, pp. 57-59) distinguishes six types of simple query that can be answered with matrixes comprising main (or linear) and inverted files. *All search strategies on matricized data are instances of—or can be constructed from—these simple queries.* In Martin's notation, E stands for entity, A for attribute, V for value of an attribute, and ? for what is sought—that is, the information to be retrieved. The basic "statement" on which retrieval is based is:

$$A(E) = V$$

That is, as in Figure 3.1, each attribute A of each entity E in the matrix has been "filled in with" or "set equal to" a value, V. Named attributes are here identical with named fields. (The problem of *missing data*—empty cells—may be serious in either information retrieval or statistical processing, but let us overlook it here.) Although Martin does not make the point, the names of entities (his E's) are simply one more attribute, but they often have the special status of being the attribute that uniquely identifies the entity—its primary key.

It will be seen in Figures 3.9 through 3.14 below that all retrievals are simply operations on different parts of the basic matrix, depending on what is known and what is unknown—the entity identifiers, the attribute names, or the values in the cells.

1. A(E) = ? asks: "What is the value of attribute A of entity E?"

Example: The student body (known A) of Brigham Young University (known E)—how big is it (unknown V)? (Figure 3.9.)

Example: What is the price (unknown V of known A) of *Jaws* (known E) in hardcover?

Physical location is a good example of an attribute that is often wanted for a particular entity whose name is known. Many works are useful for searches of the form A(E) = ? where A is physical location and the names of the E's are alphabetically sorted to permit direct access. Such works may be

Primary key	Attribute 1	Attribute 2	Attribute 3	*Attribute m*
Entity 1	Value 11	Value 12	Value 13	Value 1m
Entity 2	Value 21	Value 22	Value 23	Value 2m
Entity 3	Value 31	Value 32	?	Value 3m
Entity 4	Value 41	Value 42	Value 43	Value 4m
Entity n	Value n1	Value n2	Value n3	Value nm

The student body (A) of Brigham Young University (E)—how big is it (unknown V)?

Figure 3.9.   A(E) = ?

classed as directories if the entities are people or organizations; as gazetteers if the entities are countries; and as catalogs (or union catalogs) if the entities are published writings.

Example: Where (unknown V) is Paint Rock (known E) in relation to Dallas (known A)?

2. A(?) = V asks: "What entity E has a value on attribute A equal to V?"

This is the basic "inverted file query" underlying retrieval on indexing terms. As such it is an important concept. Any searchable field that leads to identification of entities (because it is associated with their primary keys) is called a *secondary index,* made up of secondary keys. In Martin's words (1977, p. 56), "A secondary index uses the secondary key as input and provides a primary key as output so that a record can be identified." Unlike primary keys, secondary keys need not *uniquely* identify an item.

Example: What books (unknown E) in this collection are indexed with the subject heading (known A) "Passover" (known V)? (Figure 3.10.)

Example: What books (unknown E) in this collection are indexed with the author's name (known A) "Updike, John" (known V)? More colloquially, "What do you have by John Updike?"

Example: What pages (unknown E) of this book are indexed with the

Primary key	Attribute 1	Attribute 2	Attribute 3	Attribute m
Entity 1	Value 11	Value 12	Value 13	Value 1m
Entity 2	Value 21	Value 22	Value 23	Value 2m
?	Value 31	Value 32	Value 33	Value 3m
Entity 4	Value 41	Value 42	Value 43	Value 4m
Entity n	Value n1	Value n2	Value n3	Value nm

As to subjects (A), do you have a book (unknown E) on Passover (V)?

Figure 3.10. A(?) = V

back-of-the book index term (known A) "Mercator projection" (known V)?

Example: What CIA operatives (unknown E) speak the language (known A) Tagalog (known V)?

In these examples, "Passover," "Updike, John," "Mercator projection" and "Tagalog" are the secondary keys—they can be assigned as index terms to more than one primary key that uniquely identifies a record.

3. ?(E) = V asks: "Which attributes of entity E have value V?"

Martin (1977) himself characterizes this third type of query (and the sixth, below) as "less common." The third and the sixth would seem much less important than the others in practical information work.

Example: Did Salesman Bob Lee (known E) have any month (unknown A) last year in which his earnings totaled exactly $2,400 (known V)? Which month? (Adapted from Martin, 1977; see Figure 3.11.)

Types 4 through 6 require *listings* as answers.

4. ?(E) = ? requests all values of all attributes of entity E.

Example: Give me everything we've got (all V's of all A's) on Senator Jesse Helms (known E). (Figure 3.12.)

Primary key	?	Attribute 2	Attribute 3	*Attribute m*
Entity 1	Value 11	Value 12	Value 13	Value 1m
Entity 2	Value 21	Value 22	Value 23	Value 2m
Entity 3	Value 31	Value 32	Value 33	Value 3m
Entity 4	Value 32	Value 42	Value 43	Value 4m
Entity n	Value n1	Value n2	Value n3	Value nm

In which month (unknown A) did Bob Lee (E) earn exactly $2,400 (V)?

Figure 3.11.   ? (E) = V

Example: I'd like a complete printout of all fields (all V's of all A's) for document ED600116 (known E) in the ERIC database.

Primary key	?	?	?	?
Entity 1	Value 11	Value 12	Value 13	Value 1m
Entity 2	Value 21	Value 22	Value 23	Value 2m
Entity 3	?	?	?	?
Entity 4	Value 41	Value 42	Value 43	Value 4m
Entity n	Value n1	Value n2	Value n3	Value nm

Give me everything we've got (all V's of all A's) on Senator Jesse Helms (E).

Figure 3.12.   ? (E) = ?

Primary key	Attribute 1	Attribute 2	Attribute 3	Attribute m
?	Value 11	?	Value 13	Value 1m
?	Value 21	?	Value 23	Value 2m
?	Value 31	?	Value 33	Value 3m
?	Value 41	?	Value 43	Value 4m
?	Value n1	?	Value n3	Value nm

For History 101 (known A), list all students (unknown E's) and their letter grades (unknown V's).

Figure 3.13.   A (?) = ?

5. A(?) = ? requests the values of attribute A for all entities.

Example. For History 101 (known A), list all students (unknown E's) and their letter grades (unknown V's). (Figure 3.13.)

Example: UCLA library books have LC call numbers (known A). List the individual call numbers (unknown V's) for the oversized books (unknown E's) in our collection.

6. ?(?)=V requests all attributes of all entities that have a value V.

Example: List the exercises (unknown A's) and the students (unknown E's) whenever a student achieved a score of 100% (known V). (Figure 3.14.)

Again, query types 1, 2, 4, and 5 seem to be the ones that would occur most often in practical information work with matrix files. Stated formally, as above, the query types may seem abstruse. However, they boil down to commonsensical operations:

One knows some entity's name and uses it to access other descriptive data on that entity in the file. Or, one has a description of something and uses it to

Primary key	?	?	?	?
?	Value 11	Value 12	Value 13	Value 1m
?	Value 21	Value 22	Value 23	Value 2m
?	Value 31	Value 32	Value 33	Value 3m
?	Value 41	Value 42	Value 43	Value 4m
?	Value n1	Value n2	Value n3	Value nm

List the exercises (unknown A's) and the students (unknown E's) whenever a student achieved a score of 100% (known V).

Figure 3.14.   ? (?) = V

retrieve by name all entities matching that description. One may want to retrieve additional descriptive data along with the names of the entities. The listings in query types 4 through 6 simply expand these operations.

For my part, I find it helpful to think of the operations on an entity–attribute matrix as if they were look-ups on a two-dimensional map of the world, in which the entities (the rows) correspond to lines of latitude, the attributes (the columns) to lines of longitude, and the values to places where the lines intersect. Calling these places "cities," I can concisely illustrate the differences among the six operations (these can also be traced in Figures 3.9-3.14):

1. A(E) = ?   Find the intersection of longitude A and latitude E. What city is there?

2. A(?) = V   Find the intersection of longitude A and city V. What latitude is that?

3. ?(E) = V   Find the intersection of latitude E and city V. What longitude is that?

4. ?(E) = ?   What cities lie on latitude E, and what are their longitudes?

5. A(?) = ?   What cities lie on longitude A, and what are their latitudes?

6. ?(?) = V   Find all cities named V. What are their latitudes and longitudes?

Matricization, then, imposes on the physical surface of text a system of coordinates, similar to those used in mapping the earth's surface. In each case, known information as input makes it possible to quickly "read off" corresponding unknown information—answers—as outputs of the coordinate grid. The system of latitude and longitude used in cartography and navigation is matricization at its clearest. However, the reader should see it as but one version of the overall technology of indexing and retrieval—a form of "linguistic engineering"—presented through numerous examples here.

EXTENDING THE QUERY TYPES

All of the query types above involve an equal sign: an attribute for a given entity is set equal to some value. In setting an attribute equal to some value, we implicitly declare that it is not equal to other possible values. As noted earlier, these two operations are permissible at the lowest level of measurement—classification with nominal level scales. If an attribute is measured on at least an ordinal level, we can put queries involving operators for "greater than" and "less than" a certain value in addition to those involving "equals" and "not equals." (In some applications we may also be able to use the refinements "equal to or greater than" and "equal to or less than.") This capability has many practical uses in actual retrieval.

Example: What months (unknown A's) did Bob Lee (known E) earn more than $2,400 (known V)?

Example: List all articles (unknown E's) in *Reader's Digest* whose publication date (known A) is greater than 1985 (known V).

Example: What books (unknown E's) in our collection are less than 12 cm. (known V) in height (known A)? [I want to make a display of the "tinies."]

In some applications it is also possible to use a *range* operator to imply all values from one point to another.

Example: List all women (unknown E's) in the company with birth dates (known A) from 1930 to 1939 (known V's).

What Martin calls "multiple key retrieval" involves building more complex search specifications ("search strategies") out of the simple query types above. This is done by linking the simple queries with Boolean logical operators AND, OR, and NOT.[4] It is these complex searches that are difficult

---

[4] The British mathematician George Boole (1813–1864) based an algebra on the intersection, union, and difference of sets. In online searching these operations are represented, respectively, by AND, OR, and NOT—often called "Boolean operators" or "Boolean logic." Some of the examples above implicitly contain these operators—for example, all articles published after 1985 AND in the *Reader's Digest*.

or impossible to do "manually" and that must be done by computer (or other machine) if the file is large.

Example: I want some smart men who will work cheap. List all entities which satisfy the conditions: Sex = Male AND IQ > 120 AND Expected Salary < $15,000.

Example: Use PsycINFO to get me some current writings on behavior modification in prisons. Descriptor = Convict? OR Prison? OR Penitentiar? OR Penal OR Felon? OR Imprison? OR Jail? OR Inmate? AND Descriptor = Behavior Mod? OR Behavior Therap? OR Countercondition? OR Token Econom? AND Publication Year > 1989

(Note: In this example, the symbol "?" is a *truncator.* It tells the DIALOG retrieval system to search for *any* words containing the stems shown—e.g., Prison? would retrieve records indexed with or containing the words Prison, Prisons, Prisoner, and Prisoners.)

Example: List all CIA operatives who speak Tagalog AND can hang-glide AND are expert in cryptographic analysis AND are licensed to kill.

Many textbooks, courses, and workshops exist to show how complex searches are done by computer, and so these examples will not be further developed here. Bates has more on the topic below, in her "Tactics and Vocabularies of Online Searching."

THE REPERTOIRE

It should be possible now to state the distinctive knowledge of information specialists. What they know, in a word, is matrixes—reference books and databases, whether printed or computerized, bibliographic or non-bibliographic. Furthermore, since their knowledge of these works tends to be concrete and highly structured, it can itself be modeled as a matrix. The mental activity of "calling up" a source in order to recommend it or use it on the customer's behalf can be modeled as operations on this matrix. The entities on the rows are the works constituting the repertoire—specific titles which the information specialist can quickly call to mind. On the columns are a standard set of attributes of each work (often including its where-abouts). Mental search over the attributes is triggered by components of the customer's request, as they emerge from the so-called "reference dialogue" or "question negotiation." The output of the search is titles to consult. Regarding each work, the information specialist knows:

1. Its access field(s), giving the kinds of nouns or noun phrases (search keys) with which it may be entered;
2. How these are arranged—the ordering principle;

3. Additional fields of information to be found once a work has been successfully entered—that is, once the search key has been matched;
4. Whether the work is confined to one subject area (e.g., law, chemistry, sports), or cuts across many;
5. The chronological period(s) covered by the work (e.g., classical antiquity, the 18th century, the 1950s);
6. the geographic area(s) covered by the work (e.g., the United States, Southeast Asia, the British Commonwealth);
7. The recency of the work, as given by its imprint or copyright date;
8. Special or idiosyncratic features;
9. Where the work is classed or shelved—its physical location relative to others.

These attributes are not necessarily all known in detail, but information specialists would often have a good idea of them through browsing or previous use, and the works themselves (or descriptions of them) are usually at hand if memory needs refreshing. Schools of library and information science generally introduce students to at least 100 works with matrix structure; knowledge of several hundred upon graduation would not be uncommon. (Those widely taught will be found in, e.g., Taylor and Powell's (1985) *Basic Reference Sources* .) And of course the number of known sources grows during the professional career.

This is the information specialist's repertoire, which I earlier compared to the actor's. Actors are prepared by their training to "become" or "fuse with" a part. In like fashion, information specialists' training prepares them to "fuse with" reference works and databases so as to be able to supply a desired response. Actors can "enter into" a character more quickly than non-actors. Something similar happens with information specialists as they interact with and internalize sources. They not only know better than most what sources exist, their entry points, their typical services, and their functional interrelationships; they also have a much more developed cognitive map of where things are.

It is fair to surmise that, although "everyone" is supposed to learn how to use information sources on a self-service basis, most people cannot really serve themselves well. They see the bookspines of the typical reference department as a multicolored wilderness, and being told that still more resources are accessible by computer may only confuse them further. Their ignorance is the reverse of the information specialist's knowledge: they have little or no repertoire (they may know a few trusty sources from school); they have no image of most works' internal structure (their attributes); and they cannot move swiftly to items because they lack a cognitive map of their locations. They also lack knowledge of linkages among reference works: how, for example, a particular known title, such as Sheehy's *Guide,* may be used to discover previously unknown titles. One does not shed this ignorance simply by entering a reference department open for "self-service," any more than one can immediately act *Hamlet* by leafing through a copy of the play.

The point of comparing information specialists to actors is not to borrow the latter's glamor, but to emphasize that both occupations involve *altered nervous systems;* they require not only talent and devotion to craft, but also training and practice. Once an effective source is presented, the customer may be able to use it as competently as the information specialist. It is in relative ability to reach this point that the two differ.

THE INTERVIEW

Let me sketch how the point is reached—first abstractly and then with one or two concrete examples.

As stated, the information specialist's repertoire can be modeled as a matrix. At the beginning of the interaction with the customer, nothing is known about what must be supplied from the matrix. In Martin's (1977) notation, it is a case of:

$$?(?) = ?$$

As the conversation with the customer proceeds, at least one attribute of an unspecified work emerges and takes on a known value. Such "knowns" come from the *customer's* description of what is wanted (although the information specialist may need to rephrase them). Very often, values on more than one attribute will emerge, but the basic expression is:

$$A(?) = V$$

This is, of course, query type 2, which requests something's unknown name on the basis of a known index value on some attribute. Here the entity represented by the question mark is a reference book or database. The customer cannot supply it, which is why he or she seeks help in the first place. On the basis of specified values on attributes, the *information specialist* now may be able to name at least one work that possesses the value. This entity, which the customer lacks, completes the expression, thus:

$$A(E) = V$$

To make this concrete, I will use an example from above. Imagine that a customer asks, "What is the price of *Jaws* in hardcover?" In answering, the information specialist must actually search *two* matrixes—the first to produce a likely source of the answer, the second to find the answer itself. The first search often takes place solely inside the information specialist's head. His or her distinctive expertise lies in being able to translate the customer's question into specifications such as the following: "I know that *Jaws* is the title of an American novel and that what is wanted is its current hardcover price. The title will be my search key, so I need something I can enter under 'J.' What, then, has alphabetized *book titles* as an access field AND gives hardcover price AND covers U.S. imprints AND is frequently updated?" These obviously are values of attributes that might characterize a reference book or database. In effect, since values must jointly be present for a work to be retrieved, they are indexing terms strung together with Boolean ANDs. Abstractly:

$$A(?) = V \text{ AND } A(?) = V \text{ AND } A(?) = V \text{ AND } A(?) = V \text{ etc.}$$

(I do not claim that this string or the monologue in quotes transcribes actual thought—everything is made ploddingly explicit to show content and logic—but the result is the same.) Most information specialists would know immediately that *Books in Print* possesses the values given and would choose it as a plausible place to look. Once *Books in Print* is produced, the second search, for the actual price of *Jaws,* can begin. As we saw above, this is simply an operation on a matrix of the type $A(E) = ?$: the price (known A) of *Jaws* (known E) = ? (unknown value). Customers might perform this direct look-up as easily as information specialists. But how can the latter do the first search and produce *Books in Print* ? They can because they have internalized a matrix of sources in which the following expressions of the type $A(E) = V$ appear:

An access field (A) for *Books in Print* (E) = book title (V).
The ordering principle for access fields (A) in *Books in Print* (E) = alphabetical (V).
Another field (A) in *Books in Print* (E) = retail price of hardcover (and sometimes paperback) editions (V).
The geographic coverage (A) of *Books in Print* (E) = the United States (V). (That is, it includes novels issued by American publishers.)
Frequency of update (A) for *Books in Print* (E) = at most annual (V).
The location (A) of *Books in Print* (E) = someplace known to the information specialist (V).

Typically, the information specialist would recall that the *Cumulative Book Index,* which also has most of these values, differs from *Books in Print* in a way mentioned above: files of the printed *CBI* are sorted first by the entries' year of publication, so that only if one knows when *Jaws* was published can one proceed to look for it alphabetically by title (without inefficient trial-and-error). In contrast, the computerized versions of *Cumulative Book Index* and *Books in Print* both permit one to use *Jaws* directly as a search term. They might be equally good for finding its current price; but the information specialist would know that these databases are differently "located"—at this writing *CBI* is vended only by Wilsonline, while *BIP* is vended by DIALOG and BRS.

Non-bibliographic questions are analyzed in the same way. Suppose, for example, the customer asks how George Murphy, as U.S. Senator from California, voted on the Gun Control Bill of 1968. There are several noun phrases in this question from which to choose a search key. One possibility, of course, is "Murphy, George"; but unless this particular bill loomed large in his career, even a full-length biography might not discuss it or give his vote. Without quite being able to explain how, the information specialist knows that a better choice is "Gun Control Act of 1968": "What can I enter with the year of a proposed piece of legislation AND its name AND get a roll-call of the Senate vote alphabetized by Senator (or U.S. state)?" The search through the repertoire for an item having these properties would lead many to the *Congressional Quarterly Almanac*.

Some part of the information specialist's mind, then, can be represented as in Figure 3.15, and another part as specific operations oriented to or conducted on it. The customer's request must be converted into terms that make search of the matrix possible, and then the search itself must be carried out. Perhaps the single most important thing the information specialist learns about reference works and databases is *how they may be entered*— the types of nouns or noun phrases one can use as search keys, which is roughly equivalent to what the works "cover." The most important thing the information specialist elicits from the customer is one or more nouns or noun phrases to use as search keys. Other important information for limiting the search may be explicit or implicit in the customer's remarks. The information specialist can combine such clues to produce a work in which matching the key results in an answer.[5]

Often this process is furthered by the information specialist's store of background knowledge. (The best ones exhibit high "cultural literacy," in Hirsch's, 1987, sense.) Background knowledge is drawn on to "fill in" specifications that the customer may be unable to supply, such as that Joe Orton is a *contemporary British playwright*, now *dead*; or that San Juan Hill is

---

[5] Wilson (1986) analyzes the interview from a different perspective—whether to probe beyond the initial question for "what the customer really wants." It is a commonplace among reference librarians that customers' first questions are far removed from what they really want answered. For example, they will ask for "books on Hollywood" when what they really want is Mary Tyler Moore's sign.

Figure 3.15.   'A Corner of the Repertoire'

Title	Typical services	Enterable with names of:	Geographic coverage	
Who's Who	Identifies, locates	Living persons	UK, world	
Encyc of Associations	Identifies, locates	Organizations	US	
Timetables of History	Dates	Persons, events, artworks	World	
Timetables of History	Chronicles	Years	World	
Facts on File	Discusses	Persons, events	World	
Dict of American Biog	Discusses, evaluates	Dead persons	US	
Langer	Chronicles	Periods, nations	World	
Langer	Dates	Events, persons	World	Etc.
Thomas Register	Identifies, locates	Organizations	US	
US Stat Abstract	Quantifies	Living & nonliving objects, manmade products	US	
Encyc of Philosophy	Discusses	Ideas, persons	World	
Oxford English Dict	Defines, gives etymologies & usage	English words	World	
De Sola	Translates	Abbreviations, acronyms		
Books in print	Identifies, dates, prices	Books by author, title, subject	US	
Ulrich's	Identifies, dates, prices	Periodicals by title, subject	World	
OCLC	Identifies, dates, locates	Books, serials, archives, data files, maps	World	
		Etc.		

This Refsearch-style matrix serves to indicate, in no particular order, a few arbitrarily chosen titles known to information specialists and the types of features known about them. (Sources chiefly non-bibliographic are above the line; bibliographic, below.) Other known features, omitted for reasons of space, include chronological and subject coverage, additional services and entry points, recency of imprint, and whereabouts. The figure is a sketch of "a corner of the repertoire" of many specialists, which might include thousands of titles and their features. Note that each row forms a kind of sentence when read across: e.g., "*Who's Who* identifies [and] locates living persons [in the] U.K. [and the] world." This attribute helps make Refsearch easier to learn and remember.

remembered from *the Spanish-American War;* or that iodine is *an element in the periodic table* as well as a medicine. Given a particular key, such knowledge constrains the files to be selected, or suggests alternatives that may be more fruitful than the key originally searched.

Insofar as the information specialist's expertise can be modeled as operations on matrixes—the task computers are supremely good at—it can be objectified as computerized expert systems. There is now considerable work in progress toward that end (see, e.g., Roysdon and White, 1989; Aluri and Riggs, 1990). One outgrowth of the argument advanced here, the matrix-based Refsearch system (White and Woodward, 1990), is intended to simulate the advice-giving capability of the information specialist or reference librarian in recommending sources. However, I do not believe that systems like Refsearch will soon replace information specialists, any more than systems like the well-publicized MYCIN, which diagnoses infectious diseases, will replace physicians. If nothing else, the specialist's ability to recognize the relevance of *implicit* background knowledge, and then to make it explicit on cue, has no machine counterpart and may never have. Still, nothing contributes more to the understanding of a complex task than attempts to computerize it. From the analysis underlying Refsearch, some comments may be added about *what information specialists know*— primarily on limits that constrain the material to be learned.

CATEGORIES IN THE REPERTOIRE

Access field(s). The types of nouns (or noun phrases) with which one may enter reference works are surprisingly few. Bibliographic works are commonly enterable with authors' names and with indicators of subject. Access by title is often possible (sometimes by *series* title as well). "Wordbooks" such as dictionaries are of course enterable with words *as words*— that is, all parts of speech nominalized to name themselves (which we designate by putting them in quotes or italicizing them). The great majority of the remainder— non-bibliographic reference works—may be entered with names of one or more of the following:

> Persons (real or imaginary, living or dead)
> Roles
> Organizations (profit or non-profit)
> Places (real or imaginary)
> Artworks (products of the arts—not necessarily "works of art" in an
>   honorific sense)
> Man-made products (exclusive of those from the arts)
> Events
> Times (i.e., years and other temporal periods)
> Living objects
> Nonliving objects
> Natural processes
> Human procedures
> Laws
> Languages
> Occupational fields
> Ideas

These of course need glosses and examples (for which, see my section of the Refsearch manual by Meredith, 1971). The point here is that, while other categories could doubtless be added, these few serve quite well to encompass general factbooks. Thus, if I am asked a question about *Brownian motion* or *continental drift,* I need a work I can enter with the name of a natural process.

If *minimum age for legal marriage* is wanted, I need a work I can enter with the generic name of a law. *Baptism for the dead* would be a human procedure; *the zipper* would be a man-made product; the movie *White Heat* is an artwork; *feldspar* is a nonliving object; *the Papacy* is a role. The reason general encyclopedias are so useful is that they combine several of these types of access fields (or entry categories) within one alphabet. Other works are more specialized. Many directories can be entered only with the names of persons or organizations; gazetteers, only with the names of places; chronicles or time-tables, with the names of years.

Ordering Principle(s). These, as we have seen, are mainly alphabetical or some variety of numerical. If some form of classification is used, an alphabetical index is often provided.

Additional Fields of Information. These contain the answers, initially unknown, that are retrieved by means of searches on known entry terms. The additional fields can be thought of as performing services once the work is entered. For example, in bibliographic works, "Gives publisher," "Gives price," "Gives citing papers," "Gives abstract" would be services. If one knows the fields of records in a typical library catalog, trade bibliography, abstracting and indexing service, and citation index, one pretty well knows what bibliographies can routinely do. The paradigm for services in "word-books" is set by multi-purpose dictionaries: "Defines," "Pronounces," "Gives etymology," "Illustrates usage," "Gives synonyms," "Translates foreign terms," "Translates abbreviations and acronyms," and so on.

The Refsearch analysis showed that typical services in non-bibliographic "factbooks" are:

Identifying—giving salient features that differentiate one thing from another. Features are often presented as values in fields rather than as discourse.

Discussing—presenting facts and opinions in discursive style, as, for example, encyclopedias do.

Locating—giving whereabouts (through, e.g., an address, contiguous locales, latitude and longitude, or a map display).

Dating—giving key dates in the history of something or someone (e.g., of birth and death).

Quantifying—giving numerical data characterizing something. A major subvariety of this service is giving *financial* data.

Chronicling—giving newsworthy developments connected with something in an action-by-action style that follows the order of time.

Judging—evaluating the achievements of persons, or the artistic merits of artworks, from a critical point of view.

These "answering services" constitute a version, somewhat elaborated, of what the journalist does in answering the classic questions of the newspaper story—*who, what, when, where, why,* and *how.* Such question terms are, of course, central to processes of human inquiry as embodied in language, so it is hardly surprising that reference works are structured to respond to them.

Special Services. Certain reference works are designed to perform services not readily available elsewhere. Information specialists learn to resort to sources such as *Kane's Famous First Facts* for questions about "firsts" and the *Guinness Book of World Records* for questions about "superlatives." They also learn idiosyncratic internal features of works, such as that *Webster's New Collegiate Dictionary* contains a table of the Indo-European languages; or that the online *Magazine Index* has a field in which letter grades (e.g., "A +" or "B −") sum up reviews of artworks and products. These are "tricks of the trade," idiosyncratically learned, for answering questions.

Subject Areas. Fine-grained subject analysis reveals constantly changing terminology in most fields, though the rates, of course, vary. At the higher levels of subject indication—the levels at which disciplines, professions, occupations, technologies are named—change is relatively slow. The conspectus of high-level subjects can be seen in the front matter of, for example, the *Guide to Reference Books* (whose 48 major categories are quite stable from Constance Winchell's 8th edition in 1967 to Eugene P. Sheehy's 10th edition in 1986); or the *Propaedia* to the 15th edition of the *Encyclopedia Britannica* (1974). These "outlines of knowledge" are brief enough and superficial enough that ordinary persons (of an H. G. Wellsian bent) can master them with a few exposures.[6]

Geographic Area and Chronological Period. In information work there is a natural tendency for sources to be centered on one's immediate culture (and its near neighbors), and on near as opposed to remote times. American information specialists will almost surely find that they consult works covering aspects of the U.S. most often, with Canada or the United Kingdom perhaps in second place. So, too, there will be whole works devoted to single years if they are recent—the various almanacs and yearbooks are examples—but only to longer periods, such as decades, centuries, or whole ages that are further back in time. It goes without saying that virtually all of these works will be in English, probably American English. This effect, concentric on the here and now, eliminates many potential candidates from the working repertoire—a dictionary of notables from the Tokugawa Shogunate, especially one in Japanese, would not be a prime contender for an American's list. Specific coverage of the particular works in one's repertoire is often committed to memory—for instance, it may be useful to know that

---

[6] Someone has described H. G. Wells as resembling a rice paddy—acres and acres of shining water, all of it two inches deep. But broad, shallow generalists are needed to complement deep, narrow specialists. See the final section, "Information Specialists as a Type."

the *Cumulative Book Index,* an American product, covers English-language books generally, and not just those from the U.S; or that the British *Dictionary of National Biography* includes Americans from the colonial period. Information specialists also know, however, that details of geographic and chronological coverage are given in such sources as Sheehy (1986) and the DIALOG blue sheets, where they can be looked up. One need not try to remember everything; usage will dictate what is most valuable to retain.

Recency and Physical Location. Again there is usually a concentric effect: information specialists who manage their own collections of printed sources place the most useful items, which are also generally the most recent, close to hand. Their access to computerized sources—a terminal of some sort—is usually nearby as well. The proximity of other items depends, as a rule, on how often the collection manager thinks they will be consulted—not least by the staff. Superseded items are relegated to stacks farther away.

In a Refsearch-style matrix model of what information specialists know, a work's recency is reflected by imprint date; its physical location by call number. These are solid pieces of information. But of course reality is even more vivid than the model: information specialists do not need to memorize imprint dates and call numbers, because they are physically in a room with their sources and have countless occasions to learn them as co-presences— for example, "orange-bound, black-lettered spine of volume bearing last year's date on a shelf *there."* (On a smaller scale, in computer access of data, information specialists are mimicked by read-write heads moving swiftly to a track on a disk.)

KNOWLEDGE OF COLLECTIONS

It is likely that many information specialists know their collections—what is in them and where—far better than their customers believe possible. Not a few people find it hard to imagine that anyone can learn whole collections, including many items in detail. So far as I am aware, the information specialist's or librarian's ability to memorize attributes of works, such as their titles and nature, has not been investigated. Of how many works does an experienced librarian have mental models—or "schemata"? How large a collection, in other words, can a librarian know without recourse to bibliographic tools? Drawing on research in cognitive psychology, Hirsch (1987) points out that 50,000 is the approximate number of positional patterns that a chess master can recognize, and also of words and idioms in a literate person's vocabulary. "Apparently," he writes (p.64), "a number in the range of 50,000 marks the upper limit of items to which we can have rapid [mental] access in any domain of activity....A basic vocabulary of 50,000 schemata serves merely as a quickly accessible index to a much larger volume of knowledge." If this is so, a good librarian may over time be able to learn, more or less easily, the holdings of two typical special libraries of 25,000 titles each—which is likely to astound the average customer, although it seems about right to me. (I mean "learn" in the sense of knowing that a particular monograph or serial is held, its location and possible uses—not in the sense of having read its contents.) The kinds of information one picks up automatically—many librarians learn author-title information as if by osmosis—are an interesting differentiator of persons, too little studied by psychologists. This differentiation in what one easily learns may be a reason why many potential customers fail to ask questions of information specialists, and so cannot tap their knowledge. The potentials have little image of *what is out there,* and can hardly comprehend a person who not only absorbs knowledge of sources easily but actually enjoys it.

But customers do have one insight that sustains them in going without help, and that is that answers to the really important questions in their lives, the fateful questions, are not to be found in reference works. The kinds of questions information specialists could help them with are typically *non-fateful*— unlike those brought to, say, doctors, lawyers, and clergy—and this, too, contributes to their remaining ignorant; there is no driving force of fear or trouble to make them seek assistance. (School- or work-related assignments drive some to seek assistance, but many of those with the power to make the assignments know next to nothing themselves about what might be useful, and so avoid bringing information specialists into the picture.) Given ignorance of available sources and absence of crisis, many potential customers simply never learn to put questions. The bibliographic instruction movement is an attempt by information specialists to increase laypeople's knowledge of sources, in part so that they can answer their own questions, but also surely so that they will have an image of the kinds of help with sources that information specialists can give. If people could learn *what to ask*—what can plausibly be answered with information specialists' technology—the latter might improve their usefulness, their social standing, their pay.

INFORMATION SPECIALISTS AS A TYPE

While often well read, information specialists are not usually as deeply versed in any one body of discourse as scholars, scientists, or other learned professionals. They know works designed for quick retrieval of information rather than works requiring long commitment of time and self. One might call them strategically superficial. In order to serve a wide variety of customers, they must command a wider range of writings than other specialists. This can be done only by shortening the time spent on any one item, and they deliberately sacrifice depth for breadth. Their typical mode of learning, in other words, is not protracted specialized reading, but exploration, browsing, consultation; use of indexes and bibliographic guides; brief familiarizations ("dipping into"); resort to summaries and overviews. (Matrix structure, of course, invites such behavior.) They may be as familiar with the major monographs and serials of a field as their customers, but they view them more as "sources" or "resources" for potential use by others than as messages with which they must be personally involved.

Undeniably, their superficiality is a problem. It is the only way to cope with the multitude of works and customers that confront them, but that does not matter in society's evaluation of their role. Information specialists, so called, are *generalists* where subject matter is concerned, and it may not be too much to say that society prefers either complete specialization in a subject or none at all. It is all right, for example, to be a doctor or a patient, but what is the status of the medical librarian? It is all right to be a teacher or a student, but what is the status of the school media specialist? The answer, in both cases (and all similar ones), is "uneasy." In any important matter, society wants as much *live* subject expertise as possible, and it can never be presumed that those who specialize in sources of *recorded* knowledge, and have only a smattering of their actual content, will be accorded trust or great rewards.

Another problem lies in the mindset of typical information specialists. Many of them have the humanist historian's preference for *concrete particulars*, and it is unusual for them to think in terms of *abstract data structures* of the sort written about by computer scientists. They do not think, that is, in terms of stacks, arrays, trees, queues, etc.; or of efficient algorithms for searching and sorting these structures; they think in terms of what they can do with particular sources, such as *Who's Who* or *Keesing's Contemporary Archives*. Thus they find themselves in an ironic bind: downgraded for not knowing as much content as subject experts, but also downgraded for not being manipulators of content-neutral symbols like the computer formalists.

The matter is complex, however. Information specialists exist; they are not without a social and economic mandate; society hedges its bets. Most people may ignore, as much as possible, the published records on which information specialists base their work, but there is no general inclination to throw the records away; if anything, society wants more and more recorded; witness the ever-growing numbers of publications and the millions spent on indexing to make them retrievable on demand. Moreover, a fair number of persons who read deeply in these publications, and are engrossed by a subject, are known in some sense to be constricted by the very training they undergo, so as to see only a limited range of what is available. True subject specialists are often poor "resource persons," as the information specialist understands the term. That is, they know what they learned from during the most intensive part of their educations; they know what they read or monitor now; but they are still ignorant of many reference and bibliographic works— even of many substantive writings—in their own fields. For example, every academic reference librarian can point to an English professor who, through unawareness, fails to tell his class of the *New Cambridge Bibliography of English Literature* or the availability of the *MLA International Bibliography* online; to a sociology professor who has never heard of the *International Encyclopedia of the Social Sciences*, even though she and her graduate students would benefit from its articles; to a journal editor who has his secretary laboriously compile what could be got from *Literary Marketplace* in a trice. And every day some programmer or systems analyst re-invents *indexing*, oblivious of the thousands of models, including detailed thesauri, that already exist. There may even be a sense on society's part that much of this ignorance is not innocent and corrigible, but principled and deep-dyed—*studied ignorance*, in the Catholic Church's phrase. That is why society is willing to pay some people—modestly—to know sources of information that others overlook and to be receptive to new sources as they appear. Few want to spend *more* to increase such knowledge, but few want to spend *less* either, and no one wants it to disappear altogether. In some places information specialists have even established their subject as one that students in general should learn, although usually this movement for "bibliographic instruction" is not unopposed.

The struggle between information specialists, with their broad but shallow knowledge of sources, and other kinds of specialists, with their deep but narrow knowledge of content, may well be endless. Regarding a standard journal or bibliography or reference work, the information specialist thinks, *"How can you be a professor* [or whatever], *and not know this?"* To which the reply might be, *"If I got to be a professor without knowing it, why do I have to learn it now? And why should my students learn about what I didn't and don't need?"* Underlying this reply is, *"Besides, I make more than you do—and always will."*

Whether or not one is drawn to information work rests ultimately on variables of personality and cognitive style. As yet, observers have only sketched the different configurations. One of my teachers said, approvingly, that reference librarians have "scrapbook minds." This implies openness to variety, and ability to retain miscellaneous details, but also a certain derivative and shallow quality—unoriginal contents "pasted in." It seems fairly certain that information specialists not only tolerate but actually enjoy the diversity of sources with which they work. They like, for example, being in the stacks of the typical reference section in large libraries; or they like looking at descriptions of the several hundred databases offered by DIALOG.

Many others, I would imagine, go blank or even become slightly ill in the face of such diversity. The "illness" in question is what has been called *information overload,* and the key variable differentiating people may be what brings this on, or the point at which one begins to feel it.

There are contrasting styles for coping with the diversity of stimuli that multiple information sources represent. The scrapbook-minded rove and sample widely, happily "pasting in" bits of the sources without apparent effort. Their opposites make do with *nothing* if possible, or, if something is absolutely necessary, concentrate on mastering only that. Thomas H. Martin (1974), in a metaphor too little known, calls the former types "fat men" and the latter, "thin men." The interesting thing about his formulation is that he believes the intellectual "fat men" are *pathological,* resembling persons literally obese because they have no regulators on their appetites. He has given as an example of "fat man behavior" the tendency of some at professional conferences to go among exhibitors' tables gathering pounds of brochures, announcements, newsletters, posters, catalogs—so many that they must carry them around in shopping bags, which the exhibitors also supply. His "thin men" would *never* burden themselves in this way. Not coincidentally, he characterized the "thin men" as scientists, administrators, executives; the "fat men" as...librarians and information specialists. His metaphor reminds us that the opposition of these two types is not a neutral, academic distinction. It is *visceral.* The types occur in the real world; to some degree they are aware of, and dislike, each other.

The prejudices—and the asperity—of the "thin man" are well exemplified by Sherlock Holmes, described by Watson in *A Study in Scarlet* (Doyle, 1986) as having no general stock of knowledge and wanting none. "You see," Holmes says in Chapter 2, "I consider that a man's brain originally is like a little empty attic, and you have to stock it with such furniture as you choose. A fool takes in all the lumber of every sort that he comes across, so that the knowledge which might be useful to him gets crowded out, or at best is jumbled up with a lot of other things, so that he has a difficulty laying his hands upon it. Now the skillful workman is very careful indeed as to what he takes into his brain-attic. He will have nothing but the tools which may help him in doing his work, but of these he has a large assortment, and all in the most perfect order." Watson, relatively "fat," believes one should know miscellaneous things such as the Copernican Theory and the identity of Thomas Carlyle.

The two types are contrasted extensively in Klapp's *Opening and Closing,* subtitled *Strategies of Information Adaptation in Society* (1978), which develops an entire social-psychological theory of their strengths and weaknesses. His "closers" (corresponding to "thin men") seek to avoid too much variety—

their dislike is information overload. His "openers" (corresponding to "fat men") seek to avoid too much sameness—their dislike is information underload or boredom. For example (p. 151):

> The difference between open and closed styles is mostly in the amount of scanning felt necessary before solution. The opener stays open longer—perhaps one might say he more enjoys roaming, surveying, watching what others are doing, kibbitzing, than does the closer. Staying open longer, he gains a better chance of finding everything, but also risks shallow eclecticism, even drowning in information. The closer, on the other hand, is more quickly satiated with variety, relies more on inner redundancy and intuition, empha-sizes privacy, seeks perfection from selecting facts to fit an ideal, and makes fewer kinds of things out of fewer kinds of things. But like the observer who leaves his post too soon, he may miss vital clues that the opener will catch. Yet the closer may have his design done before the opener even gets through scanning. You can't have it both ways.

Somewhat the same dichotomy turns up in a 1980 work of "neurocogni-tive" psychology—Prentky's *Creativity and Psychopathology,* which focuses on creative scientists (pp. 70, 72):

> A-type is characterized by extensive scanning that often incorporates much peripheral, extraneous information, erratic mental "threshing" of large amounts of information, and a hyper-alertness that facilitates the whole process....C-type is characterized by a constricted scan that screens out all but essential information, a narrow focus on bits of information, and a compulsive-ness that permits slow mastication, digestion, and storage of large amounts of information.

I mention these diverse sources—Thomas H. Martin, A. Conan Doyle, Klapp, and Prentky—to indicate that wholly independent observers seem, in their different ways, to be noticing the same thing. They (and other writers, e.g., Donohew and Tipton, 1973) yield the beginnings of a psychology of information-seeking styles at the level of the whole person, which has been a major gap in library and information science to date. Information specialists, for their part, seem to me to be Prentky's A-types, but without the creativity, at least as far as scientific or literary output is concerned. (Their creativity is, in the broad sense, managerial and political, involving the organization of services for people rather than new publishable writings.)

Information specialists *browse,* an old-fashioned word for what Klapp and Prentky call scanning. Browsing, in their case, does not rapidly bring on overload, nor do they usually regard it as a waste of time. It is rather a pleasant form of stimulus-seeking or novelty-seeking, related to the curiosity drive and exploratory play. (Psychologists who have studied this kind of behavior, such as D. E. Berlyne (1963), have never, to my knowledge, said anything about browsing. One would think it would have occurred to them as an example if they did it. Could they all be "thin men"?) Browsing is, of course, a quick way—some would say too quick—of learning the nature of publications. As a form of reconnaissance, it may be excellent preparation for searching. But it is different from searching in that no foreknown object, no "target publication," is sought. Instead, one presents oneself as a bundle of incipient interests for some object to trigger. Because a target publication can be more or less well described—for example, "I want a history of minesweeping"—it is possible to delegate searching to other parties and to expect fair agreement on what would be a successful outcome. In contrast, browsing, like bathing, cannot be delegated; it must be done in person, because no one else has your particular bundle of interests—ultimately, your embodied self—for objects to trigger. With browsing, you must let publications "search you." And its outcome cannot be predicted—no one can readily foresee what you would call serendipitous. Thus, browsing can be evaluated in radically different ways—as wise and happy receptiveness to what is new, or as unfocused self-indulgence, with a highly uncertain payoff.

This brings us again to our opposed types, who presumably would differ in this fashion on browsing. In the real world, they represent the poles of a continuum along which people are ranged, not exclusive alternatives. But fairly pure cases are common, I think, and attitude toward browsing is a good test with which to tease them out.

I mean browsing in the usual sense—of publications. Many people who feel overloaded when faced with the publications in a library or bookstore are quite willing to "browse" other people when information or opinion is sought. (They may be wonderful "resource persons," in a sense different from the information specialist's, if we count *people they have access to* rather than *publications they know.*) The physicist Enrico Fermi is said to have always avoided looking at the literature if he could put a question to a colleague. Prime Minister Ramsay MacDonald and President Ronald Reagan are two of many executives with a similar bent, preferring listening to reading, let alone browsing. The decisive factor seems to be that human advisers—at least some of them—not only answer questions directly and appositely, they *synthesize on the basis of knowledge about the questioner,* and thus conserve time and attention to a high degree. It may be that what sets information specialists and librarians apart is their relative tolerance for unsynthesized materials. They browse texts of all kinds (both matrixes and discourse), are content with them as wholes, and retain an appetite for further exposures.

One of their frequent complaints is that they have "too many interests," and they are sometimes at a loss as to which to pursue. Escape from indecision may lie in serving the interests of others, perhaps at the expense of really mastering anything themselves. In this sense, they could not be more different from those scientists who seek mastery of a single problem, focus intently on it, and try to simplify everything—their reading, their observations, the particular data in a matrix—to a few general statements of high explanatory power. It is as if, for information specialists, a great variety of interests—and the many particular publications that pique or satisfy them— are *equal in potential*, while scientists (and numerous others) are much more rigorous in prioritizing their interests and limiting what they will heed.

In Figure 3.6 it was noted that the entities in matrixes are roughly equal in importance, whereas in discourse they are strongly prioritized. It may be that matrixes—open-ended, relatively uncritical, unsummarized, unrigorous— express an aspect of *personality* in information specialists and librarians, at least to a greater degree than in those for whom discourse, more complex in structure and implicitly or explicitly more critical, is the natural expression. (This, of course, is highly speculative, and would admit of many exceptions.)

Whatever the case, librarians and information specialists are in the end society's guardians of the *equality of sources*. Their attitude toward the offerings of the world's authors and publishers ranges from neutral through warmly accepting; it is very rarely hostile. Seeing some merit in almost everything, they are more inclined than others to give publications equal treatment, in the sense of noting their existence and qualities, and acquiring, storing, using, and distributing them without prejudice. This is a deeply conservative position, answering society's need for conservation of publications until they have had a fair chance to prove their worth. (No one knows how long this takes.) The opposite, "radical" tendency, also very much present in society, is to compact, synthesize, dismiss, eliminate as much writing as possible in a world permanently suffering from information overload. "Science *flushes*," Belver Griffith says, expressing the thin man's approval of an enterprise that quickly consigns verbiage to oblivion. (The trouble with *social* science, in his view, is that it does not.) Where publications are concerned, most of the world's experts, to say nothing of ordinary people, would probably concur with Murphy's vulgar law: "Ninety-five percent of everything is crap." If everyone agreed on the worthwhile five percent, information storage and retrieval would be greatly simplified; but no one agrees. Thus, librarians and information specialists may have their mandate because, as a class, they are society's mildest censors, exhibiting a love not just of particular works but of publication in general. They counteract the peremptory but conflicting wishes of those who would get rid of as much as possible by the simple expedient of retaining as much as possible, as if all the others cancelled each other out.

Consider: in all the years of their activity (easily reckoned as centuries), librarians have never developed substantive theories for eliminating, abridging, summarizing, synthesizing *anything*. Their editing, such as it is, consists of selecting and rejecting publications in their entirety. Nothing is completely rejected either; copies are always placed somewhere, if only in distant or miniaturized storage. In fields outside their own, they never attempt to compare knowledge claims, eliminate some and retain others, and synthesize the results; for this kind of compaction, they rely on outsiders with subject expertise. These others may edit, summarize, critically evaluate, and generally attempt to abridge the compass of publications, but the fruits of *their* labors grow, too, and are simply added to existing stocks. So the already overwhelming stocks keep growing. Librarians and information specialists are good at browsing and searching this wilderness, and, by long tradition, they do not attempt to manage it in any other way.

Moreover, while librarians and information specialists have amassed copious data on publications and their uses over the years, they rarely try to achieve compaction through a generalizing science of their own. They tend to be atheoretical with respect to the factual data they develop. The OCLC database, for example, is the largest bibliographic matrix in history—over 20 million records and no end in sight. Yet with respect to these data they do not behave at all like scientists: there is virtually no attempt to develop general propositions from them, or discover patterns and relationships in them, or reduce them to summary statistics. Analogously, there is very little attempt by librarians to extract meaningful patterns from circulation records, or by information specialists to look for non-obvious regularities in data from online retrievals. Some researchers in information science are engaged in these tasks (the OCLC organization, for example, has a few), but they are not mainstream librarians or information specialists; and it is an open question whether the latter will draw upon the researchers' results; they seldom have in the past. Library-based information work, in short, is not conducted to establish general knowledge claims about the world; its practitioners are not scientists.

A better way of understanding them as a type is to regard their motivation as *ethical*—as essentially normative, not positive, in character. If they practice a science at all, it is a *policy science*— one concerned with framing desirable ends and choosing appropriate means, given scarce resources. Wide reading of their discourse will turn up many statements of what "should," "ought," or "must" be—normative statements. Their goal, rooted in notions of distributive justice, is *equitable access to publications.* ("Equitable" means similar privileges for those of similar rank—equals treated as equals with different statuses possible, such as students and faculty.) The more utopian among them even seek an equitable distribution of "informedness." These are ethico-political goals, expressed in statements that, e.g., support freedom of information, oppose censorship, and extend user privileges as widely as possible. Their major statement is that most political document, a *budget,* proposing outlays on a particular set of arrangements for equitable access. Again, the notion of a matrix comes to mind—a very large matrix, permanently open, permanently funded, with its proponents ever arguing, "This is the way it *should* be!" against those who would cut back, abridge, restrict, choke off—their antitypes.

Section II

Bibliographic Writing

4

Publication and Bibliographic Statements

Howard D. White

PUBLICATION

All societies at a certain level of technological development manifest their culture through publication—that is, through storing human performances in a durable medium and then releasing copies to the world.

The original storage medium is the human mind, and the original means of release is human performance or display. Before publication proper is instituted, there are direct analogs in performances from memory that others may attend (such as dances and storytelling) and performances stored in artifacts that others may examine (such as canoes, pots, and ziggurats). In both cases the contents of human minds are externalized and become potential "patterns" or "masters" that others may imitate, copy, learn. All human culture is transmitted this way; it is by definition "the learnable" (or that which is non-genetically transmitted). Technology is the subset of culture that can be broadly defined as learnable means to useful ends, and publication is a part of technology. It is the part that converts performances of human beings *as symbol users* into artifacts, with the useful end of extending their existence beyond personal limits through space and time.

The prime example of symbol use is human performance with language. Since language is the institution that integrates many other aspects of culture, it follows that publication of pieces of language is also broadly integrative. Moreover, insofar as culture can be expressed through language (or other publishable expression), publication amplifies culture, both inside and outside a society, to reach persons who might not otherwise be reached, including generations not yet born.

Among all durable artifacts, pieces of published language may be the most durable. This is because of their eminent copiability: if at all valued, they can be readily multiplied at bearable cost.

Publication rests on the idea of a master from which copies may freely be made. (The "master" may itself be a copy.) Technologically this can be implemented in various ways. (Printing is only one.) The idea unites copying technologies with a social invention—*deliberate lifting of restrictions on who may see or obtain copies, and intent to supply copies indefinitely.* So characterized, publication proper implies that "anyone"—persons unpredesignated and unknown to the author or publisher—can obtain a copy of a work.

Typically, the stages of the process are these. The work is released by its originator and accepted by an editor. The essential task of the editor is to accept or reject an entire work. More specialized *copy editing* accepts or rejects *parts* of works, such as chapters, paragraphs, sentences, commas; it is done not only with writings but also, *mutatis mutandis,* with films, phonorecords, and photographs. The work is then recorded in a master and copied (*one* copy attests to publication if the intent remains to meet further demand). Finally, it is released to anonymous persons—which is to say, a market or public.

The essential conditions of publication are the last two: copying and release. If they are met, the work is published. Usually publication also connotes *editorial quality control,* of the sort exercised by commercial publishers, and *print technology* to put a valued work in a durable storage medium. But editorial quality control and print are not *necessary* conditions of publication. Many so-called "unpublished" writings are in fact published under criteria set forth here—for example, doctoral dissertations and "near print" or "grey" literature, such as conference proceedings and ERIC reports.

While mere intent to distribute copies constitutes publication in the legal sense, there is usually a de facto distribution as well.[1] A major contrasting means of cultural transmission is widespread display. If a work has been widely seen or heard, but one cannot actually acquire a copy of it, it has not been published. Rock concerts, bowl games, and television shows, for example, may have been seen by millions but are not published in the strict sense.

---

[1] Cf. Strong (1990, p. 69): "Publication is the act of offering copies to the public. There does not have to be an actual distribution. Even if there is a distribution, it does not have to be a sale; giving copies away to the public is sufficient. The size of the public is irrelevant; handing out one or two copies can constitute publication. And though performance or display of a work is not publication in and of itself, distributing copies to a group of persons who will themselves perform or display the work does count as publication, unless those persons are your employees or otherwise act under your control."

This contrast is noteworthy. Widespread display leaves only memories (perhaps backed by records that may eventually be published). Publication, on the other hand, leaves artifacts—stored pieces of culturally valued language, often dispersed over a more or less wide geographic area—that society wants "managed," to the extent that not all become lost. Librarians and information specialists have this as a central responsibility, and bibliographic statements, as described below, are essential to the task.

WRITINGS

In information work several terms are made to stand for the cumbersome phrase "stored pieces of culturally valued language": *documents, records* (or *graphic records), "generic books," writings.* Modern technology is such that any setting of a piece of language in a durable medium may be considered a "writing," but as used here the term will mean pieces of language that, because of intrinsic interest, have been published, or at least conserved with the intent of ultimate publication.[2] Ordinarily they will have titles by which (possibly with other information) they can be identified.

These stipulations rule out a vast body of writings—for example, schoolchildren's worksheets, most people's letters and memoranda, instrumental documents like sales slips, application forms, bills of lading and computer printout—but, even so, they do not clearly set apart the kinds of writings to be considered here. For example, the messages on a soap box, or a brochure advertising woodland lots, are titled and published writings with a certain "cultural value," yet they are not generally the concern of information specialists and librarians. What will be treated as "ours" are writings that have survived the editorial process in institutions with publication as their primary intent. These institutions may be commercially motivated, but the writings themselves will be their product, rather than a means of selling some other commodity like soap or real estate.

WORKS AND TEXTS

Publications appear endlessly in many languages on innumerable subjects; they are of all lengths in a great variety of forms and genres; and the backlog from many nations and times is already immense. Society wants all of this

---

[2] It is also common for information specialists to deal with publications other than writings in the strict sense: for example, musical scores, maps, films, video tapes, photographs, phonorecords, computer programs, databases, and reproductions of pictures. Each different medium has its own terminology. I shall usually discuss written works, but the others can be taken as implied. My discussion to some extent draws on Wilson's (1968) *Two Kinds of Power.*

managed—that is, made findable and suppliable—even if great quantities of materials go unread most of the time. It would be wonderful if one could "manage" writings by reading them and learning their contents. What anyone can read, however, is a minute fraction of what appears. Publications alone are far too numerous to master by reading; there is time only for cursory examination. Thus, much of library and information work consists merely of *identifying and characterizing* publications as they appear, *locating* a particular publication, and—perhaps—*providing a copy* . This would require great effort even if all publications existed in only one version. However, it is all the more demanding because published works almost always have multiple texts.

The task of identifying and locating copies becomes clearer if one grasps *work* and *text* in a technical sense. Publications embody authors' intellectual products, commonly called *works*. Works are contributions to culture for which authorial credit is usually given. They may be published alone or with other works. Their internal order is given them by their authors; they are "creative" and not form-generated. (The closer works come to being form-generated, the less respect we have for them, as when we disparage something as "formula fiction.") They can be analyzed into fields (including a title field and an author field), but they are primarily discourse. *All Creatures Great and Small* is a work of this sort; so is Wordsworth's "We Are Seven."

Emerging from projects, works may rest on contributory matter of various kinds (e.g., notes, protocols, statistical files); the latter may or may not be considered important adjuncts. A written work consists of at least one *text* representing, more or less well, the author's performance. A *text* is an abstract piece of language existing in one or more versions. The versions are always physically embodied in some medium, but the work is independent of particular storage; it can always be recreated and stored anew in other copies or another medium (including human memory). A *copy* unites a particular physical support and a particular text.

Here is a work as embodied in a particular copy of a particular text:

Hickory dickory dock.
The mouse ran up the clock.
The clock struck one
And down he run.
Hickory dickory dock.

The reader who wishes to see that this is *one* work with *many* texts should ask several persons to write it from memory. They will produce versions with, for example, a different fourth line, different punctuation, different capitalization. Various texts of this work exist in print. It can also be shown in typescript, on a cathode ray tube, on blackboards, in skywriting; or traced on a neighbor's back. It can be translated into French, German, and so on, more or less successfully. The same is true of any text, except that (unlike short rhymes, proverbs, the Lord's Prayer, the Pledge of Allegiance, etc.), most are not found in human memories.

Among those not in memory, the great majority are unpublished. They exist only as one text in one storage medium in one copy (e.g., personal letters, lecture notes, home movies, dictaphone recordings) or a few copies (business letters, Xeroxed memos). Published writings, however, usually consist of a *family* of texts: related prepublication drafts, a manuscript or typescript submitted by the author, a text from which the publisher's master is made (copytext), the set of copies run from this master. This set constitutes an edition. If the work is highly valued, there may be subsequent editions, perhaps including translations and reworkings (adaptations, abridgements, and so on). The following schematic illustrates:

Unpublished: *Work-->text-->one copy*
Published: *Work-->texts-->master-->one edition, many copies*
Published: *Work-->texts-->many masters-->many editions, many copies*

Thus a work is an intellectual unit consisting of all valid transcriptions and translations of its text(s), in all copies. ("Valid" is relative: no published version may perfectly represent the author's *intended* text, because of, e.g., editor's cuts, scholar's or censor's emendations, printers' errors, or the author's own miscarried revisions.)

All this matters for retrieval. We need to be able to retrieve specific texts and copies of works; ask whether they meet certain criteria, such as being on a subject; and ask where copies are stored.

WRITINGS AND BIBLIOGRAPHY

Bibliography may be thought of as the language by which writings are described to make them serve our ends. It consists of statements whose referents are written works in the broad sense, as just noted. The aim of bibliography is to produce *compact representations of writings*—linguistic objects that include whatever facts we find useful, such as identification statements, or IDs plus nonevaluative descriptions, or IDs plus evaluations, or IDs plus location statements.

The statements jointly are *entries* (in a file) if they simply convey that an item exists or is owned; *citations* or *references* if they convey that it has been used in the production of some other work. Consider:

Causley, Charles, ed. *Puffin Book of Magic Verse.* London: Penguin Books, 1974.

Writing that, a trade bibliographer implies: "This book exists; here is what is copiable of it, within conventions." A library cataloger adds (implicitly): "And we own it." In the context of a best books list, the implication is "Recommended." On a teacher's list of readings, it is "Required." In a footnote or endnote of another work, the implication might be "Quoted from." All but the last would be entries; the last is one of the other work's references and a citation to Causley.[3]

Representations like the Causley example can be stored and manipulated in a variety of settings and ways. Since they reduce writings to a few significant features, they occupy far less physical space and take less time to scan than the originals. They are also separate from the originals, and more readily duplicatable. Therefore, they can enter new meaning structures. They can be sorted, for example, so as to group writings by some commonality, such as "Penguin Books" or "books of children's verse." This can be done even if the texts (as embodied in copies) are not so arranged. (If all bibliographic statements were attached to full copies of a text—on bindings, dust jackets, title pages, etc.—it would be impossible to create new meaning structures except by physically sorting *copies*—a very uninviting prospect.)

Some representations can substitute for—that is, be read in lieu of—the original texts and are called surrogates. Abstracts are the chief example. Book reviews sometimes substitute for books, as do condensations (e.g., Cliffs Notes) and what Bernier & Yerkey (1979) call *terse literatures*. Mere references, citations, and entries, of course, are bibliographic statements that cannot be substituted for the originals.

Representations in general contribute to *bibliographic control*. A good translation of this phrase is *power over writings*—the power to find (or discover) what we want, based on the indexical statements others have made about them. (The notion is a rich one; Patrick Wilson's 1968 book remains the fullest treatment.) When examining a bibliography, one should ask: What sort of power does this give me? What demands can I place on it? An ID plus a description affords some power over writings if the description can be related to one's goals. My goal, for example, might be *to obtain copies of all French translations of Hemingway's works*. Existing bibliographies could probably serve this end well. But if my goal were *to find examples of Hemingway's humor,* existing bibliographies would not serve; those passages are not identified. Or suppose I said I would like all works in a collection that would *make me laugh.* I would have still less chance of getting them; existing

---

[3] One paper might have, e.g., 10 *references* at its end, whereas Causley's anthology might have received, e.g., 20 *citations* from all papers. The different terms help keep these counts straight for those who study quantitative aspects of bibliography as part of the study of scholarly communication. It is like having two words to distinguish between shots fired and shots hitting a particular target.

bibliographies do not confer this power. In practice, bibliographic control of writings is obtained by statements that:

> Identify them to edition level;
> Indicate their subject content;
> Reveal their use histories;
> Locate them in physical space;
> Abstract and/or evaluate them.

Some ideas on these topics are presented in the next sections.

IDENTIFICATIONS OF EDITIONS

The distinguishing characteristic of bibliographic statements in the strict sense is that they identify *editions* of writings (or other records).

An edition is the union of an abstract piece of language or symbolic expression—a text—and a durable support medium. It is usually defined as all copies made from a single master. (In print technology, this is a single setting of the type. If copies are run off at the same time, they are one *impression* or *printing*.) The definition can be extended to cover records of performances other than linguistic texts, such as films, phonorecords, and photographs; for simplicity's sake I continue with editions of writings here.

Consider this mini-review:

I Am a Camera by John Van Druten. No Leica.

Whatever one's reaction to this as criticism, it is not strictly a *bibliographic* statement since it only identifies and evaluates a *work*. Works exist only in textual versions, and these in turn exist only in one or more physical embodiments. In print technology, for example, the words are spelled in certain ways and copied in a determinate order, in lines and blocks dictated by page size; they are rendered in type of a particular face and size with a specific ink on a specific paper. One can refer to, and make statements about, a published work without considering it in any particular textual version, but if embodiment makes a difference, one must go further than the author-title ID given above. Assuming that a printed version of the Van Druten play is being reviewed (and not the film or a staged performance by actors), a *bibliographic* statement would make clear which physical embodiment of the text—which edition—the reviewer used in forming an opinion. It could be an American edition, a British edition, an edition from some other country, an "acting" version (of the sort published by Samuel French), a resetting of the text for an anthology, the film script used for the movie version, etc., and while all of these could be highly similar in rendering the text as an intellectual entity, they could also differ in important ways. *In making a bibliographic statement, one gives the reader the information needed to retrieve a particular version of a text.* This is especially important in scholarship, where one's opinion may be influenced by the particular text one uses.

A work in *any* edition, of course, may be the retrieval unit. But often this is not a matter of indifference. One wants a copy belonging to a specific edition or subedition, or maybe even a particular copy (if it has special interest—e.g., belonged to a famous person, such as Coleridge's Schiller or Auden's *Either/Or*).

To *identify* something means to give enough information to set it apart from other, similar things with which it might be confused. A *work* has a name consisting of a title and (perhaps, if known) an author. Neither by itself is necessarily enough for identification. An author's name by itself merely designates a person or an oeuvre. Title alone may duplicate other titles. Here are four very different works:

> The Image
> The Image
> The Image
> The Image

If one simply refers to *The Image* without further context, it is ambiguous whether one means the history of American advertising, the introduction to "eiconics," the collection of stories by a Nobel laureate, or the quasi-pornographic French novel. To disambiguate, it is necessary to add context, such as a subtitle or the author (respectively, Daniel J. Boorstin, Kenneth E. Boulding, Isaac Bashevis Singer, Jean de Berg). But that still may not be enough. Author and title alone (or title alone) are sufficient only to identify a work embodied as abstract text. To disambiguate further, and identify the actual text read or used, one adds the imprint (place of publication, publisher, date of publication), and sometimes even more. Only then has one identified a *book*—-literally the physical support on which a version of the work is reproduced from a master copy. For example:

> Boulding, Kenneth E. *The image; knowledge in life and society.* Ann Arbor, MI: Ann Arbor Paperbacks, 1961.

In database terms, at least five fields—author, title, and the three fields of the imprint—must be filled in to create a search key uniquely identifying the copies made from a particular master. (One may also need to add, e.g., "3rd edition, revised.") The other way to identify editions uniquely is to give each a distinctive number, and that of course is what the system for assigning International Standard Books Numbers does.

Some texts are coextensive with their storage medium (e.g., novels and monographic nonfiction), but many are not—for example, most poems, most short stories, essays, scientific and scholarly papers, chapters, plays in collections. With works shorter than "book length" or "periodical length" (and thus not co-extensive with the total pages of their support medium), the identification process corresponds to that for books. Articles in magazines or journals, for example, require more than author and title for identification. They require the periodical's name, volume and issue numbers, date, and so on, if the article is to be set apart from other possible editions of it—such as in a set of conference proceedings or in a volume of the author's collected papers—that may be textually different. (Similar considerations arise in identifying works *more* extensive than their support medium, such as a novel in three volumes or an opera on four disks.)

The fields beyond those of author and title, including pagination, are obviously needed for efficient retrieval. But they are also a reminder that, when the same work is reproduced from different masters, the resulting versions may vary, and the variation may or may not reflect the author's intent. To take one example, an equation in a mathematical paper in a journal could be marred by a misprint that is corrected in an anthologized version of the paper. Hence identification of the edition that one read is important.

Most texts, it seems safe to say, appear in only one edition. The technology of reproduction being what it is, those that appear in more than one may undergo little or no important change from edition to edition, but no one knows without checking whether this is so. *Lady Chatterley's Lover, Sister Carrie, An American Dream,* and some of W. H. Auden's poems, for example, exist in markedly different versions depending on the edition we read. The films *Cabaret, The Member of the Wedding, Two-Minute Warning*, and *King Kong* differ depending on which edition we see.

Workaday makers of bibliographic statements—for example, library catalogers and most citers—usually find identification to edition level sufficient. That is, while differences *between* editions are recognized, differences *within* an edition are not. In contrast, physical bibliographers in the tradition of W. W. Greg, Fredson Bowers, and G. Thomas Tanselle may carry the identification below the edition level to particular issues, states,[4] or single

---

[4] In Belanger's words (1977, p. 98), "An *issue* is that part of an edition offered for sale at one time, or as a consciously planned unit, and an edition is occasionally sold by means of several different issues. Different issues within an edition...might, for example, have different title pages, one giving the name of a New York publisher for distribution in the

copies of text. They tend to work with texts valued as literature, and may want to discriminate finely among copies—for example, to establish the history of variants occurring in a single press run of a particular text. They may also be interested in a publisher's practices, such as binding advertising in some copies of an edition but not others. They often want to establish *definitive* versions of texts, and they accumulate extremely specific details about the transmission of texts through time. Thus, as Tanselle (1977) notes, while the cataloger describes *one* copy of a work in order to "log it in" as part of a collection, the physical bibliographer examines *many* copies of an edition in order to describe an ideal copy.

At the opposite extreme are writers, such as T. S. Eliot, who do not even mention editions in their literary commentary. Whatever the value of their *critical* statements about writings, they are not given to *bibliographic* statements, limiting themselves to the mention of authors and works—"Tennyson's *In Memoriam*"; "Twain's *Huckleberry Finn*"—without stating the editions. Their implicit message is that one edition of a text is much like another, and that only pedants bother about such things.

There is indeed a whiff of the scholar about bibliographic statements. For those who make them at all, conventions developed over many years of scholarly tradition have to be learned. Bibliographic statements need not be seen as pedantic, however—merely as careful and precise. (One wants to identify a bibliographic object uniquely, but also in such a way that others can identify it, and so resorts to standardized fields containing standardized values in a consistent order.) Bibliographic statements enable people to discuss the existence and uses of a certain text *copied a certain way*. A copy of an edition is the unit retrieved in all literature searches, even if the searcher then goes on to retrieve something *within* the copy—a work (such as a short poem), or a passage, or a single fact. Bibliographic statements make possible our retrievals on the first level, and may also lead, through page indication, to retrieval on the second.

NONCOPIABILITY AND SUBJECTS

A distinction is sometimes made between *primary* bibliography, in which statements are based on examination of a work in hand, and *derivative* bibliography, in which the compiler lacks a copy of a work and, on faith,

---

United States, the other giving the name of a London publisher for distribution in Great Britain.***State* refers to the minor differences in the printed text between one copy and another of the same book. When an error in the text is discovered during the printing of the pages, for example, the press is stopped long enough to make the correction. Sheets printed before the error was noticed constitute the uncorrected state; sheets printed after it was caught constitute the corrected state."

adopts statements about it from other bibliographies. The latter propagates errors.

Even in primary bibliography, however, not all statements are equally easy to make. Some—generally, the easier ones—are *copiable* from the work in hand; others, discussed below, are not. Copiable elements are words and phrases that can literally be taken over from the work, such as title, author, genre, place of publication, publisher, imprint or copyright date, edition, impression, blurbs from the jacket, an existing abstract or summary, pagination, and price. There are problems associated with such transcription, but they are well understood.[5] For the most part, straightforward copying works very dependably in making useful files. Incidentally, the distinction between copiable and noncopiable elements, while fundamental, is not in wide use—I suppose because it may be somewhat embarrassing to the copyists. Much expertise in systematic bibliography and descriptive cataloging consists merely of knowing what to transcribe, how to handle missing (or otherwise imperfect) data, and how to arrange the results. The possibilities are more complex than non-initiates realize; book-length codes such as the *Anglo-American Cataloging Rules* and the *ALA Rules for Filing* are needed to handle them. However, I would agree with the common impression that such work is not—and cannot be—very creative. With some exceptions, it is reducible to algorithms and, ultimately, will be delegable to machines. This is not to deny its necessity, merely to describe it without illusion.

Elements that are noncopiable, even with a publication in hand, include *physical* facts, such as full collation, paper, ink, and binding; and all the facts that depend on one's *perception of content*, notably subject classification and subject indexing. These two types of subject indication (on which I shall focus) have different rules and differently structured vocabularies. *Classifying* a work often means assigning it to *no more than one* position in a hierarchical scheme of subject headings; *indexing* it often means assigning it *at least one* subject heading from a list in which the headings may or may not be related hierarchically. This is done usually on the basis of as little actual reading of the text as possible. "Reading," of course, is a matter of degree, from glances at key parts (such as title, abstract, first and last paragraphs, table of

---

[5] For example, simple copying of titles may cause different *texts* of the same *work* to be separated when the titles are alphabetized in a large file, as would happen if one were called *The Arabian Nights*, another *Tales of Scheherazade*, and a third *The Thousand and One Nights*. Simple copying of authors' names may cause works by the same author to be separated when the names are alphabetized, as happens when authors write books under their own names and also pseudonyms. A different kind of problem arises when imprint date, place of publication, etc., in a work are erroneous or falsified. But these are problems for which bibliographers have long since devised solutions—uniform titles, which standardize titles of works; authority lists, which standardize authors' names; bracketed corrections of data discovered to be false, and so on.

contents), through skimming, to intense, long-term engagement with an entire text (rereadings, underlining, marginal annotation, etc.). I think it fair to assume that, because of the numbers of works they have to deal with, bibliographers are generally at the glancers' end of the spectrum. The main point, however, is that subject indication usually requires the bibliographer to go beyond mere copying in making statements. Concepts from the work must be *identified and translated into the terms available in a given subject scheme.* For this, judgment is needed; most of the "rules" are only guidelines. Some paraphrased examples:

> Choose a term that covers the whole work.
> Choose the most specific, not the most general, term that fits the whole work.
> Choose as many terms as are needed to cover salient aspects.

Such directions leave much to individual discretion. They have to: there is no algorithm in sight to bring uniformity or predictability to the process of subject indication. And in fact people differ in how they index the same writing; they may not even agree with *themselves* if they index it at two different times. (In information science, this is the problem of "inter-indexer consistency." Others in the social sciences know it as the problem of "inter-coder reliability" when data are assigned to categories by more than one judge.)

Something else emerges if we look at subject statements that people actually make. Not only are there no hard rules for choosing terms, there is also no consistent meaning to the statements. The conventions of subject indication are such that only *noun phrases,* the headings or class names, are explicit. Noun-phrase indexing is relatively quick and easy to do, and produces terms that might occur in people's questions. Such terms permit a match between a question and its possible answer in the indexed content, or between an interest and its possible satisfaction. But what is really being said with the terms—the full statement—is left for the user to infer.

Figure 4.1 is my (non-exhaustive) list of things bibliographers might be saying as they index or classify a work. The blanks in the statements are, of course, to be filled in with appropriate terms from classification schemes or subject heading lists (making grammatical changes as necessary). Similar statements, most with different nuances, are grouped within dashed lines. I have italicized the first three because the subject indicators that would go in those blanks seem copiable from the work in hand. All the rest seem noncopiable and dependent on judgment.

The last three would probably be disavowed by classifiers and indexers on the grounds that they do not attempt to predict reader's reaction or searcher's behavior. I include them because some theorists have surmised that classifiers and indexers may or should predict in this way. On the face of it, they

1. *The words_____appear in the title.*

2. *The words_____appear prominently in the front matter.*

3. *Frequently appearing nouns in this work are_____.*

4. A synonymous expression for the title is _____.

5. An alternative title or subtitle for this book is _____.

----

6. The subject of this work is_____.

7. This work is on_____.

8. This work is about_____.

9. The words_____sum up the content.

10. A major part if this work is devoted to_____.

11. The facets of this work are_____, _____, _____ [etc.].

----

12. This work belongs to the literature of_____.

13. This work most resembles those already at_____.

----

14. This work is relevant to the study of_____.

15. This work will shed light on _____.

----

16. If you want to read about_____, this work will satisfy you.

17. If you are interested in _____, read this.

----

18. I predict that anyone interested in this work will be most likely to look for it under_____.

Figure 4.1.   Possible Subject Statements

seem implausible. They would require the bibliographer not only to scan a work and translate its essence into the language of huge schedules and lists with many thousands of terms, but simultaneously to choose terms with an imaginary "typical customer" for their services in mind. Moreover, this would be a continuing requirement through statements about a endless variety of works. Under time pressure, the complications would quickly become too great, and the "typical customer" would be scrapped as a delusion, so as to get on with work that is already hard enough.

It is instructive to fill these blanks with subject indicators actually assigned to published works. We may then ask: (a) Is this what the bibliographer is saying, in that it seems true? (b) If true, is it the *best* indication of subject that can be found? One might imagine that, again and again, bibliographers simply make statements from the second group in Figure 4.1, such as "This work is about ____." However, that is not the case; different real-world bibliographers have a variety of "templates" in their heads. This is sometimes clear from their mistakes, such as placing *discussions of survey methodology* and *examples of surveys* under the same heading when separate headings are available. But, as far as I know, bibliographies containing subject statements *never* make plain what the templates were; they must be laboriously inferred.

Take as an example George Woodcock's (1962) *Anarchism: a History of Libertarian Ideas and Movements.* This is classified in the Library of Congress scheme at HX828 (Anarchism. History. 19th - 20th centuries.) and its sole LC subject heading is Anarchism—History. These duplications of the title are perfunctory but unexceptionable; if they are inserted in the blanks of the 18 statements above, most seem true. The worst that can be said is that, since access by title is possible, they add nothing to the work's retrievability. (Having the class number might lead to the retrieval of *other* works on anarchism adjacent on the shelf.)

Take next a work popular in the early 1970s, Theodore Roszak's (1969) *The Making of a Counter Culture; Reflections on the Technocratic Society and Its Youthful Opposition.* Its LC classification and three LC subject headings are:

HN17.5 Social Reform Literature, 1945-. General works.
Social history—1945–1960
Social History—1960–1970
Civilization, Modern—1950–

Roszak's book is a polemical defense of hippies, young radicals, romantic visionaries threatened by the deadening effects of science and technology. Thus these headings strike me as strange and alienated—as if the bibliographer set out to denature the work in hand to the maximum degree. When inserted in sentences 6 to 10 and 12 to 15, they produce statements that are not exactly false, but that cry out for revision in the direction of greater specificity, greater sensitivity to the author's message. Foregoing that temptation, one notes that there is no way of deciding which of the templates are meant.

Take, finally, Barbara Tuchman's (1984) *The March of Folly; From Troy to Vietnam,* a study of governmental persistence in bad policy (illustrated by sections on Troy's acceptance of the Wooden Horse, the Renaissance Popes' provocation of the Protestant secession, Britain's loss of the American colonies under George III, and America's war in Vietnam). The work is classified at:

> D210 Modern History, 1453–   . General special. Addresses, essays, lectures.

The LC subject headings assigned to it are:

> History, Modern
> History—Errors, inventions, etc.
> Power (Social sciences)
> Judgment

Inserting any of them in the blanks above produces statements that are, again, dubious at best. And again, it is difficult to know what "template" was in the mind of the person who made them. Probably statements 14 and 15 come closest to being true when so completed—for example, "This book is relevant to the study of Judgment"; or "This work will shed light on Power (in the social scientist's sense)." But even then one wonders whether, using the second criterion above, these are the *best* terms that could have been applied to Tuchman's book. (Can anyone imagine finding it through "History—errors, inventions, etc."? I said that indexers probably do not consider an imaginary typical customer when they index, but that does not mean the makers of the list of authorized terms should not.) "Folly" was available as a subject heading; so were "Errors" and "International Relations."

Second-guessing actual statements reveals, however, that my proposed terms are not *conspicuously* better than those assigned. (Both sets are more or less misleading.) It also took much time digging in the *LC Subject Headings*, 10th edition, to produce them. Thus we come to realize that, even if we could improve the lists and schedules of authorized terms, and even if we could revise the work of the bibliographers using them, the gains are slight and questionable. It often becomes a contest of "My word against yours." The gains diminish all the more because of the time they take. Subject analysis, however flawed, has already been done for millions of works, and no one has time or inclination to re-do it. Millions more will pour forth from publishers in the years to come, and no one has time or inclination to do more than "mark and park" them, in a phrase well known in information work.

The bibliographer doing subject indication—classification or indexing— should be thought of as having much in common with the worker on the automobile assembly line. Just as the worker always has parts arriving with bolts to tighten, so the bibliographer always has truckloads of books, articles, or other writings arriving for which terms must quickly be found and applied. There is no time to seek high exactitude or to customize the product. If one tried, the backlog would immediately grow intolerable, and the "line" would shut down.

The point of the examples, of course, is to show some of the mysterious things that happen when we move from copiable descriptions to noncopiable subject statements. (Woodcock, Roszak, and Tuchman, by the way, were not chosen by design; they simply were the first three paperbacks I picked from a bookcase.) Subject indication—stating in brief the overall content of a work—is the most deeply problematical part of bibliographic writing. It is not particularly difficult to *do*—people do it all the time—but it is difficult to do *well*, in the sense of knowing what one is doing and why, and getting others, both bibliographers and users of bibliographies, to share in the understanding.

Simply taking over significant phrases from the natural language of a text, whether done by copyists or the computer, is inadequate. While such natural language "headings" are useful as retrieval points, in a file they scatter writings that should be together. To bring the writings together, standardized headings are needed. That has long been known. But we are still asking what "good subject indication" is: more than a century of theorizing and empirical research, most recently in information science, has not settled the matter. It may turn out to be indeterminable.

USE-HISTORICAL STATEMENTS

The next major class of statements emerges from the histories of publications—their "careers," so to speak.

Sociologists distinguish between social status that is ascribed to a person, such as being someone's son, or white, or Danish; and status that the person achieves, such as attaining a certain level of schooling or salary. Thus, ascribed status is based on characteristics more or less fixed at birth; achieved status, on performance over time. A similar distinction can be made—although, I think, has not been—with respect to publications. Status may be ascribed to them on the basis of characteristics already introduced, such as author, publisher, or subject, which are fixed when a publication appears. These are true status characteristics in that they admit of ranking on a scale of prestige: some authors, publishers, subjects, etc., are more prestigious than others. But publications also have histories in which countable events happen, and these counts can be taken as another basis for rankings and status—as measures of achievement. Thus a literary person might automatically ascribe a Mary McCarthy novel higher status than one by Danielle Steel, but if the McCarthy novel sold only 50,000 copies to Steel's

500,000, the ranking on one kind of achievement—historical popularity—would be reversed. I would grant that terms like "prestige" and "achievement" properly apply to the persons behind the publications—to authors, publishers, writers on certain subjects, and so on—rather than to the publications themselves. Status ascribed to publications rests, in fact, on the past achievements of the persons connected with them, and to speak of publications "achieving" or "performing" is no more than an indirect way of discussing the continuing achievements of persons. But it is common to displace talk of status from the human maker to the thing made, and my extension of the sociological terms to books and other writings should cause no difficulty. Information work lacks a generic term for statements using measures of achievement; I shall call them *use-historical statements*, to indicate their basis in counts of usage over time. Categories to be discussed are:

> Counts of sales or subscriptions;
> Counts of circulations or consultations;
> Counts of citations.

Statements identifying editions and indicating subjects can be made near the "birth" of publications, so to speak, while these counts are part of their "life"; they are not to be found in standard bibliographic tools, which resemble birth registries. Nevertheless, all three kinds of statements have an important thing in common: they can be made without having read the publications in question. (This is, of course, a matter of necessity rather than choice.) Use-historical counts indicate the reception of works by various publics. Inevitably, certain works rise to the top, and one can use information about standings—their "achieved status"—to make decisions about which ones to buy, consult, recommend, retain. (It must be added immediately that such information is not available for all titles, and that other factors are considered in such decisions.)

The systematic study of use-historical counts is called bibliometrics, a subfield within information science. Bibliometricians use the counts as data in building models, often mathematical, of such time-linked phenomena as the distribution of writings on a subject over journals, the growth patterns of literatures, the obsolescence of writings as use declines with age, the publication and citation records of authors, and the interconnectedness of papers, authors, and journals as revealed by citations. De Mey (1982, p. 112) comments: "For the orthodox epistemologist, this orientation might appear atrocious since it leads to judgements upon texts derived not from reading them but from measuring them in such superficial attributes as their number, length, citation links and popularity. ... This apparently meaningless counting reveals a more structured picture of science than one would expect."

Sales and Subscriptions. Best seller lists like those in the *New York Times Book Review* are important, not necessarily because they reveal merit in an absolute sense, but because, being widely seen, they shape the demand to which librarians and information specialists respond: people often want what has been successful with other people. It would be very useful to have far more "best seller lists" than we now have, particularly for periods longer than a year. Over the past, say, 20 years, what are the best-selling titles among encyclopedias? Dictionaries? Atlases? Histories of the American Civil War? Editions of Shakespeare? Sociological monographs? Cookbooks? Yukio Mishima's fiction? While one could ask the question in hundreds of categories, it would usually be difficult to obtain actual counts of copies sold for the rankings. Publishers are not given to publicizing their internal records, and, even if they were, an agency for compiling the results— something like a central statistical office for the publishing industry—exists only embryonically. The *Bowker Annual,* for instance, publishes aggregated sales figures in certain broad categories. What is wanted, however, is a record for each individual title. (The *New York Times Book Review* does not supply sales figures for titles; it reports only their rank and the number of weeks they have been listed.) Lists of "best" or "standard" titles are plentiful, but these are based on judgments, not actual sales figures. (Sales figures presumably would inform, not supplant, judgment; some books that sell well would be judged bad on other grounds.)

A special kind of "sales" record can be found online through OCLC's international union catalog: the number of OCLC-member libraries that have purchased at least one copy of a particular edition. The bibliographic record for each title is followed by codes for libraries reporting it among their holdings; as of 1991 the OCLC Prism system includes a count of these libraries as part of the bibliographic record. Because of duplicate catalog records and multiple editions, it is still somewhat tricky to arrive at holdings counts for many works; even so, the counts are a vivid indicator of the work's reception over time. They indicate its geographic diffusion as well, since holding libraries are grouped by U.S. state. Underdeveloped now, these counts nevertheless have potential for use in a national collection management information system. For example, a list of very widely held titles in a subject class could be published as a de facto core collection, or a list of uniquely or rarely held titles in a subject class could be published as a guide to libraries with unusal strengths. At least one researcher has proposed using OCLC holdings data on journals to help managers arrive at collection development decisions.

In the case of magazines, journals, and other serials, it is generally possible to get claimed subscription figures, for example, in *Ulrich's International Periodicals Directory,* and to use them to rank periodicals in a discipline or subject, such as anthropology or photography. The difficulty is that the data are not properly sorted for comparison. Titles are sorted alphabetically in *Ulrich's*, and one must still go to the trouble of ranking them high to low, which is a small research project in itself if one's choices are numerous. (It is also rare to find library subscriptions distinguished from personal subscriptions.) Now that bibliographic tools such as *Ulrich's* appear in computerized as well as printed form, it will be increasingly easy to produce customized rankings, such as the journals of a subject by number of subscribers.

Circulation and Consultation. Circulation is to libraries what sales are to publishers. Although libraries have long kept aggregate circulation counts, they cannot as a rule supply circulation counts for individual titles without special effort—particularly if their record-keeping is not computerized. With the advent of automated circulation systems, it should be possible to learn the "achievement" of titles over time as a by-product of loan transactions. This would enable librarians to state what they now generally do not know—such facts as their 10 most borrowed titles, or the top circulators in a given subject class. It has always struck me as sad that public librarians, who need good publicity to compete for funds, cannot point to the circulation records of particular works as evidence of their "impact" in the community. Aggregate circulation figures, even when they rise, are simply boring statistics to most people, whereas being able to say "In the past six months inner-city kids borrowed *Moby Dick* eight times, the *Bible* 10 times, *Othello* 14 times," seems to me the sort of anecdotal evidence most people, including funders, like.

With non-circulating reference works and bound serials, in-house reading, consultation, or copying accounts for all use. Moreover, part of the use of circulating works comes from their being copied, read, or consulted without being checked out. When users simply reshelve the items (instead of leaving them on tables, carts, etc.), such use leaves no countable traces. This is a major problem in measuring library "output"—one with which researchers have long wrestled. I would note merely that counts of in-house use of particular titles, if they somehow became obtainable, would be a valuable addition to title circulation counts. A map librarian told me that the two most consulted works in his collection were the (London) *Times Atlas of the World* and Rand-McNally's *U.S. Commercial Atlas and Marketing Guide*. These are standard works, very well known, and therefore his impression is easy to believe. But it would be interesting to have actual data to prove him right or wrong. Probably few librarians could say with any certainty what works are most consulted or most circulated in their collections, yet the advantage of having such knowledge for management and politics is obvious.

The counts of sales underlying the *New York Times* best seller list are pooled from bookstores in many U.S. cities. It is not too much to hope that, with increasing computerization of loan records, libraries across the nation could contribute to similar pooled counts of the circulation of individual titles. Intelligently publicized—for example, through press releases appearing in newspaper feature pages—the rankings could have considerable general interest as cultural indicators. (Future historians presumably would find them interesting as well.) For instance, public librarians might report what America is reading other than current best sellers; academic librarians might report what titles were most frequently borrowed by U.S. college students. Such publicity could have the beneficial side-effect of building awareness of and support for libraries—an intangible but important political gain.

Citations. In science, scholarship, and law, authors normally cite precedent works related to their own. These linkages are the basis for *citation indexing,* in which one looks up an earlier writing of interest—for example, Plato's *Symposium,* or a judicial decision in a court case—and finds the later ones that have cited it. Citation indexing complements subject indexing, and often reveals connections between writings that subject indexers miss.

In the citation indexes produced by the Institute for Scientific Information, the *citing* works are mainly articles from the journals covered by ISI—a well chosen but necessarily restricted subset of all journals published. At this writing, ISI's database of citing articles in science dates from 1961; in social science, from 1972; and in the arts and humanities, from 1979. Within these limits, either the printed or the computerized versions of the indexes can be used to compile counts of how many times publications have been cited. The *cited* items, numbering in the millions, can be of all eras, places, and types: citation counts are obtainable for a particular author, book, journal, article, poem, play, movie, painting, and so on. They are also available for the total publications of organizations, U.S. cities and states, and foreign cities and countries. Ranked high to low, these counts enable one to demonstrate the influence or impact of comparable items within a given period. Although the counts are not infallible signs of quality (any more than sales or circulation figures), over the long run they reliably show intellectual coin being paid, and correlate well with other marks of excellence. They are valuable leading indicators, for example, of who will win Nobel Prizes, as ISI's founder, Eugene Garfield (1980, 1981), has observed. (His *Essays of an Information Scientist,* 1977- , are a valuable source of ranked citation counts in many fields.) The critics of citation analysis issue frequent warnings on how the counts can mislead; but this may stem from an inability to see them at their proper level of abstraction (or a distaste for it; cf. White, 1990, on author cocitation analysis). Bibliometrics, including citation counts, is to literatures what demography is to populations; bibliometric data are on a par with counts of natality, mortality, fertility, and nuptiality. That a certain work or oeuvre has an unusually high citation count indicates its importance *whatever the motives of the citers,* just as an unusually high marriage rate in a society is important whatever the quality of individual marriages. It does not follow, however, that lack of citations means that a work is worthless, if its importance can be demonstrated on other grounds. Used sensibly, as more resembling demographics than psychohistory, the counts do not mislead in most cases. They are the sole means, incidentally, of observing the use histories of relatively short works such as articles, poems, and scientific papers, since other use-historical data—sales and circulation figures—are available only for books and serials.

In its more sophisticated forms, citation analysis is a specialized variety of "cliometrics"—quantitative history—and may be taken as a rich source of evidence on the fate of authors and the development of learned specialties. Particularly promising is the use of citation data to create maps of papers, oeuvres, and journals within fields. The maps are created by computer from counts of how frequently *pairs* of papers (or authors or journals) are cited *together* (co-cited). Typically involving large amounts of data, these maps show intellectual interrelationships—for example, works closely related; works central or peripheral to a specialty; changes in the position of works over time—so as to complement individual judgment about key papers or authors with empirical evidence (cf. White and McCain, 1989).

LOCATING PUBLICATIONS

By its very nature, publication not only disperses copies of a work but leaves most in private hands, where they are no longer consultable by the public. In time, copies are no longer available from the publisher either; the work is no longer "in print." Since it is no longer available to anonymous persons, it is, in a sense, no longer published. The continuing problem for any society is to bring at least a few copies into public sharing systems—libraries—before the work goes out of print.

Seen in this light, libraries insure *permanent publication* by retaining some few copies to be consulted, shared, and possibly recopied by the public. (Recopying *extends* publication.) There is a market mechanism—publishers, booksellers, paperback distributors, book clubs, and so on—for "short publication," and an alternative nonprofit mechanism—libraries, clearinghouses, and archives—for "long publication." In achieving society's goal of "long publication," libraries constantly issue bibliographic statements that identify, describe, and *locate* public copies of writings. (Second-hand and antiquarian book dealers also locate public copies of writings, but they are limited to what is *for sale,* which is not necessarily what one needs or wants to consult.) If copies cannot be found and provided on demand, it does little good to have their IDs.

Actually, it would be interesting to know, through a magical device, the spatial locations of *all copies;* we could then study cultural diffusion at a high level and see what kinds of patterns appear for various works and various media. (Where are all copies of *Easyriders* motorcycle magazine? Where are all copies of the film *Easy Rider*? Where are all phonorecordings of the song?) We could also judge whether writings were *fairly* distributed; do those who should have them have them in fact? But that wish is unattainable. (It would also be open to abuse.) Therefore, we try to bring a few copies under control by giving them a public home and publicizing the address. This is done through bibliographic tools, such as libraries' joint holdings lists (union catalogs), that not only identify copies but tell where they may be found. The great advance here in recent times is the OCLC database, which locates many millions of works in particular libraries.

Overviews of location, such as union catalogs provide, are vital to library subsystems for cooperative collection development and interlibrary loan. Indeed, librarianship as a whole rests on location statements. On the practical level, librarians' fiduciary responsibility for public copies requires constant tracking—from publisher or wholesaler to the library; from the technical service department to a "home position" in public services; from this "home" to borrowers or users or the bindery and back; then eventually to remote storage or disposal. On the political level, librarians generate statements as to *what should be where* in pursuit of their goal of equitable access to publications. (They, above all, are interested in the *fair* distribution of writings mentioned above.) Both levels obviously have a geographic component.

What librarians do can in fact be considered as contributions to a kind of geography, not much studied: *the geography of publication.* Maps, the tool of the geographer, are organized by coordinates in two dimensions. The locator system of librarians also uses coordinates, not usually in maps, but in successive files. That is because the latter system has to take the user down through many different *changes of scale*— for example, from state to city to library to floor plan to stack to subject classification sequence to edition. Millions of persons—students, scholars, scientists, writers, and so on—make bibliographic statements, but responsibility for bringing them to this level of the locator system is uniquely librarians'. Statements by the author or a back-of-the-book indexer may then further refine the scale of the search to sub-mappable levels, until a particular chapter, page, passage, sentence, or word is reached.

ABSTRACTS

A particular word may be reached, but the *author's information* resides at no lower level than that of full sentences. Full meaning and implications emerge from still larger units—paragraphs, sections, the entire work, the work in relation to other works. Yet often we lack time to read something in its entirety, or need guidance as to whether reading it would be worthwhile; we want a brief version as a replacement, or at least a temporary substitute, for the original. Unfortunately, the task of *abstracting* the informative content of the entire work (leaving aside its relation to other writings) cannot be accomplished with the noun phrases of typical indexing and classification. Seeing only them, we do not even know what the indexer or classifier is asserting. (Recall the discussion of Figure 4.1.) Still less do we know what the author is asserting. Let me set out some claims about indexing and abstracting schematically:

1. Noun-phrase *indexing* is inadequate to express what either abstractors or authors actually mean.
2. *Indicative abstracts*, which embed noun phrases in full sentences, may be adequate expressions of what abstractors mean, but not authors.
3. Only full-sentence *informative abstracts* may adequately express authors' meaning. Informative abstracts paraphrase (and sometimes quote) authors' content. They, and paraphrases under other names (e.g., plot summaries), are the best brief renderings available to us; even so, they are not necessarily faithful in giving the gist of a writing.

These points can be illustrated. Consider first this subject indexing for an imaginary work:

Theft
Social Surveys

While the two headings certainly cut down the universe of discourse, and are "informative" in the sense of reducing uncertainty, considerable doubt as to meaning remains. Many constructions can be placed on the terms, singly as well as together. The Library of Congress heading "Social Surveys," for example, has been applied by indexers to works that *discuss techniques for doing surveys*, works that *report results of a survey*, and works that *contain survey instruments* (questionnaires and scales). The title of a work might, through its syntax, eliminate such confusion (e.g., *A Survey of Persons Convicted of Crimes of Theft in Ohio in 1938*), but, then again, it might not.

We do not know what the indexer means by "Theft" and "Social Surveys" unless that person obliges us with full sentences—in effect, writes an indicative abstract (whether or not it is called that). Indicative abstracts generally amplify or clarify a title, and convey, in ways subject headings cannot, what a writing is about. They have long been used with articles, somewhat more rarely with books. They are essentially a form of writing by an *outsider*—that is, someone who can impart over-all content but not necessarily qualified to select and paraphrase main points. It is often held that only persons with subject expertise can do the latter for serious non-fiction and for scientific and scholarly writing. However, the degree of subject expertise needed to select key points must vary with writings and from field to field.

Here are two indicative abstracts, either of which would accord with the subject headings introduced above (though not the "Ohio study"):

1. A methodology for identifying and surveying victims of theft is pro-posed by two sociologists associated with the Survey Research Center, Hunt University. The authors develop a means of contacting victims and show how questions can be asked to elicit their cooperation in discussing a traumatic event in their lives.

* * *

2. This report gives results of the first of two planned surveys of victims of various kinds of theft, including armed robbery, burglary, auto theft, and confidence games. During April 1985, questions were asked of a sample of 280 persons selected from New Urbana police records by the Survey Research Center, Hunt University, acting under a grant from the U.S. Law Enforcement Assistance Agency.

Obviously these abstracts refer to different works. Either would *greatly* clarify what the indexer meant by assigning "Theft" and "Social Surveys," as above. In that sense they are a clear improvement on noun phrases alone. But neither reveals, through paraphrase, what the authors actually state; neither could be substituted for the original writing. It gives nothing away to claim that abstracts of this sort can be written without reading much of the originals. They seem a rather alienated form of work, done, like subject indexing, out of necessity—even when authors write them for their own articles and papers. (When authors write indicative rather than informative abstracts of their own works, it may be because they want the reader to read their whole piece, and dislike divulging its main points shorn of context. Consciously or not, they reveal only enough to lead the reader into the full text, for which they do not intend to produce a substitute.)

Only through the informative abstract, with its paraphrase of key content, is the author's main message expressed, and for this, greater discrimination and more reading on the part of the abstractor is usually necessary. The informative abstract generally conveys methodology and, in particular, results. Here is one corresponding to the second indicative abstract above (again, the work is imaginary):

3. Victims of thefts within the past five years are not significantly different from non-victims in their desire to punish the offenders, as measured by

t-tests on mean lengths of prison sentences believed appropriate for armed robbery, burglary, auto theft, and confidence games. This finding by Hunt University's Survey Research Center emerges from samples of 240 victims drawn from New Urbana police records and contacted by telephone during April 1985, and 192 non-victims contacted by random digit dialing a month later. Victims are significantly more negative than non-victims in attitudes toward police and in willingness to turn to vigilantism, and men in both samples tend to be significantly more punitive than women (all results, $p<0.05$).

A professor I know has said that the only way to tell indicative from informative abstracts is that the indicative ones are shorter. But length aside, the informative abstract is more an insider's piece than the earlier, indicative ones. The abstractor seems knowledgeable about the theft victimization survey, and qualified to write about it on our behalf. This is hardly surprising when author and abstractor are the same, as now frequently happens in journals; but, if not, the writer of an informative abstract is supposed to read the whole report and imitate the author as closely as possible in abbreviating it.

So, must one be an expert, immersed in the literature of a subject, to write informative abstracts? Or can anyone reasonably bright—the typical information specialist —do it? Such a question moves us into the endless struggle between "outsiders and insiders"—between generalists and holders of more specialized expertise. Who is qualified to do write what, and how much reading does it take? Many subject experts regard abstracting as a chore and are loath to do it for their own works, let alone those by others. Generalists, on the other hand, may lack the acuity to pick or express main points well. Meanwhile, the publication mill grinds, and everyone lacks the time to read more than a few of its products, which nevertheless must be summarized. As with subject indexing, the art of abstracting is practiced on a staggeringly large scale—*Chemical Abstracts* alone is a huge undertaking—with indeterminate and probably indeterminable results.

Whether abstractors (other than authors) read "every word," we will never know: informative abstracts are typically reductions of scientific papers, whose well-defined structure—introduction, methodology, results, conclusions—lends itself to spot reading. How well the main points are captured is something else we seldom discover. To judge, one would have to closely compare the original with the abstract, or possibly compare several abstracts of the same work, and that is excessive labor as a rule. (It would be similar drudgery to compare plot summaries of novels or digests of "great books.") Another test, which I have not seen tried, would be to ask authors what they think of abstracts by others of their works. I have not liked them for works of mine (nor some of the subject indexing, either). It is not the same as a bad review, but one says, "Idiot!" nonetheless. While we could, with study, distinguish good from less good abstracts in particular cases, the sheer volume of summarization needed makes one less than choosy; one settles, quite quickly, for having it done at all.

EVALUATIONS

While most abstractors in the sciences do not judge what they summarize, a mixture of summary and criticism is commonplace in general reviewing, and so is evaluation without summary. Evaluation statements are essentially editorial; they come down to "This I recommend; that I don't." (No Leica.) A basic divide in evaluation is whether it is done formally, for a collective audience, or informally, for one person. In the first case, the evaluation is usually a piece of published discourse incorporating references to one or more works. It appears in well known forms, such as the annotation, the book review, the critical essay, the review of a literature. (See "Literary Forms in Information Work" below.) In the second, it is usually oral. The latter might be called "biblioloquy," a coinage suggesting personal conversation in which the relevance of a specific work (or text) to an individual's question or need can be addressed.

Like informative abstracting, however, and unlike the other kinds of statements we have considered, these forms of evaluation are predicated on having read the work—something information specialists, such as systematic bibliographers and library catalogers, seldom have time to do. Insofar as they read and formally evaluate, they do not differ from others who do the same, such as reviewers and scholars. But to read is to specialize: one can only declare interest in and commit time to a relatively small number of works. It is impossible to specialize very deeply in this way and function on the front lines of publication, where the numbers of writings are (and always will be) too vast to cope with unless one is willing to approach them in a spirit of deliberate superficiality. If societies are willing to countenance publication at present levels—and they show no signs of cutting back—then, for information specialists, evaluation of most writings must reside in the fact that they were published in the first place. There is not time—there will never be time—for them to do more. Reviews and critical estimates do get published, of course, but they are written by persons who gain time to read by ignoring the expanse of writings that confront information specialists.[6]

---

[6] Not everyone who claims knowledge of a work has earned it by careful reading; a certain amount of faking goes on. For example, writers often complain that reviewers cannot have read their work, given their remarks; and in science and scholarship some people are known to cite or include in bibliographies things they have barely looked at. But for present purposes, the ability to evaluate a work will be assumed to result from full perusal.

Do information specialists even read reviews? Most do, I suppose, as a matter of keeping up, but not necessarily for guidance in acquiring items for their collections. Many publications are not reviewed at all, and many more are reviewed too late for the opinion to be of use. Hoping to have an item on hand (or on its way) when customers learn about it, information specialists who develop collections often order on the basis of the earliest bibliographic statements they see—either bare, entry-type listings or publishers' ads.

It is a good question as to what, in the bare listings, actually prompts their orders. Do any statements in the U.S. national and trade bibliographies—the *Weekly Record, National Union Catalog* proof slips, and so on—have sufficient force to cause librarians to acquire works? If so, which ones and why? Among statements of author, title, publisher, subject matter, and so on, which *most often* cause the collection developer to decide favorably? The statements are not intended to be evaluative at all; yet some trigger purchase—a sincere form of positive evaluation—and others do not. My guess is that, for most non-fiction, it is a combination of publisher and subject, with publisher predominant. In other words, since reviews are so often unavailable (or unavailing), collections are built on the basis of *what publishers' names connote.*

Libraries, as guarantors of "permanent publication," ratify the choices of publishers generally, but of some much more than others. It would be interesting to know which publishers a given library has ratified the most over the years, in the sense of purchasing their output. Which publisher, for instance, accounts for the largest share of titles in the Research Library at UCLA? (Conversely: where, if anywhere, is the total output of a given publisher held?) Even more interesting, of course, would be a ranking of the publishers *within subjects* at a large library like UCLA's, or, better still, in large libraries nationwide.

Again, these statistical aggregations, if they ever come, will be the by-product of computerized files created for other purposes. They might eventually be generated, for example, from the OCLC database—a new kind of "cultural indicators." In this regard it is instructive to note that ISI's citation databases furnish valuable "science indicators," even though this has never been their primary function.

THE BIBLIOGRAPHIC WORK FORCE

I have argued that bibliographic statements identify editions of works, and that, once that is done, further statements can be attached—to indicate subjects, convey use histories, locate copies, and summarize or evaluate content. This way of putting it, however, obscures the origin of the statements. Many bibliographic products, particularly the massive national and trade bibliographies, are so impersonal and standardized that they seem "hardly human." They are in fact put together by persons who examine publications on our behalf, write about them in a more or less prescribed fashion, and turn in their statements to be published. A look at these origins may restore their image as ultimately personal. One reminder is the blunder. In a Bowker list some years ago, Richard Brautigan's novel *The Abortion; an Historical Romance* was put with the non-fiction under "Obstetrics and Gynecology." That was done, most likely, not by a computer or someone making a joke, but by a dutiful member of the bibliographic work force. Among those members, anything is possible, of course—from extremes of alienation and error, to high serviceability and scholarship.

To refer to "the bibliographic work force" may seem odd: it is not a standard occupational category, and neither a trade union nor a professional association exists to give it organizational identity. Nevertheless, the term is useful as a catchall for persons who, within certain conventions, write of culturally valued records by name. This work force includes makers of national and trade bibliographies (e.g., some employees of the Library of Congress and the British Library, and of firms like Bowker, H. W. Wilson, ISI, and Whitaker), professional subject bibliographers in and out of libraries, and library catalogers. It includes indexers in several varieties, abstractors, annotators, reviewers, and specialists in documentation. It also includes teachers who prepare lists of required or recommended readings, and writers who cite their own and other writers' works.

Obviously the last groups swell the ranks of this work force considerably, and many of their members would protest that they "do bibliography" only incidentally. In the strict sense, that is true. But the characterization allows us to treat any statement about any publication (or somehow derived from it) as bibliographic in tendency, and thus "doing bibliography" becomes a component in the occupational role of students, research assistants, secretaries, researchers, scientists, lawyers, clergymen, professional writers, reviewers, and many others.

It is, in fact, next to impossible to give an exhaustive list of all the occupations that engage in bibliographic work at least part time; or to estimate the size of this work force. Those whose tasks might be said to be wholly bibliographic are not well identified by the *U.S. Dictionary of Occupational Titles* (a standard source), and no count of them is made in occupational censuses. (They are hidden under relatively undiscriminating titles such as "librarians, editors, clerical not elsewhere classified; computer personnel; researchers not elsewhere classified.") Until interest in the burgeoning "information sector" of advanced economies becomes keen enough to prompt more discriminating occupational classification, the easiest way to demonstrate the existence of a bibliographic work force is to point to its products. These are very considerable, even if we omit those of students, who annually produce countless bibliographic statements in their assignments, and those of clerical workers charged with various kinds of "records management" in enterprises throughout the world. Confining our attention to published (or public) bibliographic products of the sort found in libraries—to indexed lists of entries and to citation-bearing writings—we find evidence of millions of hours of effort.

BIBLIOGRAPHIC GRADES

A status system operates in this bibliographic world, as in many others; it affects such practical activities as librarianship and information service; yet, while widely sensed, it is seldom discussed. To reveal all its aspects would be to create an entire sociology of bibliography. I propose nothing more sweeping here than a few criteria for defining and ranking levels in the bibliographic work force.

Statements about other writings can be ranked according to what, from their context, we ascribe to the person making them. The levels are at least three. On the first and lowest, the statement in context furnishes no evidence that the person has read the item—merely examined its title page and other superficial aspects. On the second, the statement allows us to conclude no more than that the person has read the item referred to. On the third and highest, the statement is taken as evidence that the person has not only read (or consulted) the item referred to, but used it in preparing a new work. As in any social system, different levels in the hierarchy are linked to different rewards, such as prestige.

In somewhat finer detail, capsule "position descriptions" in the bibliographic work force can be graded rather like those of a civil service:

> *Grade 1.* Gives written evidence of having examined particular works by copying prescribed elements in the prescribed way. Example: *Descriptive catalogers.*
>
> *Grade 2.* Gives written evidence of having examined particular works by assigning one or more alternate titles from a list of standardized alternate titles. Examples: *Subject catalogers and classifiers.*
>
> *Grade 3.* Gives written evidence of having read works by summarizing them. Alternatively, may give titles to *passages* or *sections* of a work, drawing them from the text on the basis of reading. Examples: *Abstractors. Book indexers. Indexers of articles and other publications in serials.*
>
> *Grade 4.* Gives written evidence of having read works by evaluating them. May recommend or not, explicitly or implicitly. Examples: *Book reviewers. (Reviewers of other media as well.) Compilers of annotated bibliographies.*

Grade 5. Gives in writing a systematic account of many works, choosing interrelationships to discuss. May do comparative evaluations. Example: *Authors of reviews of the literatures in various disciplines, professions, and specialties.*

Grade 6. Gives evidence of having read one or more works in the course of producing an original piece of writing. Works are referred to as discretion dictates, rather than systematically as in Grade 5. Evaluation of works referred to is discretionary and will often be implicit rather than explicit. Examples: *Scholars, critics, nonfiction writers generally if they cite.*

These occupational groups are set forth in Figure 4.2, which illustrates a system within which bibliographic statements are made. The two major dimensions on which groups differ are *autonomy in reading works* and *autonomy in writing about them.* These are not, of course, the only dimensions by which to judge. But I should anticipate here the complaint that such distinctions are snobbish. Aside from the openness of all ranks in this system—and one's sure knowledge that a good descriptive cataloger is worth two or three average professors—these dimensions and this ordering recommend themselves by what they can explain.

The dimensions say that bibliographic statements are *acts of writing* with more or less freedom, based on *acts of reading* with more or less freedom.

A key division among makers of bibliographic statements is whether they have read the item or not. By "non-reading" I do not mean total ignorance or neglect of the item; in that case there would be nothing to state. A minimum would be cursory examination of the title page. Spot reading and "glancing over" key parts such as an abstract, introduction, and conclusion would be about the maximum. The assumption is that anyone making bibliographic statements about an item could report such things as "I've only looked at the title page," or "I've read it all the way through," or "I've read it dozens of times and pondered it for years." The midpoint of the horizontal axis in Figure 4.2 (inset) lies where varieties of cursory examination pass over into varieties of reading works in their entirety.

I have called this axis *autonomy in reading* (and not just "reading") because I believe that persons toward the low end—catalogers and classifiers—*cannot* read works all the way through and still perform their duties. Compared to those at the high end, they lack autonomy both in choosing what they will examine and in how much of each work they will actually look at. In a sense they are paid to deal with *glut,* a constant oversupply of publications. Given the time available for processing, the only possible response is varying degrees of spot reading.[7] On the other side of the divide, one has—or takes—

---

[7] Catalogers and classifiers of course read *some* things—perhaps even on the job—just like everyone else; I am not suggesting they are robots or slaves. But as I said above, they are in some ways like workers on an assembly line.

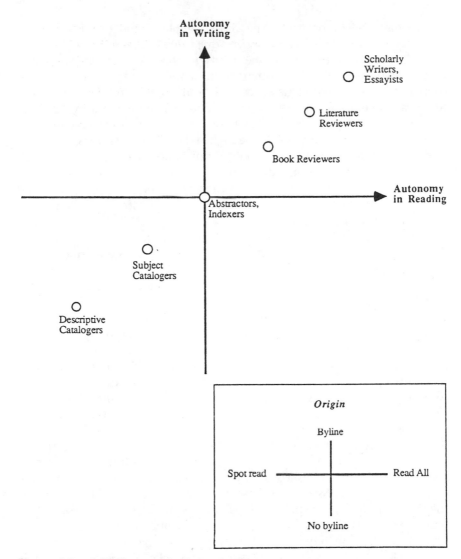

Figure 4.2.   A Bibliographic Status System

increasing freedom to choose titles and to read as much of them as one likes, as often as one likes. One becomes, increasingly, one's own editor in confronting the glut.

Persons are driven to read by desires for aesthetic pleasure, moral gratification, and subject mastery. These powerful incentives can best be satisfied if persons are free to read autonomously. Some individuals will want, further, to share information about reading that satisfies them—or perhaps fails to—by discussing the works. The more one has read in a given area, the more one may seek to claim *authority* in that area—the right to be preferentially heard or read. (The most complete modern discussion of authority in this sense is Wilson's *Second-Hand Knowledge*, 1983.) But authority cannot rest *merely* on the ability to copy or quote or paraphrase parts of what others have written; it must increasingly involve original commentary. One individuates oneself from other authors (other authorities) by contributing new work, recognized at some point by others as valuable. Authority in short is based on ability to convert autonomy in reading to *autonomy in writing*. At the high end of the vertical axis, this is the freedom to state what one likes about writings one has chosen to read, as long as at least some persons, editors in their own right, find it acceptable. At the lower end, one may only copy or paraphrase; personal expression would be out of place. (Imagine the strangeness of a catalog entry with the note, "I loved this book!")

The occupational grades traversing Figure 4.2 may be thought of as persons involved in "reading-writing systems" with definite characteristics. Catalogers and classifiers have as little autonomy in what they write as in what they read. Descriptive catalogers copy bits and pieces according to well established conventions; little reading is necessary (or possible). Subject catalogers and classifiers are slightly more free to read, so as to express overall content in a pre-set vocabulary. They are not as bound to copy their data as descriptive catalogers, but in practice they often simply adopt noun phrases from a title or summary, possibly with some variation. (Montgomery & Swanson, 1962, have called this "machine-like indexing by people.") Abstractors and indexers may have to read more, but still must follow fairly rigid rules in what they write, so as to stay close to the author's content. Book reviewers have more liberty to read and comment than abstractors; they are not constrained merely to summarize but can add commentary of their own, as can compilers of annotated bibliographies. Reviewers of literatures (e.g., the published research on a topic of the past year or some longer period) have discretion to read and comment as they like, as long as they stay within topical confines, broadly construed. They must cover their topic, however, which may mean reading and mentioning *more* authors than they would like, in order to do it justice. Finally, "essayists"—nonfiction writers of all kinds—can pick titles to read and cite ad libidem, as long as they can convince others that they know what they are doing. Basic prudence on their part dictates that they try to read and cite "the right things" so as to forestall unfavorable criticism, but they are basically free to choose as many or as few references as they like.

Where publications are concerned—and I am discussing mainly bibliographic statements that are published—greater autonomy in writing is divided from lesser by authorial credit. The midpoint of the vertical axis in Figure 4.2 (inset) is marked by *whether one gets a byline*. The lower grades, catalogers and classifiers, do not; their constrained reading and highly stereotyped writing are deemed not to merit it. The higher grades, reviewers and authors of various kinds, get bylines as a matter of course, based on their supposed authority. In the middle are those for whom bylines are irregular and problematical—indexers and abstractors. Some get bylines (perhaps as their initials); many others are credited only on mastheads or not at all. These are persons who need to read all or most of a work to do their jobs, but who labor under conventions that do not permit much individuality of expression; hence they often remain anonymous. (Book reviewers and contributors to dictionaries and encyclopedias may also share this plight.) Occasionally book indexers get authorial credit, perhaps for a fine piece of work; but this is exceptional.

Anyone may read and write with autonomy outside the publication system, but the privilege of publishing discourse, and of vying to be known as an authority, must be earned. The process people go through for degrees, from high school onwards, generally includes a series of prescribed readings; one's own ability to publish is based on submission to the discipline of others as to what must be read and mastered. (One may also need knowledge that can come only through apprenticeship.) The idea, of course, is that through intense socialization the external discipline will be internalized, so that ever after one's performance is a credit to one's teachers. This form of submission differs from that of catalogers, classifiers, and indexers in that, at a well-marked time, it is supposed to *end*, leaving one free to write creatively thereafter. For seekers of advanced academic degrees, that is what "getting to the research front" means. (The self-taught may set their own readings, but, in order to publish, they still have to do roughly what their Ph.D. counterparts would do.) The doctoral dissertation, which symbolizes the final steps to autonomy, is supposed to demonstrate competence at the top two levels of Figure 4.2. It is, first, a new contribution to knowledge that grows out of, second, a review of the literature, representing existing knowledge. And this pattern is supposed to be followed in subsequent work—each new article or book should artfully cite and review precedent literature if it is to be persuasive.

There is little doubt, however, as to which is generally more valued. A review of the literature is seldom as prestigious as a writing making some new knowledge claim, because it does not individuate its author as sharply. (A dissertation that was simply a review of the literature would probably not be accepted.) As long as the review can be described as a rehash of what others have said, it does not fully establish one's own identity and authority. Hence it is difficult to get creative scientists and scholars to write reviews of literatures. (Sometimes they refuse; more often, I would guess, they fail to volunteer.) Reviews are seen, quite accurately, as involving a great deal of reading and judgment for a rather meager reward.

Reviews of the literature do, however, have an advantage over the typical book review, in that the clever may be able to use them as a vehicle to organize a field intellectually, or to deliver a major critique of existing work. The typical book review, on the other hand, conveys the substance and merits of a single book in brief compass. As a rule it lacks the prestige of an original essay, or even a review of a literature, because it is thought to be a highly prompted form of work, and thus relatively easy to do: having read a book, one can hardly fail to have something to write about; simply retelling the argument or plot fills space. The subject is dictated less by oneself than by the author, with whom the billing is shared when the review appears.[8]

Fortunately, there are people, including very creative ones, who will write book reviews and reviews of literatures. My claim is simply that, with notable exceptions, the latter two forms of bibliographic statements are accorded lower prestige than books and articles. Certainly this is so in academia, where matters of intellectual status are highly salient.

Perhaps the least prestigious form of writing for which one can claim authorial credit is the annotated bibliography. There are of course gradations within this class as well. A specimen like the *Guide to Reference Books,* under its various editors, may well be more prestigious than truckloads of indifferent papers. But, as a class, annotated bibliographies suffer from low creativity and primitive organization—a fact noted indirectly when we say that they are compiled rather than written. They lack the essayistic quality of a review of the literature, in which various writings can be compared and contrasted in an over-all scheme; they consist instead of discrete blocks of discourse related only through categorization. (In other words, through *indexing.*) However good of their kind, there is a kind of flatness and obviousness about them: here is a literature, ho-hum, and someone has put it into pigeonholes, ho-hum. They are even less exciting when annotations are neutral. Nevertheless, many thousands have been published (with bylines); Besterman's *World Bibliography of Bibliographies,* for example, devotes four volumes to numerous free-standing ones appearing through 1963. Libraries buy and stock them in great numbers, and some must occasionally find use as reference works. As printed publications they date quickly, and the number of printed ones will probably decline as bibliographic services become more and more computerized.

As we move downward through the grades of the bibliographic work force, the writing becomes progressively less "creative" and the chance for a

---

[8] It is possible to convert a book review into a major statement of one's own position (Chomsky's 1959 review of Skinner's *Verbal Behavior* comes to mind). But this is merely to acknowledge that brilliant people with strong views will turn *any* writing assignment into an occasion for an essay; the texts they read are simply pretexts for exhibiting their own prowess at length. Contributors to periodicals like the *New York Review of Books,* e.g., Gore Vidal, have raised this form of long review-essay to an art.

byline more remote. Around the midpoint of Figure 4.2, one sees a division of labor occurring and a marked status divide. An author capable of writing articles or books might be willing to review the works of others, or to produce an annotated bibliography. The same author might also be willing to abstract his or her own work (often as a last weary chore) in order to comply with journal requirements. But that is all; one does not go—one rarely even communicates—below the divide. The abstracting of works not abstracted by their authors is someone else's responsibility. It and such tasks as indexing, cataloging, and classifying publications are left to the army of the intellectually nameless.

BIBLIOGRAPHIC LIVES

The tradition of anonymity for the lower grades is, from the standpoint of those in the upper, not unfair. Few would deny the usefulness of lower-grade work, but it is too routinized and mechanical to command the true prize— attention. And since no one is forced to do it, there is the presumption that choosers of low autonomy must be content with their lot. (If not, a way upward is always open.) Those who make bibliographic statements in publications with bylines are often quite oblivious, I believe, to those who make them anonymously for pay; but if they think about them at all, it is probably to wonder at their humility and to recoil from the perceived dullness of their work. Someone (a recoiler) has described indexing as a skill that, once mastered, is no longer worth doing. Such persons generally want *earned renown* above all, and they find it hard to imagine employment so selfless. "A realistic image of science," writes Randall Collins (1975, p. 480), "would be an open plain with men scattered throughout it, shouting: 'Listen to me! Listen to me!'" He makes it quite clear that all of their behavior, certainly including their reading, writing, and citing, is fundamentally involved in "a competition for attention." The reading-writing systems of the lower bibliographic grades—those who *make entries* rather than *cite*— virtually preclude attention, let alone fame; and the persons writing in those grades are deeply, irremediably *ancillary*. "Ancilla" means "handmaiden" — for many, a terrifying thought.

   In sum, millions of bibliographic statements are made by persons who cannot choose, and have not really read, the works they deal with, and who are free to say about them only the most rule-bound things. These same persons are also absent from, unknown to, and ignorant of those for whom they write. Their labors will not be credited. Do they care? Do they *want* more credit? What, after all, do they see as the meaning of their lives? From another point of view, of course, they are simply mass-production workers, like many others. The workers who manufacture jeans or transistor radios or white bread do not become famous either. Or rather, their fame is in the product, which they do not get to sign. Why should the production of copy for OCLC or the *British National Bibliography* be regarded as any different from work on a Hyundai car?

One wonders nevertheless. As far as I know, no one has ever studied the occupational culture of workers in the lower bibliographic grades in settings like Bowker, H.W. Wilson, and the Library of Congress. I mean "study" in the sense of a book combining ethnography and sociology, with perhaps a bit of muckracking thrown in. One suspects that the bibliographers, catalogers, and indexers working without bylines are mostly women, and that the subject might yield itself to a "women's studies" approach; but even these are question marks. Certainly no such book has been done in the field of library and information science; there are, in fact, information scientists who have studied indexing all their professional lives without ever having talked to an indexer. Meanwhile, publications pour forth; the databases grow; and their print counterparts, the multi-volume sets of the great bibliographies, catalogs, and abstracting journals, arrive year after year to stand on the shelves like monuments.

5

Rigorous Systematic Bibliography*

Marcia J. Bates

INTRODUCTION

Systematic bibliography has long been viewed as a poor relation to descriptive or analytic bibliography. The practice of making bibliographies to be used in literature searches has been seen as a simpler and humbler activity than that of creating exquisitely detailed descriptions of the physical and textual aspects of books. I will argue here, however, that systematic bibliography as it *should* be requires greater skill and sophistication on the part of the bibliographer than is customarily presumed.

My purpose is to provide a foundation for technically subtle work, in which the practical utility of systematic bibliographies is matched by the skill in searching, selection, and organization required of the compiler. The bibliographies so created will make possible a more rational search strategy for users and will contribute to bibliographic control in a way that many existing bibliographies do not.

The question of whether to do a bibliography on a topic will not be addressed here. But it should be clear that all good bibliographic work requires an assessment of the need for and likely usefulness of the resultant product. Time is too precious to waste on work lacking this base.

A second requirement, which *will* be addressed at length, is that a

---

* This chapter first appeared, in different form, as Bates (1976), © American Library Association, used by permission.

bibliography state its own specifications. This is a requirement that compilers often fail to meet. In explaining the concept I will draw extensively on Wilson's (1968) *Two Kinds of Power.*

GLOSSING THE TERMS

Vernor Clapp (1974, p. 722) has said that the aim of systematic bibliography is "to identify and describe in a systematic arrangement the books that may be suitable for a particular purpose or that have other common characteristics." He divides it further into two subclasses: "Enumerative bibliographies, whose primary purpose is to present an inventory, may be contrasted with subject bibliographies, where the primary purpose is content." He gives national bibliographies and catalogs as examples of enumerative bibliographies, and periodical indexes and abstracting services as examples of subject bibliographies. The principles of bibliography preparation to be developed here may, for the most part, be applied to both categories.

By "systematic bibliography" I mean *an ordered list of descriptions of graphic materials on a given subject or area.* Some comments on the definition follow.

Graphic materials: This phrase refers to messages recorded by human agency in some durable medium. So lists of descriptions of books, journals, journal articles, phonograph records, videotapes, films, educational kits, maps, microforms, machine-readable databases, and microcomputer software—to name some major media—can all be considered bibliographies.

List: A bibliography is composed of discrete descriptions arranged in a list, or sequence, rather than in running text.

Descriptions: Bibliographies always describe—and point to—other graphic materials. The questions of *what elements* should be in these descriptions, and *what form* these elements should take, are at the heart of bibliography and cataloging, and provoke endless writing and debate. Suffice it to say that there are roughly agreed-upon elements, in roughly agreed-upon order, that should appear in the descriptions for each of the various media. (Two of the most consistently appearing elements are *author*— the person or organization creating the work—and *title.*) The set of these elements, in order, describing an individual graphic record is often called a "reference" or "citation." Hence a bibliography could also be defined as a list of references, or citations, to graphic materials.

Ordered: To increase the utility of the list, the items on it should be arranged according to some principle rather than randomly.

Given subject or area: The word "area" is used to represent all the other criteria besides subject that may be used for defining coverage of bibliographies. Examples are geographic area, location of collection (as with a catalog that lists items to be found in a particular library or bookdealer's), form or genre of material, and "works by..."

THE USER'S STANDPOINT

Bibliographies, I noted, point to other things; for most users they do not carry the desired information, but point to where that information can be found. Let us now ask an elementary question: why should anyone ever want to use a bibliography anyway? If the bibliography only points to other things, and briefly at that, why not go directly to the book (or other item) referenced? Bibliographies, especially catalogs, are often used to facilitate *physical* access to the desired items, but why ever use a bibliography for *intellectual* access?

It must be that sheer collocation of descriptions of materials in lists aids people in their information-seeking. We assume, for example, that if one person selects out of the universe of graphic materials just those on air pollution and collocates them in a list, then the search and selection process for other people interested in that subject will be speeded up or even eliminated.

This point may seem obvious, but, in fact, its consequences are not generally carried through to their logical conclusion. If we prepare bibliographies so that seekers can find materials *selected and grouped in certain ways*, then it is crucial to the effective use of those bibliographies that the *principles of selection and collocation* be made crystal clear to all users.

In *Two Kinds of Power* (1968) Wilson states that users of a bibliographic instrument need to know its *specifications*, that is, "the rules according to which it was constructed." He adds (p. 59), "Even if I examine the contents of the instrument, item by item, I do not know what I can properly conclude about the items I find, and just as importantly, the items I do not find. My knowledge of the power given me by an instrument depends on the clarity of the rules according to which it was constructed, and on my knowledge of those rules." Specification includes detailed, precise statements (usually in the introduction) of the subject or area of the bibliography, the sources searched to create it, the arrangement of the entries, the elements within the entries and their format, and, if the bibliography is selective, the selection principles. By implication the specifications should be formulated and thought through early in the process of compiling the bibliography, so that later they may be honestly and accurately stated.

Once given the specifications, the user of a bibliography can develop a much more efficient and effective search strategy than would otherwise be possible. It may be, for example, that a bibliography is completely adequate for a particular user's needs. To prepare it, the compiler scanned the sources the user feels should be checked, and its subject scope neatly matches the user's interest. But *in the absence of specifications*, how is the user to recognize the suitability of this resource?

Without precise knowledge of the coverage of bibliographies, conscientious users will generally feel constrained to consult several sources to insure coverage of the topic. Ironically, some of the sources these users check may already have been scanned by the compilers of other bibliographies they have already consulted. For example, a compiler may have scanned ten years of *Business Periodicals Index* to prepare a bibliography. A subsequent user may not know this, however, and, in addition to consulting the bibliography, searches under the very same headings in *BPI* as those earlier scanned by the compiler. In short, the user duplicates work already done—a waste of the user's time and, in a sense, of the compiler's as well.

In any extensive search, the user is likely to want to consult several sources, even when specifications are provided. But through use of the specifications, the searcher can rank the sources by their relevance to his or her needs, and search them in that order. In some situations, two sources may cover the same territory, and so one source may be eliminated. In other cases, gaps may be noticed that would otherwise be missed. These gaps can then be compensated for by supplemental searching in still other sources.

Specifications thus enable a user to design a search that is both fast and thorough. By providing them, the compiler can, without spending much additional time, greatly improve the utility of the instrument for the user.

BIBLIOGRAPHIC CONTROL

The universe of graphic materials is very large; it is impossible in practice to search that entire universe for every bibliographic need. Thus, bibliographies may be seen as *pre-selection devices,* making it possible for users to meet their needs by searching only a tiny portion of that universe. For our purposes, bibliographic control may be seen as an activity we engage in to create and record the existence of these pre-selection devices.

Once a systematic bibliography is created, we may view some part of the graphic universe as "pinned down"—that is, organized in such a way that a user has effective access to a portion of that universe. But bibliographic control should consist not only in identifying and labeling the literature, but also in creating an integrated structure for physical and intellectual access to recorded materials.

Egan and Shera made this point in 1952. They distinguished a *macrocosmic* and a *microcosmic* view of bibliography. The macrocosmic view is represented by those "who would view bibliography as one of the instrumentalities of communication, and communication itself as an instrumentality of social organization and actions" (p. 125). Representing the microcosmic view "are those who look upon each bibliography as a separate tool...each separate bibliography having little or no acknowledged relationship to any other." They argue that the "hodgepodge" of bibliographic services available when they wrote (and with us still) is the result of microcosmic thinking.

While a universal, integrated structure of bibliographic control may remain a dream, it is nonetheless possible to improve the integration of the current "hodgepodge." A large part of the bibliographic universe is in fact pinned down, sometimes very well. The trouble is, we do not know the exact extent of that coverage; without specifications we do not know what is and is not included in the available bibliographic instruments. It is as if we have a blurry rather than sharp picture of the state of bibliographic control. Does a subject bibliography cover a certain subfield? Is it selective, and, if so, in what respect? Are all recorded media covered or only some? And so on.

In most cases, such questions simply cannot be answered. The information is forever hidden in some bibliographer's mind. It is thus impossible to state with conviction that all major aspects of a subject or area have been covered. By the same token, aspiring bibliographers, whether publishers or individual compilers, cannot determine where they can best make a contribution. Hence the labor available to produce bibliographic materials is misused, in that some areas are covered repeatedly while others are left untouched.

If, at a later time, a centralized structure is developed, it will be possible to view existing resources as building blocks, their role and place in the structure-to-be readily determined by a reading of their specifications. If those specifications are developed and described by a common set of principles, then, no matter how diverse the bibliographies, it will be relatively easy to fit them into a single structure.

In the meantime, while we cannot do anything about bibliographies already published, each individual bibliographer or publisher can greatly improve bibliographic control by stating specifications clearly within the instrument itself. As more of this is done, the picture will come into increasingly sharp focus, and the gaps and overlaps will be evident.

Because individuals and publishers generally want to make themselves look as good as possible, some will resist stating specifications. (Who wants to limit the sweep of a magnificent title?) When teaching reference courses, I have been dismayed again and again by how little bibliographies say about their coverage. It might therefore be appropriate for an organization such as the American Library Association to publish *standards for specification statements* in bibliographic instruments. Since many published bibliographies are bought almost exclusively by libraries, ALA could quickly make its expectations felt with publishers.

TYPES OF SPECIFICATIONS

Wilson gives five sorts of specifications that need to be made about a bibliographic instrument. I have altered his terms slightly to suit the practical demands of bibliography making. The specifications to be discussed here are *scope, domain, information fields, organization,* and *selection principles.* (Library catalogs are excluded from my discussion because their specifications—their organization particularly—are very complex.)

Scope and Domain. *Domain,* according to Wilson (1968, p. 59), is "the set of items from which the contents of the work, the items actually listed, are selected or drawn." *Scope* I define as the subject or area declared to be the range of coverage, or requirements for inclusion, of a bibliography.

The scope is the conceptual territory covered by the bibliography; the domain is the bibliographical territory searched to create it. Many existing bibliographies give inadequate definitions of their scope and do not mention domain at all.

A *scope statement* might take the form, "This bibliography covers journal articles in English appearing during 1981-90 on the topic of applications of high-powered widgets in industry. Their use in the automobile, airplane, and railway car industries is covered, while use in shipbuilding is excluded. Materials solely on low-powered widgets are excluded, as are articles on high-powered widgets that are not applications-oriented."

A *domain statement* might take the form, "The following sources were searched to created this bibliography:

- American Widget Association Headquarters library catalog under the heading "High-powered widgets—applications."
- *Widget Review* annual subject indexes, 1981-89, under "Transportation industry," and unindexed current issues through August 1990 under Section 2.2 "Industrial applications."
- *Widget Abstracts* online for the years 1981-90 under the full-text truncated terms "High-power Widget? AND (Auto? OR Airplane? OR Rail?)."

Note that someone coming across this bibliography two years hence can easily update it online by inputting the same search formulation and limiting it to 1991–92. It is also useful to mention unproductive locations searched in the domain statement. By doing so, one enlarges the domain, telling the user, "Nothing can be found there; don't bother."

Domain statements for locally produced bibliographies may vary from those in published indexes. The locally produced Widget example may be contrasted with the sort of statement needed in, e.g., a periodical index, where it would take the form of a list of journals scanned.

In principle, one examines each item in the domain to see whether it meets the scope. In order for this process to work, the scope must be defined through explicit subject headings. Items in the domain that meet the scope are included in the bibliography; those that do not are excluded. There may or may not be other items outside the domain that meet the scope—the bibliographer makes no claim one way or another about them (cf Wilson, 1968, pp. 59-60).

In practice, it is usually not necessary to examine every candidate item in the domain, since it is often possible to determine from titles or other available information whether items meet the scope. But when in doubt, one should personally examine dubious items. In this manner one can fairly claim to have produced a comprehensive, or exhaustive, bibliography. *All items within the domain meeting the scope have been included.* Otherwise, without delimiting the domain, a claim to comprehensiveness in this day of vast publication may be foolhardy: The compiler simply cannot know that every relevant citation has been found.

Interplay of Scope and Domain. It is important to realize that scope should be determined independently of domain. Scope should not be allowed to degenerate into being identical with domain.

Suppose one searches under "Teacher skills" and "Teacher education" in one periodical index, and "Teacher education" and "Teacher training" in another. It may be tempting to let the scope definition consist of these domain terms, and to uncritically accept all items in the domain as meeting the scope, without further thought. But, in fact, those terms have particular meaning to the makers of those bibliographies. "Teacher education" in one might cover quite different conceptual territory from "Teacher education" in the other. Or the compilers of the index using "Teacher skills" may have dumped some marginally related items in there for lack of another term in their particular thesaurus. If all items falling under these terms are uncritically assumed to meet the scope, and those domain terms are declared to define the scope, then the resulting bibliography will collect together in one place all the inconsistencies existing in the domain. Only when the scope is independently defined *before the search*, and each item in the domain judged carefully for fit, will the result be consistent and coherent.

Scope in More Detail. Scope comprises the same types of elements used in discussions of reference sources: subject, forms and genres of writings included, date ranges, geographical and language coverage, and so on. Defining scope may seem straightforward, but in fact requires considerable care. The goal is to state *explicitly* every criterion that determines whether an item is included. (No less care is needed in *holding to scope* once defined.)

Here is an example. Suppose one sets out to prepare an exhaustive bibliography on "Automatic Indexing for Information Scientists." At first that phrase alone—the indication of subject—may seem adequate to define coverage. But a close look at one's search behavior quickly shows that other criteria are operating, too. Perhaps only American items are being accepted, and since little work on automatic indexing was done before 1960, the scope is being limited to items published since then. Further thought reveals that newsy, chatty articles are being rejected, and only research-oriented items accepted.

After a hard look at the scope actually operating in one's selection of citations, it may turn out that the true, full scope statement should read, "This bibliography covers high-quality, research-oriented American books, journal articles, and technical reports published since 1960 on the type of automatic indexing known as 'derivative' or 'derived.' Materials solely on 'associative' or 'assigned' indexing are excluded."

Specification of the subject aspect of scope, in particular, often requires more detail than has been used in the examples so far. Every meaningful nuance should be included in the scope specification—every aspect that makes a difference in the decision to accept or reject items. A good way to learn whether there are as yet unexpressed scope elements is to notice those occasions when one wants to reject an item but finds that there is nothing in the scope statement that the item fails to meet. Examining what it is about the item that makes one want to reject it will reveal additional scope elements in one's decisions.

If every element of the scope has been made explicit, not only in the mind of the bibliographer but in a written statement, then it is possible to make a well-founded, consistent decision about every item considered for inclusion. In the final version of the bibliography for a given domain, every item is there because it meets the scope, and every item not there is excluded because it does not meet the scope. A resource so prepared is quite different from the hodgepodge agglomerations that sometimes go under the name "bibliography."

INFORMATION FIELDS

The information fields are the elements present in each citation in the bibliography. It is vital that consistent, complete citations be provided for each entry. The way to insure this is to use a recognized source for bibliographic formats, such as the American National Standards Institute (ANSI) Committee Z39.29 standards or *A Manual of Style* of the University of Chicago Press, at the beginning—not the end!—of compilation. Such manuals state what fields are to be included and in what form for each kind of material. (For example, the elements to be included in the citation for a journal article are quite different from those for a technical report.) Failure to determine at the beginning of the search which elements are to be included in citations of each type will mean additional look-ups to obtain missing data.

It may be tempting to invent one's own format for bibliographic citations, deciding which elements are to be included as one encounters each new bibliographic form (journal article, book chapter, symposium, etc.). This is not recommended. A great deal of thought has already been put into the standardized forms presented in manuals in order to achieve consistency and readability—more thought than the bibliographer is likely to have time to invest.

In the specifications, the user of the bibliography should be given the complete citation of whatever source has been used to determine the selection and formatting of the information fields. This tells the user that, if a model can be gotten from the source (e.g., *A Manual of Style)*, the bibliographer can be relied on to provide certain elements in a certain order in each citation. If, for example, the user notes that a journal article is cited without month, the user can safely assume that the journal does not date its issues by month. With more haphazard bibliographic practices, the user does not know what is characteristic of the original item and what is simply the bibliographer's inconsistency.

A typical "information fields" specification statement might read, "Citations in this bibliography are formatted according to the practices called for in *[complete citation of source].*"

The effort in preparing a bibliography is always to have complete, correct citations. I would say from experience that this is a good deal harder to achieve than it sounds. I have discovered errors in my own work after double and triple checking, and have also found errors in highly reputable sources. For a user, there is nothing more frustrating than a promising reference that leads nowhere. The ultimate purpose in making bibliographies, even beyond collocating materials to help users in searching, is *to facilitate information transfer.* Information specialists are facilitators in the transfer process. Every blind lead is a small clog in the flow of information—hence a small defeat for us as professionals.

ORGANIZATION

Organization refers to the arrangement of the entries in the bibliography. The specifications statement should report the following aspects of organization: access points, ordering principles, and (if practical) entry terms.

An *access point* is a field by which a searcher can search the file. Typical access points are author, subject, title, and date of publication. There may be many information fields within each entry but an access point is one by which the entries are sorted for searching. Date of publication, for example, is an access point only if the entries are arranged in publication date order, either in the main sequence or an index. (Multiple sorting principles within the main sequence, and additional, back-of-the-book indexes, may create more than one access point per work.)

Even with popular periodical indexes, access points are not always stated: one must determine access points by scanning entries. It is not immediately evident in some of these indexes, for example, whether one can get access by title.

Ordering principle refers to the way in which the entries are sorted. The most common sorts are alphabetical, numerical, chronological, and classified.

Entry terms are the specific terms (of names, subjects, or whatever) that can be used to enter the bibliography. In a large periodical index, the total set of subject entry terms would constitute the thesaurus used to index items for inclusion. In such a case, the thesaurus would generally be separately published. In smaller bibliographies, there may be only half a dozen entry terms, as when the works of several authors are gathered together, or when the subject of the bibliography is subdivided with a few subtopic headings. It is useful in these cases to state the names of authors or subtopics at the beginning of the bibliography, so that the user can see at a glance how it is organized. Exception would be made when there are nearly as many different entry terms as citations, as when a bibliography is arranged by author and most items are by different authors.

A specification statement for "organization" might read, "Entries are arranged alphabetically by subject and sub-arranged by author's surname within each subject term." Where appropriate, the statement would go on to list entry terms.

Stating the access points and ordering principles enables the user to decide quickly whether the arrangement of this bibliography suits his or her needs, and makes it possible to use the bibliography easily and effectively. Statement of the entry terms further clarifies the coverage of the bibliography, and makes it possible for the user to see quickly which section to concentrate on.

PRINCIPLES OF SELECTION

This section deals with principles used to produce *selective bibliographies,* while the previous sections dealt with bibliographies that are exhaustive within a stated scope and domain.

One suspects that "Selective" in the titles of bibliographies is sometimes a code word for "Some Miscellaneous Things I Found on the Subject of..." or "Major Index X Wasn't Available, But Here's What I Scraped Up Elsewhere on..." In other cases the word may reflect much more careful editorial principles. However, unless the selection principles are specified, the user can make little effective use of the bibliography, and its role in bibliographic control is not clear. It will be evident from this section that a good selective bibliography is not just a half-baked comprehensive bibliography, but one compiled with as much care as one in which every item meeting the scope is accepted.

Wilson originally defined "selection principles" to mean the criteria by which items are drawn from the domain. "Scope" was used for that meaning here, and "selection principles" will refer to the various ways by which items are drawn from a set of items *already meeting the bibliography's scope statement.*

What good is it to pick out only some of the items meeting a stated scope? The following selection principles correspond to various ways in which a user might want *samples* of items dealing with a subject or area.

Expert Judgment. From the items meeting a stated scope one might wish to exclude *all but the best*— for example, the highest quality, the most helpful, the best known. The results would usually be matters of expert judgment, but one might resort to statistical criteria, as when journals or books are chosen for purchase on the basis of citation counts, the "best" or "most popular" being those that receive the most citations.

A Systematic Sample. A random sample of citations meeting the scope statement may be useful in certain circumstances. "Random" is used here (as in sampling theory) to mean that every item in a population has known probability of being drawn. In the bibliographic realm, manual random samples are usually "systematic," that is, every *nth* item is chosen until the desired sample size has been reached.

In principle, it should be easy to *automate* systematic random sampling in online systems. This would enable a searcher to explore an area she does not know well. Suppose the system provided a "Sample *N*" command; that is, the system will print out every *nth* item after the searcher fills in *n*. The searcher happens to put in widely applied terms and gets back a large number of postings, say 1,225 items. But now she enters, say, "Sample 30," so that every 30th item is gathered in a subset. The resulting 40 items, since they are drawn from the entire time span of the original set, present a good picture of the subject area. If she had printed out only the 40 *most recent* items (as searchers now usually do by default), she would not have gotten as good a picture of the subject as a whole.

A Stratified Sample. A sample might also be stratified, with the intention of producing representativeness. An academic librarian could prepare a selective bibliography with this statement:

> Materials have been selected so that the number of items in each subject section is approximately proportional to the number of items on each subject appearing in the literature. This is done to provide a representative picture of research being done in each of the topics of this bibliography. Within this constraint, items available in this library have been preferred.

This method of course presumes knowledge of the total numbers of writings within each subtopic of the literature. If subtopic X has twice as many articles as subtopic Y, then section X of the bibliography will have twice as many citations as section Y. At the same time, for the convenience of the user, only locally available items have been listed. The selection is thus stratified to represent one feature (subject) but not another (journal or publisher).

Equivalence Sets. A final selection principle is to choose sets of writings (or other graphic records) that are *functionally equivalent.* Such a set is chosen so that, in the bibliographer's judgment, any item in it is as good for the user's purposes as any other: to have read one is to have read them all.

After grouping items meeting the scope into functional equivalence sets, the compiler then picks one from each set to include in the final bibliography. The user thus armed should, in most circumstances, need no further references.

Hierarchical Equivalence. This state exists when one item *sums up*—or incorporates at a higher level—several other items. In this sense, a review paper may be functionally equivalent to several research papers—i.e., only the review paper need be read. Similarly, a textbook may be functionally equivalent to many original articles or several review papers.

Substitution Equivalence. There may also be equivalence within the same hierarchical level. For example, several textbooks in elementary statistics may be considered identical in content. Or consider several research papers: each is different, of course, but if they all test the same thing, or vary the test only in some aspect of no interest to the reader, then one of them may be substitutable for all.

A Final Example. A researcher tells a special librarian that she wants to get a quick education in a certain subject field, and asks him to select a set of materials for her to read. Of several review articles on the subject, he picks the one that most closely fits the researcher's stated interests. In the review articles he notices repeated references to four seminal papers and notes them down. He assures himself that the review article plus the four major articles cover early material adequately, and he now concentrates on finding materials that have appeared in the three years since the date of the review.

Looking through the literature, he notes major themes and lines of research. He selects six or seven research articles which collectively cover the current research front. He copies the articles locally available and borrows others on interlibrary loan. A few days later, even though he does not have as much subject background as the researcher, he presents her with a dozen or so items that constitute a good introduction, and that are in all probability adequate for her purposes. In explaining his procedure, he says nothing about "functional equivalence sets," but the concept was implicit in all of his selection.

PRESENTATION OF SPECIFICATIONS

Specifications should be presented at the beginning of the bibliography in a standardized format. The order I recommend is scope, domain, information fields, and organization. If applicable, selection principles could come after domain. To recapitulate, by way of summary, some directions given here:

Scope. Report here every element that played a part in decisions to include or exclude an item—subject, bibliographic form, language, country of origin, temporal period, level of treatment, and so on.

Domain. State something along these lines: "The following sources were searched to create this bibliography..." Then identify all sources by, e.g., title, subject terms searched under, and time spans of their coverage. Include periodical indexes, other bibliographies, and any library catalogs used. Include, too, sources that seemed plausible to search but that proved unproductive.

Information Fields. At a minimum, the standard source used for bibliographic format should be cited, and cryptic elements in typical entries explained. A sample of a typical entry, with comments and illustrative data, may be useful.

Organization. State access point(s) and ordering principle(s) for the bibliography in generally understandable terms. Entry terms should be presented together here, except when they are too numerous. It may be possible in the latter case to refer the user to a separate thesaurus of authorized entry terms.

CONCLUSION

Wilson's (1968) *Two Kinds of Power* takes further many of the ideas presented here. While it is a rigorous and sophisticated contribution to reference theory, it is also somewhat removed from daily library practice. My purpose has been to translate a piece of this theory into a form that can be used by practicing information specialists and librarians. Like physicians, they are usually too busy with the immediate demands of their clients to work on basic theory or even on applications. They therefore have reason to expect, from their professional literature, articles in which theory is presented and applied for them.

I view the writing of such articles as one of the jobs of the library school professor. We are often criticized as having our heads in the clouds, but it is that very concern for theory that is our strong suit. New theoretical approaches can ultimately advance the field greatly and help us cope with new political and social realities. The problem lies in linking theory with practice. This is a problem unique to professional fields, and it is a difficult one. In this essay I have attempted to create such a link.

The day will come when we will look back and marvel at the primitive-ness of descriptions of bibliographic sources in the 20th century, the way we exclaim today over the fact that at one time libraries did not have reference librarians. The bibliography should not only list materials, but also *state its relation to the rest of the graphic universe,* which means that its introduction must convey precisely what is and is not covered. This presupposes that selection and collocation are done sensibly and intelligently enough to permit description. As we have seen, there may be a good deal more to this process than one might think.

6

Literary Forms in Information Work
Annotated Bibliographies, Bibliographic Essays, and Reviews of Literatures

Howard D. White

LISTS VS. ESSAYS

People not only *save* writings, with a kind of archival instinct; they *list* them, avowedly to increase awareness of them and to facilitate their use; unavowedly perhaps because listing writings is itself, for some, an easy and pleasurable way of creating something.

If, like the authors of this book, one teaches others to use these people's products—printed or machine-readable bibliographies—one's subject matter appears basically as *lists.* More exactly, one presents sequences of writings, often called "resources," in which each record characterizes a particular item, and the records are sorted on values in a particular field, such as author or title. The lists may include annotations—bits of commentary on each item—but that does change their basic structure. The annotated lists of reference works known to librarians as "Sheehy" and "Walford"—the *Guide to Reference Books* and the *Guide to Reference Material,* respectively— exemplify such a structure. So does the weekly account of movies in the front of the *New Yorker.*

One's problem in teaching is that, while any item on the list may be interesting in its own right, or at least interestingly described (the *New Yorker* annotations are not without art), a list is not a very powerful way of organizing subject matter. A list is not an outline. Unlike an essay, even in outline form, its separate items are not superordinate and subordinate, do not cumulate, do not tend toward a point. Thus the list has none of the coherence or cumulative logic of a good textbook in calculus; none of the narrative force or drama of a good history of Elizabethan England. Despite the potential usefulness of the listed items, the mere fact that they are presented as discrete entities, one after another, possibly in great quantities, has a deadening effect. Intellectual coherence, drama, and force and so on, are virtues associated with *discourse,* and the list is preeminently a *file* or *matrix.* As I noted in Chapter 3, the matrix is the form in which statements are not only sortable but "all on a par." How can one achieve force or drama or a coherent chain of reasoning with that as a constraint? This state of affairs must in some measure contribute to the reputation of "library science" as being vapid.

A teacher can, of course, go beyond presenting a list of resources *in alphabetical order,* the weakest linkage of all. One presents by form and purpose, by similarities and differences of coverage, by interrelated uses; one gives anecdotes of typical or unusual questions that the resources have answered—*anything* to improve the list as an organizational principle. But nothing helps much. In Gertrude Stein's phrase, "There is no there there." Or rather, there are many resources to learn and much to learn about them— a large matrix in fact!—but little that makes for good lectures. Structured exercises—*workbooks*— combined with browsing are the best way to teach or learn resources; a suitably motivated person should hardly need lectures at all.

The difficulties of lecturing about resources are directly related to my main topic, the difficulties of *writing* about them. A reasonable surmise is that one might replace an insipid form, the annotated list, with something more complex. And indeed, because of the prestige of the essay over the annotated bibliography, a hybrid has gradually developed, the "bibliographic essay." This kind of essay, however, though widely practiced, is not much of a success either. After some preliminary comments, I hope to show where the form goes wrong, in that most examples are neither easy to read nor easy to consult. I conclude by comparing both annotated lists and bibliographic essays with another important form in information work—reviews of literatures—to the latter's advantage. Some older writings are used as illustrations, in order to focus on relatively permanent principles.

PRESTIGE

Why, initially at least, do we accord more prestige to an essay than to a list? The answer, plainly, is that lists are "mechanical"; they can be generated by following a few rules for copying and arranging facts about writings. Essays cannot be generated in this way; it is harder to compose than to compile. The list-maker who makes the rules of compilation unambiguous enough can delegate subsequent tasks to assistants or a machine. The essayist's work involves a continuous play of personal, unroutinized judgment and expression; it can rarely be delegated. We value the essay over the list precisely because it involves more than repeated application of impersonal rules, and thus fewer persons are capable of it. Essays, relative to lists, are luxuries.

List-makers knows this and would argue that they work by necessity, not choice. Since writings come in multitudes, they lack the time to comment on them in depth and to organize their comments "creatively," in the essayist's mode. Put differently, lists are the output of an overloaded system—one in which input has already exceeded capacity to deal with it except in routine and perfunctory ways. Even so, *annotated* lists of writings, for all their faults, would be better left as lists than recast as "essays" of the sort criticized below.

ANNOTATED BIBLIOGRAPHIES VS. BIBLIOGRAPHIC ESSAYS

Many bibliographies, of course, are simply lists with little or no annotation. By *annotated bibliography,* I mean the familiar form in which each of a set of writings is identified to edition level, and each identification is followed by the bibliographer's personal description (perhaps including evaluation) of the writing. This produces a file of discrete prose entries, which are sequenced by the values in some field, most often alphabetically by author or numerically by ID number. Many book-length annotated bibliographies also impose a classification scheme (subject and genre categories, chronological periods, etc.) on the file.

Personal notes, of course, are not governed by a standardized code, such as the *Anglo-American Cataloging Rules*; they are written ad libitum. Librarians used to learn the art from Haines's (1935) *Living with Books*, now rather faded. The annotations made for movies and television shows are perhaps the best current models.[1] Figure 6.1 gives an entry with annotation from Patterson's (1983) *Literary Research Guide*. Patterson writes livelier notes than Sheehy (1986) and Walford (1980–1987) on many of the same materials, and might serve as a model to annotators trying for vivacity in what is, at best, a difficult business.

Both unannotated and annotated bibliographies are often published as "guides to the literature" of a subject. A guide to the literature always names

---

[1] The tradition of brisk mini-reviews represented by, e.g., Pauline Kael can be traced at least as far back as James Agee's (1964) movie columns in the 1940s. In *The Nation* for February 14, 1948, his entire review of *You Were Meant for Me* was "That's what you think."

Figure 6.1.   Annotation from Patterson's *Literary Research Guide*

B13. British Museum. *General Catalogue of Printed Books* (*Brit. Mus. Cat; BM Catalogue; BM Cat.*). 263 vols. London: Trustees of the BM, 1965. Supplement, 1956–1965 (50 vols.); supplement, 1966–1970 (27 vols.); supplement, 1971–1975 (13 vols.). Z921.B87

The main set of 263 volumes contains photocopies of the catalog cards for all books owned by the British Library, London, up through 1955. (The British Library was formerly referred to as the British Museum because the library was housed in the national museum, but in 1973 an official reorganization was announced.) It is necessary to consult all three supplements at present for subsequent acquisitions, but a cumulated edition is under way (see B14). A series of subject indexes covers the years 1881 to 1960.

American researchers and librarians use the catalog mainly for verification of factual information. It is formidable in size and inimitable in fragrance but, in general, easy to use, having a simple, alphabetical-by-author arrangement with a few exceptions such as a listing of all periodicals by city of publication under "Periodicals," and certain subject groupings such as "England" and "Ireland." Both of the latter idiosyncrasies were abandoned in the third supplement, and henceforth the *BM Catalogue* will be computer-based and machine readable. An era has ended

Source: Margaret C. Patterson, *Literary Research Guide*, 2d ed. New York: Modern Language Association of America, 1983. Reprinted by permission.

particular titles, on the grounds that they are essential to the study of the subject or that they are somehow typical of what writers on that subject produce. Quite often, such a guide will cover more than one "level" of the literature. For example, in the natural or social sciences, the primary literature is that of scholarly writings—journal articles, reports, monographs, books. Another level is sometimes discerned in the compactions of this basic output into such forms as research reviews, essays in handbooks and encyclopedias, textbooks, popularizations, and specialized dictionaries. The secondary literature, so called, comprises bibliographies, subject indexes, and abstracts of literature on the first level. The guide itself stands on a tertiary level with respect to these.[2]

Bibliographic essays, which may be of any length (from short article to full-length book), are generally guides to literatures. Unlike annotated bibliographies, however, they observe the conventions of expository prose. That is, they are not formatted as discrete blocks in mechanical order, but as paragraphs. They look as if they should possess the "single, swelling"

---

[2] In the discipline of history, the levels must be reordered because the term "primary literature" is reserved for the *sources*— official records, reports, letters, diaries, etc.—from which the historian constructs his "secondary" work. The same holds true of literary studies, in which the primary literature, such as novels, poems, and plays, gives rise to secondary critical and historical works, making bibliographic tools tertiary and guides to all levels quaternary.

exposition, "free from jerks," that Ranganathan (1961) found typical of discourse. They look, in other words, like arguments toward a point; they look as if they should be *read*. But in fact, unless one is *very* interested in the resources they cover, they are seldom readable. Instead, they often combine a lack of direction with the flat commentary of a person too overloaded to do more than copy. The overloaded cannot read or study items in detail (there is too little time); they can only suggest what *might* be read or used. This of course affects organization: items actually read would be transformed by one's sensibility before re-presentation; but these are presented from without, in crude subject (or chronological) groupings, like books on a library shelf. (I would guess that the model—perhaps the reality—of *books on a shelf* lies at their root.) What is said about them is a patchwork of separate annotations, not the essay's line of reasoning toward a point. The typical bibliographic list may be mechanical in its arrangement—for example, alphabetical or numerical—but at least it is useful for quick look-up of entries. Bibliographic essays lack even this virtue.

THE STRUCTURE OF BIBLIOGRAPHIC ESSAYS

To get down to cases, what is wrong with this form? Basically that, although it masquerades as an essay, it is still a list. In an unpublished draft paper, Bates remarked, "In general, we may say that people make files for look-up access and write discourse for reading through. While in principle, it might be possible to mix these forms of information in composition, in practice, it does not seem to happen....There are no *blends;* we do not say certain writings are *filish.*" On the contrary, that is exactly what I say. Imagine a list of books alphabetized by title and annotated; then imagine the annotations rewritten and reordered slightly so that the titles are *embedded in sentences.* This rearrangement destroys alphabetical order; the books can no longer be quickly found by title; but a kind of prose has been created. Add paragraphing, a few transitions, and so on, and before long one has the simulacrum (or counterfeit) of an essay. But it is just that, not the real thing. It is "filish writing," a confusion of genres. One good test of the real thing is directionality, or tendency toward a point: its effect, when read, is not the same backward as forward. Another is paraphrasability: the true essay has a theme or thesis and can be paraphrased; the simulacrum cannot.

These points echo those made in Figure 3.6 of Chapter 3, in which discourse and matrixes were contrasted as two highly different kinds of text. The bibliographic essay is essentially discourse in which the differences have been obliterated—*discourse whose underlying structure is a matrix.* Matrixes, even when they contain annotations, forego most of the virtues of discourse in the interest of quick retrieval. The true essay, on the other hand, enables writers to generalize and compare, in a manner inappropriate to the annotation under any single item. It allows them to bring in background material, to digress or switch subjects, to appraise at length, to trace relationships over time (such as the ancestry of a text or an idea), to mention needed as well as existing works. But the wonderfully flexible essay form also requires the writer to set the generalizations, comparisons, appraisals, and suggestions for fresh work in the context of some overriding argument.

Among verbal structures, matrixes are notable for their lack of such argument—more broadly, their lack of anything that might be called expository force or "narrative pull." By itself, this might not be fatal—a matrix consisting of a list of celebrities, their sexual tastes, and their past and current lovers would indeed be read all the way through. Typically, however, librarians and information specialists have only *bibliographic* matrixes in their heads, and these are, for almost everyone, a dull subject. (I do not say that *having and using such knowledge* is dull—merely writing about it in essay form.) Composition with matrix structure accounts for the bibliographic essay's frequent property of being unreadable. Or, rather, they read like this, from Preminger (1967, p. 205–206):

A number of retrospective and current bibliographies reflect the increasing cross-fertilization between literature and other disciplines. They include such titles as *Literature and the Other Arts: A Selected Bibliography, 1952–1958* (MLA General Topics 9, Bibliography Committee, New York, NYPL, 1959); *Literature and Society, 1950-55* and *1956-60* (so far) (MLA General Topics 6, Coral Gables, Fla., University of Miami Press, 1956 and 1962); *The Relations of Literature and Science: A Selected Bibliography, 1930-1949* (Fred A. Dudley, et al., Pullman, Wash., Dept. of English at the State College of Washington, 1949) kept current by the annual bibliographies (1950-) in *Symposium: A Quarterly Journal in Modern Foreign Literature;* and *Psychoanalysis, Psychology and Literature: A Bibliography* (Normal Kiell, Madison, University of Wisconsin Press, 1963), plus the annual bibliographies in the journal *Literature and Psychology* (1951–). All these are concerned with English literature.

The annual bibliographies in the *Abstracts of Folklore Studies* (Philadelphia, American Folklore Society, 1960) and the *Journal of Aesthetics and Art Criticism* (Cleveland, American Society for Aesthetics, 1941-) attest to the close relationship between English literature and folklore on one hand and English literature and aesthetics on the other. As for the study of the parallels between English literature and other literatures, Fernand Baldensperger and Werner Friederich's *Bibliography of Comparative Literature* (Chapel Hill, University of North Carolina, Studies in Comparative Literature, No. 1, 1950) and the bibliographies in the *Yearbook of Comparative and General Literature* Bloomington, Indiana University, 1952–) furnish ample substance.

Despite their obvious faults, many hundreds, perhaps thousands, of bibliographic essays have been published. The matrix-minded continue to write them—for whom, I don't know. I suspect that everyone politely maintains the fiction they are of use to some imaginary beginner. Any such person would do better to browse among the sources themselves. I have, as a teacher, assigned students to read and write bibliographic essays. Those assigned to read them simply stop, I think, after the briefest of trials. Writing them may not be a bad way to learn the resources of a subject or field, but it is a bad way to develop craft and character as a writer. Persons of any verbal skill discover they can quickly put together what looks like an essay by picking up reference books and copying a bit from the front or back matter of each.

Here is another typical paragraph, taken from a published guide to the literature of the social sciences by McInnis and Scott (1975, p. 128). I give as much as I dare, but the reader should know that writing like this goes on for *300 pages:*

> The five-volume *Handbook of Social Psychology* (1968-70) (3) provides a massive amount of information. Edited by Gardner Lindzey and Elliot Aronson, the present edition was compiled by 68 contributors, including political scientists, sociologists, anthropologists, and psychologists. The titles of individual volumes illustrate the broad coverage: *Historical Introduction and Systematic Positions, Research Methods, The Individual in a Social Context, Group Psychology and Phenomena of Interaction,* and *Applied Social Psychology.* Each chapter includes a bibliography. A separate cumulative author and subject index has also been published. Alfred M. Freedman et al. edited the *Comprehensive Textbook of Psychiatry* (1967) (4), a large, single-volume, encyclopedic compilation of information on neurophysiology and neuropharmacology as well as individual and group behavior. Each article is by an authority and has a bibliography. Another specialized source is *The Encyclopedia of Sexual Behavior* (1967) (5), edited by Albert Ellis and Albert Abarbanel. The work of over 90 contributors, mostly from the United States, it attempts to be "comprehensive, authoritative, inclusive of wide-ranging viewpoints, and truly international." The scope of its articles—with brief bibliographies—includes emotional, psychological, sociological, legal, anthropological, geographical, and historical aspects of sexuality.

The above passage nicely exhibits, in fact, all the faults of the prosified matrix: the absence of direction, the absence of paraphrasable argument, the choice of copiable matter over fresh statement, the loss of quick retrievability as titles are submerged in prose, the general dullness. (The book from which it is drawn does not even have an alphabetical index to authors or titles; it must be read through if notes on particular works are to be found.) Nothing is gained by converting the matrix to discourse, except, perhaps, the appearance of having written "something more than a list"—an essay. But this is illusory; the honest list is better.

CRITICISM IN BIBLIOGRAPHIC ESSAYS

Essayists often judge the writings of others. Their evaluations are convincing to the degree that they make us see and accept their critical principles. They can do this only in a field they know well—and that for most essayists means an intensely cultivated but restricted corner of a field, not its full reaches.

Take English literature, for example. Its reaches are vast, even if we omit primary works, such as novels, poems, and plays, and consider only secondary ones—critical and historical studies. The tertiary works, such as abstracts, annual reviews, and bibliographies, form another population that, if not vast, still has many members. Besides being numerous, they show the brute diversity and incompatibility of small, independent projects, each cast in its separate mold. In the absence of a theory that would allow one to review these works substantively in a true essay, one might try to make recommendations for their interrelated use. Failing that, merely listing them, with comments under citations, would have the virtue of not forcing one to resort to specious generalizations and comparisons in order to keep up appearances as an essayist. More important, the list format does not oblige one to *argue* critical comments in order to voice them.

I suggest that bibliographic essays go wrong—in particular, that they are fakes of genuine criticism—when the following conditions are met:

1. A writer is faced with a large number of disparate works, the literature and bibliography of a specialty or a field, on which to comment.
2. The writer adopts the conventions of the essay instead of the more modest annotated list.
3. Unlike some reviewers, the writer has no clear prospect of "fellow experts" as readers whose general requirements are known.
4. The writer has no explicit tests or thesis to apply to the works jointly.
5. The writer nevertheless makes summary judgments.

The type of faked judgment I have in mind is exemplified by the word "useful"—a favorite of bibliographic essayists. Rarely are we told what the "useful" opus is useful for. Flanagan (1967, p. 224) writes:

> To the professional student of American literature, the most useful tabulation of periodical material is the section entitled "Articles on American Literature Appearing in Current Periodicals" which has been a feature of every issue of the journal *American Literature* since its inception in 1929.

Johnson's (1963, p. 353) huge bibliographic appendix to the *Literary History of the United States (LHUS)* has many statements in the same vein:

A useful study of periodicals and personalities in California literature during the second half of the nineteenth century is Franklin Walker, *San Francisco's Literary Frontier,* New York, 1939; it includes material on Bierce and Stoddard and on the western variety of Bohemianism.

Bateson (1965, p. 199) in *A Guide to English Literature* catches the style perfectly:

A detailed if often superficial account of the most recent English and American criticism will be found in Stanley E. Hyman's *The Armed Vision* (1948, rev. 1955), which also has useful bibliographies.

All of these writers, if pressed, would have to say of any work, "Useful if you find it useful, but not otherwise." And in fact the usefulness of a work cannot be predicted if the requirements of the prospective user are unknown. The force of the term is weakened when it has merely an honorific sense.

Caught between the duty of covering a large number of works and the wish to be discriminating—useful—in judging them, the bibliographic essayists weaken critical usage by making what they have to say a matter of trust rather than evidence. Among their capsule judgments are "judicious," "valuable," "important," "sensible," "exhaustive," "sane," "satisfactory," and "level-headed" as words of praise; cautions include "eccentric," "pedestrian," and "unreliable." There is no particular reason to grant the writers that any of these appraisals is just, unless, upon looking at a work, we happen to find that we agree, and this is by no means a foregone conclusion.

I find puzzling, for example, Bateson's (1965) remark that *The Armed Vision* is "superficial." He could, of course, explain to me what he means, but he "does not have space" to devote more than a word or two (a few sentences at most) to any work. So with Johnson (1963) in the appendix to *LHUS;* so with Flanagan (1967) in his essay. Their critical vocabularies are unmoored to anything. An uninstructed reader might be presented with parallel passages from Johnson or Bateson, one genuine and the other identical but altered in all its critical judgments—for example, "stimulating if sometimes unreliable" replaced by "pedestrian but sound." I doubt whether the reader would be able to tell the genuine passage even after reading the work in question. What is at issue is not the accuracy of their assertions, nor whether the reader ultimately agrees with them, but the evidence the writer is able to bring to their support. As practiced, the bibliographic essay is rife with unsupported claims. That seems a good reason to question its "prestige" relative to an annotated list.

Plainly a list, too, can contain any number of unsupported critical estimates in the notes following citations. Many lists in literary scholarship, for example, contain evaluations that could be put into a scheme of "grades," like the one for motion pictures, in which a particularly admired film gets four stars. People who use grading schemes do not usually have to justify what each grade asserts; pointing to the length of the lists they have to work with, they can argue that their shorthand reduces many complex estimates to a quickly intelligible form, and that *there is no time to do more*. Lists are the output of a system in which input is dauntingly large: an overloaded system. When the rule is also to *evaluate* whatever is being listed, it reduces the overload to have a very limited vocabulary for expressing the result. Thus three stars may mean *either* "stimulating if sometime unreliable" *or* "pedestrian but sound"; it may mean a great many other things as well.

Any such rating scheme is a device for coping with overload. The rater quickly learns that summary judgments, which allow one to get on down the list, are in effect not very different from careful, fine-drawn judgments, each of which takes a long time, thereby producing backlogs. The gallant response in the face of overload (recalling that Johnson took as his province *American literature;* Bateson, *English literature*) is to go beyond not only dry, descriptive listing, but also a rating scheme with a small, fixed vocabulary. Johnson and Bateson actually appear to have read, compared, tested, and drawn distinctions between vast numbers of works. What is more, they express their findings in critic's English. If we see them basically as annotators, we need not expect them to justify what they write. That would be foolish—the list is precisely the form for arbitrary remarks. It signifies that too many items await "processing" for anything more than quick comments and summary appraisals to be made.

Unfortunately, it is hard to look on Johnson and Bateson as mere annotators, for they interleave their notes with essay-like passages and critical reviews; while Flanagan and several of his co-contributors to *Bibliography; Current State and Future Trends* can only be regarded as would-be essayists. The annotator's privilege of being arbitrary has been taken over by these writers, who at the same time string their notes together as conventional prose paragraphs. The resulting product is not only full of unargued judgments, but hard to refer to as well.

UNEXCEPTIONABLE TYPES

Before proceeding further, I should distinguish some other types of essays that might be called (or understood as) bibliographic, and exempt them from these criticisms.

The first of the types would be the essay properly called bibliometric, which involves regarding writings macroscopically, as if they were populations, and counting them according to certain attributes. (The vantage point is similar to that of the demographer with human populations.) Bibliometric essayists often group writings by journal, subject, age, language, citation linkages, national origin, or circulation histories, and make counts to learn the statistical distributions within the groups, or possibly the growth, stasis, or decline in the counts over time. Usually there is an attempt to discover regularities in the data that can be described by mathematical or statistical models. Whatever their findings, this sort of essayist does not set out to introduce us to individual works in the population, and certainly not to judge their individual merits.

At the other, microscopic extreme would be the essay in which minute particulars of a text (variant readings) or of its physical support (paper, ink, typefaces, binding, etc.) are analyzed—essays in the Greg-Bowers tradition of critical bibliography (summarized, for example, by Williams and Abbott, 1985). These often focus on a single work, just as biographers do on one person. A frequent aim is to put a specialized kind of historical inquiry at the service of literary scholars—one that conveys who printed what and how, the vicissitudes of a work as it moves from the author's hand through the editions that publishers give the world, and what in fact the best version of a particular text might be. For making claims, with evidence, about details that individuate texts, the essay is of course the natural form, just as in the parallel activity of writing about individual persons.

Then there is a large and heterogeneous group of essays that deal with bibliography as a subject—discussing, for instance, the difference between "critical" and "systematic" bibliography, or the notion of bibliographic control, or the place of bibliography in scientific communication. To these can be added the many historical or critical reviews of specific bibliographies—e.g., reviews of *Psychological Abstracts* or Lyle H. Wright's *American Fiction*. Essays in the present book belong to this mixed group, which could be called "metabibliographic" in nature. The final kind of writing to be excepted, and a very important one, is a *review of a literature* (also "research review," or "state-of-the art review"), which appears mostly in science and scholarship.

REVIEWS OF LITERATURES

The review of a literature (discussed above in Chapter 4) is not an account of one book, but a synthesis, at least implicitly evaluative, of many authors' research over a certain period. On a continuum of bibliographic content, it ranges from articles in which almost every sentence is studded with a citation, to articles, such as appear in encyclopedias, that cite only a few key works. The review is sometimes confused with the bibliographic essay because both forms refer explicitly to other writings, to which both are in some degree "guides." But in fact reviews of literatures have a markedly different function. Bibliographic essays are intended to tell what resources exist for study within a given field. Reviews of literatures, in contrast, are intended to integrate the statements in a given body of writings into a theoretically meaningful design. Reviews will be organized to answer the questions, "What do these writings allow us to conclude? What is known? What is the state of the art?" The reviewer will be concerned with assembling the various claims and counterclaims suggestively and interrelating them so as to explain some range of phenomena. Thus the reviewer may be able, after the survey, to say where expert knowledge is relatively strong and where it is weak—that is, where further research is needed. The bibliographic essayist, surveying merely what writings exist, is in no such position.

This contrast leads me again (as in earlier chapters) to distinguish between work based on subject expertise, developed through reading of texts, and work based on superficial examination of texts. This is, again, the distinction between works by *insiders* and *outsiders*. Insiders are those who have read or otherwise learned enough that they can *contribute* to a literature; they are not mute before it (as I am before the literature on, say, eutrophication of lakes). The review of a literature is an insider's piece of writing; the bibliographic essay—and all guides to literatures—the outsider's. (I, and most information specialists, could cobble together a guide to the study of eutrophication.) There is a strong parallel between the review of the literature (covering many writings) and the informative abstract (covering one writing): both presume reading in full and expert subject knowledge. Similarly, there is a parallel between the guide to a literature (covering many writings) and the indicative abstract (covering one writing): both presume only spot reading and generalist's knowledge.

REVIEWS VS. GUIDES

"Guides" in what follows, will include both annotated bibliographies and bibliographic essays. In fairness to writers of guides (e.g., Preminger, 1967, or McInnis and Scott, 1975, above), I should point out that they often discuss a field's secondary and tertiary works, such as bibliographies and directories, which are designed to be consulted rather than read. Such matrix-based works do not offer new knowledge claims. Thus it is next to impossible to treat them in the same way as works that do make new knowledge claims— articles, papers, reports, and books. Writers of reviews usually confine themselves to the latter, and have an easier time, if what they read is provocative at all, of coming up with interesting things to report. My comments below deal with cases in which both guides and reviews cover substantive primary writings of the latter types.

To grasp the wide difference between reviews of the literature and a guide to the literature, one need only look at tables of contents of book-length examples, shown as Figures 6.2 and 6.3. The one for the guide (which, in this case, is also a bibliographic essay) is made up largely of *form classes*. Librarians tend to think of literatures as divided in this way because each form class has a different function and poses different problems in collection management. For example, books, government documents, reference works, serials, monographs, maps, and machine-readable files are physically different, come from different suppliers, and require different handling and preservation techniques. The also tend to be housed separately in parts of the library that bear their names, and different librarians specialize in knowing their contents and uses. These differences would hold, moreover, whether anyone ever read them or not. Thus, guides to literatures typically embody what might be called a librarian's view of literatures—they are organized by function and physical form, which are knowable independently of reading. While the librarian's view is that of an outsider, librarians and information specialists seem nonetheless to believe that it usefully partitions the literature for the student or newcomer to a field.

They can hardly believe otherwise if the external view—by form classes—is all they can present. Figure 6.2, from Elliott's *Guide*, is largely atheoretical as far as insider's subject knowledge is concerned. (It does, of course, reflect an outsider's theory of what users want.) In contrast, Figure 6.3, from the *Annual Review of Psychology*, reveals the view from the inside, a subject analysis based on the editors' reading and integration of the literatures of their discipline. To such editors, and the authors who write the chapters reviewing particular topics, a breakdown of the disciplinary literature by *form classes* would probably seem bizarre—certainly not the way in which students or newcomers should encounter writings.[3]

There are persons who might occasionally benefit from use of the guides, just as they might occasionally benefit from a course in "bibliographic instruction," which is the curricular counterpart, taught by librarians, of what the guides offer. But in both cases scientists and scholars tend to promote socialization as insiders—that is, "read what we read"—rather than to encourage this other perspective. In their capacity as teachers, they have the right, jealously guarded, to prescribe what others should know. They do not prescribe—and often do not know of—the guides. Many, in fact, do not prescribe reviews of literatures either, and would regard courses in "bibliographic instruction," in which such things as guides and reviews are discussed, as unwarranted competition for their students' time. That is the real problem. The result is that the guides go untouched for long periods. In

---

[3] Guides to literatures may have tables of contents that at first glance look like those of annual reviews, because they are made up of topical headings. However, the subchapters under these headings will be found to be organized by form classes—a sure sign that one is not dealing with research reviews.

Preface

Chapter 1 Psychology and related subjects
            The nature of psychology
            Related subjects
            Psychological research
            Support for psychological research problems
            Psychological organisations

Chapter 2 Libraries and classification
            Classification
            Decimal Classification
                Universal Decimal Classification
                Library of Congress
                Bliss: Bibliographic Classification
            Catalogues

Chapter 3 Functions of information

Chapter 4 Documentary aids
            Periodicals
                Journals
                Reviews
                Indexes
                Abstracts
                Bibliographies
            Books
                Handbooks
                Textbooks
                Collections of readings
                Yearbooks
                Encyclopedias
                Dictionaries
                Directories
                Theses and dissertations
                Reports
        Miscellaneous other aids
                Meetings
                Symposia
                Selective dissemination of information
                National information system for psychology (US)
                Data banks
                Films and other audio-visual material
                Standards

Chapter 5 Comprehensive searching sequences
            Preliminaries
            Clarifying the area of enquiry
            Preparing the bibliography
            Retrieval and evaluation
            Reporting

Chapter 6 Current Awareness

Chapter 7 Everyday reference enquiries

Chapter 8 Miscellaneous information
            Book selection and evaluation
            Report writing
                Written reports
                Conference papers
            Preparation of indexes
            Translations
            Personal reference files

Appendix A Associations and societies
            connected with psychology
         B Some primary journals in psychology
         C Some English language journals
            which publish Oriental and Soviet information
         D Newsletters, house journals, etc.
         E KWIC index of abstracts and index titles
         F KWIC index of review titles
         G Some handbooks and similar sources
         H Foreign language dictionaries
         I English language dictionaries
         J Some guides to documentation

Index

Source: C. K. Elliott, *A Guide to the Documentation of Psychology*. London: Linnet Books &
        Clive Bingley, 1971. Reprinted by permission. The original layout has been con-
        densed, and page numbers have been deleted.

Figure 6.2.   'Psychology' as Presented in a Guide to the Literature

libraries using Library of Congress classification, hundreds sleep in the Z's.
Short guides sometimes known as "pathfinders," locally prepared and
offered free, remain untaken in display racks.

MINISTERIAL RELEVANCE

Librarians and information specialists cannot really remedy this situation,
because they lack the power to prescribe what others should know. Their

PREFACE

The objective of the *Annual Review of Psychology* is to provide expert evaluations of progress both in the main traditional areas of psychology and in important new or developing areas. In order to assure such coverage, the Editorial Committee has devised a master plan of topics, and the plan is revised frequently. The master plan of 1970 is shown below. We present it here to give information to our readers and to solicit comments and suggestions.

As the table shows, certain topics are included in each volume (those indicated by "1"), certain topics occur every 2, 3, or 5 years, and some appear only infrequently. For a number of reasons, no volume follows the plan exactly. Sometimes a chapter will reflect a more restricted coverage than that of the topic on the master plan, since authors are encouraged to be selective. In almost every volume, some planned chapters do not appear because authors defer their contribution or default. Nevertheless, the plan states our aim for coverage, and we adhere to it reasonably well. Comments about the plan and suggestions for its revision will be welcomed.

MASTER PLAN

DEVELOPMENTAL	1*	INDUSTRIAL-ORGANIZATIONAL PSYCHOLOGY	
MOTIVATION	2	Personnel Attitudes, Morale, and Motivation	2
Basic Drives	2	Personnel Selection, Classification, and	
Derived Motives	2	Job Placement	3
LEARNING		Personnel Development and Training	3
Verbal Learning and Memory	2	Engineering Psychology	3
Motor Learning	3	Consumer Psychology	X
Neurophysiology of Learning	3	ABNORMAL AND CLINICAL PSYCHOLOGY	
Mathematical Models of Learning	3	*Approaches to Psychopathology*	
Animal Learning	4	Statistical, Epidemiological, Diagnostic	
COGNITIVE PROCESSES		Approaches	4
Psycholinguistics	3	Social, Cultural, and Environment-Related	
Thinking and Concept Formation	3	Disorders	4
Cognitive Theories	X	Development and Life History Research	
Computer Simulation	X	in Psychopathology	4
Behavioral Decision Theory	X	Neurological and Physiological Bases of	
EDUCATION AND COUNSELING		Psychopathology	4
Student Development and Counseling	2	*Assessment in Psychopathology*	
Human Abilities (Individual differences)	3	Assessment of Special Conditions	2
Instructional Psychology	4	Objective Diagnostic Tests and Measures	3
COMPARATIVE PSYCHOLOGY AND ETHOLOGY	4	Projective Tests	3
RECEPTOR PROCESSES		*Intervention in Psychopathology*	
Audition	1	Individual Methods	3
Vision		Group Methods	3
Color	3	Social and Community Invention Methods	3
Spatial Vision	3	*Prevention of Mental Disorders*	4
Visual Sensitivity	3	BEHAVIOR GENETICS	3
Chemical Senses	4	PSYCHOLOGY IN X COUNTRY	3
Somesthetic Senses	4	UNGROUPED	
Vestibular Sensitivity	X	Aesthetics	X
PERCEPTION	2	Attention	X
PERSONALITY	1	Gerontology (Maturity and Aging)	X
Theory and Techniques of Assessment	X	Hypnosis	X
PHYSIOLOGICAL PSYCHOLOGY		Sleep and Dreams	X
Brain Functions	2		
Electrophysiology and Behavior	4		
Psychopharmacology	4		
SOCIAL PSYCHOLOGY			
Attitudes and Opinions	3		
Mass Communication	3		
Interpersonal Attraction	3		
Study of Small Groups	X		
Mass Phenomena	X		
Psychology and Culture	X		

*The numbers represent the intervals between successive chapters. The Xs indicate only occasional appearances.

Source: *Annual Review of Psychology*, v. 22. Palo Alto, Ca: Annual Reviews, Inc., 1971. Reprinted by permission. The original layout has been condensed.

Figure 6.3.   'Psychology' as Presented in an Annual Review

penalty for being generalists is that they are "staff" instead of "line"; they can advise but not require.

Librarians may argue that *they* find relevant documents in guides, and that others will, too, if they only look. They are correct in this, of course;

documents that satisfy criteria of relevance can be found, given time and a request that is not outlandish. But, in the absence of a request, the librarian is frustrated. He or she is in the position of a minister who can tell you, if you go to him, what passages of scripture will do your soul most good. The trouble is, you do not go to him. Even though there may be a number of Bible verses that could work your salvation if you looked for them and could tell when they were found, you may still be disinclined to search for them yourself or to ask for a minister's opinion. Much the same holds with writings that you could find in a guide to the literature. One might say that they have "ministerial relevance" to your need, and that the librarian resembles a minister of another faith, which, though estimable, you rule out.

"Ministerial relevance" is poignantly evident when persons in one group want to impart information that other groups ignore. Some years ago, for example, the Special Commission on the Social Sciences (U.S. National Science Board, 1969, p. 19) wrote in frustration, "How can the knowledge and forecasts of the social sciences be made to *command* the attention of an effective body of citizens to make them face the facts and act before disaster strikes?" The answer is, they cannot, unless knowledge is aligned with prescriptive power. Thus we come to another kind of relevance that ministers, librarians, and everyone else appreciates.

MAGISTERIAL RELEVANCE

"Magisterial relevance" exists by virtue of the fact that some persons have the power to set readings for others, either explicitly or by force of example. A great deal of library use by high school and college students occurs simply because they can be commanded to read X, Y, and Z. They read to please one or more judges, whose own reading will determine what will have magisterial relevance and what will not.

Much of our reading is done, by this account, to converge with persons whose identities and accomplishments we know. They may have recommended or required that we match our reading with theirs; or we may do so unbidden out of admiration or a sense of rivalry. The desire for convergence motivates, at least in part, much of our professional or job-oriented reading. In areas of research, such readings are set not by librarians and information specialists but by writers who are familiar, as insiders, with the concerns, requirements, and values of a particular field.

Since convergence is determinable—I know whether or not I have read what some guiding figure has read and listed before me—I will value it insofar as it appears to heighten my chance of reading to advantage. In practice, it is the surest route to advantageous reading. Further, as librarians and teachers know, it is the only route that can be *realistically* recommended as likely to help the reader. Reports of magisterially relevant writings—including those found in guides and reviews—are all that teachers, mentors, and librarians can routinely come up with. If they tried to do truly personalized evaluations of texts for individual needs, the backlog would soon stretch to world's end.

Guided reading does not guarantee success, of course. But then neither does unguided reading. Suppose one is told, "Ignore the experts, and simply follow your own interests. In both the arts and sciences, reading done without regard to others can produce spectacular results. Discoveries of relevant material no one else has adduced or prescribed are made constantly, sometimes to the extent that an entire field is overturned." Unfortunately, numerous counter-examples exist of free reading that has come to nothing. There is no assurance at all that it makes creative new work probable. Such probability can be attained only by reading convergently with experts.

On the other hand, suppose the counsel is: "Read with the experts. Find out what is most highly regarded in book reviews and reviews of literatures, and read that." As Wilson (1968, p. 35) notes, this alternative is not sure to produce results either: "We might take a request for the best books on Cretan history to be a request for those books that are most highly regarded by, say 'the experts' on Cretan history. If that is the request, it can be filled without any evaluation, for to report the popularity or standing of a writing among a certain class of men is not itself to evaluate the writing at all." In other words, the mere fact that something has been endorsed by experts does not guarantee that it will be the best textual means to an end for a particular person, with particular needs and goals.

Given this dilemma, one might generally choose a mixed strategy, combining both free and guided reading, so as to have the advantages of both. But guided reading clearly increases one's level of control. With free reading, one simply hopes for luck. With guided reading, one has a sense of *precedent* luck, in that at least some of the writings named are known to have already impressed one or more experts. The naming of what they consider relevant, moreover, yields an implicit bonus: the set of items *not* recommended or not on the list.

Magisterial relevance is social in nature, and reflects existing power relationships and reigning fashions. It is, broadly speaking, a social contrivance to *filter out* as much reading as possible, by using the critical intelligence of supposed authorities as the screen. In a sense, that is the goal of the entire educational system: teachers and mentors exist to tell us what to read, but also *what we may omit* and still pass. It is bracing to judge any information system by the degree to which it minimizes reading. The timeless question of students—"Will this be on the test?"—makes good sense (however dispiriting it is to teachers) if the teacher is regarded as a critical information system. Students want the teacher to behave not like a librarian showing them *possible* reading, but like an editor showing them *essential* reading—that is, to separate out what is really important from the total matter of the course.

This is not to deny that in many areas the minimal reading required, as judged by a critical intelligence, is quite a lot of reading indeed; one cannot become knowledgeable about Platonism or Spanish history or the Victorian novel without plowing through many volumes. But it still makes good sense to assume that each person is a reading-minimizer who wants magisterially relevant texts: those that have passed through critical appraisal and been judged as necessities. If we were not reading-minimizers, we would not need teachers; we could all educate ourselves by going to libraries. But of course that is just what most of us do not want—a glut of titles all clamoring for attention, all unranked as to potential. We want writings that screen out other, longer writings by being, as Bates says in Chapter 5, their functional equivalents.

Reviews of literatures are of central importance because they indicate how readers can read convergently with insiders' definitions of the field. Guides to literatures are, as a class, less good in this respect. The review of a literature, if good of its kind, will resemble a course given by an intelligent and critical teacher. It establishes contexts and priorities. It screens out. It synthesizes claims, perhaps even obviating the need to read some or all of the writings it covers. It is an essay. The guide to a literature, in contrast, will resemble one or more sections of a library. While not disorganized, its level of organization is not as high as the review's. It says, in effect, "If you are interested in this subject, *this* may be useful, and *this* may be useful, and *this* may be useful…etc." There is no synthesis, merely agglomeration. The guide cannot substitute for *any* of the writings it covers; it simply points to them.

There are dissolute reviews that slip toward being dull guides (the *Annual Review of Information Science and Technology* in recent years has had its share). Conversely, there are guides, including bibliographic essays, that are full of valuable and interesting commentary (often these are by scholars deeply knowledgeable about a field). An expert could prescribe either a review or a guide for one's particular case, and either would then be magisterially relevant. But in general, the review is to be preferred to the guide because it represents a higher level of intellectual power: the power of critical writing based on critical reading. Not only are works compared, but a new argument suspends them in novel relationships to each other so that, at best, we see how they fit together as knowledge, transcending author-title boundaries.

As Wilson (1977, p. 11) says, this transmutation may well go beyond any of the claims of the original works: "The striking thing about the process of evaluation of a body of work is that, while the intent is not to increase knowledge by the conducting of independent inquiries, the result may be the increase of knowledge, by the drawing of conclusions not made in the literature reviewed but supported by the part of it judged valid. The process of analysis and synthesis can produce new knowledge in just this sense, that the attempt to put down what can be said to be known, on the basis of a given collection of documents, may result in the establishment of things not claimed explicitly in any of the documents surveyed."

The review thus puts the reader closer to a research front than a guide. Almost surely, some of the writings reviewed will "light up" for the reader because they appear in a context set by a critical intelligence, with whom convergence is desirable, rather than in a mere bibliography. *If* one can set this context, one deserves more to be read than the person who merely lists and annotates. In that sense, one is more relevant.

Section III

Literature Searching

7

Searching: Strategies and Evaluation

Patrick Wilson

WHAT ARE WE LOOKING FOR?

If we are going to conduct a search for someone else, the search must be preceded by the formation of an explicit *search statement*, a description of what the search is aimed at finding. Formulation of a search statement is usually the result of discussion and negotiation between client and searcher in a *reference interview.* Here we will not ask how the search statement is arrived at, but concentrate on what to do once it has been formulated. But it is obvious that careful formulation of a search statement is an essential prerequisite for a successful search; we can waste a great deal of time by rushing into a search before we have a good idea of what it is that is actually being asked for. (On the latter, see Wilson, 1986.)

There are all sorts of searches: for writings by a particular author, for texts of a particular literary form, and so on. Here we will be concerned only with subject searches—that is, searches for material on a particular topic, or having a certain subject matter. The central part of a search statement for a subject search is a description of the topic or subject matter content of the materials being sought: the subject description. The subject description of a search statement will often be divisible into two or more conceptual components or facets. Suppose we are looking for material on the financing of opera in the United States. Opera then represents one conceptual component or facet of the request, financing represents another component or facet, the United States a third component or facet. If we were only interested in the 20th century, the subject description would contain a fourth component or facet. Many subject searches show a common pattern of conceptual components or facets: there will be one representing an object of interest, another representing a characteristic or activity or process of interest, another representing a place of interest, another a time of interest. (Faceted classification schemes are based on analysis of subject matters into patterns like these.) The "decomposition" of subject descriptions into conceptual components or facets is not always straightforward; there may be several ways to do it, corresponding to several different ways of formulating the subject description. (Would it make a difference if we had started by expressing an interest in the economic structure of *grand* opera in the United States? Or the sources of financial *support* for opera *performances* in the U.S.? There is hardly ever only one way of saying what we are looking for, and different ways of saying it will draw attention to different "concept analyses" of a request.)

In addition to a subject description, a complete search statement usually has a specification of types of material wanted. Subject searches may be qualified by many different types of restrictions, of which the following are probably the most common:

1. restriction to material in certain languages, e.g., English;
2. restriction to material published during a certain time period, e.g., the last few years;
3. restriction to certain physical or bibliographical forms of material, e.g., monographs, journal articles, maps, films, bibliographies, reference works;
4. restriction to material of a certain technical or intellectual level, e.g. popular works, scholarly works, introductory textbooks.

Any of these or other type restrictions may constitute distinct facets or components of a search request.

A third component of a search statement is a quality component. A search is either for material of a certain quality or value, or for material irrespective of quality or value. It is likely that a high proportion of searches are for material that is *good of its sort:* good textbooks on a subject, good discussions of a topic, the best current summary of the state of knowledge in a field, and so on. Such searches we will call evaluative, in contrast to the others, which we will call neutral or nonevaluative. Often the evaluative component of a search is left covert or unexpressed, and nonevaluative searches are performed for people whose real interests are in finding material that is good of its sort or good for their purposes. But ignoring or suppressing the evaluative component of a search statement means working with an incomplete and misleading search statement.

Finally, the fourth component of a search statement is a *quantity* component. Here we can distinguish three main alternatives:

1. *comprehensive* searches are searches for *everything* of the specified subject, type, and quality;
2. *partial* searches are searches for *some* but not all of the material of the specified type, subject, and quality;
3. *specific* searches are searches for a *unique* item (e.g., the latest book on a topic), or for *any one* of the items fitting the subject, type, and quality description.

It makes all the difference in the world to a searcher whether the task is to find everything of a particular sort, or some things of that sort, or a particular item. Comprehensive searches are of course the most demanding; but they are also relatively rare. Most searches are partial searches, not aimed at absolute completeness even within restrictions on type or quality. Partial searches may but need not be specified in terms of an exact number of items wanted; we do not often start out a search looking for exactly three or exactly seven items. But three or seven may nevertheless turn out to be a satisfactory number of items found.

WHAT STRATEGY SHALL WE ADOPT?

A *search strategy* is simply a description of the steps that are to be taken, or that actually were taken, in the course of a search. Formulated in advance, it is a plan that one expects to follow; formulated after the fact, it is a history of the search. Here we are interested in plans of action; we would like to be able to formulate plans of action that are likely to succeed. We must remember that an apparently foolproof plan may not work; what looks good on paper may not work out in practice. And plans almost always get modified while one is carrying them out; this is normal and to be expected. Still, we want to be able to make good plans in advance. There are five major types of search strategy that deserve discussion.

1. *Browsing* is going directly to a collection of materials and looking them over. This may not sound like a strategy, but it is, and is often the best one. A partial or specific search can often be done most quickly by browsing. If we are reasonably sure that a collection contains what we are looking for, and that we would be able to recognize the material that is wanted if we came across it (something that is not always true), the simplest thing to do is to go directly to the material.

2. _Footnote chasing_ is the way many if not most scholars conduct their searches. Starting with a particular work (book or journal article) of interest to them, they follow up the footnotes, end notes, or bibliographical references in that source, locate the items referred to, follow up their references to other works, and so on.

3. _Citation searching_ is the opposite of footnote chasing: it is chasing forward rather than backward in time. In this kind of searching, one starts with particular works, often but not always old ones, and by using special indexes, citation indexes, finds later works that have referred back to one's starting set of works. The idea is that, if a given work is of interest to the searcher, writings that refer back to that work may also be of interest.

4. _Consultation_ is simply the process of asking for recommendations from someone who is in a position to give advice. Like browsing, this may not sound like a strategy, but it is one, and often the best one.

5. _Indirect search_ is what we will call the strategy of approaching the materials we want indirectly by using catalogs, bibliographies, indexes: works that are primarily collections of bibliographical descriptions with more or less complete representations of content. This is the strategy we will be discussing in some depth.

A "pure" strategy is one that sticks to one of these five approaches; a "mixed" strategy is one that employs two or more of them. In a specific or partial search, a pure strategy may be sufficient, but in a comprehensive search, a mixed strategy is always necessary.

Let us consider when each strategy is especially appropriate.

Browsing is a good strategy when one can expect to find a relatively high concentration of things one is looking for in a particular section of a collection; it is not so good if the items being sought are likely to be spread out thinly in a large collection. Browsing is also less good if the things one is looking for are likely to be off the shelf, out on loan, in storage, etc. If the best and newest books are most in demand and always in circulation, and if one is looking exactly for the best and newest books, then browsing is unlikely to work, at least as a pure strategy. In a non-circulating reference collection, on the other hand, and for a specific search, browsing may be best. When looking for a particular piece of information, sure that it must be in one or another of this small collection of books, but unsure which one of them, we may find browsing is just the right strategy.

Footnote chasing is not adequate as the only (pure) strategy for a comprehensive search, since much of what one is looking for may simply not have been referred to in subsequent writings. Another drawback is that the literature may fall into several "streams," such as different schools of thought, that do not refer to each other's writings; if we start in one "stream," we might never find the other ones. The method is also sensitive to the initial choice of starting point. If our starting point is not a recent writing, it cannot refer to other recent writings. But footnote chasing is a useful ingredient of comprehensive searches, often completely satisfactory for partial searches, and especially useful in searches for material that does not fit into conventional indexing schemes and so cannot be easily found in an indirect search. It is also useful in evaluative searches, since people often say what they think about the worth of the things they refer to.

Citation searching is the least familiar method for general literature searches. It is useful in many different sorts of searches; in subject searching, perhaps its especial usefulness is in allowing us to look for material whose subject we cannot describe very well except by saying: it is what Smith discussed in that 1956 article of his. When we can best describe a subject only by mentioning a particular work in which it is discussed, citation searching is a strong strategy.

Consultation is sensible when evaluations are wanted and when an expert is available. It is a good way of finding a suitable starting place for footnote chasing or citation searching. It is better for unique or partial searches than for comprehensive searches; for those, it is good mainly for general advice on search strategy.

Indirect search is really the last resort for most people, the least used method of finding what they want. But for the professional searcher it is the standard method, an ingredient in most partial and all comprehensive searches. It is the one we will discuss in some detail.

SUCCESS

How do we evaluate the success of a search? This is a question we must discuss before talking further about search strategies, for discussion of the evaluation of search results will provide us with a vocabulary we need in talking about strategy.

The three search components—subject description, type limitation, and quality statement—together define more or less exactly what the objective of a search is; they specify a *target set* of items, which is simply the set or collection of items that fit the description given in terms of subject, type, and quality. The target set may be small or large; it may be empty as well, for there may be no items that fit the description. In a comprehensive search, the aim is to find all of the target set; in a partial search, the aim is to find some members of the target set; and in a specific search, the aim is to find *the* one member of the target set (if one is looking for a unique item), or *any* member of the target set.

From this, it seems to follow that evaluation of the results of a search would be easy in principle. The result of a search is a list or collection of documents; let us think of the result as always being a list (for of course it could always be made into a list). Then a comprehensive search has been completely successful if all the members of the target set are on the list; the aim was to find the whole target set, and success consists of producing a list that is indeed a list of the members of the target set. The success of a partial search is analogous; if one wanted a few members of the target set, and the list contains 8 or 10 members of the set, then one has succeeded, if in fact 8 or 10 is within the range of "a few" in the particular case. And, finally, if one was looking for a unique item, or for any member of a target set, then the search is successful if the unique item, or a member of the target set, is on the list.

So far, so good; but this is not the entire story. There are two kinds of mistake one can make. First is to miss items that should have been included in the list: this is to make an "error of omission." Next is to include items that should not be included: this is to make an "error of commission." A list that includes all it should include (therefore reflecting no errors of omission) might still include many items that it should not include (therefore reflecting many errors of commission). The usual aim of a search is two-fold: to include items that fit the search statement description, and to exclude all items that do not fit that description. In a comprehensive search, we can say that the aim is to find and list *all and only* the members of the target set. Failure to find them *all* is but one sort of failure: failure to list *only* members of the target set is quite a different sort of failure.

There is an established technical vocabulary for talking about the questions we have been discussing; three key terms are "relevance," "recall," and "precision." By convention, the items in the target set are called *relevant* items. They are the ones that should be on the resulting list.

The *recall* of a search is the percentage of *relevant* items that actually get on the list; this is the same as the percentage of target set items that have been found. If the target set consisted of 100 documents, and 50 of them are found, then the *recall* of the search is 50%; if the target set consisted of 20 documents, and 15 were found, then the *recall* is 75% (15 out of 20, or three fourths, or 75%).

High recall is always aimed at in comprehensive searches; by definition, one wants all of the target set, 100% of the relevant items. But high recall is not always wanted; in partial or specific searches high recall is expressly *not* wanted. Consider the following case: there are 100 items in the target set; we want a dozen or so; our search yields 10. Here, the recall of the search is only 10%, but success is excellent—the recall measure is a very poor measure of success. Here is a better measure of success: take the number of relevant items found, compare that with the number wanted, and let the resulting measure be our success measure. Then, if in a given search 12 are wanted and 10 are got, the success measure is 10/12 or 83%. Further, if only one item is wanted in another search, and we find one item that fits the search description, our success measure is 100%—one wanted, one found. This last would be true even if there were a thousand items in the target set for that search; the traditional recall measure for that search would be one out of a thousand, or 0.1%, while our success measure was 100%.

We will presently have to raise serious questions about the possibility of obtaining a numerical measure of success. For now, the essential point is simply that the technical term *recall* is used to mean the percentage of the *relevant* items actually found in the course of search.

Recall equals *the number of relevant items on the final list* divided by *the total number of relevant items,* with the result converted to percentage.

The *precision* of a search result is just the percentage of the items on the final list that should be there—that is, the percentage of items on the list that are *relevant.* If the list contains 100 items and 85 of them belong there, that is, are *relevant,* then the *precision* of the search result is 85% (85 out of 100). While we cannot say that high recall is the object of every search, every search aims at ending with a list all the members of which are relevant.

Precision equals *the number of relevant items on the final list* divided by *the total number of items on the final list,* with the result expressed in percentage.

RELATIONS BETWEEN PRECISION AND RECALL

One of the most important generalizations that can be made about searching is that precision and recall tend to vary inversely: the higher the precision of a search result, the lower its recall, and the higher the recall, the lower the precision. The practical meaning of this is not quite obvious. When we conduct a literature search, we will generally select and edit as we go, eliminating irrelevant items from consideration as they are spotted; as a consequence, the final list may be high both in recall and in precision. We will have "thrown away" the irrelevant items. The generalization about the inverse relation of recall and precision simply amounts to this: that, as we strive for maximum recall, we will almost certainly have to discard or "throw away" more and more irrelevant items, for the simple reason that we will be looking at less and less promising or productive sources. We will have got to the point of diminishing returns; it will take more and more work to achieve the final percentage points of recall. The first batch of relevant items may be easily found, but as the search goes on in quest of additional relevant items, by and large the relevant ones will be more thinly distributed among irrelevant ones. This is an instance of the principle of diminishing marginal returns: as we go on in the direction of high recall, equal amounts of effort are likely to result in diminishing amounts of new relevant material. If we did *not* select and edit as we went along, but simply copied or printed out everything we found under each index term we examined, then the resulting list would almost certainly show the relationship in question: the higher the recall, the lower the precision, and vice versa.

SEARCH EFFECTIVENESS AND EFFICIENCY

A good search strategy is one that leads to finding what is sought; a strategy is effective if it is successful in this way. But a good search strategy is also one that wastes little effort; a strategy is efficient if successful in this way. We can say, roughly, that recall is a measure of effectiveness and that precision is a measure of efficiency. If two people conduct searches for the same material, and both achieve the same degree of recall, they have both been equally effective. But one might have been more efficient than the other, by getting results of higher precision: discarding fewer items along the way, or producing a list that required the client to discard fewer items, a list containing fewer irrelevant items. We know that, as a search continues towards higher recall, precision is likely to drop steadily; but it may drop faster for some people than for others. The inefficient searcher is the one who wastes time and effort looking in places where there are few if any relevant items to be found.

PROBLEMS IN ESTIMATING SUCCESS

There are important practical and theoretical difficulties with the notions of recall, precision, and relevance. Neither recall nor precision can be measured exactly unless (a) we know how many relevant items there are (which is the same as knowing how big the target set is), and (b) we are able to tell, for each item we find, whether it is one of the relevant ones or not.

If we do not know whether there are a hundred or a thousand items in the target set, then we certainly cannot measure the recall of a search that produced 100 items: it could be anywhere from 100% (100 out of 100) to 10% (100 out of 1,000) or less. And if we are unsure about the relevance of half the items on our list, we cannot measure precision either. In fact it is often difficult to tell whether an item should or should not be on the list. It is practically impossible to be certain, merely from the title of a book or article, that it is about what it seems to be about, and judgments of relevance made only on the basis of titles are necessarily chancy and often inaccurate. Even when one examines the content of a work, relevance may be hard to determine. The only way of telling is seeing whether the description given in the search statement fits the content of the work. But every search statement is vague to some degree, and descriptions do not either fit or not fit, they fit *more or less well*. The fit between search statement and document content is a matter of degree. The problem in judging the relevance of an item is to decide whether the content of the item fits the search description *well enough* to deserve to be included in the final list. But it is hard if not impossible to formulate search statements precise and detailed enough to allow one to decide that matter in every case. This is often a serious practical problem, not simply a theoretical one.

To measure precision, one has only to look at the items on the final list, but to measure recall, that is clearly not enough. We must at least know the size of the target set. We have to know what is missing from the list, or how many things are missing, and we cannot tell that from the list. We do not start a search already knowing the size of the target set (at least with any accuracy), and we do not discover its exact size in the course of the search (or at least cannot be sure we have discovered it). So how do we find out the size of the target set?

It is usually said that we could in principle discover how many relevant documents there were in a collection by going through the collection item by item and deciding, in each case, if an item was relevant or not. But even in principle we cannot escape the problems of determining relevance just discussed. And even if we could escape them, the possibility of discovering the size of the target set by an item-by-item examination of an entire collection is of no practical interest; we use indirect searches just to avoid that kind of job.

In some cases there is a good estimate of the size of a target set available: someone has already made a comprehensive bibliography on the subject of our search. In that case we can compare our list with that comprehensive bibliography, and find that our list includes some percentage of the items in the comprehensive bibliography, plus maybe some not included in it. But in that case the search has been a mistake from the start. We should have found that comprehensive bibliography. As we shall note below, our search should *begin* with a preliminary survey of available bibliographical works, to discover (among other things) if our work has already been done for us (cf. Chapter 5). So it looks as if we can never in practice have a way of telling what the recall of a search is—never unless we mistakenly ignore a comparison bibliography we should have started with.

In practice, we can get an idea of the recall of a search only by more searching. After we have stopped a search, we can check on the recall of the search results so far by starting a new "test search" in what we think would be the next best source, and see if we find anything new. If we do not find anything new, we can have some (but not too much) confidence that we have found almost all there is to find. This is inconclusive, for there may be a large number of relevant documents lurking in an unexpected place. But this is the basic fact of life for the searcher: the precision of search results can often be determined fairly exactly, but recall can rarely be determined exactly.

For comprehensive searches, this is a serious difficulty; we can never be sure just how successful we have been. It is not a serious difficulty if we are doing partial searches, as we usually are; for there, high recall is not even aimed at. All we need to be able to do is measure or estimate precision. Even here, though, we cannot expect to be able to say exactly how successful a search has been. Remember that we proposed measuring the success of partial searches by comparing the number of relevant documents found with the number wanted. But there is usually no precise number of items wanted; we want *some* material, but not any definite number of items. When that is so, no numerical measure of success or effectiveness can be given.

Nor is it even true that high precision is always important. Quick searches aimed only at finding a few relevant items may be satisfactory even if their precision is low; "quick and dirty" is the ordinary way of describing short, low-precision searches. There is nothing at all wrong with "quick and dirty" searching if the results are satisfactory, as they often are. Then why bother about questions of measuring precision and recall? Because what makes a "quick and dirty" search acceptable is that it is quick: little effort has been expended, and so it does not much matter if that small effort was very efficient or not. The more effort is expended, the more important efficiency becomes. And if we do a *lot* of short partial searches, then efficiency begins to be important, for a lot of "dirty" searches may add up to quite a bit of wasted time.

Partial searches, and indeed *any* search with a strong evaluative component, can raise other kinds of problems in evaluating success. If we are looking, as we may well be, for the best introductory work on a subject, or for one that will be most helpful to a particular individual, how do we tell that we have actually found it? The usual answer would be that we leave it up to the client to decide that what we have found is what was wanted. This is not satisfactory; if I want a good introduction to a new subject, because I know nothing about it and want to learn, I am hardly in a position to tell whether I have been given the best introduction or not. To judge the success of such a search, we will have to ask someone who is in a position to do serious evaluation, or, in other words, to *consult* an expert. If we *can* do that after the search, perhaps we should have done it before, and instead of, the indirect search.

PRE-SEARCH SEARCH

We now turn to closer examination of one search strategy: the *indirect* strategy, involving the use of catalogs, bibliographies, abstracting and indexing services, and online databases. We will not consider the specific details of using particular online retrieval systems; instructions in formulating search commands in DIALOG, BRS, and other retrieval systems will be found elsewhere. We will instead concentrate on major strategic and tactical problems that arise using any kind of printed, card-form, microform, or online bibliographical file.

The number of bibliographical files is enormous, and before beginning a search we have to settle the prior question of which file to search in. The decision is often obvious, based on our prior knowledge. But very frequently we have to spend time discovering what files there are: what bibliographies are there, what indexing services, what published library catalogs, and so on. There may be no need to carry out the original search, if we find that someone else has already done it for us. Nothing is more frustrating to the searcher than to spend time and effort on a search, only to discover later that someone else had already done the work and published the result. The more one stands to lose in wasted effort by unnecessarily duplicating the work of someone else, the more careful should one's preliminary search for bibliographical works be. This means, obviously, that the preliminary search is more urgent in a comprehensive than a partial search.

How do we discover what files there are? This is itself a search problem, and to answer it we must do what we would do for any other search: choose a strategy, formulate a plan of action. Using the *consultation* strategy, we might choose to ask an expert colleague. Using the *browsing* strategy, we might choose to look on the open shelves of a reference collection. Or we might proceed indirectly, by using specialized files of files, such as bibliographies of bibliographies, guides to bibliographic and reference works, directories of online databases, or a library subject catalog, which includes bibliographical works of all sorts. *Using* files of this sort presents the same problem as does using any other files, and what we will be saying later on also applies to the pre-search for suitable files. *Finding* files of files (bibliographies of bibliographies, etc.) is itself a search problem to which what we say later also applies. The presearch is just another search (perhaps too frequently "quick and dirty").

The choice of files to search depends mainly on the *scope* of the different files. The scope of a file is simply the extent of what it contains specified in terms of subject matter, type of publication (including time period covered), quality, and quantity: exactly the same factors that go into a complete search statement. (This is no accident, since any index might in fact be the result of a prior systematic search, guided by an explicit search statement.) The choice of files reduces to this in the simplest case: we look for a file whose scope description includes (or is the same as) our search statement—i.e., what we are looking for is included in the scope of the file. If we are looking for material on the history of the railroad in the United States, we look for indexes whose scope is the same as or larger than that search description. If we find a file with exactly the right scope, our work may be done at this point; we may then have the list we want. If we find a file that includes our search description as a sub-part of its scope, we will have to proceed to select what we want from the larger mass of material. In a specific or partial search, we may need only to consult one file; in a comprehensive search, we are almost certain to have to use several files one after another. In any sort of search we may find that no single file covers all of the scope of our search, but that two or more files each cover part of its scope (e.g., one file lists only monographs on our subject, another file lists only journal articles, and we want both types of material). A very complex comprehensive search may require use of dozens of different files. But in all cases, the selection of a file is on the basis of the relation between its scope and the search statement.

The idea of a pre-search aimed at finding what files are available seems clear enough. But things get a bit more complicated when we remember that any book or article on a topic may contain a bibliography (in the form of a formal list or of bibliographical footnotes) that may be as good or better for our purposes than anything we could find in a library catalog, periodical index, or other secondary work. If you want a list of works on a subject—say, on pragmatics, a branch of linguistics—the best thing to do might simply be to find a recent monograph on the subject and look at *its* bibliography, if it has one. Why go to the trouble of searching through general linguistics bibliographies or indexes, if you can quickly find a convenient list in the back of an easily discovered book? The moral here is: consider skipping the step of looking for specialized secondary works; go directly to the subject catalog of monographs in your library, and find a recent work with a bibliography. This is especially sensible if you are looking for a good starting point; the monograph may give you all the information you need, but if more is wanted, its bibliography will lead you to it. But this is just the *footnote chasing* strategy. What is being suggested here is that it is often best to avoid indirect search *except* as a way of finding a good starting point for footnote chasing, that a library subject catalog is often a good place to find such a starting point, and that in such cases no extensive search, and no pre-search search, is needed at all.

SUBJECT INDEXES

We now turn to the process of searching in a particular file (catalog, bibliography, database, etc.). While there are many ways in which a file can be organized, we will confine our attention to only two types of arrangement and two corresponding types of search: subject indexes and free-text indexes. Subject indexes will include *both* the familiar alphabetic subject-heading system *and* classified systems. Free-text (or "natural language") indexes will include simple title indexes and also indexes to extra-title information: abstracts, full text, etc. A preliminary look at the general character of the different types of index is necessary, for decisions made about what index to search and how to search it *must* be sensitive to differences in the design characteristics of the different indexes. Efficient use of an index depends on prior understanding of its logical character.

Subject indexes essentially require two steps in their construction: (a) the selection of a number of subject categories, and (b) the assignment of individual writings to one or more of these subject categories. From our point of view, it does not matter whether the subject categories are arranged in any systematic order of a classification scheme, or alphabetically as in a subject catalog, or for that matter whether they are arranged in any systematic manner at all. The essential thing is simply that there is a definite number of different categories, each with some kind of description (index term, classification slot description, etc.), and that each document is assigned to one or more of these categories.

Terminology differs for different sorts of subject index. What are called subject headings in standard library terminology are often called controlled vocabulary terms in the context of database searching. A list of controlled vocabulary terms is called a thesaurus, which is just what would be called in library terminology a subject heading list. Terms in the thesaurus are also called descriptors; other authorized indexing terms, like proper names used as subject headings, and often not included in subject heading lists, may be called identifiers. Despite the difference in nomenclature, descriptors and identifiers are simply subject headings.

The first step in using a subject index is ordinarily to find the subject headings (or classification slots, descriptors, etc.) that correspond most closely to the subject component of the search statement. Although our overall strategy in searching subject indexes is *indirect*, we can call this "taking the direct approach" within that strategy. Another way of saying the same thing is this: the first step is to find the index description or descriptions that most specifically describe the material one is searching for. As subject catalogers follow a rule of *specific entry*, calling on them to choose index descriptions that most specifically describe the material at hand, so the user follows a corresponding rule of specific approach. To find the closest fitting index description, we look at subject heading lists or thesauri, if they are available (in print or online). If no such list is available, we proceed by trial and error in the file itself. If the subject description in our search statement is complex, there may be close approximations to single components of the description but no close approximation to the subject description as a whole. The closest approximation may not be very close, and it may be an approximation to only one part of the subject description.

DEPTH AND EXHAUSTIVITY OF INDEXING

In a subject index, each individual item is assigned to *one or more* subject categories: it is given one or more subject headings, or put in one or more classification slots. The *depth* of indexing corresponds to the *number* of subject categories to which individual items are assigned. In shallow indexes, each item is assigned to only one category, and some may be assigned to no category, even though listed in the file under, for instance, author's name. In deeper indexes, each item is assigned to several subject categories; a fairly deep index would be one in which each item was given ten or a dozen subject headings.

Exhaustivity of indexing is a related but slightly different notion. It refers to the number of different subjects or content elements in each document that are picked out by the indexer and used in making assignments to subject categories. If only the principal topic is used as a basis for making assignments to subject categories, the index is relatively inexhaustive; if sub-topics, sub-sub-topics, and so on are also used as a basis for indexing assignments, the index is relatively exhaustive. (Put another way: if parts of a book or article are represented in the index as well as the book or article "as a whole," the index is more exhaustive; the smaller the parts into which the whole is broken down for indexing purposes, the more exhaustive the resulting index.)

Depth and exhaustivity are obviously related, in that one consequence of increasing the exhaustivity of an index is to increase the number of subject category assignments, that is, the depth of indexing. But an index might be relatively deep without being very exhaustive; the subject indexing vocabulary might be set up in such a way that it took five or six separate subject headings to cover simply the "main topic" of a work. A complex Library of Congress subject headings may contain easily five or six terms in one subject heading; in another system, all headings might be "simple" one-word terms, so that it would take five or six subject headings to express what LC does with one. The one-word heading system would produce deeper but not more exhaustive indexes. But usually, depth and exhaustivity of indexing go together; an index is deep because it is exhaustive.

In general, the deeper or more exhaustive an index, the more of the writings on a particular topic will appear when one takes the most direct approach. The more exhaustive the index, the more writings on a particular topic will be explicitly shown as such. Not only whole books or articles entirely devoted to a topic will be shown, as in a shallow index; parts or segments of books and articles discussing the topic will also be shown. So recall will be better at the most direct approach, the more exhaustive the index.

SPECIFICITY

How closely one will be able to match the search statement to index terms will depend in part on the specificity of the index vocabulary or classification scheme. One term can be said to be more specific than another just in case the first refers to a species or kind of thing and the second refers to a genus or larger category of which the first is a part. So "potato" is more specific than "vegetable," because potatoes are a kind of vegetable. This is the clearest sort of example of the relation of the term *specificity;* different but analogous relationships lead to a larger concept of specificity. So "leg" might be said to be more specific than "body," because legs are parts of bodies; and "San Francisco" might be said to be more specific than "California," because San Francisco is part of California. Sets of terms can be arranged in series like Chinese boxes, the narrower or more specific terms being "included in" the wider or more general terms. An indexing vocabulary or classification scheme that has only or primarily very general terms and categories does not allow for an accurate match between most search statements and index terms; in looking for writings about potato bugs in an index that recognizes only the category of insects, but no specific kind of insects, the most direct approach may lead to a term that is more general than any of the terms in the search statement. When this happens, much of the material listed under the term is likely to be irrelevant; taking this whole set of items as a search result, we can see that the search result will not be very *precise,* because the index vocabulary is not very *specific.* This may lead people to say that highly specific vocabularies are "precision devices," ways of making searches more precise. This is not true in general; the most we can say is that if the index vocabulary is very specific, the most direct approach will yield precise results, however things go when one widens the search.

Term specificity is only one factor affecting the precision of search results on the direct approach. The other factor is the complexity of subject categories. If subject categories are subdivided in an index, forming multi-faceted subject index terms (like the LC subject headings with one or more topical or geographical or form subdivisions), one may find a very close match between search statement and subject categories on the direct approach. If the vocabulary is very specific but the specific terms cannot be combined to form complex multi-faceted categories, then the most direct approach may be to a category in which most material is irrelevant to the search, so giving low precision on the direct approach.

ACCURACY AND CONSISTENCY OF INDEXING

What we find, when we take the most direct approach, depends not only on depth, exhaustivity, and specificity of indexing, but also, crucially, on how accurate and how consistent the indexers have been. We will not find a relevant item on the most direct approach if the indexer has mistakenly assigned it elsewhere. Nor will we find it if the indexer has been inconsistent in assigning index terms, assigning an index term to some items and not to others even though they are so similar that the same index term should be applied to all of them. There is evidence that indexers are in fact not very consistent. But there is also a good deal of what we can call "pseudo-inconsistency": works quite similar in content, but different enough so that choosing the *best* fitting short index descriptions results in different index terms being assigned. Subject cataloguing and indexing practices almost guarantee that quite similar materials will be located under different index terms. Subject indexing is difficult enough that relatively small differences in point of view will lead to different index term assignments, and if the user's point of view differs from the indexer's, the user's direct approach will often fail to locate material the user would find highly relevant. Users hope to find all substantially similar works listed under the same index terms; but indexer mistakes (sometimes), indexing rules (sometimes), and differences in point of view all conspire to defeat that expectation.

FREE-TEXT INDEXES

The most familiar sort of free-text (or natural language) index is the title index in which each title is listed once, under the first word (other than an article). Online free-text indexes may not appear to resemble a one-entry title index very much, for they may list works under every significant word in titles, in abstracts (of journal articles), in assigned index entries, and even in the full text of a work. There are familiar print counterparts even to this most elaborate sort of free-text index: the *concordance* is an index to term occurrences in the full text of a single work or of a corpus of works (the Bible or the works of Shakespeare, for example). Online free-text indexes resemble concordances more than they resemble single-entry title indexes; nevertheless it is worth reflecting on the process of searching a one-entry title index, for the problems of doing that do not disappear when one is searching a concordance or an online free-text index.

In searching a title index, as in searching a subject index, one begins by trying to find the most direct approach: in this case, to find the term or terms most likely to occur in the titles of relevant works. But searching a title index differs from searching a subject index because of the lack of standardization in the title index. A subject index uses a standardized vocabulary; titles are subject to no sort of standardization beyond that provided by the language itself and by social conventions in its use. Titles may not accurately describe content, and texts with the same sort of content might have any number of different titles. If we were looking for books on, say, the economics of underdeveloped countries, there would be only one way to find each book in a simple one-entry title index: we would have to guess the first word in the title (initial articles excepted). "Economics" could be the first word of the title of a relevant work; so could "political" (as in "Political economy of the third world"), or "third" ("Third world economic problems"), or "emerging," or practically any other word, for example, "cruel" (as in *Cruel Choice,* the real title of such a book). We cannot count on finding much relevant material by looking under just *one* index entry, and we might find relevant material listed under almost *any* index entry.

Things are easier for the searcher in a multiple-entry or "permuted" title index, for instance, printed KWIC ("Key word in context") or KWOC ("Key word out of context") indexes, where titles are listed several times, under each significant word of the title. So, using the same example, we would find under the word "third" all the items containing that word *anywhere* in the title. This is a help, for it lets us find material in cases where we could not have guessed the *first* title word. It is easier to find relevant items if we only have to guess words that will occur *somewhere* in a title than if we have to guess words that will occur *first* in a title. But we pay a price for this extra help, in terms of precision: we may find very long lists of titles all containing the same word, e g , "third" or "economics," most of which are not relevant.

Modern database searching allows us to locate records containing an occurrence of a word almost anywhere in a bibliographical record, or, in full-text databases, anywhere in the text of a document. (In this last case, the online index is a concordance.) The chances that a work about the economics of underdeveloped countries will have the word "underdeveloped" *somewhere* in the record are greater than the chances that that word will occur in the title, so we have a better chance of finding relevant works by using that term as a search term online than in a single- or multiple-entry title index. But the cost in precision is likely to be very much higher: many more irrelevant items will be found, along with some more relevant items.

It is in order to reduce the cost in lack of precision that one searches online using Boolean combinations of terms, and proximity operators that specify the required linear relations of terms (that they occur, for instance, in the same sentence, the same field, immediately adjacent to each other, and so on). The effect of using Boolean operators (AND, OR, NOT) and proximity operators is to force us to specify in advance the *relevance clues* we would use in searching a single- or multiple-entry title index. It works like this. In manual search of a title index, we will start by choosing one term, scan the individual entries under that term, reject most of the entries, and select others, all on the basis of other terms we see in the titles. Having finished with one entry, we will move on to another entry and repeat the process. So we might start with the term "underdeveloped," and select out of the entries listed under that term those that also have either the term "countries" or "areas" and the term "economic" or "economics," and then move on to the term "underdevelopment" and repeat the process. (An oversimplified example!) In online searching we do just the same thing, but we try to specify in advance all the combinations of terms that would lead us to select an item out as probably relevant. So (keeping to the same oversimplified example) we ask to see items containing either "underdeveloped" or "underdevelopment" and either "countries" or "areas", and either "economic" or "economics." (The request can be simplified by using truncation in the first and third components, but the nature of the process shows up more clearly if we ignore truncation for the moment.)

In searching a printed index, all we need to do is select one or more starting terms. The other title words we need not select in advance; we can count on our ability to recognize words when we see them that provide good clues to relevance. The job in online searching is to choose these clues in advance, which makes online searching more difficult than manual searching. We cannot count on being able to produce in advance all the terms whose clue-value we would recognize if we came across them. We may forget about variant spellings of words, and about different grammatical forms of words: remember "theater" but forget "theatre" and "theatrical," for instance. We may not be able to think of all synonyms that might be used for a term: remember "drama" but forget "stage." The problem is very much worse if we are searching a multilingual database. Even if we know a little French and German, we may be unable to produce in advance the French or German terms we could recognize as relevance clues if we saw them. So success in online searching is likely to be less than it would be in manual searching. But it is likely to come much quicker, which is the main point. And of course we may not need to specify more than a few clues to relevance; for a partial search, a few obvious clues may suffice.

We have seen that the result of taking a direct approach in subject indexes depends heavily on the depth, specificity, accuracy, and consistency of the indexing. We can extend these notions to free-text indexes. If depth of indexing is simply a matter of number of index entries, then a single-entry title index is of minimum depth, a permuted-title index is of greater depth, an index to titles and abstracts is much deeper, and a full-text index is of maximum depth. (In an online index we may be able to choose the level of depth at which we search, deciding to search only in titles, in titles plus abstracts, or in all parts of a record. In printed indexes we seldom have such alternatives.) Natural language allows the full range of degrees of specificity, so considered as an indexing language, it is as specific as possible. But authors may not take advantage of its possibilities, and may produce titles that are far from being specific descriptions of content. As to accuracy: it is well known that titles are often misleading if taken literally as content descriptions. And any problems of consistency that exist in subject indexes are dwarfed by the massive inconsistencies among different authors' descriptions, in titles and abstracts, of the same subject matter.

This way of looking at free-text indexes emphasizes the difficulties that come from lack of standardization. But there are subjects and fields of study in which natural language is itself fairly standardized: where terminology is relatively well defined and uniform throughout a population of authors, where linguistic convention leads to the adoption of a uniform way of speaking, so that different people writing about the same things can be fairly confidently counted on to use the same expressions. This is more likely to happen in the physical and biological sciences than it is in the social sciences and humanities; hence the common view that the vocabularies of the former are "harder" than those of the latter. Hardness and softness of vocabulary are matters of degree rather than matters of sharp distinction; still, there are degrees of hardness, and the harder a vocabulary, the more it resembles a controlled indexing vocabulary, and the more satisfactory free-text searching will be. Where the standardizing effect of subject indexing is not crucial because natural language is itself fairly standardized, the advantages of the subject index over the natural language index are less pronounced than where natural language is soft and unstandardized. This is probably not apparent to many searchers, who by experience learn that consistency of indexing is a serious practical problem for "soft" subject matters. The point is not that subject indexes are highly satisfactory for such subject matters, only that they are *attempts* to standardize what is not standardized in natural language.

CHOICE OF FILES AGAIN

Let us return briefly to the question of selection of a file in which to begin a search. We can restate the problem this way: which file should I choose, if I want to get the best result with a direct approach? Knowing what kinds of results we can expect in files that differ not only in scope but also in depth and specificity of indexing helps to answer that question. The direct approach in a shallow subject index will be likely to turn up only a fraction of the material in the file that is relevant to our subject, but it may be just the material we want. Subject catalogs of library monograph collections are, whether manual or online, extremely shallow indexes to the collections they represent. The average number of subject headings assigned to books by the

Library of Congress (and accepted by most libraries) is less than two. In a periodical index, a two-page discussion of a topic might be separately indexed, while a hundred-page discussion of the same topic in a book might not show up in a library catalog at all, there being only a single subject heading covering a much broader topic. This is bad if it is comprehensiveness we want, but it is not bad if we are looking for books wholly devoted to a topic, which is what the subject catalog mainly shows. Looking for a lot of material (high recall), we will prefer files with deeper indexing; but looking for a small number of works—looking, for instance, just for a good *starting point*—a shallower index is probably preferable.

WHICH INDEX?

Given this understanding of the characteristics of subject and free-text indexes, we can now ask the first question that needs to be answered when one approaches a bibliographical work: which index should one use first? Where should one start one's search?

The answer seems to be obvious: start a subject search in a subject index. If there is a separate subject index, use it; if you are searching online, use descriptors and identifiers, not free-text indexes to other fields of the bibliographic record. The point of subject indexes (remember that we are including classified indexes under this heading) is to describe the contents of a collection of materials systematically by application of a standardized vocabulary of description. Taking the direct approach means picking out the closest equivalent to one's search description from the standardized vocabulary and using that as one's entry to the index. If the indexing has been done well, we should be able to count on finding relevant material for our search when we take the direct approach.

While it is generally best to start subject searches in subject indexes, there are plenty of cases in which we can be reasonably sure in advance that search of free-text indexes is better. First: it takes time for subject index vocabularies to reflect new subject matters. A look at the thesaurus (subject heading list) for a catalog or bibliography or database may quickly reveal that there is no established terminology available in the thesaurus to describe our subject. In such a case, free-text indexes may be preferable to subject indexes. Second: if the indexing vocabulary in use is a very general one, not allowing extremely specific description of subject matters, free-text indexes will offer the possibility of more specific approaches. Third: the subject index may be too shallow to give us the recall we want; free-text indexes may offer deeper (though unstandardized) access; this is perhaps the main advantage of free-text search capabilities in online indexes. Fourth: what one is looking for may fall outside the subject indexing system entirely: if, for example, subject cataloguers do not explicitly indicate the *approach* taken in a book (arguably, an aspect of the subject matter), do not indicate which works are written from Marxist, or deconstructionist, or psychoanalytic perspectives, free-text indexes may provide the best approach to finding material of the sort we want.

So we have to qualify our general rule of starting a subject search in a subject index: do this *unless* you have a good reason for thinking that the subject indexing system is going to fail in this particular case. But don't we need a still further qualification? Are there not cases in which it probably doesn't make any *difference* which index one uses first? Of course there must be such cases. In many partial or specific searches, where we are looking only for a few relevant items or for *any* work of a given sort (any recent book on magic, say), we may do equally well in either subject or free-text index. Choice depends on our guesses about likelihood of success, and we may often guess (and be right in guessing) that it makes no difference which index we use. But if it always or generally made no difference, there would be no point in systematic subject indexing; the attempt at standardizing content descriptions would not be worth the effort. The belief that subject indexing *is* worth the effort it takes leads directly to the general rule of starting subject searches in subject indexes.

In online searching, one has the option of searching both subject index and free-text index simultaneously. If descriptors and identifiers are broken up into one-word units and included in a "basic" index (as is the case in DIALOG), then searching with unqualified terms in the basic index will yield items having the terms occurring as free-text terms *or* as terms in assigned indexes (descriptors, identifiers). For searches in which high precision is sought, search in the subject index alone is usually advisable (unless it is known that the subject indexing vocabulary is inadequate in this case); for more comprehensive searches, search of subject and free-text indexes simultaneously is better.

This is one example of a "mixed" search, using both subject and free-text indexes. Another kind is this: we find a single best-fitting descriptor which we use as a one-term family for one facet; for the others, we form families of terms from the free-text index that would be used as clues in searching a manual file under our chosen subject index term. This is similar to what we would actually do in searching a manual file; the subject index term is the term we would choose as the most direct approach to a file; the free-index terms in the other facet families are the terms we would use as clues to relevance in scanning the items listed under the subject heading.

MANUAL VS. COMPUTER SEARCH

The same bibliographic files may be available in two forms, as a printed catalog, bibliography, or abstracting/indexing service, and as an online database. In that case we have to decide which form to use in the search. The decision will depend on costs and on local policy, but there are some general considerations relevant to a decision.

1. If the printed equivalent of an online database is less up-to-date than the online version, and up-to-dateness is what we want, the choice is clear.
2. If the online version has a deeper subject index than the print version, and index depth is what we want, the choice is clear.
3. Likewise, if deep free-text indexing is wanted, the online version is preferred.
4. If manual search would require scanning many separate volumes, while the database is a single cumulated file, online search is preferable.
5. If manual search would require scanning large files under very general or common terms, online search taking advantage of the combining capacity of the computer is probably to be preferred.
6. If we need a deep free-text index to make up for the deficiencies of (manual or online) subject indexing, online search is probably unavoidable.

The advantages seem wholly on the side of the computer. But it is not always so. If, for instance, a search is difficult to formulate explicitly, and/or if one counts heavily on finding relevant material by browsing and rapid scanning of large amounts of text, manual search may be much preferable. If a shallow subject index is all we need, a partial search may be completed as easily and quickly in a printed index as in its online counterpart. It may be possible, but complicated, to get what we want from an online file; in other cases, the same will be true of printed sources. Neither kind of file has a monopoly on all advantages.

DIRECT APPROACH

The first step in searching an index is ordinarily the selection of what we may call the most direct approach or most specific approach. This sounds simple and often is, but particularly in online searching, there are many alternative ways of taking the direct approach. The first problem is this: given that we start with a search description containing a subject description as well as other specifications (form, date, language, quality, etc.), how much of this information do we try to incorporate into our direct approach? The subject description of a search statement consists of one or more facets or components; the type, quality, and quantity components can similarly be formulated as a number of distinct components or facets: for instance, a publication date facet, a language facet, a literary form facet, and so on. The question now is: which of these does one use in searching?

The answer is, of course, that one tries to use all of them, but in different ways. In a printed or card-form catalog or index, one has to look under one heading at a time—ordinarily this will be one subject component (one subject heading, one title word entry)—and use the other components of the search statement to select from the items listed under that heading. In online searching, one can use several components simultaneously; that is the great power of online searching. Which components one will be *able* to use simultaneously depends on the system, and the database, one is searching. (Can you ask simultaneously for items having both of two subject headings, and in a certain language, and published in a certain year? It will depend on the database and the system.) Which components one *should* use simultaneously is a different question. Which ones should be built into one's online *command* is the question. In searching manually, we look under one heading and use *all* our other information to pick out the items listed under that heading that are of interest. In searching online, we *can* "look under" several headings at once; the question is, shall we try to look under as many as possible at once, or shall we look under only one or two, using our other information to select from the list of items we find in that way?

First, we often *cannot* use all facets. The evaluative component of a search is most clearly one that generally cannot be used in formulating search commands; we cannot generally ask for *good* books or articles on a topic—that is one of the main problems with catalogs, bibliographies, and abstracting/indexing services. (But see the next paragraph; if we choose, as the first file to examine, a bibliography of "best books," then quality is implied by the content of the file. In other cases, however, evaluations are generally absent, or, if they are present, are given in annotations and not effectively searchable.) We may be looking for works of a particular literary form: review articles, for instance. In some files, we may be able to specify that this is the type of work we want, but in others, there may be no way of specifying this. The construction of the file sets limits to the amount of information we can use in formulating our search statements.

But we should not even make it a general rule to use all the information we *can* use. First: we can often ignore one facet entirely because it corresponds to the entire content, or the major content, of a catalog or database. Looking for something about music in a music index or bibliography, for instance, we take it for granted that most of the material listed will be about music, and so do not specifically *ask* for items on music. We use the content of the file as an *implied concept;* that is, terms corresponding to the major or entire content of the file do not need to be specified; the very fact that you are looking in *that* file implies that you are interested in material of the sort contained in it. There are other ways in which selection of a database can automatically imply one of the facets of the search description. If we want only works in English, and are searching in a database with only English writings, we need not specify the language restriction, for it is automatically fulfilled. Similarly if the database is *mostly* English language material, we can simply ignore the few non-English items. Time restrictions work similarly.

Second: even if there are several facets or components in the subject description, it is often enough to use only one of them. Terms in both subject and free-text indexes differ widely in frequency of use or occurrence; one term may be used 10 times in a file, another may be used hundreds or thousands of times. If you want items having both a "rare" and a "common" term, it will often be sufficient to ask only for items having the "rare" term, for there will be so few of them that precision will be high, and the elimination of irrelevant items quick and easy. So the general rule is: if one facet corresponds to rare terms, use only that facet. In general the more specific a concept, the rarer will be the use of the terms expressing that concept, so the rule can also be stated: if one facet represents a very specific concept, use only that facet.

This rule is of no help if none of the facets corresponds to rarely occurring terms—if the terms of interest are all common, the concepts all general ones. Do we then use all facets? Not necessarily. We want to use terms that will distinguish relevant from irrelevant items, and many terms simply fail to do that. The vaguer, and the more general, a term, the worse it is likely to be. Some facets may not correspond to any available descriptors, and have to be omitted in searching a subject index. Some may correspond to available descriptors, but descriptors whose use by indexers is likely to be inconsistent or very specialized: for instance, looking for *research* on a topic, one will often worsen rather than improve recall and precision by trying to specify the idea of research in one's search statement. Looking for material on the *relationships* between two phenomena (smoking and cancer, say), it will be best to omit the concept of relationship in one's search statements—the concept is so general and so likely to be inconsistently treated by indexers that adding it is likely to worsen rather than better things.

These cautions are hard to follow at first, for we may have to learn by bitter experience which sorts of terms are bad search terms, which sorts of concepts are better left out of search commands. We may in practice do about as well, at first, simply by following this guideline: use as few facets as possible, and prefer more essential to less essential facets; prefer relatively specific to relatively general facets. The danger is in trying to use too much information, and the remedy is to steer ourselves in the direction of under-specifying rather than over-specifying the materials we want. We do better to try to make search commands as simple as possible, rather than as complex as possible. With practice we may ultimately figure out how to make them *just right,* but there are no simple rules to tell us how to do this.

WIDENING A SEARCH

If the direct approach does not give us all that we want (and in a comprehensive search it never will), then we proceed to widen the search. We can do this by altering our approach while staying with the same file, or by changing to a different file, or both. Let us first consider altering the approach in the same file. All the steps we have already examined are candidates for reexamination in the decision what to do next. We can switch from subject index to free-text index, or stay with the index we were using and change the approach. What might we do if we started in a subject index and decided to stay with it? One of the main alternatives is that of using the cross-reference apparatus of the indexing vocabulary: the "see also" references given in a thesaurus or subject heading list or the related terms in an online thesaurus. There are three varieties of related terms: *broader* terms (terms that are generic to the terms we start with, as "vegetable" is to "potato"); *narrower* terms (terms more specific than those we start with, as "White Rose potato" is to "potato"); *overlapping* or *related* terms (terms that partially cover the subject matter represented by our starting term, as "potato marketing" or "potato cookery" overlap "potato").

Indexes that supply cross references ease the job of widening the search, but one should not assume that the cross references given in a list are all that need be considered. Knowledge of the particular subject matter, and imagination, may suggest more and better terms. A search can be expanded by moving upwards, downwards, and sideways; most failures of recall are due to failure to move in one of these directions. (Of course movement in all three directions will not always be possible—for instance, movement downward will not be possible if one started at the most specific level.)

In searching a printed or card-form subject index, moving along the cross-reference structure is the natural way of widening a search in a file. In searching online, substituting related terms within one facet of a search command is the analog. We can change several facets at once, but it is possibly better to make changes one facet at a time. If recall on the direct approach has been poor, and we have used several facets of the subject description in our search command, we may suspect we have demanded too much; in that case, dropping a facet entirely—the least essential, most general, or most "suspicious" facet—is a promising next move. If recall has been poor in the subject index, we may proceed to use a mixed approach, searching both subject and free-text indexes simultaneously.

If we started in a free-text index and want to widen the search, again we have several options. First, we can search more *deeply:* if we first asked for terms from titles only, we can now ask for terms occurring anywhere in a record. Second, we can add alternatives to the list of terms we are looking for: if we started by asking for items containing either the terms A or B, we can now ask for terms A or B or C or D—and we can do this for one facet of the search or for several simultaneously. Third, if we first used proximity operators, asking for items where term A occurred next to term B, we can relax the requirement, accepting items where the terms occur farther apart. Fourth, we can drop a facet entirely, as we can in subject index searching. Fifth, as in subject index searching, we can change the level of specificity of terms being used, substituting more specific or more general or overlapping terms for those with which we started. And of course we may do several of these things simultaneously.

These choices can be re-addressed any number of times, as one goes on trying out new approaches, successively enlarging the pool of relevant items found.

As we expand our search, step by step, we may want to find out how much *new* material we are finding. No problem in manual searching, this can be a problem online, where we may find ourselves retrieving large sets of items, too many to look at one by one. There is an easy way of segregating the *new* items found in later steps of an online search. Suppose an initial approach has yielded a set of items containing some but not enough relevant items. We then try a wider search, and get a larger set of items. Question: how many *new* items have we found by this second try? To find the answer, use the Boolean NOT operator: ask to see only the items that are in the second set but not in the first. This is a way of *subtracting* sets from sets, taking from the second (bigger) set the items that are also in the first (smaller) set. Looking at the result, we may find that we have caught few new relevant items, or on the other hand that we have got all the new ones we need.

A favorite method of searching in cases in which one is uncertain about what subject headings (descriptors) are the right ones to use is this: try a title-word search in hope of finding at least one obviously relevant work; then display the indexing assigned to that work and choose descriptors from those assigned. Descriptors assigned to this obviously relevant work are likely to be assigned to other relevant works as well. The procedure can be repeated (iterated). Using a newly discovered descriptor, one locates one or more further obviously relevant items, looks at their assigned index terms, and chooses from among these. In this case, the first approach has been a shallow free-text approach (title words only); the next step has been a wider search using descriptors found in the first step. (As an alternative: having found one or more obviously relevant item at the first step, go off line, get copies of the articles, and use their footnotes in a change of strategy. A recent monograph or review articles on a subject may give us more than we could otherwise find without much wasted effort.)

The number of alternative ways of widening a search itself presents a problem: with so many alternatives, how can one decide which is best? How does one identify the *next best* approach after the direct approach? There is probably no general answer to this question. Sometimes it will be appropriate to proceed by making successive small changes, but sometimes the failure of an initial approach will suggest that a radical change of approach is called for. Unhappily, the problem of deciding what change of approach to make seems to be one for which no simple and general rules are available.

NARROWING A SEARCH

In searching manual indexes, one picks out likely relevant items found under an index term (subject heading, title word) for future examination or inclusion on a list. In searching online indexes, we might do the same thing: display everything found by a command and then pick out the promising items. But often an initial command will uncover very large numbers of items, sometimes thousands of them; and rather than look at each item retrieved, one will try to reduce the number of retrieved items before inspecting them all.

This can be done by adding new conditions—for instance, by limiting the retrieval to recent publications, or publications in English only, if we have not already used these non-subject facets in the direct approach. We may add a new subject facet, which can have dramatic effects on both recall and precision—precision can improve greatly, but recall can also drop drastically. (In a small partial search, this may not matter.) In general, we proceed by using manoeuvres that are just the opposite of those we use to widen a search. Instead of relaxing requirements, we tighten old ones and add new ones; instead of increasing alternatives, we decrease them. We may subtract alternatives from a family of free-text terms, thus reducing the number of ways a document can get into the retrieved set. If we started in a free-text index, we may switch to a subject index; if we were searching deeply, we may switch deliberately to a more shallow search (accepting terms only from titles, instead of from anywhere in a record, or accepting only major descriptors, if the database distinguishes major from minor descriptors). Adding facets or narrowing what will be accepted within facets will refine the search output (but perhaps refine it out of existence). Again the number of alternatives is very large; we can try them out one by one in successive reformulations of our approach. Also again, there seem to be no simple and general rules telling us the sequence in which to try out the alternatives. It takes practice, including practice in analyzing one's own failures and inefficiencies, to learn to choose good sequences of moves.

ENDING A SEARCH

There are two questions about ending a search: (a) how do we know when to stop widening a search in a particular file? and (b) how do we know when to stop, period? At the point at which you have found what you were looking for, you stop; that may be after the first step (direct approach), or after the tenth or twentieth. A partial or unique search may take only one or two steps in one index. A comprehensive search will always take more steps; it is in connection with comprehensive searches that we run into difficulties with stopping a search. But even a partial search may require switching files. If recall is terrible on the first step, the alternatives are to widen the search in that file or to switch to a new file. If we stay in the same file and attempts to widen the search are disappointing, the balance tilts in favor of switching to a new file, if there *is* an alternative file accessible to us that is of the right scope. In a comprehensive search, on the other hand, we may have no option but to stay in a particular file until we are sure we have found everything in it that is relevant to our search. Then we switch to the next most promising file.

How does one know when to stop a comprehensive search? The answer is that one doesn't know, in the sense of coming to a point at which one can be certain that further search will uncover nothing relevant. Sometimes we stop because our time is up, sometimes because the point of diminishing returns has long been passed, and the value of continuing the search does not seem worth the cost. And sometimes we get to the point where further search is turning up nothing new at all, and so decide that we have probably found all there is to find. But we never *can* be quite sure that our comprehensive search has been completely successful. The next file we look at may reveal new material.

SEARCH RECORD

The longer a search, the more important it is to keep a detailed record of the steps of the search, including (a) all the indexes that have been consulted, and (b) all the index headings that have been examined in each index. This is important because it is frequently necessary to go back to files that have already been examined—for instance, to look under new headings that have been suggested by the use of another index. If one is not sure which indexes have already been used, or (a more frequent occurrence) which headings have been examined in a particular index, much time can be wasted in repeating work already done. So, if one began with a written search plan, the plan should be annotated to show what unplanned steps were taken; if one began only with a plan in one's head, a written history of the search should be maintained as one goes. In a short, partial search, none of this may be necessary; in a long, comprehensive search it is vital.

AVOIDING THE INDIRECT STRATEGY

Since we have spent so much time on the indirect strategy, it will be a good idea to end by emphasizing that it is only one strategy out of several, and often not the best one. As noted earlier, it is not the favorite strategy for people other than librarians and professional searchers; other people tend to prefer browsing, chasing footnotes, and consulting. In an online search we can, in a few minutes, produce a bibliography on almost any subject we like; but why suppose that what we do in a few minutes will be a better guide or introduction to the literature of the subject than the bibliography that a serious student of the subject provides as an appendix to the book or journal article that results from the serious study? A quick and dirty partial search may turn up some good-looking material on the finances of opera in the United States; but will it turn up the *best* material for the client? The best material might not be discovered on the direct approach, which may be the only approach in a partial search. (We wouldn't find the best material if it was listed in a subject catalog under the subject heading "Performing Arts— Finance" while we stopped after finding material listed under "Opera— Finance.") The subject search through bibliographies, catalogs, online databases is frequently not an effective strategy at all, and often less effective than other strategies. We must try to learn to use it effectively and efficiently, but must not trust it too much, or think it is always the best strategy to use.

8

Search and Idea Tactics*

Marcia J. Bates

INTRODUCTION[1]

For all the developments in automated information retrieval, nothing yet matches the ability of experienced human searchers—whether known as information specialists or reference librarians—as they move among an enormous range of resources to develop bibliographies or answer questions.

While we cannot yet say completely what an experienced searcher knows that the beginner does not, this chapter attempts to inventory the "moves" of the professional (some of which Wilson introduced above). The concepts of *search tactics* and *idea tactics* are presented, and various particular tactics are named and described. The tactics shown here make up the *strategies* of both bibliographic and reference searches, whether manual or online, and apply across all types of questions and subject fields.

Search tactics, discussed first, are concerned with the search proper: monitoring the search (that is, keeping it on track), threading one's way through the file structure of the information facility to find desired sources, and fitting the search as conceptualized to the vocabulary of the sources. *Idea tactics*, discussed later, are ways of generating ideas to unblock a stymied search.

A few of the tactics are well known in the library and information science

* This chapter is a revision of material that first appeared as Bates (1979a and l979b), © John Wiley & Son, Inc., used by permission.

literature; others may be used but are not consciously articulated; and still others may be unfamiliar to most searchers, instructors, and researchers. It is a premise of this chapter that to name and define a tactic makes it more available to the searcher's mind and thus more readily applied. Moreover, even those already known and used may benefit from systematic presentation in an inventory.

SEARCH TACTICS

"Strategy" and "tactics" are terms best known for their military uses. *Webster's New Collegiate Dictionary* defines them as follows:

> *Strategy:* The science and art of employing the armed strength of a belligerent to secure the objects of a war, esp. the large-scale planning and directing of operations in adjustment to combat area, possible enemy action, political alignments, etc.; also, an instance of it.
> *Tactics:* 1. (usually construed as sing.) The science and art of disposing and maneuvering troops or ships in action or in the presence of the enemy. 2. (usually construed as pl.) Hence, any method of procedure; esp., adroit devices for accomplishing an end.

Strategy, then, deals with overall planning; tactics deals with short-term goals and maneuvers. Let us now adapt these terms for use in information searching. The definitions are simple and general, and may be refined in later theoretical development. (See Bates, 1981, for a review of some precedent literature.)

Search tactic: A move made to further a search.

Search strategy: (In searching.) A plan for the whole search. *(As an area of study.)* The theory, principles, and practice of making and using search strategies and tactics.

Every move a person makes toward the goal of finding desired information is seen as a tactic. There can be good tactics and bad ones. The measures of goodness are assumed to be *efficiency* (speed to completion of search) and *effectiveness* (amount of material discovered that is deemed useful by the requester). The purpose of this model is to suggest tactics that are thought likely to improve the effectiveness or efficiency of a search, independently of particular systems of indexing or classification. Further development of the model may make it possible to state the circumstances under which certain tactics are most likely to be helpful.

The following 29 tactics, grouped in four sections, are adapted from my own experience and thinking, from the literature, and from the comments of colleagues and students. They are presented in brief verb form, which one may think of as infinitives (TO CUT) or commands (CUT!).

Monitoring Tactics

These keep the search on track and efficient.

CHECK. To review the original request and compare it to the current search topic to see that it is the same.

WEIGH. To make a cost-benefit assessment, at one or more points of the search, of current or anticipated actions. Among other things, the searcher might consider whether any other approach would be more productive for the effort.

PATTERN. Frequent experience with a type of question may lead to a habitual pattern of search. If, for example, a common request in an academic library is for addresses of researchers, then the librarian may soon develop a sequence of sources to search, arranged by their likely productivity. To PATTERN is to make oneself aware of a search pattern and redesign it if it is inefficient or out of date.

CORRECT. To watch for and correct spelling and factual errors in one's search topic. These may exist in the topic as presented originally by the user. They also may slip into the searcher's thinking in translating a verbal request, or in remembering (without having in hand) a written request. Spelling errors and word confusions particularly beset searchers. One librarian, for example, had a request on "neuroglia" and searched instead on "neuralgia," a very different concept.

A clue to errors in the request as stated may be provided by suspicious coincidences. Josel (1971, p. 46) states as one of his "reference commandments" that *Coincidence is no coincidence.* He adds, "When a patron wants to have a biography of Saint Edmund Hall, born 1226, and you find the same name listed as a college of Oxford University, and 1226 as its date of construction, do not doubt the patron needs further talking to."

RECORD. To keep track of trails one has followed and of desirable trails not followed up or not completed. In complex searches it is sometimes necessary to return to a source of information or citations obtained earlier in the search. For example, after recording some citations from a periodical index, the searcher may then attempt to retrieve the articles cited and find a blind lead. The citation needs to be checked again in the original source. But unless the volume, date, and subject term searched under were recorded, the searcher may have to go through the entries under a dozen terms or in several volumes to locate the desired citation. Similarly, if productive online and manual bibliographic search formulations are retained, later repeat effort may be saved.

Carlson (1964, pp. 29-30) noted the following in his observations of librarians:

> They are not consistent in recording what they find or what they intend to
> check later. In many cases, they will find cross references and state that they

will check these cross references later. Unless they make some written note, they never seem to check them. Each librarian studied, at sometime during the search, noticed some discrepancy either in an item being scanned, or in an item recorded as acceptable, and made the verbal comment that he would check this later. Once again they almost never made a written note about this and when they did *not* write a note, they never did check the item. The discrepancies which arose during the search were thus not clarified.

The searcher may *choose* not to follow up a side trail or problem, but it appears that such choices are often made by default rather than deliberately.

File Structure Tactics

These are techniques for threading one's way through the file structure of an information facility to the desired source, or to information within it.

BIBBLE. One way to cope with the file structure is to find a way to do without it altogether. BIBBLE, the only neologism among the set of tactic names, is based on the abbreviation "bibl." for "bibliography." To BIBBLE is to look for a bibliography already prepared, before launching into the effort of preparing one. More generally, to BIBBLE is to check whether the search one plans has already been done in a usable form by someone else.

SELECT. To break complex search queries down into subproblems and work on one problem at a time. This tactic is a well-established and productive technique in general problem solving. As each subproblem is solved, the parts can then be knit into a solution to the larger problem.

SURVEY. To review at each decision point of the search the available options before selecting. Carlson (1964, p. 35) notes: "There is almost no look-ahead in the human search procedures. All of the librarians studied exhibited to some extent this lack of look-ahead. They would often scan each entry as they came to it and then encounter a heading which would alter the search procedure." He concludes: "Here the lesson is very clear: humans should scan over a reference document before making any detailed searches through it." Psychologically, this is a problem of "going for closure" too soon, that is, settling on a source or approach prematurely.

In employing SURVEY one resists this temptation and presumably achieves a more effective search. For example, instead of going for the first index that comes to mind in a bibliographic search, one thinks of all the major indexes in the subject and then picks the best one for a particular query. Instead of moving immediately to a subject entry term within the index, one first scans through the thesaurus to find the best terms for the subject.

CUT. When considering several ways to search a given query, to CUT is to choose the option that eliminates the largest part of the search domain at once. This tactic is of fundamental significance in our field, and is relatively little known or discussed. Here are some examples. When looking up a book written by Smith and Brzustowicz, the search will be much briefer if one looks under Brzustowicz (assuming the file has entries under co-authors). In most files there would be far fewer entries under the latter name. Thus one has cut out a larger part of the search domain than would be the case when searching under Smith.

Similarly, in a subject search, other things being equal, one should look up the most limiting elements of the topic first. For example, in using an index that permits search on all significant terms in titles, the searcher will find material on "Research in Retinopathy" much faster under "Retinopathy," because there will be fewer entries.

STRETCH. In general, it may be assumed that the most efficient searching involves using sources for their intended purposes. But when such approaches fail, answers may still be found by putting in the harder work to ferret out information incidentally provided. Thus, to STRETCH is to use a source for other than its intended purposes. However, it should be kept in mind that to STRETCH the searcher must first *think* differently—that is, about all the information in a source (in non-indexed fields, in the introduction, etc.) and not just about the ordinary uses of it.

For example, after searching unsuccessfully through many directories for the address of an engineer, the searcher may recall that *patents* contain the business affiliations of inventors, since a patent is usually owned by the inventor's employer. If the engineer has patented anything, then the address should be available in the nearest patent file.

SCAFFOLD. When the building is finished, the scaffolding is torn down, but the building could not have been built without it. In information searching, it is sometimes the case that the shortest route through the file structure leads to a dead end. In that case one may build a roundabout path to the answer by going through files or sources that may seem to have nothing to do with the question. One may acquire an additional piece of information that does not contribute directly to the answer but which makes it possible to search for the answer in some other source. Thus, to SCAFFOLD is to design an indirect route through the files and resources to reach the desired information. For example, after unsuccessfully seeking information on an obscure poet, the searcher may find out who the poet's contemporaries were and research them in hopes of finding mention of the poet.

CLEAVE. To employ binary searching in locating an item in an ordered file. In binary searching one looks first at a record in the middle of an ordered, e.g., alphabetized, file. One then determines the half of the file in which the desired record must lie. Then the middle record in that half of the file is looked at, and the quarter of the file in which the record must lie is determined. Then one looks at the middle record in that quarter of the file, and so on, through progressively smaller splits, until the desired record is discovered. In each case, the file is spilt in two; hence the term "binary."

Formally, binary searching is more efficient than serial or random searching. Yet a rigid adherence to this principle would probably be wasteful, since human beings have additional, contextual knowledge about many files. A searcher looking for the telephone number of the Ajax Corporation will not start the search in the middle of the white pages. On the other hand, a general awareness of binary search may enable searchers to improve efficiency, particularly when confronting large and unfamiliar files.

Search Formulation Tactics

These aid in designing or redesigning the search.

SPECIFY. To search on terms that are as specific as the information desired. Specificity is one of the crucial concepts in systems of information access. Almost all systems of classification and indexing require that descriptions assigned to materials be as specific as the content of the materials and the indexing system itself allows. Sears and Library of Congress subject headings use the "rule of specific entry," which requires entry of materials under the most specific terms that still encompass the content of the item. Coordinate indexing achieves specificity by conjoining as many separate terms as necessary at the time of the search.

Thus, specificity at the time of indexing requires specificity at the time of retrieval. An indexing system may or may not allow entry under broader terms as well, but it will almost always require specific entry. It is probably the case that starting with specific terms in all kinds of searches (both bibliographic and reference) will be the most productive approach.

EXHAUST. To include most or all elements of the query in the initial search formulation, or to add one or more of the query elements to an already-prepared formulation. Both EXHAUST and the next term, REDUCE, deal with the number of elements in the query that are ANDed together. The more exhaustive a formulation, the more elements of a complex request have been included. For example, the searcher interested in "training of teachers of mathematics for the elementary grades" has a four-element problem, and an exhaustive search would include all four. The more elements included, the more stringent the requirements, and thus the *fewer* the documents likely to be returned.

While this tactic is probably most useful for Boolean searching, it is also meaningful for other kinds of searches. In a catalog using Library of Congress subject headings, for example, one can decide between searching under the main heading only ("Women in Art") or, more exhaustively, under the main heading *plus its non-topical subdivisions*, such as geographic names ("Women in Art—United States") or literary form classes ("Women in Art—Anecdotes and Facetiae").

REDUCE. The opposite of EXHAUST. To minimize the number of elements of the query in the initial search formulation, or to subtract one or more of the elements from a formulation already prepared. This tactic reduces the number of ANDed elements in the search formulation, making it less stringent and thus *increasing* the number of documents likely to be returned.

PARALLEL. To make the search formulation broad (or broader) by including synonyms or other conceptually parallel terms. PARALLEL and the next term, PINPOINT, deal implicitly with elements in a query that are to be ORed together. Though these tactics are most readily applied in online searching, they may also be applied in manual searches. For example, in manually compiling a bibliography, one may look over subject headings in catalogs or terms in periodical indexes and expand the number of similar terms searched under, either at the beginning of the search or after gaining experience with the type and quantity of materials under each term.

PINPOINT. The opposite of PARALLEL. To make the search formulation precise by minimizing (or reducing) the number of parallel terms, retaining the more perfectly descriptive ones.

BLOCK. To reject, in the search formulation, items containing or indexed by certain terms, even if it means losing some relevant documents. This tactic makes use of the Boolean NOT (or AND NOT), familiar to online searchers. Again, however, the concept extends beyond online searching. For example, in doing a manual literature search, one may chose to reject all items from a certain school of thought (e.g., by ethnomethodologists) even though they are "on target" otherwise. BLOCK as a name draws attention to the tricky side of the NOT command—that, in eliminating documents that contain an undesired term, one may also block out desirable material that happens to be found in the same document.

Term Tactics

These aid in the selection and revision of specific terms within the search formulation.

SUPER. To move *upward* to a more general (superordinate) term in a hierarchical classification scheme or thesaurus. There may be explicit pointers, or searchers may have to rely on their own knowledge.

SUB. To move *downward* to a more specific (subordinate) term in a hierarchy.

RELATE. To move *sideways* to a related (coordinate) term in a hierarchy.

NEIGHBOR. To seek additional search terms by looking at neighboring terms, whether proximate alphabetically, by subject similarity, or by some other criterion. Many years ago, Coates (1960) pointed out that all manual (and, we would say today, most automated) retrieval systems do two fundamental things: locate and collocate. The primary function of such systems is, of course, to enable the searcher to *locate* desired materials. However, such systems also necessarily *collocate* entries. In any ordered file everything must be the neighbor of something else. Many of the historical arguments over the relative merits of classification and indexing systems were about collocation. Consider, for example, the old debate over providing subject access to documents: should one put the subject indexing in classified or alphabetico-specific order? A classified catalog collocates entries by their conceptual relationships (usually hierarchical); an alphabetico-specific catalog collocates entries by alphabetizing their subject indexing. These two approaches have different strengths and weaknesses, and different consequences for search strategy.

To use NEIGHBOR is to expand the search by examining the terms collocated with one's search term, whatever they are. In online searching one examines these in the online thesaurus. (NEIGHBOR, incidentally, is the command for looking at a term's neighbors in the ORBIT search language.)

The use of NEIGHBOR may be extended beyond term selection to resource selection. Since classification systems collocate books, it is easy to extend a search by examining reference or circulating materials shelved near an initial choice in the stacks.

TRACE. To examine information already found in order to obtain additional terms for the search. One way of doing this is to retrieve citations through online searching and scan their assigned descriptors. Another way is to scan the subject headings at the bottom of the catalog entry of a known book. (Because these headings help librarians trace their records for an item in the subject catalog, they are called "tracings"; hence this tactic's name.)

VARY. To alter or substitute one's search terms in any of several ways. Some specific variations follow.

FIX. To try alternative affixes (prefixes, suffixes, or infixes). Online, several may be done at once through truncation routines.

REARRANGE. In any system where terms may contain more than one word, word order may make a difference in retrieval success. To REARRANGE is to reverse or permute the words in search terms in any or all reasonable orders. One might have success, for example, with both "Oral Contraceptives" and "Contraceptives, Oral" in the same file.

CONTRARY. To search for the logical opposite of the term describing the desired information. For example, one may want information on "Cooperation" and, after an unsuccessful search, change the term to "Competition." This could bring relevant material by implied or explicit contrast.

RESPELL. To search under a different spelling. CORRECT dealt with maintaining correct spelling, among other things. But with RESPELL the concern is not with correctness, but with effectiveness. Particularly in current online systems, there are many spelling variations that show up in the citations, e.g., "Sulfuric Acid" and "Sulphuric Acid." One must incorporate the spelling variations to insure good recall. RESPELL is occasionally needed in manual systems too, where, for example, one needs to change from U.S. to British spelling ("Tire" vs. "Tyre"; "Center" vs. "Centre") to search successfully.

RESPACE. Spacing, particularly in hyphenated words, or words that appear with various spacings, can be critical in search success. To RESPACE is to try spacing variants. For example, in online files of the Institute for Scientific Information, Derek de Solla Price becomes DESOLLAPRICE D; Margaret Bourke-White becomes BOURKEWHITE M. While spacing problems are most glaring online, such problems can also be serious in manual files. The two fundamental variants in filing rules—word-by-word and letter-by-letter—differ on how the blank space is to be treated. Both of these rules are in wide use. The searcher who is thinking in terms of one filing rule, and enters a source that uses the other, may miss desired material.

Some Implications

As experience is gained with these tactics, leads for increasing our knowledge of search strategy should emerge. Some that have already come to mind follow.

(1) Various tactics form *clusters* as responses to situations in which a search yields too many or too few documents. Where too few documents are produced, the searcher might try SUPER, RELATE, REDUCE, PARALLEL, NEIGHBOR, TRACE, and VARY, among others. Too many documents might lead to the use of SUB, EXHAUST, PINPOINT, and BLOCK. It may also be possible to distinguish typical stages of searches. If the searcher is aware that a small cluster of tactics is most likely to be useful at a given stage, then she or he can concentrate on just those few at that stage.

(2) WEIGH suggests a sub-area of investigation. WEIGH is a name for on-the-spot cost-benefit assessment. In library and information science, cost-benefit analysis often implies lengthy evaluations involving mathematical models. WEIGH, on the other hand, deals with what people can evaluate *in a few seconds in their heads*. They need rules-of-thumb concerned with, among other things, how to choose among several sequences of action or among several sources. For the latter, the rules might take into account the likely productivity of the source and the effort in using it. Jahoda (1974, p. 155) recommends as one step in the reference process, "Select sequence of specific titles to search." Thus, "SORT," to mean sorting the sources responsive to a query from most to least likely to be of help, might be seen as a tactic to be used in this phase.

(3) Tactics can be developed for parts of the reference process that have been left out here. The complexity of the reference interview has been recognized in recent years, and a considerable literature has emerged in that area. It might now be possible to state tactics for the interview process, dealing with, e.g., establishing the importance of the query, or the degree of exhaustivity desired in the search. In many cases, too, the reference interview continues into the search itself, as the searcher returns with partial material to show the requester. User feedback during the search adds another dimension of complexity, and feedback-related tactics should ultimately be included in any comprehensive view of search behavior. Tactics to aid in the evaluation of relevance of retrieved materials would represent yet another part of the reference process.

As the ultimate goal, one envisions creating a single, comprehensive set of tactics. The set would incorporate all parts of the reference process, from initial interview with patron to final determination of relevance and final negotiation with patron. It would provide a unified view of the reference process, and could constitute the core of a course for reference and information specialists.

IDEA TACTICS

For many searches, the experienced information specialist has no difficulty answering the question posed or determining the items to search. The names of appropriate sources (or types of sources) come readily to mind, and the retrieval process is fairly mechanical thereafter. But many other searches prove difficult. At some point along the way the searcher is stumped and needs to think of a new way to attack the problem. Alternatively, the searcher can think of a way to solve it, but that way is tedious and time-consuming; a faster way is needed.

At such points, *idea tactics* come into play—tactics to help generate new ideas or solutions to problems in searching. The searcher may employ them at the beginning of the search, to try to find a good approach right away, or later, when more ordinary means have failed. (No tactics are suggested here for the person who is flooded with ideas and cannot decide which to select.)

If the approaches one has tried so far have failed, then there must be another way to deal with the problem—hence, the name "idea tactics." However, what is not so obvious is that new ideas are often blocked or limited by one's current thinking. All one's ideas have emerged from the particular way in which the problem is viewed. Ideas, in fact, are not homeless little wisps floating around in our minds; they arise out of a context, a set of presuppositions, a point of view. When one is stumped, genuinely new and different ideas may not come so long as current mental patterns are in place. Thus, *bringing these patterns to awareness and breaking them* may be as important to finding a solution as thinking up new ideas per se.

Ideas and Pattern Breaking

There are 17 tactics below. The first six emphasize idea generation, and the remaining 11 emphasize mental pattern breaking.

The latter can be conducted in at least two ways. One may seek to become aware of certain mental patterns and then *deliberately* break them. However, if one does not know what needs changing, or is unwilling to introspect and find patterns susceptible to change, a quicker but riskier form of pattern breaking is to *arbitrarily* select a part of one's thinking or behavior and change it. The shift in perspective that results from the breaking of any patterns may provide a flash of insight or inspiration.

The difference between these two kinds of pattern breaking is analogous to two approaches in solving a personal problem. In the first, one introspects and analyzes the problem, trying to step out of it and break accustomed ways of thinking about it. In the second, one goes on an ocean cruise and hopes that a change in environment will provide a different perspective. Though the distinction should not be rigidly made, it can be said that, of the 11 pattern-breaking tactics, the first six are the "introspective" sort; the remaining five are more the "arbitrary change" sort.

In addition, some of the search tactics mentioned earlier may also be seen as change tactics, particularly those under the "search formulation" and "term" headings. For example, the term tactics SUPER and SUB, moving respectively up and down the subject term hierarchy, may be used as change tactics—arbitrary moves made to change perspective, even when one does not particularly expect to find suitable terms elsewhere in the hierarchy.

The Importance of Location

There is another theme implicit in idea tactics. The psychologist George Miller (1968) mentions many kinds of situations in which people are able to remember and find things by *where they are located*. We use our strong memory for physical location often. In fact, it has been made use of in memorization schemes. In the centuries-old "method of loci," one calls to mind a familiar scene, such as the view from a window. Then, in order to facilitate memorization of a list of items, one mentally places each item at a specific place in the scene. By hooking the items into the superior capacity for remembering physical location, one improves recall of the list (cf. Yates, 1966).

The importance of location for information work was reinforced for me when a highly skilled reference librarian mentioned that she remembered things best by location. She recalled one library in which a certain set of reference books had been moved twice while she worked there. To locate one of the reference books, she would first remember where the materials had originally been stored, then where they had been moved the first time, and then where they had been moved the second time. She found retracing this string of moves in her mind to be more natural than, say, looking up a book in the catalog to find its most recent location.

Following Miller, one may suspect that physical location has a very important role in the mental processing of information about resources, and in searches in general. Location is a theme that shows up in the discussions of two tactics below, WANDER and BREACH.

Idea Generation Tactics

THINK. To stop, think about the search, and try to come up with new ideas for solving search difficulties. Obvious as this tactic may seem, much time and effort has been lost in searching, as in other areas of life, through failure to employ it. IBM's slogan "Think" has become well known. If the advice is not redundant in IBM's case, it is not likely to be so in information searching.

BRAINSTORM. To generate many ideas and to suspend critical reactions until the ideas are well-formed and can be fully evaluated. Clark (1958, p. 91) points out the importance in brainstorming not only of generating ideas but of *not blocking* them. It is the anticipation of negative reactions, either from within or from others, that commonly blocks creativity. He cites a number of "killer phrases," such as "Somebody would have suggested it before if it were any good," that typically nip ideas in the bud.

The whole procedure of brainstorming during a search is telescoped into a few minutes. The difference between nipping an idea in the bud and giving it a chance to flower may be a matter of *seconds,* but that time is crucial to receptivity. New good ideas (as well as new bad ones) generally look strange at first. They take getting used to; early rejection thwarts that process.

MEDITATE. This is to use rational and intuitive capacities together in solving search problems. The different functions of the left and right hemispheres of the brain are becoming increasingly well understood. As J.L. Adams (1976, pp. 37–38) notes: "The left hemisphere of the brain (which controls the right hand) contains the areas which are associated with control of speech and hearing and involved with analytical tasks such as solving an algebra problem. The right hemisphere (which controls the left hand) governs spatial perception, synthesis of ideas, and aesthetic appreciation of art or music." He adds: "The right hand has traditionally been linked with law, order, reason, logic, and mathematics—the left with beauty, sensitivity, playfulness, feeling, openness, subjectivity, and imagery."

There are societal pressures on the male to be rational and on the female to be intuitive. These may reflect innate tendencies as well. In any case we are led to rely on one mode of thinking more than the other. Yet both modes may contribute to the solution of a problem. The searcher works on bringing the rational and the intuitive modes into parity, where both may be applied to a problem, jointly or in quick succession.

I have used MEDITATE—a term employed loosely these days—because the process of calling forth *one's lesser used function* may have meditative qualities. How does one actually do this? It should be kept in mind that we already use both modes, but less deliberately than proposed here. There is no great skill required in learning to use the other mode; rather, one must be open to the possibility of using it in unaccustomed circumstances. One must "get the feel" of entering it self-consciously instead of accidentally.

An experienced reference librarian whom I interviewed related the following: "Someone will come to the desk and ask me a question, and it will be of such a nature that offhand I have no idea where to look for an answer. I tell the person that I'll see what I can do, and then more as a way to stall for time than anything else, I'll turn and walk toward the books in the stacks of reference sources behind the desk. I'll raise my hand and reach for a book, any book, and it will be the right one. I will have had no conscious sense of knowing what the book was or of going for it. But the one I pick out 'randomly' will answer the question. For me, it's intuition. I don't do all my searching this way—usually I know where to look—but at times this is surprisingly effective."

CONSULT. To ask a colleague for suggestions or information in a search. Comments by practicing information specialists and librarians indicate that this is a valuable and much-used tactic.

RESCUE. The feeling of disappointment can lead to ineffective thinking in many situations. "Throwing out the baby with the bath water" is a colloquial way of putting it. The searcher may take a general tack that contains several specific sequences. After trying one or two paths without success, the searcher may give up entirely. To RESCUE is to check, in an otherwise unproductive approach, for productive paths still untried.

This tactic is adapted from a discussion by Berlyne (1965, p. 322). He has examples of both human beings and apes giving up an approach prematurely, apparently out of a sense of disappointment with early failures. Berlyne also warns of the opposite danger, of pursuing a path too long: "Both failure to follow up one direction long enough and excessive obstinacy in pursuing inauspicious leads have often been mentioned as causes of inefficiency." The pattern-breaking tactics below should help the searcher avoid pointless persistence. The idea-generation tactic RESCUE, on the other hand, is a way to overcome misjudgments due to disappointment, and thereby reinstate fruitful possibilities.

Josel's (1971, p. 146) second "reference commandment"—*When you know the answer is in a source, it is* —can be viewed as a specific variant of RESCUE. He says: "There are times, and we have all had them, when after checking all the possible places for an answer, one source stands out as the most likely key to the problem. But a check of the source helped not at all. Take heart: the answer *is* there, it will just take some proper page-shaking before it falls out. Admittedly, this course will occasionally fail, but if it does, the fault lies not in the stars, but in your choice of source."

WANDER. To move among one's resources, being receptive to alternative sources and new search ideas triggered by the materials that come into view. It has been noted in research on problem-solving that *physical proximity* of the elements of the solution makes it more likely that people will find the solution. In our own field, Menzel's (1959) work has demonstrated the importance of serendipity—the making of useful discoveries by accident—in information gathering by scientists. Putting these results together, one may hypothesize that to WANDER promotes serendipity and enables the searcher to get ideas and encounter useful sources that would not be discovered otherwise. (In this volume, cf. White and Wilson on *browsing.*)

Pattern-Breaking Tactics

CATCH. Earlier, it was noted that both pattern breaking and idea generation are important in finding new approaches to search problems. However, in order to engage in either of those processes one must first notice in specific instances that they are needed. Inertia, or a half- conscious feeling that there are no reasonable alternatives, may keep one doggedly pursuing an unproductive path. The realization that there is a problem puts one halfway to the solution. Thus, CATCH represents a kind of preliminary pattern breaking—a realization that a change in approach might improve one's results.

How can one CATCH oneself? Usually such moments of insight, when they come, feel accidental or arise from acute frustration with a path that has long since proved wrong. But idea tactics are *intentional* remedies. With CATCH, as with the other tactics presented here, articulating and giving a name to a method of getting ideas may enable the searcher to do deliberately and efficiently what ordinarily happens accidentally and inefficiently—or not at all. In other words, *awareness of the idea of catching oneself* may make it more likely that one will do so, and sooner rather than later.

There is another kind of situation where CATCH is needed. Sometimes one may indeed be aware of a problem, but have a wrong idea of its nature and determinedly seek to solve it through misassumptions. For example, the searcher may have an incorrect citation to a journal article. It so happens that the issue for the incorrect citation is missing in the library. The searcher then initiates an interlibrary loan or a claim for the missing issue when, in fact, the desired article is sitting on the shelf. In this sort of situation it is particularly difficult to CATCH oneself, but, again, awareness that some thing like this could happen may improve the chances of doing so.

BREAK. Frequent experience with a type of question may lead to a habitual pattern of search. If, for example, a common request in an academic library is for addresses of researchers, then the librarian will soon develop a sequence of sources to be searched, arranged by their likely productivity (as in PATTERN, above). These habitual patterns can be very useful, but they can also be traps. In some cases, the common pattern will simply be unsuited to the problem at hand. The searcher needs to be open to the possibility of *not* following the pattern. To BREAK is to halt a habitual way of searching—that is, put it aside temporarily, in order to take a tack more suited to the problem.

BREACH. Discussing mathematical problem solving, Polya (1965, p. 65) notes: "We do not look for just any kind of solution, but for a certain kind, a kind within a limited outline. We do not look for a solution just anywhere in the world, but for a solution within a certain limited *region of search.*" In our field, this region may be defined both intellectually and physically. Some delimitation of an information search must occur, or else the searcher would be moving randomly through anything and everything. It may also be the case, however, that the answer lies outside the particular region of search one has chosen. A question that appeared to be in medicine may turn out to be in chemistry (a different intellectual region). Or it may be that the best answer to a question may be found by calling an expert outside one's own facility (a different physical region). A circumscribed region is necessary to the searcher's thinking, but as an outer boundary beyond which the searcher does not go, it can also imprison. To BREACH is to widen one's concept of the limits, intellectual or physical, placed on response to a query.

REFRAME. Question negotiation comprises a major area of tactics not developed here. REFRAME is presented, however, since it is a question-negotiation tactic that is also valuable as a pattern breaker.

The patron's question is always formulated and presented to the searcher within *a frame of reference.* This context may be subtly or greatly different from one person to another. Since the context is conveyed implicitly with the question—through word selection and phrasing, tone of voice, etc.—the searcher may uncritically accept it. Obstacles to successful completion of the search may arise not because of problems with the question, but because of mistakes or distortions in understanding the patron's frame of reference. To REFRAME is to examine the frame-of-reference information implicit in the user's query, to deal with it explicitly, and to negotiate changes to eliminate distortions.

NOTICE. In a complex search, numerous sources will be examined in the process of finding the best or most complete response. This intermediate information may provide many clues about the nature of the ultimate answer. It may even indicate that the original question is nonsensical as phrased and must be revised. To NOTICE is to watch for clues that revise one's notions of the nature of the question or of the answer. Sometimes these clues may be very subtle; they come in the nuances of the phrasing of the information, not in specific contradictions to the searcher's assumptions. Dogged persistence in the original way of thinking about the search may blind one to these nuances.

JOLT. When a searcher is really stumped, the ordinary patterns of searching and even of breaking patterns will not suffice. In these cases, it takes ingenuity to find a novel, dramatically different approach. To JOLT is to think "laterally," as de Bono (1969, p. 237) calls it. It is to completely redefine a problem. His description: "Lateral thinking has to do with rearranging available information so that it is snapped out of the established pattern and forms a new and better pattern....The established patterns which determine the flow of thought can be changed by lateral thinking, as can the established patterns which control how things are looked at."

In information searching one may JOLT by trying to think as another person: how would a child see it? A person in a different discipline? Alternatively one asks: how can I completely change my assumptions about the nature of the information desired or about the sources where it may be found?

CHANGE. To change something, anything, in one's search behavior—to try a different source, a different term, a different subject field, and so on. This automatically breaks a pattern. The new behavior may either lead directly to the desired results or suggest productive ideas. This tactic can be employed with various degrees of arbitrariness; in most cases it will be reasonably related to the query, but it may also be quite random.

FOCUS. To look at the query more narrowly: (a) to move from the whole to a part, or (b) to move from a broader conceptualization to a narrower. This and the next two tactics are semi-arbitrary ways to change one's search formulation, as a way out of an impasse.

DILATE. To look at the query more broadly: (a) to move from a part to the whole, or (b) to move from a narrower conceptualization to a broader.

SKIP. To shift laterally in one's view of the query: (a) to move from searching one part of a complex, multipart query to another part (see SELECT above), or (b) to view the query from, and search on, another angle, that angle being neither narrower or broader but simply different. For example, one might move from searching with subject headings to searching with cited authors as a way of capturing a topic.

STOP. To cease searching temporarily and do something else. The following experience is common with creative people: after a period of intense but unsuccessful work, they give up in disgust and go on to something else. The mind apparently continues to work on the problem at an unconscious level. While they are still doing something else, or when they return to the problem, the solution—or at least another approach—comes to mind. Information searchers do not always have the option of suspending work on a query, but when they do, STOP may be seen as a potentially productive tactic, not as a sign of failure.

GENERAL MODELS

In proposing and elucidating both search and idea tactics, at least four different models can be distinguished. An *ideal* model specifies optimal search patterns on the basis of mathematical, system analytic, or other formal criteria. *Representation* models exist for the purpose of describing, and ultimately predicting and explaining, human information searching behavior; these models represent what people actually do or think in searching. A good *teaching* model is one that makes it easy for people to learn to search. A model for *facilitating* searching is one that helps people search more efficiently or effectively.

Conceivably, a single model could be found that would be optimal for all four purposes. But it is more likely that different models will have to be found. For example, system analytic or mathematical theories of optimality, while good descriptions of ideal searching, may be of little practical interest or help to the typical information specialist, whose mathematical background is limited.

The tactics presented here are intended primarily as a *facilitating* model and secondarily for *teaching*. Experience and testing will determine whether the model is useful in these categories. Persons attempting to represent search behavior may find it useful as well. The concept of the tactic, and particular tactics, may be found appropriate for describing the behavior of skilled searchers.

While our goal over the long term may be a parsimonious few, highly effective tactics, our goal in the short term should be to identify and understand as many as we can. Then we can test them and select the good ones. If we go for closure too soon, that is, seek the parsimonious few prematurely, we may miss some valuable ones.

In fact, it may be that a larger set of tactics, including overlapping ones, makes a better facilitation model. I suggest that, for psychological reasons, this is likely to be the case. The use of these tactics is a form of creative problem-solving. The mind so engaged may not work in logical, regular patterns. It may come at a problem from many different levels and angles. It may use one tactic on a particular type of problem one time and a different one on the same sort of problem the next time. In other words, we may find that the requirements of a good facilitation model include some redundancy, and that an across-the-board application of parsimony (economy of logical formulation and expression) is more appropriate to ideal and representation models.

These tactics are not guaranteed to work in every situation. They are seen as heuristic: they may help. Thus the ultimate test of their facilitative value will need to be sophisticated enough to detect whether, on the average, the total effort involved in learning and applying them, and sometimes getting nowhere, is counterbalanced by sufficient benefit in searching to make their application worthwhile.

9

Tactics and Vocabularies in Online Searching*

Marcia J. Bates

INTRODUCTION*

The tactics presented in the previous chapter can be used in both manual and online searches. People who saw my discussion in earlier papers have told me that they found it intriguing but wanted more guidance in use of the tactics online. In this chapter I have selected some tactics that are particularly useful for that purpose. I identify the points in the search when they are likely to help, and proceed to an extended example that illustrates them at work, with emphasis on how to increase or decrease the size of the sets retrieved. This leads to an account of how the size of an output set is determined by the customer's goals, and how to avoid fallacies regarding appropriate size. I turn finally to the types of controlled vocabularies that condition what is possible in database searching, and show, with examples, how to relate one's search tactics to them.

TACTICS TO USE EARLY

To BIBBLE is to see whether the searching one plans to do has already been done by someone else—that is, whether a "bibl." (bibliography) already

* This chapter is a revision of materials that appeared first as Bates (1984), © American Library Association, used by permission; and Bates (1987 and 1988), © Online, Inc., used by permission.

exists. When a client asks for information, one's first impulse may be to launch into an extensive search, but such effort is unnecessary if the work, or part of it, has already been done.

Many of the articles, reports, or books covered in online databases contain extensive bibliographies—for example, research reviews, which are surveys of large bodies of current research literature. Free-standing bibliographies, both annotated and unannotated, are often covered as well.

Databases vary in how well they identify bibliographic sources. Some routinely assign terms like "review" or "bibliography" as part of the indexing. In such cases, one need only identify these terms, input them all as an ORed set (known as a "hedge"), and then AND them with the topic of interest to get a listing of the pertinent bibliographic materials in the database. For example, one might create and permanently save an ORed set of terms such as "Bibliography OR Review OR State of the Art," plus any other terms for bibliographically rich sources in that database. (Sometimes such terms appear as "document type" codes, instead of descriptors.) Then, the first thing one does in any search is to call up that BIBBLE set and AND it to the terms representing the topic of current interest. Thus one can quickly run a search that produces other people's literature reviews or bibliographies.

If the database is not indexed by terms indicating bibliographically rich items, then it will be necessary to look for these materials in other ways. For example, journals and annuals with title terms such as "Review," "Advances in..." or "Progress in..." usually publish review articles, and one might AND the title of one or more such publications with one's topical terms.

Once bibliographies or reviews on the topic are found and retrieved in hard copy, they may reveal most of the material the requester needs. The rest of the search then merely involves updating what has already been found, and doing some supplemental searching if the found items do not exactly match the request—a cheaper proposition than conducting a full search and printing it out. In organizations that do a lot of online searching, local "bibbling" may be possible by retrieving the actual printout of earlier searches (or records previously downloaded in machine-readable form) from their recipients.

The tactic RECORD is to keep track of the trails one has followed. A searcher in a large industrial organization told me of a search that she had great difficulty in formulating; she revised it several times and still was not happy with it. Finally, she felt that she had done the best she could. She sent on the results to her customer—a researcher in the organization—and tried to forget all about it. A few days later she got a note from him. He was ecstatic with her results and wanted her to perform searches for him on the topic regularly. The only trouble was, she had not kept a record of her search formulation! In online work it is easy to have all formulations "echoed," or logged, by a printer attached to the terminal, and this should be routine practice.

SURVEY: This tactic is to review, at each decision point of the search, the available options before selecting. For example, before beginning an online search, one's natural inclination may be to start searching on the "obvious" database, and to use only the terms supplied by the requester. Nevertheless, it should take only a brief while to review what other relevant databases are available. In surveying these other options, one may find that a foreign, full text, or citation database would be more suitable for the query than the ones usually consulted. The bit of effort spent reviewing these other possibilities can eliminate expensive search time spent on a database that has some but not the most relevant materials.

SURVEY is also a valuable technique for selecting search terms. At first only one or two terms may seem to apply to the topic, and it is tempting to jump right in with them only. But a moment's reflection, or a look at the cross-references in a thesaurus, will often produce several more terms of value. If one uses SURVEY, the search formulation can more effectively express the topic *from the start*, which saves valuable time.

One of the main tasks early in an online search is to identify good terms to search with. If one searches on only one or two apparently relevant terms, and gets back a postings set of the "right" size, it is tempting to stop there and give the requester the output set as is. (More on this illusory "perfect" search below.) But such searches are often inadequate because they miss the best terms for the topic. So, except where the search is specifically limited for some reason, it is best to manipulate the search formulation until it appears to be the best for the stated need.

Several tactics can be used to generate additional terms to enrich the search formulation. To NEIGHBOR is to find additional search terms by looking at neighboring terms in alphabetical or classified lists—a familiar technique in systems using commands such as Expand in DIALOG or Root in BRS. To TRACE is to examine records already found in the search, so as to find *additional* usable terms. In manual searching one looks at the tracings on a catalog card; in online searching one prints out sample records in full and examines their descriptor lists and abstracts.

Three additional tactics for generating search terms involve moving about in the hierarchy, or "family tree," of subject terms between broader (more general) terms and narrower (more specific) ones. It is very important to remember that a given topic may be discussed in documents that are (a) devoted wholly to it, (b) devoted to a broader topic of which it is part, or (c) devoted to a narrower topic, which is part of it. Documents of all three types may be of interest to the requester, but only those of the first type will be retrieved if neither broader nor narrower search terms are used. Thus it is a good idea to try to locate terms that are on several levels of specificity.

One can expand or alter a search formulation by using three tactics for moving around the hierarchy: SUPER, moving upward to a broader (super-ordinate) term; SUB, moving downward to a more specific (subordinate) term; and RELATE, moving sideways to a coordinate term. The searcher may simply think up broader, narrower, or coordinate terms, but it is more systematic to search through a manual or online thesaurus that links one's chosen heading to additional headings noted as BT (broader term), NT (narrower term), or RT (related term). In the ERIC database on DIALOG, for example, use of the Expand command in different ways can produce terms that are either *alphabetically* close to a chosen term or *conceptually* close to it, as revealed by the BT, NT, and RT notation.

Two other tactics are helpful in identifying terms. Every searcher is familiar with the case in which a widely used term mysteriously produces no postings, or far fewer than could reasonably be expected. Usually this occurs because the database uses a spacing or spelling variant other than the one that occurred to the searcher. "Polyvinyl chloride," for example, may appear as three words, two, or one, or as "PVC." Sometimes the situation is reversed: the version the searcher has used is the most popular one, but other documents may be found under less common spellings or spacings. The tactics RESPELL and RESPACE imply looking for spelling and spacing variants of the terms in one's formulation. These tactics are good to keep in mind at all times, and especially when a given term produces suspiciously few postings.

TACTICS TO USE LATER

Combining search terms with Boolean logic[1] is at the heart of online searching. In order to search effectively using Boolean logic, it is important to be aware of the difference between a *term* and a *concept,* since the two are treated differently in search formulations. *One* concept may be expressed by *several* synonymous terms, each of which may consist, in turn, of one or several words. For example, the single concept of "a type of teaching resource" may be expressed by two different two-word terms, "Instructional Media" or "Audiovisual Aid." Synonymous terms expressing a concept are combined with the operator OR, while different concepts are generally combined with the operator AND.

For a search on "creationism in high school biology curricula," four concepts can be identified—creationism, biology, curriculum, and high schools—which we would expect to AND together. But one might also wish to express any of these concepts with more than one term. For example, creationism may show up as a topic in documents on science curricula in

---

[1] The British mathematician George Boole (1813–1864) based an algebra on the intersection, union, and difference of sets. In online searching these operations are represented, respectively, by AND, OR, and NOT—often called "Boolean operators" or "Boolean logic."

general (which include mentions of biology or "the life sciences") and in specific discussions of zoology curricula (the part of biology most likely to be concerned with creationism). So the biology component could be expanded with additional terms to read Biology OR Science OR Zoology OR Life Sciences. One might turn up these alternatives by employing NEIGHBOR, SUPER, and the other term-generating tactics mentioned above.

With this basic pattern in mind—ORing term variants of a concept and ANDing concepts together—one can see that several tactics can be used to manipulate the search formulation until it produces the postings set desired. Through the use of these tactics, the searcher can manipulate the formulation in powerful ways—to increase or decrease the output, and to improve precision or recall. Specifically, one can add conceptual elements by ANDing them into the formulation, which is to EXHAUST, or one can REDUCE the number of concepts by dropping ANDed elements. In the creationism example, one could REDUCE the query by subtracting any one of the four concepts. This would usually retrieve *more* documents. Conversely, if one had earlier entered only two or three of the concepts, one could EXHAUST by adding another. This would usually result in *fewer* documents because the specifications the documents must meet are now greater.

To BLOCK is to NOT out a term from the search formulation. NOT is really short for AND NOT; that is, NOT is another form of AND. In searching a NOTed term, the system first finds all documents in which the term appears, just as it would for an AND, but then drops them all rather than including them all as it would for an AND. Consequently, BLOCK has an impact like that of EXHAUST: to add a NOT to a search formulation is like adding another concept, and usually results in fewer documents retrieved.

Next, any given concept can be broadened by ORing in additional variant terms, which is to PARALLEL. In the example above, if one started solely with "Biology" to indicate a concept, the addition of the parallel terms Science OR Life Sciences OR Zoology would cast a broader net. In contrast, the search could be made more precise and specific by *dropping* one or more variant terms, which is to PINPOINT.

Another way to create additional variant terms is through the use of truncation or FIX. To search on the truncated term "Librar?" is implicitly to search on an ORed set of all the terms starting with that stem—for example Library OR Libraries OR Librarian OR Librarians OR Librarianship, etc. So FIX works like PARALLEL—it tends to broaden the search.

EFFECTS ON PRECISION AND RECALL

The more concepts one ANDs in, the more stringent the formulation will be. In other words, the more concepts required to be present (EXHAUST) or absent (BLOCK), the fewer documents are likely to include, or exclude, all those concepts. Similarly, the fewer ORed terms one lists for each concept (PINPOINT), the fewer documents there will be that match the request. So EXHAUST, BLOCK, and PINPOINT, each working in a different way, tend to *decrease* the number of retrievals produced by a search formulation. Such precise and specific search formulations are likely to *increase precision* and to *reduce recall.*[2]

On the other hand, REDUCE, PARALLEL, and FIX, each in a different way, tend to increase the number of retrievals from a search formulation. Fewer concepts (REDUCE) and more term variants (PARALLEL, FIX) tend to *increase recall* and *reduce precision.*

If one finds, late in the search, that too many or too few documents are being found, some of the "early" tactics can also be used at this stage. Narrower, more specific terms tend to have fewer postings, because terms of narrow scope are usually applicable to fewer documents. So if one is retrieving too many postings, SUB is a good tactic to use. Either with the help of system cross-references or on one's own, one should try to identify terms narrower than the ones already appearing in the search formulation.

If too few postings appear, RELATE and SUPER may help one discover coordinate or broader terms so as to increase the retrievals. Also, any time a plausible term draws very few documents, one should suspect that a variant spacing or spelling is preferred in the database and try RESPACE or RESPELL.

Finally, as noted in Chapter 8, these techniques were originally developed for use regardless of whether the search was conducted manually or online. Thus, two specifically online tactics were not introduced: use of field delimiters and free-text searching. In general, limiting the search to matches on specific fields (descriptors only, title terms only, etc.) improves precision. The use of free text—that is, any natural language expression, whether authorized as a descriptor or not—may improve both precision and recall. Since this chapter is confined to techniques presented in the earlier essay, field delimiting and free-text searching will not be discussed further but should be mastered and kept in mind for practical work online.

In sum, the following tactics are recommended as situations arise:

- Too many postings; try EXHAUST, PINPOINT, BLOCK. Find more specific terms to search on by using SUB. If truncation has already been used (FIX), remove it.
- Too few postings; try REDUCE, PARALLEL, FIX. Generate more terms for PARALLEL by using NEIGHBOR, TRACE, RELATE, SUPER.
- No postings; try RESPACE, RESPELL, plus the tactics for too few postings.

---

[2] As Wilson notes in Chapter 7, *precision* is the ratio of relevant documents retrieved to all documents retrieved. *Recall* is the ratio of relevant documents retrieved to all relevant documents in the collection.

A SEARCH USING THE TACTICS

In the example that follows, which simulates a search on the DIALOG system, the particular sequence or combination of tactics should not be taken as a recommended overall strategy. I have deliberately used all the tactics I could, in order to demonstrate them; one is more likely to use only some of them in any given search.

Many different factors can influence recall and precision, and one can vary a search in several ways at once, with possibly mixed effects on the outcome. So as to keep down confusion, the search below will use only the tactics being demonstrated at each stage, one effect at a time. For simplicity's sake, search terms will be limited to descriptors. Use of free text, field delimiters, and DIALOG's "Limit" commands, while common in practice, will be left out. Keep in mind, however, that the tactics can be used with these other capabilities as well.

Offline. Let us suppose that we have this query: "I am interested in the social adjustment problems of the deaf and partially hearing when they are mainstreamed in high school." Offline, we would first analyze the query into its distinct concepts:

Concept 1	*Concept 2*	*Concept 3*	*Concept 4*
Deaf	**Mainstreaming**	**Social Adjustment**	**High Schools**
Partial Hearing			

As noted earlier, we formulate searches by ANDing distinct concepts and ORing term variants. So our formulation thus far would be:

(Deaf OR Partial Hearing) AND Mainstreaming AND Social Adjustment AND High Schools

To be deaf and to be partially hearing are different conditions, of course; these terms are not strict synonyms. But for our purposes in this search, they can be seen as variations on the same concept, because we are interested in documents discussing either or both conditions.[3]

---

[3] Note that parentheses are put around the ORed expressions. This is a general requirement when multiple terms are ORed and then combined with ANDed terms. By convention, DIALOG software implements first, operators in parentheses; second, NOTs; third, ANDs; and fourth, ORs. *Without* parentheses in the example above, the computer would first go to the ANDs and form the set of all documents indexed with Partial Hearing AND Mainstreaming AND Social Adjustment AND High Schools. Then, moving to the OR, it would add that set to the set of all documents indexed with the term Deaf—clearly a mistake. We want, of course, the documents indexed with either Deaf or Partially Hearing (or both) as long as they have all the rest of the terms. The parentheses cause the ORed "impaired hearing" set to be formed *before* being intersected with the terms joined by AND.

Now that we have a sense of the query, we want to SURVEY databases to search. ERIC (the Educational Resources Information Center database) may come to mind first, but a moment's thought—perhaps helped by examining an online service's catalog—may suggest several other good possibilities: Exceptional Child Education Resources, PsycINFO, Medline, LC MARC, Books in Print, Social Scisearch (either the citation or "title term" portion of the database), and possibly others.[4] Because ERIC on DIALOG is so well known, we will use only it in this example, but some or all of the other databases might be chosen in practice, depending on the needs of the client.

Next, we SURVEY terms to use in the search formulation. Looking in the *Thesaurus of ERIC Descriptors,* we find that Deafness, Partial Hearing, and Hearing Impairments are the descriptors to use, both for these conditions and for the people having them. We find also that Mainstreaming, Social Adjustment, and High Schools are the valid terms for these concepts. We also note that Secondary Education deals with both junior high schools and high schools and might also cover material of interest. So now our modified search formulation looks like this:

(Deafness OR Partial Hearing OR Hearing Impairments) AND Mainstreaming AND Social Adjustment AND (High Schools OR Secondary Education)

We have learned from experience, however, that no matter how carefully we review possible descriptors in thesauri, there are often other descriptors that did not occur to us to look up. The best way to discover these other descriptors is to use the TRACE tactic. We can do this with what has been called by Markey and Cochrane (1981) a "brief search."

Online. In this case, suppose we input just the essential terms in the query, without worrying about completeness. After logging on and selecting ERIC, our brief search formulation is:

Select Mainstreaming AND Hearing Impairments

We then use DIALOG's format 8 to print out only the titles and subject indexing of a half-dozen or so retrieved records. At this point we just want to find more search terms, so this format applies. Examining the descriptor lists of these records, we identify three more terms for the Social Adjustment concept: Interpersonal Competence, Emotional Adjustment, and Peer Acceptance.

---

[4] PsycINFO is the online version of *Psychological Abstracts;* Medline, of *Index Medicus;* Social Scisearch, of *Social Sciences Citation Index.* LC MARC is Library of Congress cataloging of books worldwide, while online *Books in Print* covers only books currently for sale from American publishers. See the annual database catalog from DIALOG for fuller notes on all of them.

Suppose that Emotional Adjustment is a term we had not thought to look up in the thesaurus while offline. So now, online, we decide to see if there are additional useful terms related to this one. On DIALOG's ERIC, we can NEIGHBOR this term by inputing:

Expand Emotional Adjustment

We will then get an alphabetical listing of descriptors and free-text terms that begin with the word "Emotional":

Ref	Items	RT	Index-term
E1	11403		Emotional
E2	2		Emotional Abuse
E3	1265	11	•Emotional Adjustment
E4	0	1	Emotional Behavior
E5	1		Emotional Concepts
E6	1		Emotional Content
E7	1		Emotional Control Card
E8	1165	15	Emotional Development
E9	3		Emotional Distress
E10	3353	26	Emotional Disturbances (persistent, serious emotional disorders and...)
E11	456	6	Emotional Experience
E12	1		Emotional Expression

Alternatively, we can input the same statement enclosed in parentheses:

Expand (Emotional Adjustment)

and get back a listing of the conceptually related terms—that is, be shown a portion of the *Thesaurus of ERIC Descriptors:*

Ref	Items	Type	RT	Index-term
R1	1265		11	•Emotional Adjustment
R2	0	U		Emotional Maladjustment (1966–1980)
R3	4129	B	33	Adjustment (to Environment)
R4	109	R	10	Adaptive Behavior (of Disabled)
R5	550	R	14	Affective Measures
R6	1742	R	19	Alienation
R7	3353	R	26	Emotional Disturbances
R8	900	R	17	Emotional Problems
R9	1695	R	15	Morale
R10	797	R	15	Psychiatry
R11	889	R	18	Psychopathology
R12	1941	R	34	Psychotherapy

This capability in ERIC enables us to exercise the term-generation tactics of SUPER, SUB, and RELATE. Under "Type" the letter codes state whether a term is broader than, narrower than, or related to our initial term. (NT is not found in this particular listing.) So in one listing we can go in all three directions to find additional, possibly relevant terms for the query.[5] In this case, we identify two new terms for the Social Adjustment concept: Adjustment (to Environment) and Adaptive Behavior (of Disabled). When these are added in (with nested parentheses), the query looks like this:

> **Select (Deafness OR Partial Hearing OR Hearing Impairments) AND Mainstreaming AND (Social Adjustment OR Interpersonal Competence OR Emotional Adjustment OR Peer Acceptance OR Adjustment (to Environment) OR Adaptive Behavior (of Disabled)) AND (High Schools OR Secondary Education)**

Inputting this query, we get six document citations back. We print out a few, and they seem promising. It is possible, however, that some other combination would be still more promising, and we shall try various others.

Before doing so, we want to see whether there are helpful literature reviews or state-of-the-art papers that would cover all but the recent literature. In other words, we want to use the BIBBLE tactic. If we have searched regularly on ERIC, we may have created an ORed set of terms relating to bibliographies and literature reviews—a so-called "hedge"—which we can now call up as a saved search. If not, we can create the hedge now.

Let us suppose we have two BIBBLE hedges in ERIC. The first is a long, high-recall one covering bibliographies and literature reviews of every type, in both descriptors and document-type codes, such as:

> **DT=070 OR DT=071 OR Annotated Bibliographies OR Citations (References) OR Literature Guides OR Literature Reviews OR Research Reviews OR State of the Art Reviews**

The second is a short, high-precision one:

> **Literature Reviews OR State of the Art Reviews**

At this point it is not clear which BIBBLE hedge will work out best, nor how detailed we should be in the description of the topic. For example, while we are interested in the specific topic of the social adjustment of the deaf and partially hearing mainstreamed in high school, it is quite possible that

---

[5] The "U" in front of "Emotional Maladjustment" means "Use for"—that is, use the entered term, "Emotional Adjustment" instead of "Emotional Maladjustment." Note that the latter term, not being legitimate, has no postings under "Items."

valuable reviews exist at other levels of specificity. A book-length review covering all of mainstreaming could have a lengthy section on mainstreaming of the hearing-impaired, and thus be valuable even though its topic is far broader than ours.

So we experiment with various combinations of terms in the subject query and with the two BIBBLE hedges until the printout of the first few records looks highly promising. The final formulation we settle on is:

Select Mainstreaming AND (Deafness OR Hearing Impairments OR Partial Hearing) AND (Literature Reviews OR State of the Art Reviews)

This BIBBLE search produces several records such as *Exceptional Pupils: A Review of the Literature* (1981, 338 pp.) and *Research and Development Concerning Integration of Handicapped Pupils into the Ordinary School System* (1980, 176 pp.). With any luck, these two long reviews will suffice to cover the literature up to about 1980, so that subsequent searching can be limited to the post-1980 period.

We have used various tactics to identify good search terms as well as earlier literature reviews so that we do not repeat other people's work. We have thus applied most of the tactics appropriate to the early part of the search. Now let us experiment with tactics described for the later part.

It was said above that EXHAUST and REDUCE are opposites that involve increasing and decreasing, respectively, the number of ANDed concepts in a search formulation. EXHAUST tends to promote precision, and REDUCE, recall. Let us see, then, the impact of changing the number of ANDed concepts.

Rather than repeating all the term variants, let us simply call the concepts Mainstreaming, Hearing Disability, Adjustment, and Education. (Keep in mind, however, that each component contains the full number of term variants appearing above—e.g., Adjustment includes Social Adjustment, Interpersonal Competence, and so on.) The following concepts were actually searched on DIALOG's ERIC and produced document sets with the following postings counts:

Mainstreaming 4107
Mainstreaming AND Hearing Disability 328
Mainstreaming AND Hearing Disability AND Adjustment 41
Mainstreaming AND Hearing Disability AND Adjustment AND Education 6

It will be seen that, no matter which concept we start with, adding ANDed concepts (EXHAUST) causes the size of the output set to go down. In fact, adding ANDs always leads to sets that are the same size or smaller. As noted above, each additional NOTed term (BLOCK) also leads to sets of the same or smaller size, since NOT is another form of AND. Conversely, the dropping of ANDed concepts (REDUCE) always leads to sets of the same size or larger. We can see the effects of PARALLEL and PINPOINT in a similar way:

Emotional Adjustment   1265
Emotional Adjustment OR Social Adjustment   2432
Emotional Adjustment OR Social Adjustment OR Adaptive Behavior
(of Disabled)   2531

Here, when we add ORed term variants (PARALLEL), the size of the output will stay the same or be larger. Truncation (FIX) in effect adds terms with OR logic, so FIX, like PARALLEL, increases the size of the output set:

Deafness   2444
Deaf?   3756

In contrast, when we drop ORed term variants (PINPOINT), the output count will stay the same or be smaller. All of these facts lie in the nature of Boolean logic, not just in practical experience.

Now that we have seen the effects of each of these tactics one at a time, let us see how they might work in practice with a more realistic sort of search modification. Suppose that, fearing a high output, we had begun the search with a formulation aimed at high precision—that is, we had included all the distinct concepts we wanted and used only a few term variants:

Select Mainstreaming AND (Deafness or Partial Hearing) AND Social
        Adjustment AND High Schools NOT Junior High Schools

With this formulation we run the risk that, in NOTing out junior high schools, we might eliminate some documents that discuss both high schools and junior high schools. But if, fearing very large sets, we eliminate documents discussing both kinds of school, we are sure to get only documents wholly devoted to the topic—a reasonable choice if high recall is not sought. However, the above search, run on DIALOG's ERIC, produced zero retrievals—a null set. So let us use REDUCE and drop the NOT Junior high schools.

Select Mainstreaming AND (Deafness or Partial Hearing) AND Social
        Adjustment AND High Schools

As it turns out, we still get a null set. Now we can REDUCE the formulation by dropping yet another concept; or we can add further PARALLEL terms with OR in the remaining concepts—possibly both. Using the *Thesaurus of ERIC Descriptors* on- or offline, we might at this point discover the term variants for Deafness and Social Adjustment, as well as the term Secondary Education. ORing those into the formulation would get us the six documents noted earlier. Seeking to increase this number, we might drop the Education element (REDUCE), on the assumption that any discussion of mainstreaming the hearing impaired, whether in a school setting or not, might be of value. Doing so, we would get back the 41 postings found above. Still other capabilities remain to be tried, such as free-text searching of the natural-language titles and abstracts of the records.

The important principle to understand is that these tactics can be used singly or in combination to increase or shrink output sets. We are not helpless when search formulations produce results that are, for some reason, unacceptable. With practice, and the habit of spot-checking records online, one can use these tactics in powerful ways to produce effective searches.

THE SIZE OF OUTPUT SETS

It is possible, of course, to master the tactics yet fit them into naïve strategies. To dispel over-simple notions of when the tactics are effective, we turn now to some fallacious decisions that searchers can make.

Imagine the following situation. Seated at an online terminal, a searcher inputs a careful formulation of the client's query, then sits back and awaits the results. There are 1,282 postings. What happens now? Most likely, the searcher groans and says, "I've got to cut that down—1,282 is far too many." Where does this response come from? What, in fact, constitutes "too many"?

One source of that response is the client's limitation of the search, either to a certain maximum number of references or to a maximum price. The latter restriction is common in academic libraries where the client pays for the search. Even where the client does not impose restrictions, the searcher is likely to try to reduce the search output to a "manageable" number. As a teacher of online searchers, I have noticed what is apparently a spontaneous tendency on the part of students, in the absence of any stated maximum, to consider search output "too large" if it is much in excess of 75 or 100 items. Conversations with more experienced searchers suggest that they feel more flexibility than this; they key search size to a combination of factors, but often still find the need to alter initial search output sizes, particularly in the direction of reducing output.

There is more to the question of what constitutes a good output size than first meets the eye. This matter will be explored here by examining a fallacy in thinking about searching and search modification. Taking a figure comfortably under the abovementioned 75- to 100-item limit, we shall call it the fallacy of the perfect 30-item online search. While beginning searchers in particular may find the discussion instructive, experienced searchers, too, may find it useful to consider the nuances of determining good output size.

THE FALLACY OF THE PERFECT 30-ITEM SEARCH

The fallacy lies in assuming that somewhere in the database there exists a high-quality set of 30 items (or *n* items, whatever *n* is for the searcher), and that, if one is just clever enough, one can produce it for the client. To put it differently, the fallacy lies in gearing the search to the size of the output desired rather than the topic to be searched. *It may simply be the case that the documents on a given topic in a database are not the same number as the searcher or client would like.*

The fallacy can occur in two ways. In the first, the searcher judges the initial output to be the "wrong" size, and goes to great lengths to adjust it. In the second, the searcher judges the initial output to be the "right" size and therefore stops immediately, without determining whether the initial search formulation is indeed the best one for the query. The two will be taken up in turn.

Overcutting. Since a "wrong-sized" retrieval is most often considered too large, this form of the fallacy will be called the "overcutting version." In this case, cutting down the output drastically may yield a final set that is unrepresentative of all the documents relevant to the query. Its prime virtue may be, not that it is a good or complete response, but that it contains only 30 items. Thus, in trying to get an output of a certain size, the searcher may violate the topic itself.

It may be argued, of course, that the search *has to* be limited, since clients frequently put a ceiling on output, either by preference or because they do not want to pay for any more. I am not suggesting that clients be swamped with citations they do not want. But it may be possible to produce searches of a higher quality than is likely when the fallacy is operating. Some suggestions toward this end will be offered below.

An output set of the "wrong" size can also be too small. It is possible to scrape the bottom of the barrel in order to bring a small set up to a desired size, but the dangers of producing poor output are less here. Because the searcher tries many variant search formulations, this approach is not likely to overlook potential "hits," or to burden clients with many irrelevant items. Therefore, this possibility will not be considered further, beyond noting the danger that the searcher may waste the client's money searching for nonexistent citations. There comes a time when the searcher needs the confidence to declare that nothing on the topic exists in the database: the barrel has no bottom to be scraped.

Quick and Dirty. The second form of the fallacy can be called the "quick and dirty version." It may be that to do a thorough, careful job, the searcher should OR in related terms and try variant terms in addition to (or instead of) the expression first used. But such experimentation often produces larger retrieved sets. So the searcher operating under this fallacy simply *stops*, without further trial, if the output produced by the initial formulation has the desired size.

Fenichel (1981) has noted a tendency on the part of many searchers to make little use of the feedback and search modification capabilities of online systems. Such searchers go in with just the terms asked for by the client in simple, brief formulations. There are times when such quick searches are in fact what the client needs, but other times they constitute the quick and dirty form of the fallacy. The latter mistake is reminiscent of the "anchoring" problem discussed by Blair (1980), in which online searchers are reluctant to alter the initial terms of their search formulations.

HOW DOES THE FALLACY ARISE?

It is worth going into the causes of the fallacy in the searcher's and client's thinking in some detail because they point to ways of avoiding it.

There are a lot of things about information retrieval that the typical client does not know and probably has not even thought about. The simplistic assumptions brought to the pre-search interview may be presumed to have a strong influence on the demands and expectations placed on the searcher. The searcher, on the other hand, may attempt to meet inappropriate demands that arise from the client's limited knowledge of the system.

There are three points in particular where misunderstandings are likely to arise:

- Complexity of indexing.
- Limits of Boolean logic.
- The trade-off between recall and precision.

Complexity of Indexing. Most people do not realize that a given topic may appear in an information system under many different descriptors (Cf. Bates, 1977). They have little awareness of the complex problems involved in subject indexing and the variety of ways in which any given topic is likely to be described. In its simplest form, their mental model is likely to be that a topic that interests them will be found under a single term; all documents found under that term will be relevant to their query, and no other relevant documents will be found elsewhere in the system. Thus, they expect that, in principle, it should be possible to get a response set with 100% precision and 100% recall.

When clients demand high precision for their search output, as they often do, they may be basing this demand on such a naïve model of online systems. They may assume that any request on their topic—especially in an auto-mated system, which is usually thought to be more sophisticated than manual retrieval systems—will automatically produce a set of documents all of which are relevant to the query.

Limits of Boolean Logic. In fact, not only is subject indexing more problematic than most clients realize, but the online systems themselves are not as sophisticated as clients may assume. It has long been argued that Boolean logic is not ideally suited to be the basis of term combination in information retrieval. The OR is too weak and brings in too many documents, and the AND is too stringent and cuts down output sets too severely. Boolean logic is simpler than natural-language syntax and also rides roughshod over many grammatical distinctions that make a difference in the relevance of a document to a request. Consequently, irrelevant retrievals ("false drops") are built into online searching.

Trade-off Between Recall and Precision. Above all, clients are not likely to understand the trade-off between recall and precision. Searchers are generally aware of it, but may not recognize its full practical implications for online searching. It is one of the best established results of information science that the tricks one uses to improve precision tend to lower recall, and vice versa. Lancaster (1979, Chaps. 11–12) has an excellent discussion of this. Let us demonstrate with one of his examples.

Suppose an aeronautical engineer wants a search on "slender delta wings." This is exactly what interests the engineer, not other types of wings. The chances are that a search on this term will produce a high precision set as output. But it may be that, for all sorts of reasons, there are documents relevant to this request under other terms as well. Slender delta wings may be discussed in documents on delta wings in general (and indexed under "delta wings"), or even in documents on wings in general. Good material may also be found under synonymous or closely related terms such as "narrow delta wings." These other terms may reflect a necessary variety in the information retrieval system, or may arise because of sloppy vocabulary control, changes in terminology over time, or other reasons.

In order to improve recall and retrieve relevant documents indexed under these other terms, it is necessary to search under them as well. But in doing so, it is likely that a higher proportion of the documents indexed under these more distant terms will be irrelevant to the request than is the case with the initial, highly precise term. In other words, in casting a wider net to improve recall, one also pulls in *disproportionately more junk.* Consequently, when recall goes up, precision goes down. The same things happens, of course, in reverse: if one reduces the search formulation to only the most precise terms, precision will be improved, but recall will fall.

The practical, and virtually unavoidable, result of the recall-precision trade-off for online searching is that, when recall is important to the client, there will usually be a substantial proportion of irrelevant citations retrieved in even the best-designed search. Where cost is an important factor, it may be particularly puzzling and irksome to the client to get an output set with dozens of irrelevant citations. In response to the client's dissatisfaction, the searcher may retreat to the overcutting version of the fallacy—producing high-precision searches for clients who really want high recall.

MANUAL VS. ONLINE SEARCHING

Habits and expectations formed with manual searching may carry over inappropriately to online searching. Let us compare these two forms of searching and note two important differences.

First, the number-of-postings output from an online system in response to any query is likely to be far larger—often by an order of magnitude or more—than the output of a manual search on the same topic. The typical manual search segments the output into yearly or biannual chunks, corresponding to the published volumes of the abstracting and indexing service, whereas the typical online database covers many years and produces postings for all the years at once. The total number of citations is actually the same, of course, but, psychologically, getting them all at once makes the searcher feel that the output of the online search is larger.

Another factor adds to this feeling: the postings reported in an online search are a count of the citations indexed by a term *before the searcher has had a chance to select out the potentially relevant items.* In a manual search we record only the most promising citations, not all those listed under a term. In an online search, on the other hand, a well-stated, carefully worked-out formulation produces the *initial* set from which choices are made, not the *final* set of items chosen.

The client, however, still wants the same low number of citations gotten previously from manual searches, and/or wants the online output especially low in number because of the cost. The poor searcher is thus squeezed between two contrary pressures: the output from any given online search is going to be, on the average, quite large, but the client has as much desire for small output sets as ever.

Now to the second point of difference between manual and online searches. In an online search, because of high print costs (on- or offline), the searcher usually must find a way to select out the most promising subset of the database *while looking at no more than a tiny sample of the citations matching any given search formulation.* In other words, the searcher must select the final output set virtually sight unseen. Probably because the online search thus involves a lot of decision-making without full knowledge, Standera (1978) found that developing and modifying the search formulation were the two points of greatest stress in 17 identifiable phases of online searching.

Someone may counter that it is much easier with online systems than I have made out, because they have many capabilities not available in manual sources. These capabilities can be used to design initially precise search formulations, and to cut down or increase the size of the response set so as to get the 30-item output the client wants and expects. In addition to using the tactics for expanding or contracting subject access that were examined above, the online searcher can limit output by characteristics such as publication date, accession number (reflecting how recently the item was added to the database), language, country of origin, document type, and so on. These are powerful capabilities; they allow many options for clever search design and modification. Use of them may indeed lead to drastic modification of the size of output sets. But the fact remains that, in practice, they are mostly carried out "blind." Through design and modification of the search formulation, the searcher selects the potentially relevant citations and rejects the probably irrelevant ones for the client without seeing the overwhelming majority of those citations.

The nature of searching and search modification is thus quite different for online and manual searchers. In both cases the client may set a comparatively low limit on the number of citations wanted, but the danger of unwittingly rejecting large numbers of highly relevant documents is much higher in online searching. Since the client asks for a small set, and may have to pay for the output on a per-citation basis in an online search, the searcher is determined to find ways to reduce the output—and thus may slip into the fallacy. We will consider ways to deal with this problem in the next section.

STRATEGIES FOR DEALING WITH THE FALLACY

In order to identify strategies, it will be helpful first to distinguish three common types of search. Markey and Cochrane (1981), following ideas developed originally by Charles Bourne, describe the high-recall search, high-precision search, and brief search. The first two emphasize the retrieval values for which they are named, while a brief search (already mentioned above) "is done in response to the need for retrieving a few items either to lessen expenses or to perform a rapid survey of the file before a more comprehensive and lengthy strategy" (p. 8).

The purpose of a recall search is very clear; the client needs everything that can be found on the topic for, say, a dissertation or review paper. In the case of precision searches, the client insists that the size of the output be limited and that irrelevant documents be minimized. Those of us with a library background may assume that high recall is important. People in other fields often do not. Many researchers, in fact, take a casual attitude toward the literature searches they do for articles they are writing. They see the background survey at the beginning of articles as a tiresome, if necessary, task. They merely want to show where their work fits into the stream of research; and it is enough for this purpose to mention some typical articles, not everything that has been done. If this is the attitude taken by the client, then a precision search is indeed called for.

But there is another possibility—that the client who is apparently asking for a precision search really wants a recall search. This can come about for reasons discussed in the previous section. Ignorant of the recall–precision tradeoff, the client may think that irrelevant documents are of course not wanted; the output should be limited to relevant items only. Presumably the fancy automated system can easily produce such a result. The client may even assume—this is common—that when the search is limited to 30 items, the system will produce the 30 most relevant items, i.e., a ranked output. Thus why waste money on more citations?

Furthermore, the client may make the same carryover from manual to online searches that was discussed above for searchers. The client's manual searches as a student may have produced, after scanning and selecting, only a few items. This output could have been especially low if he or she was ignorant of the complexity of indexing and the variety of bibliographic sources available in most fields. This client, in other words, may actually want high recall, but assume that the most references there could possibly be on any subject is about 30. So if the upper limit is set there, the client thinks, the search output will contain all the relevant items that exist.

How can one tell whether the client really wants a precision search or a recall search? We may presume that everyone would like to minimize irrelevant citations retrieved. What really is at issue is the importance of recall. So the crucial question to put to the client is: "Do you want everything we can find on this topic, or just some examples, some typical references?"

Now, assuming that the searcher is able to identify true recall and true precision searching in the interview with the client, what strategies should be used to avoid the fallacy? I suggest that different strategies should be used for recall and precision searches. Following our earlier practice, we may call the tactic at this point to TRADE—that is, to deliberately trade recall for precision, or vice versa, in line with the tradeoff between them. In both kinds of searches, modification by subject characteristics is often necessary *initially* so as to home in on a formulation that is both a good representation of the query and a good match with available terms in the database. But after these initial changes, precision searches should be modified by *further modification of subject characteristics*. Recall searches, in contrast, should be modified by *secondary, "non-subject" characteristics*, such as date, language, and document type.

Why suggest these different approaches for the two types of search? As noted above, a good recall search will often have an extensive formulation, with many marginal terms included. It will generally produce a large output with a comparatively large number of irrelevant documents. It is thus particularly tempting to use modification by subject characteristics to reduce output size and the percentage of irrelevant documents. For example, one might drop marginal subject terms, broader terms, and truncation if already used. Once one is confident, however, that the search formulation is a good one for the query and for that database, the use of extensive subject modification later in the search, solely to reduce output size, simply introduces covert precision searching when a recall search is wanted. A good recall search requires those marginal terms, broader terms, and so on. To drop them is to convert the recall search into a precision search *inadvertently.*

But how then is one to deal with the client who insists on limiting the size of the output for a recall search? If practical exigencies require what is really a contradiction in terms, there are two main options: (a) work out a narrower fallback topic with the client in the pre-search interview, and/or (b) arrange to cut down on the postings by modifying the search on secondary (non-subject) characteristics.

On recall searches, either of these approaches is preferable to running the risk of overcutting through subject modification and hence missing many relevant citations. When a recall search is restricted by date or other non-subject characteristics, the client knows that nothing will be retrieved prior to the stated date or outside the limit. Most importantly, the client knows that the searcher has gotten the highest recall possible within the stated limits. On the contrary, when extensive subject modification is used to cut down the output of a recall search, especially considering that the modification is mostly done blind, there is no way to know just what sort of relevant documents have been shut out as well. Thus, in such a case, what is ostensibly a recall search may, in fact, have poor recall.

In a precision search, on the other hand, we expect to TRADE away some relevant documents in order to maximize precision. (If the client cannot bear to lose those relevant items, then a recall search is what is really wanted.) With a precision search, there is less danger of overcutting, so the searcher can pull out all the stops to modify the search formulation by subject characteristics. The options for doing this are many and varied, as we saw in the discussion of tactics. By using subject modification the searcher gives the client a set of references on the precise topic desired, and across all years, languages, bibliographic forms, and so on. Of course, if the client wants the search limited by date or other secondary characteristics, the limit should be used.

When there is heavy subject modification, there is still some possibility of overcutting even in precision searches, and care should be exercised. Consider the case in which a searcher gets an initial output in the high hundreds (or even thousands) of postings—perhaps because, though precision is sought, the topic is broad and has produced a genuinely large literature. In reducing this to a small requested set, such as 30, the modification may be so drastic that it cuts out whole sub-areas or branches within the stated topic. Thus the searcher may want to arrange a narrower fallback topic in this case as well.

So far in this section the emphasis has been on avoiding the overcutting version of the fallacy. What about the quick and dirty version? Here the problem is one of accepting as final the output of a simple, off-the-top-of-the-head formulation because it produces the desired small number of citations. In cases where the client actually wants a "brief search," and the searcher is confident that good terms are being used, this approach is adequate. Otherwise, some initial experimentation with subject modification is always advisable to be sure no better combination of terms can be found.

DATABASE VOCABULARIES

Having frequently alluded to "terms," "descriptors," "subject modification," etc., we turn, finally, to a more detailed examination of the actual vocabularies from which bibliographic databases are constructed. It has long been recognized that powerful retrieval in online searching can be gained through the combined use of natural language and controlled vocabularies. Here we will focus on their interplay, with emphasis on the latter.

The idea of a "controlled vocabulary" does not, however, represent a single theory or approach to indexing or classification. There are actually many types of controlled vocabularies in databases. Often a single database will contain several types. They usually date from the days when the databases were print products only, and represent a variety of theories on indexing and classification. Effective use of these vocabularies requires a strategic understanding of which types of classification and indexing are involved, in that one must take advantage of the particular mix of vocabularies in a given database to achieve optimum retrieval.

In this section I will first describe and explain seven common types of subject vocabularies in databases, and then move on to specific search techniques for exploiting the strengths of particular types of vocabularies. Last, I will suggest an overall strategy for identifying and using vocabulary types when approaching a new database.

THE SPECTRUM OF SUBJECT DESCRIPTION

Figure 9.1 lists seven major types of subject description that can be found in online (and CD-ROM) databases today. For convenience of discussion, these

Figure 9.1.   Array of Subject Description from General to Specific

Hierarchical classification
Category codes
Subject headings
Descriptors
Faceted classification
Post-controlled vocabulary
Natural language

types are arrayed from broad to specific—that is, typical terms or categories in types higher on the list are broader and more general than typical terms or categories in types that are lower. For example, a typical category in the hierarchical classification of the NTIS (National Technical Information Service) database may be an entire academic discipline, such as geography or civil engineering, while a typical descriptor in a science thesaurus might be a particular metal alloy or chemical compound.

Note that there exists a large number of types of controlled vocabularies: in fact, almost every specific vocabulary has some unique features. With some particular vocabularies, therefore, the order of types in Figure 9.1 would be different. I am grouping and generalizing types for the sake of simplifying what is, in fact, a very complex topic.

Controlled Vocabulary and Natural Language. The top six types of vocabulary in the list can all be considered forms of controlled vocabulary, while the last, natural language, is the text as prepared by the original writer of the document or abstract. Such text follows the rules only of ordinary, "natural" speaking and writing; it is not an artificial language designed just for information retrieval. "Controlled vocabulary" refers to index terms or classification codes that have been created to provide consistent and orderly description of the contents of documents or records. Such vocabulary may be controlled in one or more ways:

- by limiting many of the normal linguistic variations in natural language (regulating whether terms appear in singular or plural, permitting only certain verb endings, etc.);
- by regulating the word order and structure of phrases; and
- by cutting down the number of synonyms or near-synonyms, so that only one way of describing a given topic is allowed in the vocabulary.

In addition, aids to indexers and searchers may be provided in the form of cross-references between terms and scope notes defining terms closely. (Still other features, to be described below, can be found in classifications.) Typically, with a controlled vocabulary, a list or thesaurus of allowable terms or categories is developed, which both indexers and searchers consult.

Post-controlled Vocabulary. A disadvantage of typical controlled vocabulary lists, however, is that they are rather inflexible with respect to new terms and topic areas when they appear in a rapidly changing discipline. New vocabulary cannot be included until it has been evaluated and integrated into a new edition of the thesaurus.

A post-controlled vocabulary, on the other hand, has some of the advantages of natural language and some of those of controlled vocabulary. Typically, with a post-controlled vocabulary, indexing is not limited to an established list. Rather, natural language terminology is permitted as it appears in new, incoming documents, but indexers then do something to that vocabulary to assist searchers. For example, they may create lists of closely related terms, or hedges, so that the searcher may see at once and enter easily a whole list of ORed terms on a topic. In this way the searcher expresses a topic well without having to think up a dozen other related terms to ensure coverage.

The BIOSIS keywords are an excellent example of a post-controlled vocabulary. These terms are drawn from the natural language of the titles of documents indexed in BIOSIS. Frequently appearing terms are listed as keywords in the Master Index of the *Search Guide—BIOSIS Previews Edition*, and serve as prompts for the searcher. Moreover, any natural language term, whether listed in the Master Index or not, may appear in document titles and consequently be a searchable keyword. Both term frequencies and related controlled vocabulary ("Concept Codes" and "Biosystematic Codes") are given next to the keywords so that the searcher may decide which is best to use in particular instances. In addition, BIOSIS indexers add some "controlled keywords" to ensure complete coverage. (See the "Content Guide" of the *Search Guide* for information on these supplemental terms.) Because the post-control done by the indexers adds some consistency, subject searching on this vocabulary can be expected to be more effective, as a rule, than pure natural language searching.

Subject Headings vs. Descriptors. Differences between these two forms of index terms are summarized in Figure 9.2. Subject headings date back to the 19th century and have been the traditional form of subject description used by the Library of Congress (e.g., in the LC MARC and REMARC databases) and by academic libraries for books. Other databases that use subject headings include the H. W. Wilson indexes (*Readers' Guide, Applied Science and Technology Index*, etc., available through WILSONLINE), the Magazine Index, and COMPENDEX (the online *Engineering Index*).

Subject headings often contain a main heading followed by one or more subdivisions, as in "United Nations—Armed Forces—Juvenile literature" (from *Library of Congress Subject Headings*). Subject headings are thus "precoordinate"—that is, all the subject elements are coordinated into a single heading by the indexer *before* the first search is done. The idea is to describe

Figure 9.2.   Differences Between Subject Headings and Descriptors

Subject Headings	Descriptors
Pre-coordinate	Post-coordinate
Whole document indexing	Concept indexing
Designed for alphabetical index	Designed for Boolean searching
Average 1–5 headings per document	Average 5–25 descriptors per document

Example databases	Example databases
Library of Congress databases	ERIC
WILSONLINE databases	INSPEC
COMPENDEX	NTIS
	PsycINFO.....plus many more

the whole document in that one heading, or at most, in a handful of such headings. (We shall get to "post-coordinate" headings shortly.)

Descriptors, our other form of subject indicator, got their big boost after World War II, when science information specialists realized that subject headings were insufficiently detailed to describe highly specific scientific articles and reports. They experimented with a variety of different forms of manual access, with names like "peek-a-boo cards" and "edge-notched cards." Quite a number of indexing theories were involved, and some descriptors were quite broad, while others were very specific. However, the principal heritage of this stage of development of subject description is that, in many indexing languages, individual descriptors were intended to describe *a single concept used within a document,* rather than the whole document—hence the phrase "concept indexing."

Along with the concept indexing approach went the idea of Boolean searching. It is sometimes forgotten that Boolean searching originated with manual information retrieval systems and antedated online searching by decades. Since any one index term did not describe the whole document, retrieval was designed so that searchers would use Boolean logic to combine whatever set of specific concepts they wanted for their query *at the time of search,* and then see which documents contained that particular combination of concepts. This type of indexing was called "post-coordinate," because the searcher combined the elements of the subject description *after* the need for a search had arisen, instead of the indexer's doing it before.

The topic of a whole document may be broad or specific, and individual concepts within a document may be broad or specific. Therefore, reflecting this range, individual subject headings and descriptors will vary in specificity. The difference in breadth between subject headings and descriptors shows up not in single terms, but in the overall pattern of indexing. Descriptor systems apply far more terms, as a rule, than subject heading systems do, identifying numerous individual concepts rather than describing the whole document in one or two headings.

Examples of subject headings and descriptors are given in Figure 9.3, on the topic of sports as a part of education. Note that the headings from *Education Index* are pre-coordinate, and so more than one subject element appears in most of them, whereas the ERIC descriptors are not to be combined until the time of the search. Note, too, that while the subject headings can attain high specificity through "dash-on" combinations, the permissible combinations are strictly limited. If such a combination as "Athletes—Bribery" (or "Bribery—Athletes") is not authorized, there may be no single expression to describe a report on, say, college players who take money to throw games or shave the point-spread. One must be content with at least two separate headings, such as "Athletes" and "Sports—Ethical aspects," neither of which captures the topic exactly. (Both, moreover, would place the report, when filed, with other writings that are somewhat dissimilar, assuring "false drops" when retrieval takes place.) The descriptors, in contrast, can be combined in any way—e.g., "Athletes" AND "Bribery"—to express the topic exactly. (This, of course, assumes that the necessary descriptors have been authorized, which is not the case with "Bribery" in ERIC.)

Figure 9.3. Subject Headings and Descriptors

Sports Subject Headings in WILSONLINE'S *Education Index*
Athletes
Athletes—Health and hygiene
Athletes—Nutrition
Athletes—Physical examinations
Athletes—Psychology
Athletes—Scholastic achievements
Athletes—Training
Athletes—Wounds and injuries
Athletics
Athletics—Administration
Athletics—Equipment—Catalogs
Athletics—Intercollegiate
Athletics—Intercollegiate—Finance
.....
Sports—Accidents and injuries
Sports—Accidents and injuries—Prevention
Sports—Accidents and injuries—Statistics

Sports Descriptors in ERIC's *Thesaurus*
Athletes
Athletic Coaches
Athletic Equipment
Athletic Fields
Athletics
.....
Sports psychology
Sportsmanship

Classifications vs. Indexing Vocabularies. What distinguishes a classification scheme from an index term vocabulary? There are many practical distinctions, but a more theoretical distinction is actually the most important for understanding such systems for online searching. The goal of classification schemes, not always achieved, is to have distinct conceptual categories that are mutually exclusive and jointly exhaustive. That is, there should be no overlap in meaning between categories of a classification (mutual exclusivity) and no areas left uncovered by the categories (joint exhaustivity). Indexing vocabularies, by comparison, simply reflect the linguistic usages of authors, or paraphrase them as faithfully as possible. Such language has many phrases and words that overlap in meaning, even when synonyms and near-synonyms have been purged through vocabulary control. For instance, "Emotional Adjustment" and "Emotional Problems," both legitimate terms in ERIC, have some overlap in meaning and some distinctive aspects of meaning. Because both are useful in capturing nuances of documents, both are authorized. A rigorous classification scheme would probably exclude one or the other as categories.

In order to define categories rigorously and to exclude overlap in meaning, it is sometimes necessary to label categories with lengthy and awkward names, different from those we would use in natural language. For example, the BIOSIS Concept Code "Tropical and Semitropical Fruits and Nuts; Plantation Crops" is not the sort of phrase that would ordinarily appear in an index language, but rather defines a carefully demarcated conceptual category. In both printed works and online databases, a compact notation often stands for such categories.[6]

Hierarchical and Faceted Classifications. Classifications are generally further organized in hierarchies or faceted schemes. Indexing languages are sometimes built on hierarchical principles: we have seen that terms in thesauri may be explicitly linked to broader terms (BT), related terms on about the same level (RT), and narrower terms (NT). Terms may also be organized by facets—for example, they might be classed depending on whether they bring out a document's topic, literary form, geographic origin, or temporal period. But again, in indexing languages there is less emphasis on creating a full, mutually exclusive and jointly exhaustive set of categories in advance of use. Creators of indexing languages tend to go by "literary warrant," adding and relating terms ad hoc, as the literature dictates. Classificationists tend to *pre-supply* the categories as parts of a logical structure, believing that they can foresee all future possibilities and provide either a niche for each publication or a place for a new category to be added on.

---

[6] The presence of codes does not necessarily indicate a classification. In PsycINFO's *Thesaurus of Psychological Index Terms*, for example, codes have been assigned to index terms to cut input time in searching, but the thesaurus contains a true index vocabulary, not a classification.

Figure 9.4.   Hierarchical Classification

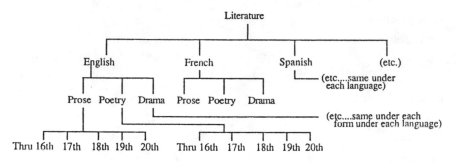

(Figures 9.4 through 9.7 based on C.D. Needham, Organizing Knowledge In Libraries, 2d rev. ed., London: Seminar Press, 1971. Used by permission of Gower Publishing Co.)

A hierarchical classification is the traditional "inverted tree," in which each category is broken down into smaller and small subdivisions, according to some clear characteristic of division at each step. A simple illustration appears as Figure 9.4. The categories are distinguished on the first level by the characteristic of language, on the second by literary form, and on the

Figure 9.5.   Labeled Categories for Hierarchical Classification.

100 English Literature
   110 English Prose
      111 English Prose thru 16th Century
      112 English 17th Century Prose
      113 English 18th Century Prose
      114 English 19th Century Prose
      115 English 20th Century Prose
   120 English Poetry
      121 English Poetry thru 16th Century
      122 English 17th Century Poetry
      (etc.)
200 French Literature
   210 French Prose
      211 French Prose thru 16th Century
      (etc.)
   220 French Poetry
      221 French Poetry thru 16th Century
      (etc.)
   230 French Drama
      (etc.)
300 Spanish Literature
   310 Spanish Prose
      (etc.)

Figure 9.6.   Faceted Classification

A Language

  a English

  b French

  c Spanish

B Form

  a Prose

  b Poetry

  c Drama

C Period

  a through 16th Century

  b 17th Century

  c 18th Century

  d 19th Century

  e 20th Century

third by historical period. In using such a scheme for classifying materials, a distinctive notation is assigned to each possible category created by the hierarchy. Figure 9.5 has examples.

A faceted classification, on the other hand, creates a separate, free-standing list for each characteristic of division. Figure 9.6 illustrates by converting the components of Figure 9.4 into an imaginary faceted scheme, with notation. A classifier would create a class code for a document by selecting a piece of notation from each facet and stringing them together, as in Figure 9.7.

Figure 9.7.   Labeled Categories for Faceted Classification

Aa	English Literature
AaBa	English Prose
AaBaCa	English 16th Century Prose
AbBbCe	French 20th Century Poetry
AcBaBb	Spanish Prose and Poetry
AcBaBbCb	Spanish Prose and Poetry of the 17th Century
BcCd	19th Century Drama
Ce	Literature of the 20th Century

Faceted classification has been little used in the United States for manual information systems, but something like it is coming to be used in online databases. In the latter, indexers usually assign the facet elements independently and do not combine them into a single notation. This approach leaves the searcher free to combine the elements with Boolean logic as he or she wishes at the time of search, which makes for the same flexibility as concept indexing. It also gets around a problem that has long beset faceted classification schemes when they are used in print—namely, the problem of which element (or elements) to sort on in creating the file. Unless *all* the facets can be sorted on in turn, one is faced with trying to pick the most useful order for presenting them, and this is by no means obvious.

The online searcher, fortunately, can choose to combine any of the facets in any order. Figure 9.8, for example, shows that in Predicasts a searcher can choose one code from an industrial Products facet, another from the list for Events with respect to products (or their manufacturers), and a third from Geographic regions. One then ANDs them together to produce a specific, detailed search formulation, such as "production management of cyclic amines in European Community countries."

In practice, it is easier to create very specific categories with faceted classifications than with hierarchical classifications. We can see why when we consider what it would take to represent the Predicasts categories in a hierarchical scheme. With the faceted approach, any element in any facet can be combined with any element in any other facet. Imagine how many tens or even hundreds of thousands of possible combinations there are. Each product code can be combined with every single geographic code and/or event code From zero to several elements can be drawn from a single facet and ORed together. And so on. The number of possible highly specific descriptions that the searcher can create is almost astronomical.

Conversely, in a hierarchical scheme each allowable combination is specified in advance, and given distinctive notation. (This is sometimes called an "enumerative" scheme, because all possibilities have been explicitly enumerated.) If that were done with Predicasts, the search manual would be vastly longer than it is now, so as to be impossibly unwieldy.

We can better see the difference between these two approaches to classification by comparing a "Chinese" to a "Western" menu. The Chinese menu tells you to select one item from each of several lists. The total number of possible combinations that result from this approach is quite large, even though the lists may be fairly short. In a Western menu, all the permissible combinations of dishes are specified in advance (often with the statement, "No substitutions, please"), and the customer is consequently limited to fewer possible meals. While in principle one may create as many categories as one wants in a hierarchical scheme, and set them out in a lengthy list, in practice it is so tedious and expensive that it is usually not done. Thus, most

Figure 9.8. Sections of Predicasts Facets

EVENT CODES

12 Organizational History Formation Private to Public Co Reorganization Bankruptcy Liquidation Expropriation Headquarters Data Public to Private Co Organizatnl Change NEC **13 Subsidiary-to-Parent Data** Parent owns 100% Parent owns 80-99% Parent owns 50-79% Affiliate-to-Parent Data Division-to-Parent Data Joint Venture-to-Parent Data Parent Information NEC	**22 Planning & Information** Planning Management Policy & Goals Operations Research Venture Analysis Management Consulting Model Building Information Gathering Information Dissemination Planning NEC **23 Production Management** Supervisory Management Production Planning & Control Plant Engineering Safety Management Materials Handling Environmental Management Energy Management	**33 Product Design & Development** Product Development Prototype Built Product Testing Market Testing Product Introduction Product Applications Product Discontinued Products NEC **34 Product Specifications** Mechanical Properties Chemical Properties Electrical Properties Structural Properties Functional Properties Energy per Unit (Properties) Process Health Hazards Price/Performance Data

PRODUCT CODES

28664	**Aromatic Hydrocarbons**
286641	Cumene
286642	Divinylbenzene
286644	A-Methylstyrene
286645	Alkylbenzenes
2866451	Dodecylbenzenes
2866452	Methylbenzene
2866453	Ethylbenzene
286647	Styrene Monomer
286648	Polymethylbenzenes
2866481	Mesitylene
2866482	Durene
2866483	Pseudocumene
286649	Aromatic Hydrocarbons NEC
2866491	Stilbene
2866492	Methylnapthalene
2866493	Anthracine
2866494	Coumarone
2866495	Methyl Styrenes NEC
2866499	Misc Aromatic Hydrocarbons
28665	**Cyclic Amines**
286651	Aniline
286652	Aniline Derivatives
2866521	Dimethylaniline
2866526	Oxydianiline
286653	Heterocyclic Amines
2866537	Aminopyridines
286655	Diphenylamine
286656	Benzidines & Toluidines
2866561	Benzidine
2866562	Dimethylbenzidine
2866563	Dichlorobenzidine
2866565	Dianisidine
2866566	Dimethyl-p-Toluidine
2866567	Toluenediamine
2866568	Toluidine
2866569	Benzidines & Toluidines NEC
286657	Cyclohexylamine
286658	Xylidines
2866585	Xylenediamines

GEOGRAPHIC CODES

EUROPE

4	All codes beginning with 4
4 .E	Europe
4 .F	Europe ex USSR
4 .G	Central Europe
4 ..L	Southern Europe
4 .M	Mediterranean
4..N	Northern Europe
4..T	OECD Europe
4 .W	West Europe
4 CO	COCOM
4 EC	European Community
4 NA	N Atlantic Treaty Org
4BEJ	Benelux
4BEK	Belg-Lux Econ Union
4BEL	Belgium
4DEN	Denmark
4FRA	France
4GRE	Greece
4IRE	Ireland
4ITA	Italy
4LUX	Luxembourg
4NET	Netherlands
4UK	United Kingdom
4WGE	West Germany
4ZEC	Other EC

WEST EUROPE EX EC

5	All codes beginning with 5
5..W	West Europe ex EC
5.EF	European Free Trd Assn
5.SC	Scandinavia
5AND	Andorra
5AUT	Austria
5FAE	Faeroe Islands
5FIN	Finland
5GIB	Gibraltar
5GRL	Greenland
5ICE	Iceland
5LIZ	Liechtenstein
5MAT	Malta
5MON	Monaco
5NOR	Norway

hierarchical classifications contain far fewer of the total possible categories than is the case with faceted classifications.

Category Codes. This is the label I have given to descriptive systems that have some classificatory features and some index term features, and can therefore be considered a mixed type. BIOSIS "Concept Codes" as re

Figure 9.9.   Concept Codes from BIOSIS

CC54512   NONPARASITIC DISEASES

CODE FREQUENCIES   Major (5280)   Minor (1610)

CODE APPLICATIONS   This code retrieves studies on *plant diseases* caused by *non-biological factors—harmful conditions* and *substances.*

EXAMPLES—STUDIES ON   • Pollution • weather • plant nutrient deficiencies or toxicities • toxic effects of pesticides on plants • soil waterlogging • genetic and developmental disorders

STRATEGY RECOMMENDATIONS
   • For studies on genetic disorders, use this code and the *Plant Genetics and Cytogenetics* code CC03504.
   • For studies on the adverse effects of radiation, use the *Plant Physiology, Biochemistry and Biophysics Radiation Effects* code CC51516.
   • For studies on diseases caused by climatic factors, use this code with the *Bioclimatology and Biometeorology* code CC07504.
   • For physiological factors relevant to plant disease development, use this code and relevant *Plant Physiology, Biochemistry and Biophysics* codes. See Directory, page B-13.
   • For studies relating environmental pollution with plant pathology, use this code and the *Air, Water and Soil Pollution* code CC37015.
   • For ecological changes in vegetation due to abiotic factors, use this code and the *Plant Ecology* code CC07506.

CC54514   PARASITISM AND RESISTANCE

CODE FREQUENCIES   Major (6510)   Minor (770)

CODE APPLICATIONS   This code retrieves studies on *plant host susceptibility* and *resistance* to *diseases.*

EXAMPLES—STUDIES ON   • Breeding for resistance • genetic, physiological and morphological factors relating to plant resistance

STRATEGY RECOMMENDATIONS
   • For studies relating plant genetics to disease resistance, use this code and the *Plant Genetics and Cytogenetics* code CC03504.
   • For studies on plant resistance to entomological pests, use this code and relevant *Economic Entomology* codes. See Directory, page B-7.
   • For plant resistance to fungi, algae, bacteria, and other agents, use this code and relevant *Phytopathology* codes. See Directory, pages B-12 and B-13.

These are two of the ten codes within the broader area of phytopathology, or plant disease. Note the extensive scope notes and carefully worked out strategy recommendations. Though these "concepts" are formed like index terms, they also have classificatory features in that their coverage is made rigorously mutually exclusive and jointly exhaustive.

produced in Figure 9.9 are an example. They are a mixed type because, on the one hand, the concepts are carefully defined and given code numbers, in the manner of classification categories, but, on the other hand, they are not embedded in a hierarchy or highly structured set of facets.

Array from Specific to Broad. To review, the types of vocabulary in Figure 9.1 are increasingly broad as one moves up the list. Natural language, at the bottom, gives the most specific of all subject descriptions, because it allows the full range of variation in vocabulary, orthography, and syntax that is found in written language. Post-control seeks useful groupings of natural language, and remains closer to its specificity than descriptors or subject headings. Because relatively short lists of facet elements can be combined in many different ways, faceted classifications can easily be quite specific. Faceted terms, descriptors, and subject headings unite what natural language scatters by standardizing the ways in which concepts are expressed; but in so doing they depart from natural language to some degree. Descriptor systems apply relatively many terms reflecting individual concepts. Taken overall, they usually give a fuller sense of a document than subject heading systems, which seek to describe the whole document in a few headings at most—often only one. Category codes and hierarchical classifications, in which combinations of elements are formed in advance, are usually the broadest, most generic indicators of content. They attempt to capture the entire message of the document in a single position on the subject scale.

OPTIMAL USE OF CONTROLLED VOCABULARIES

In this section I will discuss ways of using these various types of subject description to good effect in searching online. Nothing will be said here about the benefits of natural language searching, since we are concerned with the use of controlled vocabularies. (The main benefit of post-controlled natural language has already been mentioned.)

Hierarchical Classification Codes and Category Codes. Broad to medium-broad hierarchical classification codes—for example, those of NTIS, COM-PENDEX, and RILM Abstracts—can seldom be used by themselves. Such codes usually retrieve hundreds or thousands of documents. However, they may be used effectively in combination with other more specific terms. Classification codes of medium breadth, such as those used in INSPEC and MathSci, and the category codes (BIOSIS "Concept Codes") can sometimes be used by themselves, or, more often, used in ANDed sets with other codes or more specific types of search vocabulary.

In addition, there are three particular circumstances where broad to medium subject categories may be very useful:

(1) Current awareness. Researchers like to keep up to date by scanning a wide range of journals and other literature, representing both their specific specialty and closely related areas. The online equivalent of this can be done by entering a broad to medium classification code for the general research area and ANDing it with the code for the latest update of the database. This combination achieves the researcher's goal by producing a list of citations that covers only the most recently entered materials in a broad subject area. At the same time the list is normally not too long, because the retrieval is limited to the most current items. For example, searching INSPEC in DIALOG, one can input the category code for "Information storage and retrieval" and AND it with the code for the latest update as follows:

Select CC = 7250 and UD = 9999

(2) Unsettled vocabulary in a new research area. This approach is also good on those occasions when a research topic is so new that there are no generally agreed-upon descriptors in use for it yet. Provided that the new topic is generally understood to fall within a broad area of research, one can

enter the code for that broad area, AND it with codes for recent updates in the database, and scan for relevant articles. In this manner the classification serves as a backup for handling the limitations of descriptor vocabulary.

There are at least two other options for dealing with this situation. First, one may do free-text searching on a "hedge" of ORed natural language words and phrases that have been used for the new topic. This approach is frequently to be preferred as the most straightforward. However, it is in the nature of new research areas to contain some confusion; in such a case, it may not be entirely obvious which articles are relevant. Preselecting citations by searching only on recognized terms in use to date may limit retrieval more than one wants. In some cases, giving the researcher a chance to scan through a list of the most recent items in the broader topic area may be a surer way for him or her to identify all the relevant items.

Secondly, one may search on one or more key references in a citation database, such as SciSearch or Social SciSearch. When a publication is used to retrieve articles that cite it, it functions like an indexing term, since the citing articles presumably share its subject matter (or methodology). Retrieval by cited reference (CR) enables one to leapfrog the vocabulary problem entirely. For example, someone interested in discussions of search tactics could enter the following string in Social SciSearch

Select CR = Bates M.J, 1979, V 30?

and retrieve all the articles that have cited my original presentation (Bates, 1979a) since it appeared. Obviously this gets around expressing the subject with descriptors or natural language. At most, one needs to know the author, year, and journal volume number of an article in which one is interested. (In some cases, one would add the beginning page number, "P 205," to the search string, but here the truncator is used so that *any* version of the page number will be allowed.)[7]

(3) Distinguishing different word meanings. Homonymic terms may be used in a variety of different ways in a database, particularly in databases covering many areas, such as NTIS. "Bond," for example, can be used with different meanings in materials science, chemistry, anthropology, and finance. By ANDing the specific term (whether controlled vocabulary or natural language) with the classification category of interest to the searcher, any other meaning of the term can be automatically ruled out. In NTIS, 71 is the code for Materials Science, and subsection B of that category is "Adhesives and sealants." The following search statement will restrict the retrievals on truncated "Bond" to the field of adhesives and sealants:

---

[7] One can now also search by cited author (CA) alone and by the titles of cited works (CW) such as books and reports.

Select SH = 71B and Bond?

NTIS covers a very wide range of disciplines, but this procedure is useful in databases with narrower coverage, too, where terms may be used in subtly but significantly different ways. These multiple meanings can be eliminated through clever use of classification codes.

Subject Headings. Subject headings were not originally designed to be used with Boolean searching—the searcher was supposed to hunt in alphabetical catalogs or indexes for the complete heading. Many systems of descriptors, on the other hand, were intended from the beginning to be used with Boolean logic, and were designed accordingly. The question of whether subject headings work as well for online searching as descriptors do has never really been resolved in research. (It seems unlikely.)

With subject heading systems, the searcher often does not know which subdivisions may legitimately be used with which main headings. ("Sports—Accidents and injuries—Statistics" in Figure 9.3 is an authorized string, but many other potential combinations would not be.) This problem is particularly acute with Library of Congress subject headings. The list called *Library of Congress Subject Headings* is quite confusing on this matter to the uninitiated; in many cases only trained catalogers can make the determinations. Consequently, a controlled-vocabulary search on a main heading plus subdivision can be a gamble. Is that combination in fact in use? The use of free-text proximity searching with natural language may be both simpler and surer. On the other hand, where heading and subdivision can be identified, or only a main heading is needed, one can enjoy the same benefits that generally accrue with controlled vocabulary. Searches on main headings alone may prove quite broad in what they retrieve; one may wish to AND in more specific free-text terms as well. On the whole, subject headings are more useful when somewhat broader topics are wanted.

There is another important fact to keep in mind about subject headings. Since, as a rule, far fewer headings are assigned to each item than is the case with descriptors, combining several subject headings in a controlled-vocabulary search formulation is more likely to produce a null set—zero retrievals—than is the case with descriptors. This, again, is more likely with Library of Congress databases, in which very limited numbers of headings are assigned.

Since subject headings often contain several subdivisions, a vendor may mount a database so that the searcher can search on individual sections of the heading, or on the sections in combination. DIALOG does this with its versions of COMPENDEX and LC MARC. In COMPENDEX, for example, DIALOG treats the heading "Light—Brillouin scattering" as two headings, to enable searchers interested in either topic to find documents indexed under either. The (L) operator in DIALOG enables the searcher to require that the two elements appear together in the same heading—i.e., "Light(L)Brillouin scattering"—so that one does not retrieve documents with "Light" as a part of one heading and "Brillouin scattering" as a part of another.

WILSONLINE calls the entire heading—that is, the main heading plus subdivisions—a "descriptor string" (ds) and each element a "subject heading" (sh). Thus, as in DIALOG, one has the option of searching on the whole heading or its component parts. WILSONLINE examples:

Find   mathematicians/Soviet Union/biography (ds)
Find   mathematicians (sh)

Descriptors. Recall that in concept indexing no one descriptor describes the entire document. The numerous descriptors name several concepts that *jointly* represent the topic. This contrasts with subject heading systems, where a single heading is supposed to describe the whole document.

Beginning searchers sometimes believe that their job is to find a single topic label and input it in a simple one-word or one-phrase formulation. Research has shown this misconception to be common among ERIC searchers, for example. Both poor recall and poor precision result, since this approach runs counter to the way descriptor-based systems are designed. From the beginning, even before online searching was available, it was assumed that with descriptor systems the searcher would identify the key concepts in the search query and search on them in Boolean combinations. Though one does occasionally find a single descriptor that exactly fits a topic, usually descriptors must be assembled with ORs, ANDs, and NOTs to represent it.

In searching a descriptor-based database, prospective formulations that contain only one or two terms should be reviewed with these questions in mind: "Are all the important concepts ANDed in? Are there significant term variations that could be ORed in?" (These are instances of the tactic SURVEY, introduced above.) One's strategy in dealing with a descriptor system may contrast sharply, therefore, with the strategy used for a subject heading system.

ERIC and PsycINFO are typical of controlled vocabularies designed as concept indexing terms. ERIC, for example, often provides several terms relevant to a given topic. These terms sometimes partially overlap. In a thorough search, clusters of these terms should be ORed together (the PARALLEL tactic). Furthermore, auxiliary information is indexed, such as grade-level of students involved or type of document, so that it is possible to AND terms for the central topic with other terms representing the auxiliary information (the tactic EXHAUST) and gain much more precision in the output set. We have seen this before, but here is another example:

> Select Athletes AND (Academic Achievement OR Student Improvement OR Academic Standards) AND (High Schools OR Secondary Education) AND Bibliographies

Faceted Classification. The formulation above is, in a sense, a search for documents classified by facets, in that it combines descriptors representing subject (academic performance of athletes), grade level (high school), and desired document type (bibliographies). Great specificity is possible by combining elements from each of several facets.

Such power, moreover, is not restricted to bibliographic databases. In Figure 9.10 we see an example from the DIALOG "bluesheet" for *American Men and Women of Science,* a biographical directory. Bluesheets show, among other things, the nature of the Basic Index and the Additional Indexes for every file. Here, each Additional Index represents a facet of information about the biographees. Combining elements from various facets makes it possible to home in on a highly specific subset. For example, using the Prefix Codes (translated on the bluesheet), we may search for the set of all Nobel Prize winners in the state of California:

> Select HA = Nobel AND ST = California

Thus, we not only quickly locate profiles of all Nobel laureates in California, we also find out (assuming the file is complete and current) how many winners there are. The latter piece of information is a "postings count" that grows out of the compilation of the file; it is not explicit in any particular record. As more and more directories and other traditional reference books are brought online, it will be possible to do powerful faceted searching in many ways with these additional indexes.

VOCABULARY TYPES IN A NEW DATABASE

Identification. To take advantage of the controlled vocabularies in a database, it is first necessary to identify what types of subject description are available in it. To do so, it is important to examine the documentation put out by the creators or publishers of the database as well as that provided by the vendor. In order to provide a common format across various databases, online services such as DIALOG and BRS generally provide common labels for subject elements, such as "Descriptor" or "Classification code," regardless of the type of vocabulary involved. Thus, if only the vendor's document is examined, it is difficult to tell what types of vocabularies are being used. The publishers of databases, on the other hand, generally describe the unique features of the indexing provided in their databases, and often publish thesauri and other term lists as well. (The online time saved through proper

Figure 9.10   Additional Indexes of American Men and Women of Science

ADDITIONAL. INDEXES

PREFIX	FIELD NAME	EXAMPLES	
AD=	Institution and Street	E AD=SMITHSONIAN	S AD=CARNEGIE(W)AD=INST
BS=	Birth Statistics	E BS=FRANCE	S BS=CINCINNATI(F)BS=OHIO
CD=	Children Statistics	E CD=2	S CD=3
CN=	Country Name	E CN=MEXICO	S CN=UNITED KINGDOM
			S CN=WEST(W)CN=GERMANY
CP=	Concurrent Positions	E CP=CONSULT	S CP=PROF(W)CP=JOHNS(W)CP=HOPKINS
CY=	City	E CY=BALTIMORE	S CY=LOS ANGELES
			S CY=RAPID(W)CY=CITY
DC=	Discipline Code	E DC=03002007	S DC=02002000
EC=	Employment Classification	E EC=ACADEMIC	S EC=CONSULTING
ED=	Education	E ED=PHD	S ED=UNIV(W)ED=CHICAGO
EX=	Professional Experience	E EX=INTERN	S EX=PASTEUR(W)EX=INST
HA=	Honors and Awards	E HA=NOBEL	S HA=BORIS(W)HA=PREGEL(W)HA=AWARD
HD=	Honorary Degrees	E HD=PURDUE	S HD=UNIV(W)HD=CHICAGO
LP=	Language Proficiency	E LP=SPANISH	S LP=CHINESE
ME=	Memberships	E ME=CHEM	S ME=NAT(W)ME=ACAD(W)ME=SCI
MS=	Marriage Statistics	E MS=80	S MS=57
NA=	Biographee Name[1]	E NA=ACKEMAN	S NA=BROWN, DONALD D
ST=	State/Province	E ST=BC	S ST=MD
SX=	Sex	E SX=F	S SX=M
YB=	Year of Birth	E YB=19	S YB=31
ZP=	Zip Code	E ZP=60601	S ZP=21210

[1]Also searchable in the Basic Index.

use of available subject vocabularies can quickly make up for the cost of a $50 or $100 set of producer's documentation.)

So when first working with a new database, one should examine both the producer's and the vendor's documentation to identify unique features, as well as to discover the variety of forms of subject access. It is quite common, particularly in the sciences, for databases to have both an index vocabulary of some kind and a classification scheme. Figure 9.11 displays the types of subject description available in several major databases.

Figure 9.11.   Forms of Subject Access in Various Databases

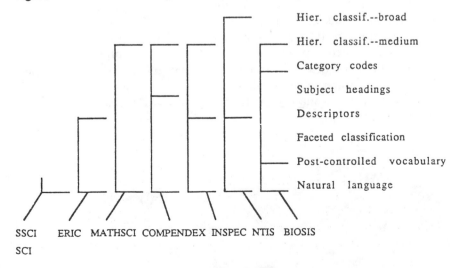

Hier. classif.--broad

Hier. classif.--medium

Category codes

Subject headings

Descriptors

Faceted classification

Post-controlled vocabulary

Natural language

SSCI   ERIC   MATHSCI COMPENDEX INSPEC NTIS BIOSIS
SCI

BIOSIS, for example, has a hierarchical classification in its Biosystematic Codes, category codes in its Concept Codes, post-controlled vocabulary in its Keywords, and, of course, natural language. COMPENDEX, with its CAL Codes, has a medium-broad hierarchical classification, subject headings, and natural language. For subject (as opposed to citation) searching, SciSearch and Social SciSearch are limited to natural language terms from titles, but have the advantage of covering many disciplines at once.

Use in Searching. In using these types of vocabularies in searching, the basic principle to keep in mind is first to identify what type of controlled vocabulary a database uses, and then use each type in a way that corresponds with the query. Specifically, after picking any database as suitable, one goes through the following steps:

- Identify each distinct search concept in the query.
- Assess how broad or specific each concept is.
- Determine which types of vocabulary are available in the database.
- Use the type of vocabulary for each concept that corresponds with its breadth.
- Combine terms in normal Boolean fashion in the search formulation.

This series of steps is similar to those recommended for preparation of BIOSIS profiles. This approach can be used with all databases, however, once one knows how to recognize the controlled vocabulary types. Once one has identified the sorts of controlled vocabulary a database contains, as in Figure 9.11, one can use the level or breadth that is appropriate to each concept in the query.

As a last example, suppose that one is searching INSPEC for applications of general systems theory to the design of information retrieval systems. INSPEC has a classification code for the first term, a descriptor for the last term, and the middle term can be entered free-text. In this way, the searcher uses terms from the database producer's vocabulary that more or less match the specificity of concepts in the query. ("Design," the middle term, is not very specific in this case.) The results can then be manipulated to increase or decrease output, and to eliminate false drops, in ways presented above. Use of appropriate tactics and vocabulary in this way will increase the quality of searches overall.

10

Pragmatic Bibliography*

Patrick Wilson

INTRODUCTION

What a bibliographer does can be analyzed into four basic processes: search for materials (books, journal articles, newspaper articles, and so on), selection of materials, description of materials, and organization of the descriptions. Any bibliographic job involves some combination of these processes, but not necessarily all of them. Within a library one may specialize in collection development, the bibliographic job of search for and selection of materials, or in cataloging, the bibliographic job of description of materials and organization of the descriptions. Making a bibliography usually involves all four of the basic operations. These operations have traditionally been at the core of the professional librarian's work. It is common to contrast reference work with bibliographic work, but I don't think the contrast is important. Most reference work consists of making a bibliography that consists of one item, and then reading something from that one item. Most librarians are basically bibliographers, though they are certainly not the only bibliographers. (I take this as an historical fact about librarians, not as a necessary and eternal truth.)

The two kinds of bibliographic work that I want to contrast can be called *wholesale* bibliography and *pragmatic* bibliography. Wholesale bibliography—more conventionally called comprehensive bibliography—is best illustrated

* This chapter first appeared, in slightly different form, as Wilson (1983b), ©American Library Association, used by permission.

by the making of national and trade bibliographies and library catalogs on the one hand, and, on the other, the bibliographies and abstracting and indexing services that inventory the scholarly or scientific output of an academic or professional field. The *National Union Catalog*, the *British National Bibliography*, *Chemical Abstracts*, and the MLA *Annual Bibliography* are examples of wholesale bibliography. They are big, highly organized, continuing activities, resulting in printed lists and computerized data bases; the results are general purpose bibliographies, made for anyone and everyone who may want to use them, but in a sense aimed at nobody in particular.

Pragmatic bibliography, by contrast, is best illustrated by the activity of one person who is engaged in a specific limited inquiry, scholarly or scientific or purely practical, and who takes time and effort to find materials that will be of help in the inquiry. The inquiry might be an attempt to discover something new, or might simply be an attempt to find out what, if anything, is already known on a subject. But in any case the bibliographic job is done to aid something else; it is not done for its own sake.

The differences between the two kinds of bibliographic work are striking. Wholesale bibliography by definition results in lists; pragmatic bibliography may have no visible result at all. If a list is part of what eventually results (for example, references in a published paper), the list may bear no close or direct relation at all to the preceding bibliographic work; I might end up citing nothing I did not already know about before I started work. As to procedure: wholesale bibliography can be simply a job of processing material that arrives automatically under standing arrangements, hence involving no search or selection, but simply description and organization. Pragmatic bibliography by contrast centers on search and selection. Wholesale bibliography is a full-time job for specialists—catalogers, abstractors, indexers, for instance; pragmatic bibliography is done occasionally by most research workers as well as by librarians, teachers, professionals of all kinds, and notably students, especially graduate students.

THE VIEW OF THE RESEARCHER IN A SPECIALTY

What about the relations between pragmatic and wholesale bibliography? One might think that pragmatic bibliography, whenever properly and efficiently done, would simply consist in making judicious use of wholesale bibliography. Is it not the point, or the principal point, of making those large, expensive works of wholesale bibliography, to facilitate the work of the pragmatic bibliographer, the person who wants to find material that will be of use in his or her own work? Let us stipulate, as they say in law, that this is so. And no doubt there are many cases in which pragmatic bibliography can and should be simply a matter of identifying the appropriate wholesale works and making intelligent use of them. But this is not the general rule; and it is important to be clear that it is not.

Let us focus on the bibliographic work done on their own account by academic research workers. The academic researcher is a member of an academic discipline, interested in some sub-discipline within that discipline, doing work probably confined to one or two specialties within the sub-discipline. Those working in the same specialty form a community, often a tiny community; the other members of the community form the primary audience for any one individual's work. The kind of work one does is likely to be very similar to the kind of work done by others in the same specialty: the kinds of problems selected, the methods used to address the problems, the kinds of solutions considered acceptable, the whole style of work are likely to be shared by most if not all members of the specialty. And what the individual does is done with one eye on the other members of the group; they are the ones who are going to judge the work, and unless it fits their notions of what is interesting and good work, it will be without effect. The community's judgment extends to the use one makes of others' work, and so to the kinds of bibliographic work that will be required.

Now we have to think of particular pieces of pragmatic bibliography as embedded in a continuous process of trying to maintain a satisfactory degree of familiarity with the world of learning. The active research worker is intensely self-centered; what others are doing is of interest primarily as it affects one's own work, and what doesn't affect one's own work can be ignored. Satisfactory familiarity with the world of learning is not familiarity with everything, but with what is likely to affect one's own work.

First, you will want to have, and will have acquired over time, an adequate grasp of the useable past of work in your specialty: not a detailed historian's knowledge of the past, for most of the past might be irrelevant now, but a knowledge of so much as still makes a difference. Second, you will want to be familiar with work that can contribute to your own work, though it is in a quite different area and style. Others may provide intellectual tools that you can use, or theories or evidence or examples that you find helpful, or may simply stimulate your thinking by offering ideas, questions, hypotheses to explore.

Now useful items might be found almost anywhere, and one might think that finding them would be a very arduous job. But in fact you will have an idea of where useable ideas are most likely to be found, and you will ration your attention to various fields according to how likely you think it to be that a field will produce something you can use. One field you will look into very occasionally, not really expecting to find much; another field you will keep an eye on constantly. You do not need to maintain the same degree of familiarity with every field of inquiry. You want to maintain the highest degree of familiarity with work in you own specialty: *expert* familiarity, in the area of your greatest expertise. You want to maintain a *working* familiarity with those lines of inquiry in which useful results are most likely to occur: working familiarity, meaning enough familiarity to allow you to understand what's happening and how it can be used in your own work. And you want to maintain a *nodding* familiarity, a rough idea of what sort of thing is going on, with less promising lines of work. Quite unpromising lines of work you can forget about entirely. So you have a map of the world of research, very detailed in a few parts, fairly detailed in others, sketchy in more, and with large areas left quite blank—labeled "science" or "humanities" or the like, depending on where you are.

Now you maintain the desired degrees of familiarity by reading and talking: scanning, looking at footnotes and references, and sometimes actually reading articles in specialists' journals, general journals, book reviews, or new books; and talking to colleagues. This is a constant monitoring activity, a sort of directed browsing. *And it is against this background of continual monitoring that any piece of pragmatic bibliography is undertaken.* The setting in not one of blind ignorance but of an already-detailed picture of the world of research. That picture is not simply one of who's doing what and who has already done what; it is a highly colored picture of reputations and of social standing, both of ideas and of people. It's a picture of work some of which is now thoroughly discredited and rejected, and some of which is now accepted and admired; it's a picture of activity some of which is thought hopelessly old-fashioned, and some of which is coming into the height of fashion; it's a picture of work some of which is thought trifling and pedestrian, and some of which is thought brilliant. It's a picture in which a few pieces of work occupy a large space and in which most occupy practically no space at all, being eminently forgettable. This highly colored picture of the world of learning guides you when you decide that it would be useful to know more about some part of that world with which you have only a nodding familiarity.

What will you be looking for, and how will you find it? I think librarians tend to believe that what one wants is a complete bibliography of the literature of the new field, the result of a comprehensive literature search. This is a big mistake. You want working familiarity with the results of research, but don't want to have to get it by reading everything. You'll want to start with summaries, reviews, syntheses, overviews that will organize and evaluate the often bewildering mass of original works of research. A single good starting place is what you want: a single good review or summary, which, if it doesn't tell you all you need to know, will direct you to the important parts of the primary literature. You may already have come across such a single good starting place, in the course of your monitoring activity. Or you may be able simply to ask a colleague who is familiar with that literature, and who can be that single good starting place, referring you to specific works in the light of what he or she knows about you as well as about the literature. Whatever you subsequently do is most likely to consist simply of following up footnotes and references. Footnote chasing is *the* preferred method of conducting a bibliographic inquiry.

Librarians often seem to be disappointed or shocked by how little use scholars and scientists make of the apparatus of wholesale bibliography; but no one has shown that the latter's method of bibliographic search, entirely bypassing wholesale bibliography, is always, or usually, or even often worse than reliance on wholesale bibliography. If one tries to educate future specialists to rely on wholesale bibliography, one is trying to get them to do what they won't need to do and probably will prefer not to do.

NON-SPECIALISTS AS SEARCHERS

But not everyone is a specialist doing research, and not everyone is going to be one. Let's turn now to the situation of the non-specialist, not engaged in a continuing line of professional research, but making a single, isolated foray into the published literature to aid in doing some single job. The variety of possible cases is endless; to simplify things, let's think of three degrees of ambition. First take the case of what I will call the Reporter, who simply wants to find out what has been written on some subject, in order to get a picture of what is thought about some matter by those who have explicitly studied it. This is the sort of case for which wholesale bibliography seems intended and most suitable. If we suppose that the ambition is not to discover every last word that has ever been said on the subject—an ambition that the shallow indexing we provide could not satisfy—but simply to find major discussions explicitly directed at the given subject, then judicious use of wholesale bibliography seems just the thing. The most judicious use will still be to look for someone else's summary, if one exists, or someone else's evaluative bibliography giving recommendations for reading in major sources, if one exists. But this is the sort of thing one can do in standard wholesale bibliographic works.

The second case is that of the Commentator, who wants to do the same job as the Reporter but then wants to add a critical appreciation of the situation, a critical evaluation. This opens up new kinds of questions. It calls for adopting some critical stance or position, some basis for criticism. Unless one simply decides to use one's own common sense and already acquired stock of knowledge and opinion and value, it opens up the possibility of searching not for more discussion of the subject of interest but for anything that would provide or suggest a critical position: an ill-defined job for which wholesale bibliography seems hardly promising as an aid. But let's skirt that difficulty and go on to the still more ambitious jobs. For in practice the possibility of searching for new critical positions or principles probably doesn't arise in the mind of the Commentator, who is quite satisfied with the stock of views he or she already has.

Now consider the job of the Investigator, one who proposes a question to the literature and undertakes to see what answer can be given, not simply from what people have said explicitly on the topic, but from whatever they have said on anything that might contribute to an answer. The aim is to satisfy oneself about what *can* be said, using what *has* been said, not only explicitly on the question but on anything that can be seen or made to be relevant to the question. In this kind of case, the texts for which you are looking are texts that are *functionally* related to your question, but they need not be *topically* related. You want material you can use, and the things you can use may well have topics that are apparently quite unrelated to the topic of your question. For example, I recently came upon a paper on misleading metaphors in linguistics that I find enormously useful in understanding certain problems in information science. No train of see-also references could be expected to connect these topics.

If you have to rely on wholesale bibliography, you are having to rely on works whose primary basis of organization is topical when what you want and need is something whose primary basis of organization is functional. Straightforward search strategies, starting from a narrow description of your question and gradually widening it, are not likely to work well. The difficulty of the job is not only that the bibliographic works are not designed to show the kind of functional relations you are interested in. It's that the job is an intrinsically ill-defined, even indeterminate one. The job of the pragmatic Investigator is one that is, as often as not, tentative, exploratory, experimental. One's notions of what one is looking for change in the process of looking. One's ideas of possible uses change, as one learns more, through successes or failures. One thing leads to another, in unforeseeable ways. And it would often be better to speak of *making* things useful than of finding them useful. One makes connections, constructs bridges. Spotting potentially useful texts is very much an exercise of imagination and insight. And it's much dependent on luck, and on timing: a work found at the beginning of a search may have no apparent relevance at all, while if found toward the end, it would have large and obvious relevance. And the job is an open-ended one; there is usually no clear stopping point; a pragmatic search of this Investigative kind could go on forever, and does not go on only because it is pragmatic, subject to the limits of time and energy allotted to the job.

There is a further crucial problem in this kind of bibliography. Having spotted a text that one thinks one could use, the question remains: but should one use it? Can it be trusted? Will it bear the weight I want to place on it? We tend to assume that this must be decided solely by evaluation of the text on its own terms, by a kind of internal criticism: by examining the methodology, the technique, the strengths and weaknesses of the arguments, and so on. But this is certainly not the whole story even for the mature scholar, and cannot be the whole story for the non-specialist. Everyone is an outsider to most subjects of study and relies on the word of others as to whether something can be trusted, taken seriously, relied on or not. Of course this crucial question of reliability, of cognitive standing, is not something that wholesale bibliography can help us to answer; the whole-salers are neutral, noncommittal. So having to rely on wholesale bibliography would mean having to rely on what was arranged the wrong way and unhelpful about the value of the things it listed.

SPECIALISTS VS. FREE SPIRITS

I have intentionally pictured this sort of bibliographic job as one that is ill-defined, ill-structured, chancy, risky, messy. And so it often is, at least in my own experience. But there are two ways of approaching the job, and one of them simplifies it considerably. You can try to do this job as if you were a member of a specialist group, trying to imitate their ways; or you can do it as a free spirit, an independent operator not interested in imitating the conventions and prejudices of a particular specialist group. Graduate students certainly, and undergraduate students sometimes, want to take the first approach: to act as novice specialists. If they can discover the cognitive map of the world of research that is shared by members of the specialist group they want to imitate, they will know where to look for useable materials and what kinds of materials are considered useable; and if they can discover the social standing of the ostensibly useable materials they find—the reputation of an author or of a particular text, the views of the insiders about the acceptability or unacceptability of the work—they can safely accept or reject it. The aim of the novice specialist is not to exercise his or her own judgment, but to get it to conform to that of the specialists; and that is the aim of specialists as well, in their role as teachers. The initial stages of education, which can last well into graduate school, are enforcement of conformity; only after one has shown that one has learned the rules of the game and correctly applies socially accepted ideas of what is good and bad can one be set free to exercise one's own judgment, now properly molded. Though this is not the way either specialists or novices would put the matter, the initially ill-defined task of Investigative bibliography can be made relatively manageable if the novice can attain the narrow-mindedness of the specialist: the specialist's views about what can be entirely ignored and what is most promising.

The free spirit, the independent operator, is clearly in a different position. He too wants to have a cognitive map of the world of research, wants to figure out where to look for useable materials and whether he dare use what he finds. But these things he has to decide and discover for himself, not by imitating so far as possible the attitudes and practices of a particular specialist group. When it comes to selection, the novice will try to guess at the received view; the independent will decide for himself. Note that there are no universal canons of utility and value that the independent investigator can apply; there are no universal "methods of research" for him to learn. Rather, different specialties have different and wildly various notions of what the value of other people's work is and how and where it can be used. If you put yourself outside the ranks of any particular specialty, there is nothing to hang on to in the way of universal standards. This is a dizzying situation, avoided by those who attach themselves as novices to a particular specialty. Life is simpler inside than outside.

If, as I claim, wholesale bibliography is not well suited, because of its topical arrangement and value-neutrality, to the work of the Investigative bibliographer, what use *can* he make of it? Sustained and systematic use of the wholesale bibliographies is often, I think, a great waste of time; but a series of brief *raids* into them, exploring different fields, approaches, leads, possibilities, will often be smart strategy. A long and systematic search may be pointless, where a quick raid, getting out as fast as possible with a few references that may provide further leads, may be rewarding. What the active researcher accumulates over years of directed browsing cannot be accumulated briefly by novice or independent; but perhaps the best alternative, or one good alternative, is to move rapidly from one bibliography to another, briefly sampling, tasting, and trying to enlarge one's sense of structure and possibility, and finding the occasional reference that may itself lead one in a rewarding direction.

IMPLICATIONS FOR BIBLIOGRAPHIC INSTRUCTION

I draw no firm conclusions from all this about the final utility of wholesale bibliography; but I am led in two directions: first, toward thinking that novice specialists have to get their more advanced bibliographic instruction from specialists, and this they will get not by explicit instruction but by osmosis; second, toward thinking that librarians really do have something to offer the independent Investigator beyond the most elementary introduction to bibliographic work. Because they are not committed to any specialist line on the organization of research or the utility of work done by this or that group to the answering of particular questions, librarians may be the best able of any group to help people orient themselves to novel situations and explore unknown territories. If they can suppress their tendencies to think in terms of making complete, topically oriented bibliographies, and keep firmly in mind that the ideal form of bibliographic organization is functional and not topical, they may help the independent Investigator learn to make effective, fast, and light-handed use of unwieldy instruments. And *that* would be well worth trying to do.

Section IV

An Integrative View of the Field

11

External Memory

Howard D. White

INTRODUCTION

A fundamental problem of all human societies is how to keep useful information from being lost. Technologically advanced societies have dealt with this problem by developing complex systems that externalize memory beyond the limits of individual minds. Vast amounts of information are now externalized and stored, but problems of finding and sharing *useful* information remain. They require human intervention and mediation in systems that are social as well as technological. The field of information studies adopts an interdisciplinary approach to understand these systems, to prepare people to take part in them, and to contribute to their improvement.

What follows are sketches on the nature and interdisciplinary relations of this ("our") field, specifically for those identifying as information specialists, present or prospective.

A THEME FOR INFORMATION STUDIES

In order to define information studies, it is useful to bracket, for the time being, the multiple meanings of terms like "information system" and to look for one with high cogency. There are reasons why different specializations exist within the field, and reasons why they nevertheless belong within it and not elsewhere. Thus, the discussion should account for major divisions of subject matter, but should also show the distinctive nature of information studies vis-à-vis other disciplines.

A major division in information studies lies between library and information science (L&IS) and information systems (IS). Both fields are equally affected by the state of the art in computing and in telecommunications, so that is not a difference. In practice, both fields deploy resources—certainly including human beings—to answer questions or satisfy interests (a) routinely (b) for a range of customers (c) by design. Both fields have a common intellectual core in the technology of databases. (Important fore-runners of databases are, on the "library" side, printed reference works and, on the "systems" side, office forms and files.) Both fields apply (and to some degree contribute to) the arts of systems analysis and operations research. Both have a direct interest in cognitive psychology (the discipline that studies attention, learning, memory—human "information processing" generally); and in the types of research sketched in such books as Gardner's (1985) *The Mind's New Science* and Machlup and Mansfield's (1983) *The Study of Information*. Again, these are commonalities, not differences.

Perhaps the chief commonality is that, unlike cognitive psychology, both fields are concerned with *external memory*—that is, with the creation, organization, and use of messages or performances stored in durable media other than the memories of living persons. In other words, they are concerned with *records*. Etymologically, a *record* re-brings something to mind (literally, to heart [Latin, *cor*]); compare Fellini's film title *Amarcord*—"I remember," and the old expression for memorization, "to get something by heart." A record is an externally stored, content-bearing memory. The biologist J. Z. Young (1971) uses "extra-somatic memory" for this notion. The phrase "external memory," which has the same sense, is briefly discussed in Herbert Simon's (1981)*The Sciences of the Artificial*. It is also evoked by "Memex," Vannevar Bush's 1945 name for a device that has remained a vision of L&IS ever since; and, more recently, by the product whose advertising asks, "Is it live or is it Memorex?"

External memory is a phrase rich with implications. Properly understood, it sums up the subject matter of information systems, library and information science, archival science, and, to some degree, communications studies. (More on this in closing.) It also suggests a complementary relation to cognitive psychology, in which the study of *internal memory* (and its cognates learning, representation, imaging, imagining, etc.) is paramount. Persons in information studies are not cognitive psychologists, but we share their further links to workers in cognitive science—in artificial intelligence and certain areas of philosophy, linguistics, and anthropology. Indeed, the notion of "memory" is implicated in all of science and scholarship—in all of human culture!—so it is no wonder that we are inherently interdisciplinary, not to say overextended.

From the viewpoint of the individual in literate societies, there are *two* forms of external memory—that of other people, which we might call social or collective memory; and that stored through human artifice in records. Social memory—that is, other people regarded as stocks of knowledge, lore, and opinion—is of the utmost importance; it is the source to which most persons, including the very learned, turn most often when uncertainties arise, as countless studies in IS and L&IS attest. One way of putting it (Wilson, 1977) is that, for most persons, sources of information other than people are not a *main stock,* but a *reserve stock,* to be used only when necessary (and often not then). Nonetheless, while fully recognizing the importance of social memory in their accounts of the world, IS and L&IS are irrevocably committed to understanding and improving the performance of the other, more refractory kind—the kind stored in graphic records. Unless otherwise noted, "external memory" will refer to the latter kind throughout this essay.

For a very long time, the *only* way to store cultural information outside one's own body was to establish folk traditions and technologies that would pass by word of mouth or physical example. With the invention of writing, speech itself became artifactual, existing outside the speaker and possessing properties of durability and transferability independent of the speaker's own memory. With the invention of printing, these properties were greatly extended; if copies can be indefinitely multiplied, a record's chances for survival—and for being influential—are greatly increased. The advent of various forms of telecommuncations increased transferability—that is, external memory's physical range. Finally, the computer changed external memory from relatively static to relatively dynamic. The actual content of the stored messages could be operated on, as long as the operations were well understood and completely specifiable. It could also be transformed into new messages more quickly than with the earlier technologies of writing and printing—so much so as to produce a qualitative change in the nature of human capabilities.

The fields of computer science and artificial intelligence are presently engaged in externalizing as many human intellectual capabilities as possible by embodying them in software and hardware. With their focus on external memory, information systems and library and information science are part of this larger enterprise. However, IS and L&IS, like the older field of librarianship, are unique in regarding external memory not just as a receptacle to be filled, or a set of processes to be abstractly modeled, but as a vast repository of pre-existing *content*—as recorded language, sound, and pictures. The external memory addressed by L&IS is exceedingly rich; in fact, it is coextensive with all areas of human culture—science, history, art, *The Poky Little Puppy,* everything. Moreover, the two fields regard this content as grist for a technology, which is to say, under human control for useful ends.

As an ultimate technological goal, IS and L&IS seek to convert content-bearing records into something resembling actual human memory. They seek, that is, an instrument outside any person, yet with the mind's supple capacity for replacing outdated with current messages and for producing content on demand. In familiar terms, these are capacities for *forgetting, remembering,* and *answering.* Since the facticity of records is what drives IS and L&IS, they do not attempt to design external memory that is largely content-free; that is left to more abstract specialties within computer engineering and computer science. Rather, they grapple continually with content: how to represent it in brief compass, how to marshal it, how to make it yield itself up. The criteria for success lie, shiftingly, in the internal memories of persons for whom external memories are designed. It is these persons who furnish the interrogative prompts—the interests and questions—that activate systems beyond their own bodies, and it is their powers that external memory systems are supposed to amplify.

For many centuries there was a technology for strengthening *internal* memory by artificial means—the so-called "mnemotechnics" that goes back through Cicero (106-43 B.C.) to Simonides (*ca.* 556-468 B.C.). As cultivated by public speakers, this consisted of associating images of subject matter *(res)* with recallable places *(loci)*—for example, the rooms of a building—such that an imaginary stroll through the building recapitulated the desired order of the subjects and helped one order one's points in a speech. (The Greek word *topoi,* originally "places," came to mean "subject-places"—our word *topics*—through mnemotechnics.) The historian of this tradition, Francis A. Yates (1966), says that, while it ceased to exert much of an influence in Europe in the 17th century, both Bacon and Leibniz studied it. (It had grown very elaborate, and persists in some forms to this day.) Leibniz is usefully symbolic in this regard, because, in his own lifetime, as both a librarian and encyclopedist, he participated in the crossover from oral culture and old-style "mnemotechnics" to print culture and the new technologies of external memory—17th century L&IS.[1]

Leibniz is said to have been the last genius to have mastered all contemporary knowledge. But, under the information explosion of the times, even he spent much effort in devising what would now be called schemes for information retrieval—for example, a classification scheme for books. The old mode of arranging one's topics in an imaginary building inside one's head gave way to ideas, such as his, for grouping real volumes by topic in a real building, the library; and to providing various alphabetical indexes as additional finding tools.

---

[1] Influenced by the mnemotechnic tradition, Leibniz devised a notation to accompany abstracts of published works, research in progress, etc.—the whole to form a cumulative encyclopedia, synthesizing all knowledge—and it was in manipulating this notation that he invented the infinitesmal calculus. A later encyclopedic genius, George Bernard Shaw, put great energy into a more barren invention, a phonetic alphabet for English.

If the subject matter of the fields IS and L&IS can be reduced to a phrase, it might be something like "relations between persons and external memory." (Even that is wordy; "external memory" implies "internal memory," which implies "persons"; but let it go.) Such a formulation differentiates information studies from the disciplines that bracket the *content* of external memory, or that do not see that content in terms of a technology of remembering, forgetting, and answering. Cognitive psychologists working on internal memory, learning, and so on, generally ignore the reality of the vast external memory. The artificial intelligence community, working on externalizing human problem solving ability, pattern recognition, speech recognition, and so on, remains unconcerned with the already-existing external memory stores per se. Only IS and L&IS address the problems and properties of external memory as a store already incalculably large and growing, which no person and no group of persons can know in its entirety, but from which various contents (sometimes called "sources" or "resources") must be retrieved on demand.

It is the content-laden nature of the two fields, particularly L&IS, that puts off formalists of all stripes. Formalists want to manipulate abstract, general models (the more content-neutral, the better) and the librarians' side of L&IS keeps bringing in *existing literatures*, with all their unparsimonious particulars—even to the point of insisting that external memory includes stories and folktales that are best retrieved through telling rather than reading. Thus one may see such odd conjunctions as a course in "Database Management" and a course in "Folk Literature and the Oral Tradition" in a single L&IS curriculum.

Anthropologists, for their part, might call what I have called *content* "symbolic and expressive culture," "mentifacts," or "the ideational superstructure," and they would study it as they find it in a particular society. But they do not see it primarily under the metaphor of memory, with the concomitant responsibility of being able to retrieve it on demand; they lack the "engineering side" of IS and L&IS. Their nearest approximation to a content retrieval system currently is the Human Relations Area Files, which, one gathers, many anthropologists relegate to whatever part of external memory corresponds to the Unconscious.[2]

---

[2] There are many suggestive parallels between the internal memory of an individual and artificial, externalized memory, and they should be pursued for all they are worth, particularly as a schema for making sense of our rather diffuse field. But I do not see either as an exact model of the other. Artificial memory in records is in many ways closer to what I called social memory—the memories of all persons other than oneself—than it is to one's own memory as an individual. For example, it shares the vastness and multiplicity of social memory—the diversity of content that includes much that is not now and never will be inside any one person's head. How far parallels between internal and external memory can be pressed—for example, whether, except as a joke, external memory can be meaningfully

REMEMBERING WORLD 3

The "engineering side" of IS and L&IS can be characterized in a way that may reveal them in a new light. The philosopher Karl Popper (1972) argues persuasively that the world of human mentifacts—externally stored content—has a life of its own, independent of the lives of human individuals. He calls this *World 3*, in contrast to

> *World 1,* the physical world, and
> *World 2,* the world of subjective experience.

World 3 he identifies particularly with such things as mathematical theorems and scientific explanations embodied in written form; World 3 contains not only them but also their *implications,* even if the latter have not yet been discovered by any human observer. Popper also refers to World 3 as *objective knowledge.* John Ziman's (1968) account of science as *public knowledge*—knowledge externalized in records even if it presently exists in no one's head—is similar. The idea can be extended to include other stored forms of human expression, from the very utilitarian, like telephone numbers and stock quotations, to the supreme triumphs of religion, science, music, literature, art. Popper's World 3 objects are what many in L&IS would call *works*—abstract intellectual entities that nevertheless, as he points out, have histories and that interact with both the physical world and the world of subjective experience.[3]

Now, suppose we ask an innocent question, "Where is World 3?" Where, for instance, is Mozart's Jupiter Symphony? Where is the Pythagorean theorem? Well, everywhere and nowhere; such things as symphonies and theorems exist independently of any particular realization of them. But they do have embodiments in World 1, the physical world. The Jupiter Symphony is realized not only in performances; it is stored as potential music in recordings and scores. The Pythagorean theorem is stored not only in people's heads (World 2), but externally in, for example, a copy of Euclid's *Elements,* a copy of Jacob Bronowski's *The Ascent of Man* (book or videotape version), a copy of the movie *The Wizard of Oz* (it is what the Scarecrow recites when he gets a brain). These occupy physical space and can be located, even to the point of being given spatial coordinates. So can World 3 objects that

---

said to have an "Unconscious"—remains to be seen. It is, however, provocative to extend Freudian terminology so as to think of external memory as the "Postconscious" (a coinage I do not find in the psychological literature). One is reminded, for example, that censorship of certain "postconscious" materials by society bears a well known resemblance to repression of "unconscious" materials by the individual. What other interesting resemblances might emerge?

[3] Fuller interpretations of Popper's relevance to L&IS will be found in Brookes (1980), Neill (1982), and Swanson (1986).

are merely utilitarian, such as telephone numbers, want-ads, and nurses' notes on types of baths given to hospitalized patients. *A major "engineering" task of IS and L&IS is the mapping of World 3 objects onto World 1 in such a way that they can be found when wanted, on presentation of a World 2 description.*

Less cumbrously, if external memory is to work *as memory*, it requires not only records but a control system for remembering where the records are—their addresses. It also requires that the control system respond to the query langauge of the questioner or translate it into language it can accept. These are things that human answerers can do more or less at will when asked the proper question. However, to get external or artificial memory to do them requires human enterprise on an ongoing basis. External memory can be seen as an automaton that performs only some of the functions of a human respondent. While it can retain, perfectly, much more than any person, it is helpless when asked to supply an answer not anticipated by its designers.[4]

The content of the "main stocks" of external memory is largely a given—*data* in the root sense—for IS and L&IS; it is whatever human beings from all walks of life want to retain. Beyond all else, IS and L&IS are concerned with the *control* systems of external memory; their "ongoing enterprise" is to render accessible the content (or data) supplied by others. In some cases practitioners from the two fields design and create such systems; in others, they study, evaluate, or use existing arrangements for control.

In *The Society of Mind* Marvin Minsky (1985, p. 158) posits equivalent control systems in individual persons: they consist, he says, of "memory-control memories" that coordinate the "flow of information" among short-term and long-term memory units. To do this, the control systems have to respond, in some measure, to commands—either their owner's or those of other persons. How they do so remains a mystery. All we can say is that they deploy and re-deploy content from short-term and long-term stores so that persons can do such things as answer questions.

When we leave individual heads for the realm of external memory, the control systems become explicit: we can see them as structures, often very large, made of language—the "verbal matrixes" I wrote of earlier. (Studying them may not be easy because of their large size.) In traditional systems, the language structures are ordered records (or ordered descriptions of records) and indication of their whereabouts; instructions for human searchers and updaters may also be present. (These instructions always leave unsaid much of what actually goes on as human beings work.) In newer, automated control systems, the descriptive and locative statements remain, but part of the human capability in updating or searching—the ability to scan, to match

---

[4] Unless, of course, questioners are clever: as a new task for online information retrieval Swanson (1990) has proposed that we search World 3 for logically related scientific claims that have common natural language, but that are *not* linked by citations because the propounders themselves are unaware of the implications of their ideas.

search keys, to accept or reject items on the basis of editorial criteria, and so on—has been stated in such detail that it can be transferred, through programming, to the computer, which can simulate (and improve on) more human intellectual skills than any other device.

It will be evident that the last remark characterizes present-day database technology. Although a variety of technologies contribute to the design of external memory (e.g., reprography, telecommunications, ergonomics), database technology seems clearly central at this time. It does not merely model data structures in the abstract, nor merely convert operations on these structures into algorithms; it gives one control of actual content by making it producible. Both IS and L&IS draw on it; they gain their unity from using it in common. L&IS, for example, uses it to organize our records of publications (which are themselves records) and to produce answers about them; when "bibliographic control" is mentioned, the ability to answer standard questions about publications is what is meant. Skills vital to traditional librarianship—the ability to create and use catalogs, bibliographies, and reference works—and these physical products themselves are immediately intelligible now as parts of database technology. (The fact that "memory-control systems" in librarianship, such as card catalogs, have so long been implemented with *print* technology should not obscure the current reality.) IS, for its part, uses database technology to organize records of everything *besides* publications (and sometimes them as well); it can be thought of as "general records control" or "general large-file management."

Neither IS nor L&IS is exclusively confined to database technology, of course. Both employ other technologies now, and may gravitate to new ones in the future. However, the set of concepts and skills associated with databases defines the current state of the art in the "external memory professions," and so should be the foundation of any curriculum that trains practitioners to enter them.[5] This common foundation is the rationale for offering courses in both IS and L&IS within one professional school or college. Nor is the commonality unremarked: it is the reason that many leading schools of *librarianship* (or library science) have added courses, first, in *information science* and, later, in *information systems* over the past 25 years.

WHY "EXTERNAL MEMORY"?

Above, I have often used "content" in preference to "information," and "external memory" in preference to "information system." There is a reason. Information in the strict sense should be *truthful* content. An ideal information system delivers answers that are not only meaningful, new, complete,

---

[5] For a corroborating independent account, see the chapter "Electronic Memory" in Bolter (1984).

concise, and relevant to one's request, but true as well. External memory may contain such answers, and if so, it contains information, in the strong sense of factual statements or accurate representations. But, like our own internal memories, it also contains untold numbers of opinions, untested beliefs, speculations, fictions, lies, mistakes, statements no longer factual, inaccurate representations, jokes, folklore, poems, sermons, fantasies, and so on. Beyond that, it implicitly contains all that can be inferred from these. A system for retrieving any of these things has virtually the same design features as one for retrieving "information" in the strict sense of factual statements. Unless we have control over the input such that we can assure its veracity—no mean feat—*a misinformation system cannot be distinguished from an information system.* And in fact, in IS and L&IS we rarely design a system that separates out pure information from misinformation (or opinion or nonsense or whatever); we only design systems that retrieve mixtures. In other words, we design and use *memory* systems. Some of these may approximate pure or ideal information systems—for example, displays of flight schedules in airports—but many of them retrieve messages that lack truth, novelty, relevance, and so on, or that even intentionally mislead (disinformation systems). Others retrieve messages that we value for reasons other than informativeness—for example, as entertainment. One can call anything retrieved "information"—many do—but that further scatters the sense of a word already quite various in meaning.

It is also, incidentally, a word beloved by writers of cant. For example, when one reads high-sounding statements like *"Information is a resource that must be managed,"* one naturally asks, "How? In what ways?" A plain answer (by no means typical) would be: "Hide some things and let others be widely known. Keep some things and get rid of others." These are old-fashioned matters of access and retention. If we add, "Tell the truth—unless it seems better to lie," we have added quality control, and given three essentials of what is now called information resources management.

So put, it will be seen that IRM has been practiced throughout history. People have always decided who should have access to what and for how long. The only novelty is to back them up with database technology and seek new titles for them as managers in corporations. One of the charms of the term "external memory" is that it may re-focus the thought of those given to phrases in which "information" has become very nearly meaningless.

THE WORD "INFORMATION"

Although all sense data can be called "information," this usage includes vast amounts of data that simply convey *maintenance, continuity of states, little or no change.* Often we reserve the term "information" for *that which changes what the recipient knows or believes.* The word "news" (and the seldom-heard "tidings," cognate to German *Zeitung*, "newspaper") usually has this sense; there is no direct antonym, such as "olds," for the unchanging. Information (news, tidings) alters memory, the recipient's internal image or representation of the world, with greater or lesser impact (cf. Boulding, 1961). All information, including misinformation and fiction, does this: for example, our image may be changed as much, at least initially, by a message that misleads us as by one that does not. (A *novel* is a kind of news, as its name implies—*imaginary news;* those familiar with the conventions of fiction would give it special status as "information," but some would still hold that a novel can mislead—i.e., worsen the behavior or attitudes even of those who do not believe it literally true.) Marilyn Levine (1977) has tried to measure the impact of new information on people's images in units she calls "whomps." B. C. Brookes (1980) holds that if we could actually take the difference (Δ) between an earlier knowledge state (KS_1) and a later, higher knowledge state (KS_2), we would have a measure of cognitive impact—that is, information—and be able to solve the fundamental equation of information science, $\Delta = KS_2 - KS_1$. Obviously, we are far from being able to plug in numeric values.

A more specialized use of the word "information" is *that which reduces uncertainty.* If one has a more or less structured set of expectations, one's uncertainty is reduced by learning which of the expectable messages has been received.[6] Of course, the message might be simply that some state of affairs has continued, but even that reduces uncertainty when continuity is in doubt. Thus it is informative to have one's expectation of *no change* confirmed (for example, about a flight time or an illness) even if notice of change would have more impact still. "No news" then becomes merely a special case of "news," in the sense above.

We are not, however, mere receivers of information; we are senders as well, through speech, writing, and other communicative acts. External memory may be altered by our output, just as internal memory may be altered by what we take in. In the present context, it is tempting to regard information as *the medium of exchange between internal and external memory*—as a two-way (or multi-way) flow—though the formulation is vague. External memory here would include both social memory (other people) and artificial memory (records).

In information studies we generally further restrict the term "information" to *symbolic data,* particularly the data of language. Yet another restriction is that we usually mean symbolic data stored in a durable

---

[6] An airless literature stemming from the work of communications engineer Claude Shannon illustrates this notion with examples that allow uncertainty reduction to be measured in bits. These examples usually involve receiving a message from a finite set of messages whose probabilities are known: information in this sense is maximized when all messages are equally probable, and hence equally uncertain.

medium—for example, language or numbers stored in print or electronically. Other forms of symbolic expression can be similarly stored, such as pictures on film and sound on phonorecordings, and these, too, would readily be called "information" although they are not propositional. We do not by any means rule out human memory as a durable storage medium; we recognize ourselves and other persons as important sources of information, frequently the most important, as noted above. But the term "information" tends to imply to us symbolic expression stored outside the human body through artificial means.

Information (of the sort we mean) often inheres in statements or propositions. According to Wilson's (1978) "Some Fundamental Concepts of Information Retrieval," propositional information in the *weak* sense includes statements (or other representations) that are *about* a topic of interest, whether true or in some way less than true (e.g., misinformation, fiction, disinformation, unfounded opinion). I may consider myself informed about, say, Robert F. Kennedy or Salt Lake City, even though some of what I think I know is dubious or false. Information in Wilson's *strong* sense comprises statements with high truth value or warranty.

The following conditions characterize "incoming" propositional information, even in the weak sense. It is:

- *meaningful*—intelligible statements about something (real or imaginary) in the world.
- *new* to the recipient (or, more likely, a complex mixture of new and old).
- *relevant* to the recipient's question or interest. The supposition here is that data *become* information by being marshalled on behalf of the questioner or interessee. The person can be thought of as a "directed consciousness" actively seeking certain kinds of input and ignoring others; no such person, no information. There are also logical relationships between question and answer, or between interest and satisfaction, and they must hold if we are to speak of information as being relevant.[7]

---

[7] The best brief account of relevance will be found in Wilson's (1978) "Some Fundamental Concepts of Information Retrieval." His "Situational Relevance" (Wilson, 1973) and *Two Kinds of Power* (1968, chap. 3) are also rewarding. He notes that while "relevant" in one sense means "bearing as evidence for or against a claim," that sense is not usually what is meant in information retrieval. If if were, relevance would be objectively determinable. In information retrieval, however, "relevant" simply means "retrieval-worthy," based on a customer's subjective criteria. This raises the question, how can a document be judged *not relevant*, as is often the case, if its indexing matches the customer's search terms exactly? The answer lies in the endless ambiguities of search terms. They often can be taken in multiple senses both singly and in combination—for example, the combination "Theft" and "Social Surveys" from Chapter 4. The customer using these terms in an online search would want what *she* means by the pair—perhaps surveys of victims of thefts. But that may not be the sense in which, with equal legitimacy, an *indexer* used the pair—perhaps to cover a survey of

Propositional information in the strong sense is, further:

- *true,* in the case of closed questions. This could be modified somewhat to include degrees of epistemic standing, such as "highly probable."
- *authoritative,* in the case of open questions. By strict test, this would be opinion or judgment that events confirm; a more lenient test might be whether an opinion is useful or fruitful.[8]

Information *systems,* as understood here, routinely answer questions and satisfy interests; somewhat more unpredictably they may generate new questions and interests. A typical systems design involves persons acting as informants for other persons under shared rules or conventions as to types of information legitimately provided. "Bibliographic" (or "documentary") information systems more or less satisfy interests by providing pointers as to what to read. "Factual" information systems give more or less warranted answers to questions of limited and generally foreseeable kinds. The answers are propositions as described above (unless they are pictorial, musical, etc.), but the requirement that they be true is difficult to meet consistently.

INFORMATION SYSTEMS VS. LIBRARY AND INFORMATION SCIENCE

Having offered a sketch of what unifies IS and L&IS, I turn now to some ways in which they are separate. Where do the differences lie?

One might ask initially why the name "information systems" is reserved for just one field, since L&IS obviously deals with information systems also, as do other specialties, such as mass communications. The answer is that "IS" has a restricted sense when used to mean a field of practice and study; it does not cover every sort of system associated with informing people. For example, when Peter G. W. Keen (1987) writes: "The mission of Information Systems research is to study *the effective design, delivery, use and impact of information technologies in organisations and society,*" it is clear that he is not speaking primarily of research on television, non-fiction publishing, newspaper journalism, film documentaries, school media centers, or radio talk shows. IS exponents and practitioners use "information systems" to mean computers and related technologies such as telecommunications, in the

---

thieves, or a scandal involving thousands of completed questionnaires stolen from a national pollster. Presumably the customer would reject documents on the latter topics as irrelevant—not "retrieval-worthy"—even though their indexing exactly matched her search terms.

[8] On open and closed questions and on "authoritative" statements, see Wilson (1983), subtitled *An Inquiry into Cognitive Authority.*

service of organizations. (These may be private or public, profit or non-profit, but the dominant impression is one of large, complex bodies in which coordinating the work of many specialists is a major endeavor.) IS personnel are typically links between less technical and highly technical staff (or the machines themselves); they may also liaise with customers. IS personnel may be called analysts, designers, programmers, managers, coordinators, or whatever, but they are not usually thought of as "media people," oriented toward audiences or publics. Within organizations, those who *are* thought of in this way, such as writers, editors, press agents, technical information specialists, photographers, layout artists, librarians, etc., belong to "information systems" of a different order—those of the world of *publication*. And here we reach the great divide.[9]

L&IS is primarily oriented toward *publication* as a social institution and toward individual publications. The latter by their very nature transcend individuals and organizations; they are meant to be available "anywhere" and to "anyone." IS, in contrast, is primarily oriented toward *sources of information within organizations*—sources not published beyond organizational limits and perhaps restricted even further, such as memos, correspondence, working papers, and reports; likewise—in typical databases—records of employees, equipment, inventory, production, billings, purchases, suppliers, customers, competitors, and funders. These unpublished sources are not necessarily proprietary or confidential or personal—although they may be—but their content is not put abroad for "everyone," often because it would lack external interest (except perhaps to competitors). In some cases—relatively few—their content may be destined for publication, although not yet released. Such sources may be viewed as forms of intra-organizational intelligence, marshalled by staff to help the organization carry out its objectives.

When only print technology is available, these sources are often, in effect, in-house "reference works" (that is, meant to be consulted in part rather than read in full), produced by employees of the organization. When computer technology is available, they are still "reference works," but of a more dynamic sort: more quickly updated, more readily transformable into new arrangements, and thus new, customized products. Typically nowadays

---

[9] As a rule, corporate librarians and information specialists deal with publications from outside the organization (sometimes by organization members as well), while the others usually *produce* publications for internal or external audiences. The contrasting emphasis of IS is shown by Buckingham et al (1987). In their 120-page description of a 44-course [British] curriculum in this area, Buckingham et al. allude only briefly to publications—either those generated within the organization, such as house organs and newsletters, or those generated outside it. Much the same can be said of model information systems curricula of the [U.S.] Association for Computing Machinery and the Data Processing Managers Assocation, discussed by Davis (1987) in the same volume.

they are in-house databases, perhaps conjoined with software that, for example, simulates human reasoning powers in giving advice under complex contingencies (expert systems) or answers questions of the "what if?" type (decision-support systems). Some databases, of course, are useful beyond organizational bounds, and the lure of profits (or at least cost-recovery) may lead to their publication.

With its emphasis on publications—on works that, as a rule, pass through a process of editorial quality control before release to the world—L&IS tends to be oriented toward content that is quite *stable* over time, as far as individual works or records are concerned, whether they are published in print or electronically. Updating occurs by adding items to (and, more rarely, deleting items from) an over-all stock. The bibliographic files that mirror the world's publications, a major intellectual concern of L&IS, are a good example: they are updated through addition and deletion of records. Information *within* bibliographic records is changed relatively seldom—in many instances, never—once it is entered. The major problem, since bibliographic files are often very large, is finding what one wants. Hence the importance of various kinds of indexing—by subject, author, title, publisher, and so on—that the earlier chapters of this book have stressed. Since publications can be considered the permanent memory of humankind, it is obviously important to be able to retrieve them, under various indexing, on demand; and L&IS has a long history of work on this problem.

In contrast, IS deals, to a greater degree than L&IS, with sources that are internally *volatile* in content—updated not only by the addition and deletion of records but by actual change of content within fields of those records (or even change of the fields themselves)—for example, in payrolls, parts inventories, balance sheets, transaction accounts, schedules, and personnel files. The major problem with this sort of source is keeping the data both accurate and current. The various forms of normalization taught in database management courses become important when one is dealing with volatile files.

As the phrase beginning "payrolls, parts inventories..." suggests, IS deals with sources having many different units of analysis. So, however, does L&IS: the reference works in libraries are highly varied in the kinds of entities they refer to—people, places, organizations, events, words, and so on. Hence their common reliance on database technology, which is quite inclusive in the types of entities it call handle. The difference is one of emphasis. More than any other field, library and information science concerns itself with sources having publications (or their parts) as the unit of analysis—with *bibliographic* sources. While IS can accommodate bibliographic data—many information systems in the real world do—information systems *as a field* de-emphasizes this part of external memory, possibly because so many of the people whom IS serves, such as executives and managers, want immediate answers to their questions rather than references to other writings. Their tolerance for extended searching and reading tends (like many people's) to be low.

The in-house records of organizations do not get published unless they are associated with some kind of news story (in which case they may be stolen or "leaked"). IS thus confronts, to a greater degree than L&IS, problems of privacy and security of data. Much of the data with which IS deals is not only unpublished, it is not meant to be published. It is meant to be used in-house, perhaps by only a predesignated few. In addition to the usual restrictions on who may change the content of a file, there may be further restrictions on who may look at the file, in whole or in part. If it is available throughout the organization, there still may be conditions for release of data to outsiders. This, of course, is the antithesis of publication, which involves lifting all restrictions on who may have access to a copy.[10]

There is one area, however, in which IS personnel may be highly involved with publications—that of *published software*. While IS personnel must keep up with new software in any case, the need is intensified if they belong to an organization moving from centralized data processing to decentralized end-user computing (as is common nowadays): they may be called on to help end users adopt software effectively. Some librarians and information specialists also do this, and so the line between IS and L&IS may appear blurred. Typically, however, persons in IS would work with more specialized and advanced clienteles (for example, adult engineers as opposed to students). It remains true, too, that practitioners in L&IS still devote most of their attention to publications other than software.

ACCESS

Other contrasts between IS and L&IS could be drawn, but enough has been said to show that the two fields divide on the degree of accessibility of records they handle. Access is a dominant theme in any discussion of external memory, just as it is in discussions of internal memory. For example, only some of the contents and operations of our own minds are accessible. Moreover, not being in telepathic communication with others, we can know "who knows what" in relatively few cases, and, in those, only a fraction of

---

[10] Libraries, ideologically oriented toward publication, open access, freedom of information, and the anti-censorship position, nevertheless are organizations in their own right, with their own jealously guarded in-house files. One of these is the circulation file: many libraries will not release records of who borrowed what to outsiders, even powerful outsiders like the FBI. All of what I have said about IS, in fact, holds true for IS in libraries; it should not be supposed that they differ from any other type of organization in their need for and use of internal, unpublished data to carry out their goals.

what they know. Our access to external records—through browsing, searching, reading, watching, listening, etc.—is similarly partial and circumscribed.

Expressions like "physical access" and "intellectual access" pervade writings in IS and L&IS. Intellectual access to works is provided by indexing, about which a great deal has already been said; it is independent of their physical placement. Physical access has to do with where, and under what conditions, recorded works are available. It is grounded in social agreements (and controversies), but these give rise to real spatial distributions: not-yet-published or deliberately unpublished records are typically found in one place (or at most a few places), whereas published records are typically found in many places. Publication, in other words, involves not just making copies from a master but their geographic dispersal.

Thus we can meaningfully speak of and study a geography of access, and relate both IS and L&IS to the field of human geography, in which social and spatial data coincide. Because so many human variables have spatial coordinates, human geography overlaps all the other social and behavioral sciences (even cognitive psychology, as in studies of mental maps and environmental perception). Its overlap with IS and L&IS—and external memory—becomes clear as we consider such questions as "Who should have access to a particular work? How can a particular work be distributed usefully? Justly? Profitably?" These questions are inseparable from the physical placement of works, which rests, in turn, on number of copies (from one to many millions). The more dispersed the copies, the less control on further copiability and general use. Elaborate social arrangements—security clearance systems, editorial gatekeepers, copyright laws, price and fee mechanisms, censorship boards, etc.—are made to preserve differential access to records, and differential access is the main theme of welfare geography, which focuses on the equity or inequity of spatial distributions of goods (cf. Smith, 1977). In this sense, although the claim is novel, many information professionals deal in *applied welfare geography,* and the time may be ripe to bring the research techniques and concepts of that field to bear on IS and L&IS. If this is done, ideas associated with *degrees of publication* will very likely be central.[11]

By their very nature, records raise questions of access. In many cases, the decision is that *anyone* should be able to get a copy, which is tantamount to a decision to publish. In many more cases, publication is seen as premature or

---

[11] Geographic treatments of library services have appeared sporadically in the literature since Louis Round Wilson's *The Geography of Reading* (1938); see, for example, Palmer's (1981) review. But the geography of *publication* is still inchoate, despite the availability, in various online databases, of information from which maps could be made. Recall again the notion of mapping Popper's World 3 objects onto World 1.

undesirable or permanently unsuitable. (This may go without saying, or someone may decide.) While "unpublished vs. published" is a serviceable distinction, there is actually a continuum of states. *Unpublished* records range from ultra-secret documents through items that, while not secret, are too limited in interest ever to publish (inventory figures; last week's grocery receipts) through items on their way to publication or borderline cases (such as a large company's manuals). Control of this sector of external memory is largely given to IS, which, as noted, organizes unpublished records on behalf of people in organizations. Computers and private telecommunications are central to this effort, but many unpublished organizational records are still in older media, such as print or typescript, and they, too, may be organized for access by IS—or by archival science.

Whether printed, Xeroxed, or electronically stored, *published* records range from items copied a few times, neglected and obscure, to "ordinary" publications; thence through mass-circulation magazines and best-sellers trumpeted worldwide, to works enshrined at the center of cultures, like the Bible or the Koran. "Publication," moreover, should connote not only books and serials, but other kinds of records such as films, pictures, sound recordings, online databases, and computer software. In a sense, the ability to tape radio or television programs and Hollywood movies off the air makes publications of these as well. (Movies and some radio and television shows are also published now in the strict sense, since it is possible for anyone to buy a copy on cassette.) Beyond publication are television broadcasting and, for movies, theatrical display—technologies that do not leave physical copies, but that are even more powerful in giving whole nations access to certain records. The latter achieve the same end as furnishing multiple copies of publications by multiplying the number of places in which a single copy may be received. In this sense they simply add places to the geography of access, and any account of external memory must include them.

LIBRARY SCIENCE, INFORMATION SCIENCE, LIBRARIANSHIP

Just as the distinction between *unpublished* and *published* records separates information systems from L&IS, so the distinction between *literatures* and *collections* separates information science from library science. Unpublished and published records, however, are largely disjoint sets, whereas literatures and collections are simply different ways of partitioning the same set—of publications. Both literatures and collections, moreover, are represented in the same way—as files of bibliographic data. Hence, unless one is interested in nuance, it makes sense to run library science and information science together as the ungainly "L&IS."

As a field of applied knowledge, L&IS is above all concerned with uses of bibliographic data—in a nutshell, with *bibliographic modeling of human interests.* That, at least, is its distinctive intellectual terrain, to which much space has been devoted in this book. Since publication is a human institution (in the sociological sense), and since libraries are a part of that institution, both can be studied with methodologies drawn from virtually all the social sciences (including history). There is a large, shaggy literature attesting to this in the Z's of academic library stacks. This, too, can be called L&IS if one wants to be inclusive.

It is tempting simply to equate the "library science" in L&IS with librarianship; many do. The composite L&IS can be distinguished from librarianship, however. (I have not been scrupulous in doing so above.) It is useful to think of L&IS as a *discipline*—a body of knowledge taught in established schools and added to by published research—and of librarianship as a *practice*. Librarians learn some L&IS (e.g., techniques of managing and using publications) during their pre- and post-professional training. But, as professionals, most of them do not produce new knowledge in the manner of natural or social scientists, and their stock of existing knowledge is widely— and probably justly—believed to be for the most part commonsense. (For these reasons, "library science" falls on some ears as a euphemism similar to "domestic science" or "mortuary science.") Most librarians, moreover, read little of the L&IS research literature once they are finished with school. But that is because *they do not need to;* or, as they would claim, because it does not tell them what they need to know. Librarianship is a world of practical service; it involves the management of real collections on behalf of real people in an environment that is endlessly political. The mandate of librarians to keep certain segments of external memory alive is essentially a political task, calling for knowledge that is ethical and situation-specific, rather than technical and general in the style of L&IS research. Aside from their bibliographic expertise, the "science" of working librarians is mostly *policy,* expressed as codes and conventions, budget requests and justifications, plans, statements of local procedure, and normative articles in their own press (saying what "should" or "ought to" be).

There is, nonetheless, a body of research that could be called "library science" (as opposed to librarianship) in a fairly strict sense. I have in mind various quantitative studies (often surveys) of the use of library catalogs, collections, and services. While often specific to particular libraries, these studies also contribute to a generalizing science. Collections, after all, are simply those parts of literatures that libraries own, and it is not surprising that they have much in common with literatures as objects of study, or that library science and information science uncover similar patterns (see, for example, Metz, 1983).

Literatures can be identified in many ways—for example, by language, national origin, form or genre, or citation linkages. Probably the most important for information science is by subject. All of these are ways of *remembering* individual writings, and of *answering questions* about them— particularly of forming useful subsets in response to some person's request. Put another way, they are ways of indexing writings so as to facilitate retrieval. (A major goal in information science has always been to understand indexing and retrieval in sufficient detail so as to *automate* as much of them as possible.) One can also discover properties of publications aggregated in various ways—for example, growth rates, citation rates, distributions of indexing terms within subsets. Note that these concerns bear on the *management of publications in the aggregate,* and have little to do with readers' responses—aesthetic, critical, or otherwise—to particular writings. This sharply sets off information science from other sciences and humanities, in which the focus is on response to individual texts.

The other essential thing to grasp about literatures is that, once defined by means of standard categories of bibliographic data, such as subject headings, they can be studied independently of where physical copies of the constituent writings are held. Information science has no responsibility for copy provision; librarianship does. Similarly, information science may shift its focus from literatures to people as users of literatures (and of other sources of information) without considering them as patrons who have to be served. It largely escapes the ethical and political problems inherent in librarianship, such as devising and implementing the systems by which public copies may be shared.

INFORMATION SPECIALISTS AND EXTERNAL MEMORY

Against this backdrop, it is fairly easy to characterize typical information specialists and to set them apart from others. Information specialists are persons whose own memories are fused with external "memory control systems" for publications—with bibliographies, indexes, and indexical works such as are often found in libraries. (Libraries of course also house the "memories" themselves—the pieces of discourse, sound, and imagery that these "memory control systems" retrieve.) While most information specialists are expert users of libraries, and acknowledge L&IS rather than IS as their parent discipline, they are not necessarily librarians: only some develop or record or interpret a collection in a particular setting. Others retrieve items from literatures or contribute various bibliographic statements in settings outside libraries. In any case, the great majority are practitioners who find and marshal existing publications, rather than researchers who publish new opinions and knowledge claims.

Since persons from many walks of life know something about finding, acquiring, and using publications, information specialists are sometimes said to lack one of the marks of professional status, a distinctive knowledge-base. However, information specialists are *quite* distinctive in the degree to which they have assimilated memory-control systems known only sketchily to others, and in their appetite for assimilating more. In a real sense, they are enamored of making external memory work by means of their own relational powers. This predilection, however, would not set them altogether apart from scholars such as historians. What further differentiates them is their willingness to invoke the contents of external memory *at the request of other persons*. To do so successfully, they need not only broad culture but a fund of intellectual sympathy, so as to be able to act on behalf of many different questioners. The corollary is a selflessness that is hardly universal among those who might otherwise be adept at information work. Hence, if you have ever been served by a good information specialist (too few have), you know it: it is a distinctive experience.

It is also just as well that they are willing to serve, since external memory is far from being an autonomous source of answers—records are not yet, and may never be, within the ken of artificially intelligent beings, such as C-3PO, with whom one can converse and who even initiate conversations. The memories stored in records can only "speak" or "answer" when powers of understanding have been supplied by the questioners themselves or by intermediating information specialists. These powers are notoriously difficult if not impossible to externalize. It is not likely we will soon see a machine that combines vast stores of recorded content with the ability to answer questions like "Are there any *funny* mistakes in your records?"[12]

What can be foreseen is an evolving partial union of external memory, artificial intelligence, and time-honored human capabilities, with occasional advances in what is possible. It seems fairly certain that these advances will not, by and large, generate systems that can guarantee information in Wilson's strong sense—that is, that can reliably separate true statements from everything else that external memory contains.

In certain highly constrained domains it may indeed be possible for information systems to deliver "the truth, the whole truth, and nothing but the truth," like someone on the witness stand. But, as I have noted, most so-called information systems are really just content-delivery systems. Incorporating human information specialists into them does not necessarily change them for the better, because the specialists themselves often cannot distinguish truth from the many varieties of non-truth. Information specialists are really just adepts in tapping external memory, not in converting what

---

[12] See Dreyfus's (1979) *What Computers Can't Do*. Dreyfus's position is caricatured in Casti's (1989) otherwise laudable summary of the debate on whether machines can think.

they find into critically evaluated intelligence. What they deliver is "information" in Wilson's weak sense—content that may or may not be truthful.

The courtroom formula for getting the truth from witnesses also sheds interesting light on information specialists' ability to retrieve *relevant* publications. In the ideal literature search, all relevant documents in the literature are retrieved (perfect recall), and no irrelevant documents are retrieved (perfect precision). But this is exactly like the injunction to tell the whole truth (perfect recall) and nothing but the truth (perfect precision). Except in very limited domains, it cannot be done, by information specialists or anyone else. Just as what is delivered may or may not be true, it also may or may not be relevant.

INFORMATION STUDIES, TRACY AND HEPBURN

A quick way to explore internal-external memory relations is to watch a 1957 movie now available on videotape: *Desk Set* (1990). Set principally in the library of a broadcasting corporation in Manhattan, it stars Katharine Hepburn as an information specialist and Spencer Tracy as a "methods engineer"—we might now say an information systems designer. (External memory reveals that, in 1957, Hepburn was 50 and Tracy, 57; casting them as romantic leads made this movie, even then, mildly embarrassing to watch. Given the lines and the plot, Doris Day and Rock Hudson would have been about the right ages for the parts.) The conflict is between lovable Kate and the unlovable computer (Emmarac or "Emmy") that Tracy wishes to install, complete with officious female operator, in the library. Originally *Desk Set* was a 1954 Broadway comedy by William Marchant, and in both play and movie the computer is now quaintly large. Libraries, on the other hand, look much the same.

Insofar as it is not about snagging a man, *Desk Set* is about memory, aided and unaided. The title is a punning allusion to the department's female reference librarians, who use traditional look-up skills. Hepburn, their chief, has a scrapbook mind and an excellent natural memory—for example, she can recite *Hiawatha* on request, and knows by heart the names of Santa's reindeer (one of her reference questions). In a scene with Tracy it becomes apparent that she "chunks"—that is, retains small details by seeing them as higher-level patterns with mnemonic associations. "I associate many things with many things," she says. Having taken "a library course at Columbia," she also knows sources. (The *Times* index, the *Farmer's Almanac*, and the Bible—"Book of Amos, Chapter One"—are mentioned.)

Tracy, in contrast, has the memory of an engineer. Possessed of "a Ph.D. in science from MIT," he seems to have credentials in systems analysis, computer programming, operations research, and psychological testing, but when he tries to answer the reindeer question, he mixes up their names with those of the Seven Dwarfs. He is shown to be absent-minded, too. Apparently he welcomes computerized information retrieval because (like his real-life counterparts) he does not know or cannot believe that people like Hepburn exist. In the play (Marchant, 1956), his character classifies hers on a intelligence scale that includes "Slow—Alert—Totally Receptive—Total Recall," and concludes that she belongs in the final category, "Freak."

Tracy represents the technocratic faith in mechanization of human powers; Hepburn, the rival faith in cultural literacy and common sense. (Even today, most reference librarians would feel closer to her than him.) They must get together in the end, of course; Tracy proposes marriage. The larger implication is that each has something the other lacks: librarianship must marry computerized information science to become newfangled L&IS and, eventually, information studies.

It turns out that Tracy does not see his "electronic brain" as replacing the librarians (their great fear)—merely as freeing them to answer more complex questions. (I have used the same line myself in proposing the expert system Refsearch.) Hepburn, for her part, knows the machine cannot replace her as the spirit of the library, even though it has been fed, on punched cards, the texts of all the reference books. "There are too many cross-references in this place," she says; she and her staff are walking indexes no machine can match. Her foil is not so much Tracy—he must remain sympathetic—as prissy Miss Warriner (played by Neva Patterson), who is devoted to the computer but who, like Tracy, lacks a powerful, cross-referenced memory. She is more concerned with protecting the machine from cigarette smoke and dust. Miss Warriner is Emmy's "human element."[13]

In a fact-retrieval contest, librarians vs. computer, Emmy wins the first round by answering in a few seconds a question that took the staff weeks to answer: the annual damage done by the spruce budworm to American forests. While Hepburn, who has a head for figures, can remember the amount in dollars, the computer gives the cost down to the last cent, thereby proving but not endearing itself as a calculator. But on the next two questions, Miss Warriner's search strategies are wrong. Asked whether the king of the Watusi drives an automobile, she ANDs the name of this African tribe with "king" and gets a review of *King Solomon's Mines,* an MGM movie in which the Watusi are featured. (Hepburn recognizes the false drop the

---

[13] Marriage is the stereotypical mark of success in this comedy. Marchant (1956) writes in his stage directions: "Miss Warriner is not yet thirty, and she is modishly dressed in a gray suit but a certain brisk efficiency in her demeanor suggests that a permanent spinsterhood is most certainly to be hers." In the play Tracy's chararcter calls Hepburn's at one point "an unreconstructed old maid." One of her loyal staff members then calls him a "robot"—the most devastating rejoinder she can think of.

instant she hears the citation, and knows how to correct it.) Asked next for all available information on Corfu, Miss Warriner guesses "Curfew" and retrieves a definition of the word. (RESPELL, as Bates would say; but even "Corfu" might not avail, since some reference books now call this Greek island Kérkira or Kérkyra.) Another librarian (played by Joan Blondell) triumphantly produces the Corfu data from a book, while Hepburn chants "Curfew Shall Not Ring Tonight," the full text of which the computer has also retrieved. Miss Warriner leaves in a tizzy as Emmy burbles, flashes lights, and spits punched cards and printout. External memory is only as good as the internal memory it is paired with.

Moments later Hepburn tries her own online search in response to the question "What is the total weight of the earth?" Suddenly displaying powers far beyond those of any machine today, Emmy responds with an ominous gag-line: *"With or without the people?"* Another computer in the payroll department has already mistakenly fired everyone by sending out pink slips with their Christmas paychecks. The 1950s message is clear: computers can take on a life of their own and are not to be trusted. But it is equally clear that, in accepting Tracy's proposal, Hepburn will become Emmy's new soul; everything is all right as long as the right information specialist—the right person—is in charge. Thus one might characterize Tracy's long-term goal—and the long-term goal of information studies—as the creation of systems that in some ways resemble Katharine Hepburn.

SIZES AND THE RESNIKOFF-DOLBY SCALE

Hepburn in her library, I in my office, even Vannevar Bush at his imaginary Memex—all of us are environed by records. Those in my home or office are organized by placements that over the years I have idiosyncratically devised. The "memory control memories" by which they may be found are *my* memories, *my* associations—a system only partially visible to or inferable by anyone else. (It was this personal associational system that Bush proposed the Memex should capture.) The degree of organization depends largely, of course, on the size of the set to be organized. For my 3.5-inch microcomputer disks, I have no system beyond labeling and so must flip through them every time I want something. While this is rather stupid—it is our old bugaboo *serial scan*—there are still few enough disks (40 or so) that I find it easier to flip than to arrange. But in any case, quick retrieval of anything depends on me—I am the *genius loci* here, as no doubt the reader is somewhere else.

The effect of collection size on "memory control memories" is crucial. In my office I store archival materials in labeled folders in 10 large filing drawers, and there are more folders for more-or-less "active" items in my desk drawers and on and around my desktop. I also have other archival caches around my office (looseleaf binders, magnetic tapes, old punched cards, computer printouts, computer manuals, publishers' blurbs, Xeroxed articles). All are indexed by my memory alone; and although I am at the point where I sometimes lose things or forget what I have, in the main the system works well enough, and I do not need externalized indexing for efficient retrieval. The books and journals on my shelves I know, too—some from years of use—so that the idea of recording their natures and locations in indexes outside my own memory seems a waste of time. Needless to say, I am the sole user of this collection, which another person, lacking an index, might view as impenetrable. The key fact about my books and journals, however, is that, even though they constitute the largest office collection in my college, they number less than 2,000. At that size, I can rely wholly on internal memory for their control, and in this I am no different from thousands of other professors, and millions of other people in offices.

Where, then, do *things change?* A striking answer has been set forth by Resnikoff and Dolby (1972), from whose study Figure 11.1 is adapted. In their abstract they write, "It is the purpose of this study to provide fresh insight into the nature of library problems by systematically studying the question of size in various information contexts." Their argument, which should be read in detail, equates levels of *average* collection sizes with powers of 30, thus:[14]

Level	Size	
0	30^0 =	1 volume
1	30^1 =	30 volumes, average size of an encyclopedia
2	30^2 =	900 volumes, average size of a personal library
3	30^3 =	27,000 volumes, average size of a junior college library [or a typical special library]
4	30^4 =	810,000 volumes, average size of a university library
5	30^5 =	24,300,000 volumes, average size of a [world-class] national library

Each level is an order of magnitude greater than the last, and each can be taken to represent a typical collection within a range of collection sizes at that level, as Figure 11.1 shows. For example, my collection of ca. 2,000 items is larger than a typical personal library (30^2 or 900 volumes), but definitely of the same order of magnitude, Level 2. *Things change,* or real qualitative differences are perceptible, as one reaches the point at which one

---

[14] Actually, the value is 29.55 or $(2e)^2$, where e is about 2.7183, the base of natural logarithms. Resnikoff and Dolby themselves often round it to 30, and, for journalistic purposes, I am presenting rounded approximations of all their values, including those in Figure 11.1. Where orders of magnitude are concerned, the discrepancies are small.

Figure 11.1   The Resnikoff-Dolby Scale

Number of Volumes

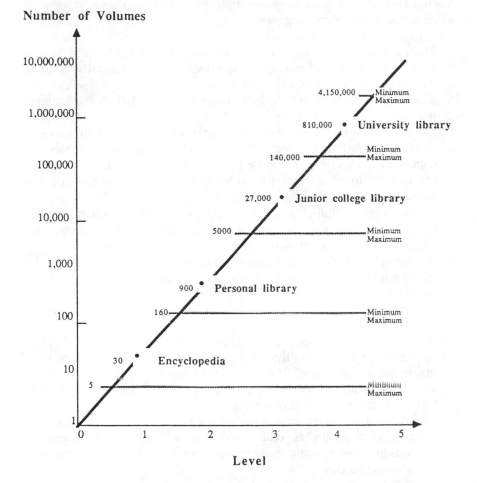

order of magnitude shades into another—the"maximum-minimum lines" of Figure 11.1.

For present purposes, the point of greatest change lies at the boundary of Levels 2 and 3, which marks the transition between personal libraries and what, generalizing Resnikoff and Dolby, I will call the "communal" libraries at the upper levels. This point corresponds to about 5,000 volumes—not too far above what I would get if I combined all the publications (books mainly) and all the file folders (or other archival "volumes") in my office. The 5,000-point would represent a large personal collection and a small communal collection. (For example, many elementary school libraries and children's departments in public libraries would exceed 5,000 volumes). Level 3 ranges from about 5,000 to about 140,000 volumes (Resnikoff & Dolby, 1972, p. 12.) Within Level 3 (and of course above it), some interesting things happen, all as consequences of increasing size:

- The collection no longer fits a "personal" space (such as a faculty member's office), and requires a space of its own, generally at some remove from the workplaces of its users.
- Economies of scale require maintenance of the collection for multiple users.
- "Memory control" of the collection can no longer be left to someone chiefly occupied with something else (such as a professor). "Memory control memories" must be lodged in external devices, such as catalogs and indexes. In other words, formal bibliographic control begins, complementing one's unaided powers of recollection.
- The prospect of multiple users (as opposed to one) necessitates explicit devices for controlling the indexing vocabularies, such as author and subject authority lists, thesauri, and classification schemes.
- Economies of scale dictate standardization of "memory control" devices—for example, uniform practices in cataloging, classification, indexing, and automation of bibliographic records across organizations.
- Librarians and information specialists emerge as full-time managers of "memory control."
- An alienation effect appears. Potential customers underuse the collection because of barriers both physical (e.g., distance) and psychological (e.g., unfamiliar or uncongenial indexing). When possible, they seek to stay within the smaller "shells" of external memory immediately around them—their personal collections and other persons.
- Librarians and information specialists try to counteract user alienation through such means as online retrieval services and bibliographic instruction. They become spokespersons for what others perceive as a labyrinthine machine.

The Resnikoff-Dolby scale suggests a way of relating collection size to human preferences—more abstractly, a way of relating external to internal memory. There seems to be considerable evidence that most persons do not want, or are not comfortable with, large "shells" of external memory around them. This would hold particularly for publications; somewhat less so for utilitarian unpublished records. People generally seek either to get rid of records or to abridge them. Failing those possibilities, they ignore them as much as they can. Essentially they are defending against information overload.

As far as books are concerned, the largest single category of people seem to prefer an environment of *none*. Many others will tolerate an environment of *one to a few.* For example, many persons in the U.S. have a Bible; it is also common to have a telephone directory, a cookbook or two, a book on childcare such as Dr. Spock's. Students typically have a small bundle of textbooks. Less common, but still fairly numerous are persons who own a multi-volume encyclopedia. ("We bought it for the children.") In the overall population, one would expect a fairly regular falloff of persons holding *x* books as one proceeded along a scale of personal collection size from 0 to 5,000. Those holding personal collections in the Level 2 range would be relatively few and disproportionately from the ranks of the college-educated (professionals, intellectuals, and the like); books after all are their badge.[15]

Even among bookish types, one would frequently encounter sentiment that the number of publications in any field is excessive. (I noted this tendency in discussing intellectual "thin men" above.) Desire for reduction by at least one order of magnitude is commonplace, and, for many persons, 30 is an upper, not a lower, limit to the items they want to examine. I am fairly sure, for example, that some scientists believe any collection of 900 volumes in their field could be reduced to a golden (if not Little Golden) encyclopedia of 30. Bates's choice of 30 in "the fallacy of the perfect 30-item search" (see Chapter 9) was not prompted by knowledge of the Resnikoff-Dolby scale, but it bespeaks an intuitive grasp of the same phenomenon. She of course was discussing literatures rather than collections, and her point was that, since many literatures are in fact larger than 30 items, searchers artificially cut to that number at their peril. But, far from being capricious, searchers do this *because* they sense about 30 items to be the maximum tolerable load on most customers' attention. Furthermore, what many customers really want is not 30 articles (let alone 900), but *one* article (a good review of the literature that summarizes all the rest); not 30 books, but *one* book (a single volume that tells them all they need to know). They want to go from Level 1 to Level 0 on the Resnikoff-Dolby scale.

---

[15] Wilson's (1977, pp. 94-99) interesting discussion of "studiousness" can be integrated with this account: "Those unwilling to study at all are studious in the degree zero. Those prepared to study a single source, but no more, are studious in the first degree. Those willing to use together any number of documents are studious, as we say, in the *n* th degree....A small number of people are highly studious, a large number are studious in the first degree, and a large number in the degree zero." It is slightly awkward that, in a power scale like Resnikoff and Dolby's, Level 0 corresponds to *one book* (30 to the 0th power is one), whereas Wilson's *degree zero* really means *no books*. That aside, the two accounts complement one another nicely. According to Wilson (pp. 94-95), the reason many people do not want to go beyond one book on a single subject is that, "If we use two sources together and both tell us the same thing, the second source has added nothing except, perhaps, a degree of confirmation. If the two tell us different things, however, the work of using them is greater than the work of reading and understanding the two, for the additional job of comparison, reconciliation, and decision of which to believe is added." A history of undone intellectual work lies in that last remark.

With regard to their use of bibliographies, Wilson might have been speaking of them in Chapter 10 when he urged, "A long and systematic search may be pointless, where a quick raid, getting out as fast as possible with a few references that may provide further leads, may be rewarding." So, too, even if they own a multi-volume encyclopedia or a multi-volume run of a serial, they very likely do not read it in its entirety, but "raid" it from time to time for what eventually amounts to about one volume's worth of materials. Again, the tendency is to want to go from "too many" items to one or a few (Level 0).

While 30 is not, of course, the upper limit to the number of items one can *learn*, it does seem a reasonable estimate of the mean number of items one comfortably *treats as individuals* in any current project. Perhaps it measures what we might call the typical "interest-span" for most persons: somewhere beyond 30, items tend to lose their individuality and blur into a mass. Resnikoff and Dolby (1972) note that the average class sizes in many schools tend to be around 30. The average number of bibliographic citations in scientific and scholarly papers is somewhat less. Slater (1981) says that a ratio of one information specialist to 30 users, while "mythical," has appeared in the literature for years as an ideal. The number of subdirectories that people maintain on microcomputers probably does not go much beyond 30 before they either literally reduce them or divide them "psychologically" into current vs. archival files. I observe that, among the file folders of papers on my desk, *one* occupies my attention at any given time, while the number I keep at hand for quick retrieval (on the desktop rather than in filing cabinets) is in the neighborhood of 30. Similarly, I observe that my personal collection of books is not at all monolithically on one subject, but breaks down into subcollections averaging 30 items for each of my interests (Japan, Russian literature, American studies, political science, human geography, and so on). This was not deliberate. Rather, it is as if there is a "natural" point to which I collect before an interest is satiated and tapers off.

These speculations about the psychological side of the Resnikoff-Dolby scale help to refine certain themes that have emerged from the foregoing chapters. It is now possible to move to a summary interpretation of what information specialists do, what distinguishes them as professionals, and why they are less successful than they would like to be. The account advances—but also squares with—the conventional wisdom about them and their potential customers.

INFORMATION SPECIALISTS AND REDUCTION OF OVERLOAD

For the great mass of people, external memory does not yet work very well, except as a bringer of mass entertainment, once they go beyond their personal systems. Rather than speaking to them like a counselor, it is simply "noise without signal" or, to use the other common metaphor, overload. As I said in Chapter 3, "the key variable differentiating people may be what brings [information overload] on, or the point at which one begins to feel it." Among people who have any publications around them at all, the great majority are comfortable only at Level 0 or Level 1 on the Resnikoff-Dolby scale. A smaller but still considerable group, essentially the educated elite, have personal libraries in the Level 2 range. The fascinating thing about information specialists is that they apparently are comfortable *at Level 3 and higher.* A collection of 27,000 items, the typical Level 3 communal library, does not faze them; indeed, they may feel reasonably familiar with a collection twice this size.[16] Moreover, they routinely deal with bibliographic files reflecting literatures or collections numbering in the hundreds of thousands and even millions.

Thus, the chief distinction of librarians and information specialists seems to be a high tolerance for what others call overload, and their chief professional claim is that they can reduce it to manageable proportions, not only for themselves but for others. As far as I know, research has never shown precisely why they possess their distinctive tolerance, nor the psychological mechanisms by which they cope with so much diversity. While there is anecdotal evidence that they have happy recollections of libraries from childhood (unlike many people), this could well be an effect rather than a cause. It seems likely that, where publications are concerned, they "chunk" in the manner of Hepburn's character in *Desk Set*—that is, retain detail by assimilating it into larger patterns. But are these "chunks" subject categories or something else? It would be wonderful if cognitive psychologists turned their attentions to this area. (Admittedly, it is closer to personality psychology than they like and may even involve affect.)

I would guess that if what information specialists do could be demystified, it would involve three main abilities, none exclusively theirs.

The first is the ability, won in part through browsing, to regard any large collection as hundreds of small, interesting subcollections. In other words, collections at Level 3 or higher are for them simply aggregates of companionable Level 1's. Many of these subcollections will contain items they have personally used and with which their intellectual lives are bound up, just as mine is with the books in my office. Of course, classification schemes such as Dewey and Library of Congress are *supposed* to partition large collections in just this way—supposed to bring them, regardless of size, down to comfortable subsets of Level 1 magnitude. But many people apparently find these schemes unhelpful (if they are aware of them at all), and critics have justly

---

[16] In this vein, it is interesting to take the collection size in a large library and divide it by the number of librarians who must interpret the collection to the public; results in the neighborhood of 50,000 volumes or more per librarian will not, I think, be uncommon.

faulted them on many counts for years. Amazingly, they seem to work for information specialists, perhaps because the latter's interests are so open that almost any deliberate grouping of works gives them a sense of buoyant serendipity, and they come to love what the categories bring them. They also, like Hepburn's character, come to associate "many things with many things" thereby counteracting some of the failures of classification schemes (and other indexing) to connect related items properly.

The foregoing ability is not really teachable, but a matter of temperament, personal cultivation, and gifts. However, to some degree it underlies skill in searching, which *is* teachable and whose nature has been at least broadly conveyed by this book. This second ability involves knowing how to reduce the complexity—the overload—of external memory through appropriation of "memory control memories" in the form of bibliographies and reference works, and to do it even when one is initially unfamiliar with their contents. Ideally, one not only knows how to find good instruments and bring them to bear in new situations; one has also come to believe, perhaps because of the first ability, that successful search is possible rather than unlikely. Such a belief, though obviously useful, is by no means shared by everyone. (Hence the science teacher's gibe, "Remember, kids, a month in the lab will save you an hour in the library.")

These first two abilities enable information specialists to perform their main task, which is *to move people quickly in the desired direction on the Resnikoff-Dolby scale.* (Information specialists would not put it this way, of course, but I think it useful to suggest the magnitudes involved. "Quickly" means "more quickly than the people could move themselves.") The desired direction will usually be *downward,* with the reduction from ca. 30 items to ca. one probably the most common partition of all. Much of this book has been about how external memory is designed to permit such partitioning operations, and how persons combine with particular tools to carry them out. In some cases the reduction will span several orders of magnitude, as when one moves from a Level 4 literature, such as everything in the ERIC database, to a list of 25 works on moral education for teenagers (Level 1), or from a Level 5 collection, like that of the Library of Congress, to a single family history (Level 0). Moreover, the Resnikoff-Dolby scale can be extended still lower (and in their presentation is), to incorporate access to *parts* of a single work through indexes or indexical arrangements, and so further reduce what is to be scanned or read. (One might move, for example, from the family history's index to a sentence on a particular ancestor). Conversely, it is sometimes desirable to move *upward* on the Resnikoff-Dolby scale, from smaller to larger sets of items, as when one scans the footnotes in a few scholarly papers to generate 25 related articles, or enlarges an online retrieval from 50 books on Utah to 800 through a more inclusive search strategy. This, too, the book has dealt with.

The third ability, sometimes based on a literature search, relates to a better way of reducing overload than merely decreasing the number of items to be read. That is *reducing them in length while preserving their intellectual content.* Compaction of this sort is not cost-free: someone must "ghost-read" items on behalf of others and then abstract or synthesize them. But the result is that others may absorb the content of many items in the time they would ordinarily spend on one. The various forms of compaction, such as abstracts, encyclopedia articles, and reviews of literatures, provide a way of moving down the Resnikoff-Dolby scale, perhaps by an order of magnitude or more, while retaining some of the information of higher levels; thus they are attractive to the many persons who find the original literatures excessively large. If information specialists have the necessary time, writing skills, and subject competence, they may be able to create useful compactions them-selves. It is more likely, however, that they will learn to find those already written by others. The provision of works that make the reading of additional or longer works unnecessary (because they are, in Bates's phrase, "func-tionally equivalent") is probably the most valuable service information specialists can perform. It is their third ability, as evidenced by the universal emphasis in their training on the forms of compaction, which have also been discussed at some length in this book.

CUSTOMERS AND THE REDUCTION OF OVERLOAD

To summarize, information specialists routinely filter publications on behalf of a clientele, perhaps rewriting them into the bargain. This is necessary because publications are an unusual resource: not only growing, but not consumed in use. In fact, publications can be thought of as consumers themselves, and what they consume is *us*—human attention. Plato, for example, is still consuming attention, yet neither he (as a body of writings) nor the ever-growing literature on Platonism is consumed. Yet we would consume a great deal of our lives if we tried to read it all. The total stock of attention in the world is finite. The total stock of expert attention—of highly trained, highly paid "heed"—is more limited still. Everyone needs strategies and tactics for conserving heed, a scarce (and, in the case of individuals, dwindling) resource. To do that, one needs a screening or filtering system that minimizes unnecessary reading.

It would seem, therefore, that information specialists' abilities should meet with approval—Herbert Simon's (1971), for example, when he claims that "An information-processing subsystem...will reduce the net demand on the rest of the organization's attention only if it absorbs more information previously received by others than it produces—that is, if it listens and thinks more than it speaks" (p. 42). While Simon's talk is a classic statement on information overload and attention as a scarce commodity, Russell Ackoff (1971) puts it even more plainly: "If...one sees the manager's information problem primarily, but not exclusively, as one that arises out of an overabundance of irrelevant information, most of which was not asked for, then the two most important fuctions of an information system become *filtration* (or evaluation) and *condensation*" (p. 265). These functions could be directly served by the abilities noted above.

Nevertheless, a common strategy for avoiding overload seems to be to avoid information specialists. Elsewhere in this book I have said they are "fat men" where others are "thin"; they lack a societal mandate to prescribe readings and so are only "ministerially relevant." The real problem may be that they are *neurologically different* from most of their potential customers— differently wired, so to speak—and that what seems a sharp reduction in overload to them remains for others an imposition. Information specialists think it useful to be able to reduce some large literature or communal collection to, say, a few items, but even that small set is dispensable to people who insist on the adequacy (if not superiority) of their own information systems—the shells of external memory they have personally gathered around them. While such insistence may come across as arrogance (ask any reference librarian), it is arrogance of a highly functional kind, intended to protect their own styles of conserving heed. (One may read it as a tripped circuit-breaker.) It is also an abiding part of their personalities, no more to be lightly changed by information specialists than membership in a church. I would imagine that converting most people to regular use of communal library services would be about as easy as making Catholics of Protestants, or vice versa. (Why else has more than one writer called for librarians and information specialists to be *missionaries?*) Many potential customers, it would seem, believe firmly in managing overload on their own.

Observations to this effect are provided by psychologist Karl E. Weick (1970), from whose pioneering essay on overload mangement in science the following tactics are adapted. (His account is much fuller and more complex.) Scientists—and most of the rest of us, too—cope by:

- Ignoring as much of the literature as possible. Generating one's own theories and attempting to confirm them rather than attempting to confirm the theories of others if the latter would enlarge the backlog of unread items.
- Relying as much as possible on peers and other human informants for word of new developments and for evaluations of what is important. Using personal contacts to avoid "print dependency."
- Equating what is read willingly with what is relevant. Reading, in effect, to discover relevance rather than to get through a list of titles deemed relevant in advance.

- Revising priorities on what to read, dropping or postponing an item whenever something more interesting appears.
- "Textbooking"—that is, mentally embedding "a fragmentary piece of information in a plausible body of related findings" (p. 101) that give it context and thus increase its retrievability. Akin to "chunking."
- Using secondary sources such as abstracts and review articles rather than the primary literature whenever possible.

This last tactic would seem to play to information specialists' strengths. However, it should not be forgotten that, in this relatively affluent time, many scientists and other professionals can buy secondary sources (and computerized literature searching) themselves, or have them supplied by their employers for direct, unmediated use. This does not mean, of course, that they have actually solved the problem of overload, any more than the persons who are willing to turn to information specialists. It merely means that they want to cope in their own way.

Such resistance militates against systems like H. G. Wells's (1938) "World Brain," which was to have been a gigantic organization of wise heads and learners on behalf of humanity, who would keep track of and synthesize the best that is known in every field and supply it to inform actions, especially by decision makers. Wells wanted his league of super information specialists to provide intelligence or popular science that, while of high quality, was brief enough to be absorbed by busy leaders or even the man in the street—a kind of customized encyclopedia in constant revision. The world did not have that in the 1930s, when he wrote, and it is no less utopian now. In 1970s dress, it reappears in Charles L. Bernier's plea for the establishment of "terse literatures" (Bernier & Yerkey, 1979). Bernier is more of a realist than Wells in that he does not presume eager receptivity to information services on the part of all potential customers. In fact, he states that *professing disbelief in the problem* is one of their chief ways of avoiding overload. (Like Weick, he also mentions ignoring the literature or *skipping.*) Typical dismissals he has heard include: "I am [already] educated." "The literature is junk." "I am keeping up." "It is a paper explosion rather than an information explosion." "My colleagues keep me informed." "By the use of my ingenuity, skill, wisdom, and hard work, I do not need to keep up." He is mainly quoting engineers, but his account independently reinforces Weick's. Unfortunately, his proposed solution—highly cogent, highly compacted literatures—has not yet caught on, and one may doubt whether it would overcome the resistance he so well characterizes, any more than Wells's idea of a "World Brain."

In truth, all such schemes to master external memory by distilling its essence seem destined to fall short. We are faced with something for which the social psychologists' term *selective attention* seems too mild. Something harsh and northern, like *heed guard*, better conveys the psychological visor through which people confront and screen external memory. While each person's visor may be unique in the full range of what it admits or blocks, ways of guarding heed probably fall into stable patterns. Aside from the legions who lack skill or interest in reading and so block out *anything* information specialists might do, there is an interesting minority whose resistance is principled: it may derive from a belief that, without subject competence to recognize what is wanted, information specialists will supply only more, not better, items. There is another interesting minority whose *receptivity* is principled, on the grounds that information specialists really do help them manage overload. Both are guarding their heed, but why they are so differently visored remains a mystery—part of the wider mystery of people's different styles in dealing with records.

A PARTITIONING SCHEME

As I look at the records around me, some basic distinctions emerge that suggest a final way to characterize the work of information specialists and the field of information studies. Let me start again in that well-worn place, my office.

It is usually easy for me to decide whether something has been published, despite gray areas in the continuum. Beyond this distinction, I can say whether I personally own an item and whether I am currently using it. The opposites, respectively, are "communal" ownership (for example, by the university that employs me) and archival status—items no longer in use but stored in case they should be wanted. These three dichotomies—unpublished vs. published, personal vs. communal, and current vs. archival—generate a scheme with eight categories when cross-tabulated as in Figure 11.2. With them I can classify all the records in external memory, whether they are at hand or various removes away. For example, this month's electric bill on my desk is unpublished, current, and all mine, whereas the files for the 1983 class of students in the college where I teach are unpublished communal property, stored archivally in the basement. Among the publications I own "archivally"—that is, have not read and am not currently reading—is *The Mill on the Floss* (will I ever?). If I display the ORBIT version of *Science Citation Index* on my modem-equipped microcomputer, I am calling a communal, published file into current use. And so on, through various "shells" of external memory around me.

Suitably glossed, Figure 11.2 yields a framework for constructing the house of information studies. Though of no particular depth, the scheme is unusually comprehensive in its implications. The next few figures reproduce it, with different substructures emphasized through arrows and shadings. The shadings represent stocks of records in various categories; the arrows, flows of records between stocks. Other details will be explained; but let me

Figure 11.2   Eight Categories for Describing Records

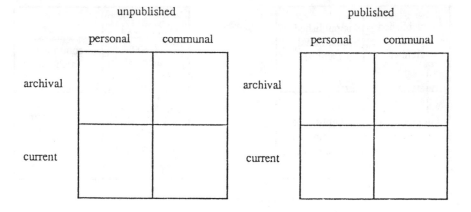

immediately illustrate the eight types of stocks with further examples, since the schematic language is rather glassy:

1. **Unpublished, personal, current:**   Active records in any home or personal office (e.g., unpaid bills, today's checks).
2. **Unpublished, personal, archival:** Inactive records in any home or personal office (e.g., old income tax forms, last year's checks, my album of baby pictures).
3. **Unpublished, communal, current:** Active records shared by persons in an organization (e.g., personnel files, inventory files, library circulation files).
4. **Unpublished, communal, archival:** Inactive corporate records of little historical interest (e.g., microfilmed library circulation files). But also, papers of important people or organizations saved for their historical value (e.g., the Theodore Dreiser papers, the archives of the Univesity of Pennsylvania).
5. **Published, personal, current:** Personally owned books, journals, software, etc., currently being read or used.
6. **Published, personal, archival:** Personally owned books, journals, software, etc., no longer being read or used.
7. **Published, communal, current:** Contents of newspaper and magazine stands, movie theaters, television channels. Contents of bookstores, record stores, software stores, video rental stores, and possibly of libraries, information centers, and clearinghouses. Contents of latest issues of subscription periodicals and latest updates to published databases. Contents of current bibliographies.
8. **Published, communal, archival:** Contents of library stacks. Older segments of databases.

Figure 11.3.   Personal Information Systems

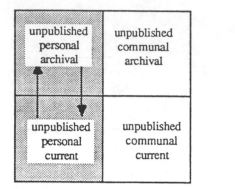

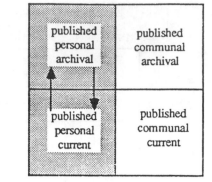

The View from Anyone's Office

Figure 11.3 recapitulates my—or anyone else's—office system insofar as personally owned records are concerned. It is also a reminder that, in any account of external memory, personal infomation systems are a good place to start.[17] Figure 11.3 shows the circulation of unpublished and published records from current to archival status and back. As noted, there are always some books and other publications that I am currently reading, and some files of unpublished materials—letters in draft, students' papers, computer printouts, etc.—receiving my active attention. At any given time, I know which items are current and which are not, although nothing shows it beyond occasional faint "positioning" in the space of my office. When most publications lose currency, they are simply returned to my shelves, where they may sit for years. Unpublished items are either destroyed or placed in files I consider "psychologically remote." The upward arrows in Figure 11.3 reflect these moves to archival status, connoting lessened attention. The downward arrows convey the fact that archival status is not necessarily permanent, and that items are sometimes recalled into current use.

The category of unpublished, personal, current records also contains another sort of materials—those created in order to be published. That is the state of the manuscript now before me, which the reader will see as *For Information Specialists,* and the state of all individually authored works while they are in draft. Figure 11.4 is a simplified diagram of one of the central concerns of this book—the publication process, in which intellectual

---

[17] On people as the all-important complement to records in personal information systems, see Wilson (1977, chap. 2).

products pass from their creators' personal attention to communal ownership and currency. The arrow's second origin at left is a reminder that many
works are communal rather than individual property even before they are
published—for example, books of corporate authorship, versions of symphonies by particular orchestras, and Hollywood movies. The lines the arrow
crosses may be thought of as editorial processes on the part of creators and
publishers—various decisions that produce the work that will finally be
released.

It is convenient that this scheme allows us to talk about both the state of
"non-publication," in which concerns such as privacy and security of records
may be important, and the state of publication, in which restrictions are
lifted and a recorded work is released to the world. Figure 11.4, incidentally,
is the only one in this set that shows the flow of records from *unpublished* to
published; the length of the arrow evokes (for me at least) the long task of
moving a work through the process. The arrow is also, of course, one-way:
once publication has been achieved, attempts to "de-publish" a work
through censorship (or even destruction of copies) almost never succeed.
Neglect is better; but republication—and hence renewed dissemination—is
always possible.

CURRENT VS. ARCHIVAL RECORDS

The distinction between unpublished and published records is clear enough,
and so is that between personal or communal ownership, if the latter is taken
to mean something like "held in common" or "available to multiple users."

Figure 11.4. The Publication Process

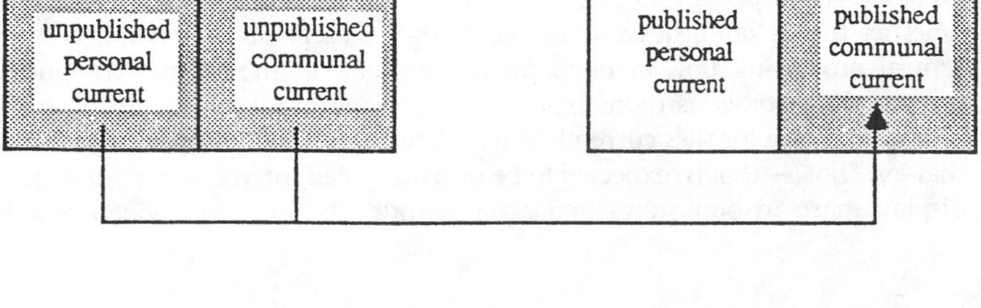

However, the "current vs. archival" distinction is vaguer and needs inter-preting before all three are used to describe the disciplines of information studies.

For a time records are new and, as such, the focus of whatever attention they initially receive; and then they are older and subject to whatever fate awaits them—lessened interest, a pattern of alternating neglect and revival, oblivion, and so on. I have called the first state *current* and the second *archival*. Respectively, these states bear some resemblance to short-term focal awareness and long-term memory (or permanent storage of learned items) in human beings. However, the time-scale of external memory is not what we as persons are used to—depending on the example we choose, something might remain unchanged in current display for several years; in archival display, for several centuries.

The currency of records under almost any definition will vary widely. Weather and traffic bulletins may change hourly. For serial publications, the term is generally announced on the cover—daily, weekly, monthly, quarterly, annually, and so on. (The real frequency of appearance may differ.) For many private documents such as letters or school notes, there is just one version, never updated; so is it for vast numbers of published documents, like novels. The matter is complicated because different copies of the same work can have different fates; some might be displayed as active while others have been relegated to deep storage.

Current records differ from archival in that they occupy the limited, central storage spaces to which maximum personal or societal attention can be devoted, and for which there is always competition. They are relatively easy to discover simply because they *are* in high-attention locales. (The latest *Time* magazine, the latest hit movie, tonight's offerings on TV are seemingly everywhere and very easy to find—until they disappear from privileged display.) Archival items are less easy to discover because they occupy a larger, more labyrinthine world, in which far more is hidden to the eye; hence the elaborate indexing systems needed to bring them forth. The ultimate limits on exposure in *current* external memory are set at any given time by the stock of human attention available, and that, as Herbert Simon notes, is always a scarce resource. There is less competition for archival space because, not claiming as much attention, there is incalculably more of it.

The limits on current display can be readily demonstrated. With un-published records, only so many can occupy prime storage space at a time, whether this is one's desktop, or the filing cabinets close at hand, or the central processing unit in one's microcomputer. In mainframe computer centers, disk storage is more expensive than tape precisely because it is so often the choice for files currently active. With published records, only those that are "hot"—that is, expected to be of widespread interest—get privileged display space in bookstores, magazine stands, record stores, video rental shops, software catalogs, and so on. (There are gradations, too, even in current displays; some items are highlighted more than others. The front page of today's newspaper makes a story more visible than an inner page; so does the back cover of this month's *Cosmopolitan* for an ad. Bookstores, record stores, video rental stores, libraries, etc., separate "new arrivals" from older shelf stock.) When newer items supervene, the older ones lose their prime positions. They are far from lost, of course—merely consigned to relatively unrestricted archival storage. (Deliberate purge, such as shredding or "deep-sixing," and accidental loss or destruction are other possibilities.)

Archival storage is inherently less "hot," less in the foreground of attention. This does not necessarily connote diminished value; it may simply mean "no longer new." Many important works exist for the most part archivally. (Here, too, gradations in currency are possible, from "most recent" shelf stock to "least recent" items in remote storage.) A typical pattern would be one in which works are periodically recalled from storage for users and then retired again, the whole cycle going on indefinitely. Some unpublished items have this kind of existence in single locations—that is, literal archives. Vast numbers of published items have it in multiple locations—the libraries and shops where they are dispersed as copies. There are also untold numbers of works in archives and libraries that are used seldom or never, though they are kept permanently available in case they are ever needed.

It may be hard to decide when a record leaves *current* for *archival* display. Nevertheless, for any recorded work, there is usually a point at which we can say that it has passed (or copies of it have passed) to permanent retention or to oblivion. For example, at some point most television shows no longer command air time, even as re-runs; they are either stored somewhere or lost. (Where is *Lost in Space* ?) Electronic records of prices in volatile markets—commodities, stocks, futures, etc.—often pass from current to archival status very quickly, but the transition can still be marked. The changeover point in the much slower-moving world of printed serials might come when recent individual numbers are bound as volumes or microfilmed. For books (or software, sound recordings, etc.) it might come when they are out of print—not available from publishers but only from libraries or second-hand dealers. For unpublished records (written or electronic) it arrives when they are literally relegated to personal or organizational archives. And so on. Even if it is difficult to judge the status of *all* copies of a work—they may simultaneously occupy *several* categories of Figure 11.2—we can almost always judge it for individual copies.

In these examples, the loss of currency usually involves moving a record physically to some other location, in order to retain it permanently. The item moved could be a work that has appeared in one version and remains unchanged (a novel, one's old class notes), an older version of a work

superseded by a newer (mail order catalogs, directories, military regulations), or past issues of a serial that are not necessarily superseded (many
scientific and scholarly journals, literary magazines, indexes). However, in
some cases the "relocation" model has become outmoded. With computer
technology, works such as directories need not be split between current
displays and relocated "back files." In machine-readable form, the starting
file can simply be updated or purged indefinitely to make one perennially
current work. The result, a bane to historians, is a work that leaves no
archival traces as it passes through time.

Talk of purging and updating brings us to a difficult area: the relation
between *currency* and *quality of content* in records. Presumably the ground for
purging something is that it is no longer of use (or an embarrassment); the
ground for updating is that missing or invalid data can be corrected. Broadly,
these are editorial powers. But who decides what to retain, and what to
purge or correct? In earlier terminology, who decides what external memory
should remember and forget so as to provide good answers? My discussion of
"currency" has been superficial, as if it were merely a matter of keeping track
of the *date* of records and calling the most recent version or update or
replacement "current." Indeed, that is all many records managers can do, so
swamped are they by the volume of material they must handle. As everyone
knows, however, the most recent version of anything is not necessarily the
best version. The best—the most truthful, accurate, profound, beautiful,
helpful, or whatever—may reside somewhere in archival storage, but may
still be *current* in the sense that nothing better has appeared. A valid
scientific claim published in 1948 is not superseded by a less valid claim
published in 1952.

To judge currency in this sense is the job of specialized human intelligence
in every field—people exercising whatever critical authority they can as
editors, reviewers, and revisers of their own work and the work of others. (I
am not suggesting that they literally have these titles.) Unfortunately, their
assessments of quality are hard to get except by word of mouth; records
deposited in external memory rarely come "pre-tagged" with them. There
are, it is true, critical reviews of various sorts to help one choose among
published (and, occasionally, unpublished) sources; but these in many cases
simply add to one's reading load without in fact answering the real
questions. Records disclose themselves only gradually. We must spend time
to get them to reveal their contents, just as we do with human beings. The
upshot is that, unless we know the best answer or source already, we cannot
quickly retrieve from external memory what we really want; it is simply not
indexed so that "the best," however defined, is readily discoverable. Only
persistent search, and the information specialist's or customer's good luck,
may avail.

Figure 11.5.   Interrelated Disciplinary Fields

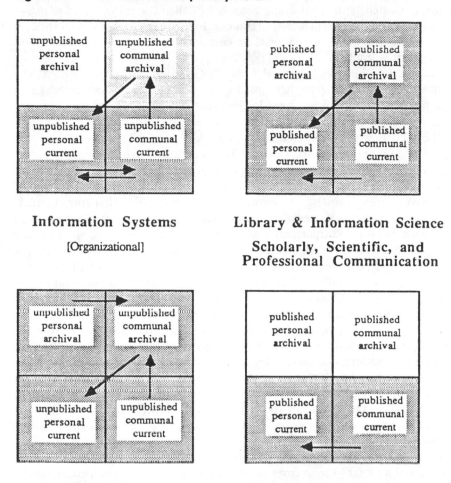

Information Systems
[Organizational]

Library & Information Science

Scholarly, Scientific, and Professional Communication

Archival Science

Mass Communications

FOUR INTERRELATED DISCIPLINES

Figure 11.5 uses the scheme to summarize some relations of information systems and library and information science with each other and with two associated fields, archival science and mass communications. All four are concerned with the content of external memory at a more concrete level than computer science and artificial intelligence. All four seek to understand specific content in relation to the interests and questions of persons. All four would benefit from a psychology of information-seeking styles, and all four are implicated with what might broadly be called the *psychology of editing*—that is, with problems of selecting content. In Figure 11.5, again, each time an arrow crosses a line, an editorial process such as filtering (acceptance and rejection) is implied.

There is, I believe, a general sense that the four fields are related. The intent here is to articulate that sense to the point where one can see why two or more of them might co-exist in the same college. However, by no means all of the possible relationships are captured by the diagrams or examples (the scheme is complex enough as it is).

Mass Communications. Three of the diagrams have a diagonal arrow implying movement of records from a communal archive to some person for current use. (Since the opposite process, return to the archive, seems relatively unproblematic, its arrow has been omitted.) This movement is classic information retrieval, and it is a major commonality of information systems, library and information science, and archival science. Single-arrow mass communications, in contrast, lacks the focus on problems of retrieval of "past" or "back" records. As an academic discipline it investigates the motivations that lead very large numbers of individuals to become publics or audiences, and the effects of transferring communal messages to their personal stocks in an eternal *now.* Because the messages have broad interest, are heavily publicized, and appear though well-known systems, the problems of "finding" them are relatively slight; in general, market forces will transfer them without massive index files or mediating information specialists.

The diagram has this as a transfer of *publications,* which would imply such things as newspapers, magazines, sound recordings, and trade books—a formulation that may seem too narrow. Mass communications deals with nothing if not radio, movies, and television, and these media transmit content directly to internal memory by means other than publication—that is, without the dissemination of copies. I would admit that the scheme is stretched a bit far here to cover all the mass media. As mentioned, however, since radio and TV programs can now be copied at home, they can be said to be published as well as broadcast, and movies are now published in ownable copies after (or sometimes without) theatrical release. In any case a field called information studies cannot fail to take all the important modalities of communication into account, even if it focuses on problems of information retrieval.

Scholarly, Scientific, and Professional Communication. The broad disciplinary area called communication is conventionally divided into two major sub-areas—mass communications and interpersonal communications—in its own scholarly press. However, there is a third important sub-area, scholarly, scientific, and professional communication, that overlaps library and information science. I have put it with the latter's diagram.

Mass communications is overwhelmingly oriented toward whatever news and entertainment are "uppermost" today. Scholarly, scientific, and professional communication differs in that it involves flows not only from publishers' and vendors' *current* stocks, but from *archival* stocks of literature—libraries—as well. In the language of information specialists, it may involve retrospective literature searches as well as current awareness services; it may involve fact-checking in older as well as newer sources. Also, the messages generally require more sophistication, more specialized training, to comprehend than those of mass communications, which are chosen to cut across all educational levels.

It is too bad, in a way, that one cannot call this sub-area elite communications, meaning those specific to occupational groups with relatively high levels of education. However, that name would connote political elites to some, and in any case, though neutral in intent, it would run afoul of levelers everywhere. So we may be stuck with the more cumbersome alternative.

Library and Information Science. Three of the cells in this diagram are shaded to imply record stocks of roughly equal importance. The arrow upward denotes the movement of publications from vendors' current stocks to archival status in libraries—essentially the editorial process of collection development.

This status need not connote mustiness. Many libraries offer publications (e.g., magazines, newspapers, and best-selling books) while they are still current in non-library channels. But libraries do connote lessened discoverability of records. Hence the presence of many indexing services and also of mediating information specialists, who try to make the public copies of publications more findable. "Obviously," write Egan and Shera (1952, p. 127), "mass communication has little or no use for bibliography, which is a means for locating a graphic record of the *content desired by the prospective receptor.*" Mass media content, they note, is controlled not by the receptor but by the communicator.

The arrow showing the transfer of publications from current communal to current personal stocks registers the important process of "keeping up." Libraries assist in this process for some, but of course they are not the only providers of current materials. It is worth pointing out that, as a discipline, library and information science is concerned not merely with the management of libraries, but with *the total publication process,* including non-bibliothecal channels such as journal subscription services, clearinghouses, and bookstores. (Recall, for instance, that "librarie" means "bookstore" in French.) There is a considerable literature in infomation science on how various professions get and use new information, much of which has been found to come from sources other than libraries. In fact, this literature established an important result that Figure 11.5 cannot even convey — namely, the primacy of informal *oral* channels in transmitting news and criticism before publication occurs.

It is also important, however, not to let informal "talk" overshadow the formal written record. Both are integral parts of a complex communication system. And since new publications do not always find their audiences unaided, information specialists can and do help the process with their current awareness and document delivery services. Respectively, these are services for delivering bibliographic news about new publications and then supplying copies on demand.

Information specialists of course play another role as well. The diagonal arrow refers to the transfer of "published, communal, archival" records—i.e., older library holdings—to current personal stocks. More than a century of information systems design in libraries has been devoted to making this transfer possible through self-service. But many potential customers, as we have noted, are not really capable of self-service; they regard archival external memory and its "memory control memories" as dauntingly complex. At the same time, publications are, broadly speaking, more important to society than unpublished materials; they have been more painstakingly judged and validated. For both reasons, information specialists have a societal mandate to assist in the process of finding and filtering older materials—that is, to be experts in retrospective literature searching and provision.

One last note: until records (old or new) are somehow empowered to speak their own contents, information specialists will be among those who serve as external memory's voice. In this, they re-embody the question-answering capabilities of the records' creators. Thus the "current, personal stock" to which answers are transferred may be one's own memory and the transfer, as indicated by the arrows, may be made directly by speech rather than writing. Someone recorded in a reference book that Neva Patterson played Miss Warriner in *Desk Set* (it is not evident in the credits), and years later that someone answered my question through a proxy—a reference librarian. But of course only a person with an information specialist's skills could have become that proxy and spoken on the original writer's behalf.

Information Systems. This diagram is intended to capture features of organizational information systems, primarily workplaces, which often exhibit the creation, alteration, and replacement of *unpublished* records at a relatively brisk rate. Generally, these systems are designed to solve problems in the interchange of current "in-house" information between personal and communal stocks.

The cell for communal archives has been lightly shaded to imply that, in organizations, they are generally less important than records in current status. The arrow upward reflects the retirement of once-current records, a routine organizational practice. Presumably, most of these records would have little or no historical interest; they are archived simply in case questions, problems, or lawsuits arise.

As implied by the diagonal arrow, retrieval from archives would consist of producing for current use such records as a 1980 student application, an employer's 1975 payroll deposits, or the microfilmed blueprints and specifications for a 1970 nuclear reactor. These correspond to information specialists' retrievals from published literatures. However, in many organizations, retrieval of unpublished archival records is not a full-time specialty but an ad hoc activity that depends on available indexing, which may be nothing more than the recollections of a secretary or clerk. On the other hand, a records manager or database administrator may have developed a fully externalized system and may function like an information specialist in it.

The flows shown by the arrows in this diagram are very similar to those in library and information science. The one difference is that current unpublished records flow in both directions, from personal to communal stocks and back. For example, the records manager in a college might create a class enrollment list in a university-wide database, retrieve it later to change the values in certain fields, and then return the amended file for further communal use. The relative ease with which in-house records may be created and altered, as well as received as output, is a distinctive feature of organizational information systems. The route to publication, as suggested by Figure 11.4, is more difficult.

Archival Science. While many non-current records will never again be consulted, certain archives exist to preserve unpublished materials that may eventually be published or at least read by biographers and historians. Such materials are in the purview of professionals whose discipline is archival science. Presumably the "memory control" they exert is somewhat more extensive than is usually the case with organizational records. (Since it is typically based on the records' provenance, it is also different from the subject and citation indexing used by librarians.) The main tasks of archivists are implied by the arrows: selecting materials for retention from current communal stocks (such as the minutes of committees) or from personal archival stocks (such as the papers of famous authors), preserving them physically, and then transferring them on demand, as the diagonal arrow indicates, to the current working collections of interested parties such as biographers. In the latter task they function much like information specialists.

CONCLUSION

Jointly, then, the diagrams of Figure 11.5 display the field of information studies, comprising disciplines whose subject matter is *external memory.* I argued earlier that library and information science and information systems complement each other in this union; it is no accident that both have been conjoined in the curricula of what once were simply "library schools."

Archival science can also readily be subsumed. Mass communications is a somewhat more difficult fit, particularly as it shades off into journalism in various media, but some of its research concerns, such as content analysis, are relevant to L&IS. Moreover, the sub-field I called scholarly, scientific, and professional communication has long been a concern in both L&IS and communications research, and observers in both fields have found theoretical and empirical connections.[18]

One final point needs emphasis. Information studies, however construed, must increasingly become a part of psychology. Figures 11.2 through 11.5, which apparently focus on records in various conditions, should be taken to imply *a total psychology of external-internal memory,* still far from being realized. While records are interesting units of analysis in their own right, the ideal unit of analysis would capture *the interaction of records and persons.* The arguments developed above, in which external information systems are seen as extensions of personal or social memory, are intended to suggest a framework in which such interaction can be studied. There have been contributions toward an interactive psychology—for example, research on why management information systems fail, on preference for oral sources (social memory) over written, on judging the relevance of documents to a request, on uses and gratifications of television viewing, on information overload (the volume by Havelock et al., 1971, provides an early synthesis)— but nothing yet has reached critical mass. The numerous researchers in cognitive psychology tend to be interested in processes at a less molar level than those seemingly at work when people interact with external memory. For example, since so many cognitive psychologists (not to mention AI researchers) shun the study of affect, there is not yet much useable work on *interests,* which emerge at the level of the whole person. Studies of cognitive styles, learning styles, selective attention and retention, and epistemic curiosity are in the right direction, but still rather jejune. We are dealing with nothing less than how people edit their worlds. This area lacks a name, but may be roughly co-extensive with what Jesse Shera (1968) called *social epistemology.* Its most wide-ranging theoretician now is Patrick Wilson, whose writings, listed in the bibliography, extend and deepen the interpretations of this book at almost every point.

---

[18] See, for example, Rice (1990), Paisley (1990), and the editor's introduction in Borgman's (1990) *Scholarly Communication and Bibliometrics.*

References

Ackoff, Russell. (1971). "Management Misinformation Systems." In *Information Technology in a Democracy*, Alan F. Westin, ed. Cambridge, MA: Harvard University Press. 264-271.

Adams, J. L. (1976). *Conceptual Blockbusting*. San Franciso: San Franciso Book.

Agee, James. (1964). *Agee on Film; Reviews and Comments*. Boston: Beacon Paperbacks.

Aluri, Rao, and Donald E. Riggs, eds. (1990). *Expert Systems in Libraries*. Norwood, NJ: Ablex.

Bates, Marcia J. (1976). "Rigorous Systematic Bibliography." *RQ* 16: 7-26.

Bates, Marcia J. (1977). "Factors Affecting Subject Catalog Search Success." *Journal of the American Society for Information Science* 28: 161-169.

Bates, Marcia J. (1979a). "Information Search Tactics." *Journal of the American Society for Information Science* 30: 205-214.

Bates, Marcia J. (1979b). "Idea Tactics." *Journal of the American Society for Information Science* 30: 280-289.

Bates, Marcia J. (1981). "Search Techniques." *Annual Review of Information Science and Technology* 16: 139-169.

Bates, Marcia J. (1984). "The Fallacy of the Perfect Thirty-Item Online Search." *RQ* 24: 43-50.

Bates, Marcia J. (1986). "What Is a Reference Book? A Theoretical and Empirical Analysis." *RQ* 26: 37-57.

Bates, Marcia J. (1987). "How to Use Information Search Tactics Online." *Online* 11: 47-54.

Bates, Marcia J. (1988). "How to Use Controlled Vocabularies More Effectively in Online Searching." *Online* 12: 45-56.

Bateson, F. W. (1965). *A Guide to English Literature*. Garden City, NY: Doubleday Anchor Books.

Belanger, Terry. (1977). "Descriptive Bibliography." In *Book Collecting; a Modern Guide*, Jean Peters, ed. New York: Bowker. 97-115.

Berlyne, D. E. (1963). "Motivational Problems Raised by Exploratory and Epistemic Behavior." In *Psychology: a Study of a Science*, Sigmund Koch, ed. New York: McGraw-Hill. v. 5: 284-364.

Berlyne, D. E. (1965). *Structure and Direction in Thinking*. New York: Wiley.

Bernier, Charles, and A. Neil Yerkey. (1979). *Cogent Communication; Overcoming Reading Overload*. Westport, CT: Greenwood Press.

Besterman, Theodore. (1965-66). *A World Bibliography of Bibliographies and of Bibliographical Catalogues, Calendars, Abstracts, Digests, Indexes, and the Like*. 4th ed., rev and enl. Lausanne, Switzerland: Societas Bibliographica. 5 v.

Blair, David C. (1980). "Searching Biases in Large Interactive Document Retrieval Systems." *Journal of the American Society for Information Science* 31: 271-277.

Bolter, J. David. (1984). *Turing's Man; Western Culture in the Computer Age*. Chapel Hill: University of North Carolina Press.

de Bono, Edward. (1969). *The Mechanism of Mind*. Baltimore, MD: Penguin Books.

Borgman, Christine L. (1990). "Editor's Introduction." In *Scholarly Communication and Bibliometrics*, Christine L. Borgman, ed. Newbury Park, CA: Sage. 10-27.

Boulding, Kenneth. (1961). *The Image; Knowledge in Life and Society*. Ann Arbor, MI: Ann Arbor Paperbacks.

Brookes, B. C. (1980). "Measurement in Information Science: Objective and Subjective Metrical Space." *Journal of the American Society for Information Science* 31: 248-255.

Buckingham, R. A., et al. (1987). "Information Systems Curriculum: a Basis for Course Design." In *Information Systems Education; Recommendations and Implementation*, Richard A. Buckingham et al., eds. Cambridge, UK: Cambridge University Press. 14-133.

Bush, Vannevar. (1945). "As We May Think." *Atlantic Monthly* 176: 101-108.

Carlson, G. (1964). *Search Strategy by Reference Librarians*. Final Report on the Organization of Large Files, Part 3. Sherman Oaks, CA: Advanced Information Systems Division, Hughes Dynamics.

Casti, John L. (1989). *Paradigms Lost; Images of Man in the Mirror of Science*. New York: Morrow.

Chomsky, Noam. (1959). "A Review of B. F. Skinner's *Verbal Behavior*." *Language* 35: 26-58.

Clapp, Verner W. (1974). "Bibliography." *Encyclopedia Americana*. v. 3.

Clark, C. H. (1958). *Brainstorming*. Garden City, NY: Doubleday.

Coates, E. J. (1960). *Subject Catalogues: Headings and Structure*. London: Library Association.

Collins, Randall. (1975). *Conflict Sociology; Toward an Explanatory Science*. New York: Academic Press.

Davinson, Donald Edward. (1980). *Reference Service*. New York: Saur.

Davis, Gordon B. (1987). "A Critical Comparison of IFIP/BCS Information Systems Curriculum and Information Systems Curricula in the USA." In *Information Systems Education; Recommendations and Implementation*, Richard A. Buckingham et al., eds. Cambridge, UK: Cambridge University Press. 134-145.

Desk Set . (1990). New York: CBS/Fox Company. (Videocasette release of a 1957 motion picture starring Spencer Tracy, Katharine Hepburn, Gig Young, Joan Blondell. Director, Walter Lang; producer, Henry Ephron; screenplay, Phoebe and Henry Ephron, based on the play by William Marchant.)

Donohew, Lewis, and Leonard Tipton. (1973). "A Conceptual Model of Information Seeking, Avoiding, and Processing." In *New Models for Mass Communication*

Research, Peter Clarke, ed. Beverly Hills, CA: Sage. (Sage Annual Reviews of Communication Research, v. 2). 243-268.

Doyle, Arthur Conan. (1986; many other eds. available). *A Study in Scarlet* in *Sherlock Holmes: the Complete Novels and Stories.* v. 1. New York: Bantam Classics.

Dreyfus, Hubert L. (1979). *What Computers Can't Do; the Limits of Artificial Intelligence.* Rev. ed. New York: Harper & Row.

Egan, Margaret E., and Jesse H. Shera. (1952). "Foundations of a Theory of Bibliography." *Library Quarterly* 22: 125-137.

Fenichel, Carol Hansen. (1981). "Online Searching Measures That Discriminate among Users with Different Types of Experience." *Journal of the American Society for Information Science* 32: 23-32.

Flanagan, John T. (1967). "American Literary Bibliography in the Twentieth Century." In *Bibliography; Current State and Future Trends,* Robert B. Downs and Frances B. Jenkins, eds. Urbana: University of Illinois Press. 214-236.

Gardner, Howard. (1985). *The Mind's New Science; a History of the Cognitive Revolution.* New York: Basic Books.

Garfield, Eugene. (1977-). *Essays of an Information Scientist.* Philadelphia: ISI Press. (A continuing series of collected reprints from his column in *Current Contents.)*

Garfield, Eugene. (1980). "The 250 Most-Cited Primary Authors, 1961-1975. Part II. The Correlation Between Citedness, Nobel Prizes, and Academy Memberships." In his *Essays,* v. 3 (1977-78), 337-347.

Garfield, Eugene. (1981). "The 100 Most-Cited Authors of 20th Century Literature. Can Citation Data Forecast the Nobel Prize in Literature?" In his *Essays,* v. 4 (1979-80), 363-369.

Haines, Helen E. (1935). "The Art of Annotation" in *Living with Books; the Art of Book Selection.* New York: Columbia University Press. (Chapter somewhat revised in 2nd ed., 1950.)

Havelock, Ronald C., et al. (1971). *Planning for Innovation through Dissemination and Utilization of Knowledge.* Ann Arbor: Center for Research on Utilization of Scientific Knowledge, Institute for Social Research, University of Michigan.

Hirsch, E. D. (1987). *Cultural Literacy; What Every American Needs to Know.* New York: Houghton Mifflin.

International Organization for Standardization. (1983). *International Standard ISO 5127/2: Documentation and Information—Vocabulary—Part 2: Traditional Documents.* 1st ed. Geneva, Switzerland: ISO.

Jahoda, Gerald. (1974). "Reference Question Analysis and Search Strategy Development by Man and Machine." *Journal of the American Society for Information Science* 25: 139-144.

Johnson, Thomas H. (1963). In *Literary History of the United States: Bibliography,* Robert E. Spiller et al., eds. 3rd ed., rev. New York: Macmillan.

Josel, N. A. (1971). "Ten Reference Commandments." *RQ* 11: 146-147.

Katz, William A. (1978). *Introduction to Reference Work,* 3rd ed., v. 1. New York: McGraw-Hill.

Keen, Peter G. W. (1987). "MIS Research: Current Status, Trends and Needs." In *Information Systems Education; Recommendations and Implementation,* Richard A. Buckingham et al., eds. Cambridge, UK: Cambridge University Press. 1-13.

Klapp, Orrin E. (1978). *Opening and Closing; Strategies of Information Adaptation in Society.* Cambridge, UK: Cambridge University Press.

Lancaster, F. Wilfrid. (1979). *Information Retrieval Systems: Characteristics, Testing and Evaluation.* 2nd ed. New York: Wiley.

Levine, Marilyn M. (1977). "The Informative Act and Its Aftermath: Toward a Predictive Science of Information." *Journal of the American Society for Information Science* 28: 101-106.

McArthur, Tom. (1986).*Worlds of Reference; Lexicography, Learning and Language from the Clay Tablet to the Computer.* Cambridge, UK: Cambridge University Press.

McInnis, Raymond G., and J. W. Scott. (1975). *Social Science Research Handbook.* New York: Barnes & Noble.

McLuhan, Marshall. (1964). *Understanding Media: the Extensions of Man.* New York: McGraw-Hill.

Machlup, Fritz, and Una Mansfield, eds. (1983). *The Study of Information; Interdisciplinary Messages.* New York: Wiley.

Marchant, William. (1956). *The Desk Set; a Comedy in Three Acts.* New York: Samuel French.

Markey, Karen, and Pauline A. Cochrane. (1981). *ONTAP Online Training and Practice Manual for ERIC Data Base Searchers.* 2nd ed. Syracuse University, ERIC Clearinghouse on Information Resources.

Martin, James. (1977). *Computer Data-Base Organization.* 2nd ed. Englewood Cliffs, NJ: Prentice-Hall.

Martin, Thomas Hughes. (1974). *A Proposed Ideology and Methodology for the Critical Information Scientist.* Ph.D. Dissertation, Stanford University.

Menzel, Herbert. (1959). "Planned and Unplanned Scientific Communication." In *Proceedings of the International Conference on Scientific Information.* Washington, D.C.: National Academy of Sciences, National Research Council. v. 1: 199-243.

Meredith, Joseph. (1971). *Reference Search System (Refsearch) Users' Manual.* Institute of Library Research, University of California, Berkeley. (ERIC Report ED 060 918).

Metz, Paul. (1983). *The Landscape of Literatures; Use of Subject Collections in a University Library.* Chicago: American Library Association.

de Mey, Marc. (1982). *The Cognitive Paradigm; Cognitive Science, a Newly Explored Approach to the Study of Cognition Applied in an Analysis of Science and Scientific Knowledge.* Dordrecht, Netherlands: Reidel.

Miller, G. A. (1968). "Psychology and Information." *American Documentation* 19: 286-289.

Minsky, Marvin. (1985). *The Society of Mind.* New York: Simon & Schuster.

Montgomery, Christine, and Don R. Swanson. (1962). "Machinelike Indexing by People." *American Documentation* 13: 359-366.

Needham, C. D. (1971). *Organizing Knowledge in Libraries.* 2nd rev. ed. London: Seminar Press.

Neill, S. D. (1982). "Brookes, Popper, and Objective Knowledge." *Journal of Information Science* 4: 33-39.

Osborne, Charles. (1979). *W. H. Auden; the Life of a Poet.* New York: Harcourt Brace Jovanovich.

Paisley, William. (1990). "The Future of Bibliometrics." In *Scholarly Communication and Bibliometrics*, Christine Borgman, ed. Newbury Park, CA: Sage. 281-299.

Palmer, E. Susan. (1981). "The Effect of Distance on Public Library Use: a Literature Survey." *Library Research* 3: 315-354.

Patterson, Margaret C. (1983). *Literary Research Guide*. 2nd ed. New York: Modern Language Association.

Polya, G. (1965). *Mathematical Discovery*, v. 2. New York: Wiley.

Popper, Karl R. (1972). *Objective Knowledge: an Evolutionary Approach*. Oxford, UK: Clarendon Press.

Preminger, Alex. (1967). "English Literature." In *Bibliography; Current State and Future Trends*, Robert B. Downs and Frances B. Jenkins, eds. Urbana: University of Illinois Press. 186-213.

Prentky, Robert A. (1980). *Creativity and Psychopathology; a Neurocognitive Perspective*. New York: Praeger.

Prytherch, Ray. (1984). *Harrod's Librarians' Glossary of Terms Used in Librarianship, Documentation, and the Book Crafts*. 5th rev. ed. Aldershot (Hants.), UK: Gower.

Ranganathan, S. R. (1961). *Reference Service*. 2nd ed. London: Asia Publications, 1961.

Resnikoff, H. L, and J. L. Dolby. (1972). *Access; a Study of Information Storage and Retrieval with Emphasis on Library Information Systems*. Final Report. Los Altos, CA: R and D Consultants Co. (ERIC Report ED 060 921).

Rice, Ronald E. (1990). "Hierarchies and Clusters Among Communication and Library and Information Science Journals, 1977-1987." In *Scholarly Communication and Bibliometrics*, Christine Borgman, ed. Newbury Park, CA: Sage. 138-153.

Roszak, Theodore. (1969). *The Making of a Counter Culture; Reflections on the Technocratic Society and Its Youthful Opposition*. Garden City, NY: Doubleday Anchor Books.

Roysdon, Christine, and Howard D. White, eds. (1989). *Expert Systems in Reference Services*. New York: Haworth Press. (Also issue 23 of *The Reference Librarian*).

Rugh, Archie G. (1975). "Toward a Science of Reference Work: Basic Concepts." *RQ* 14: 293-299.

Sheehy, Eugene P. (1986). *Guide to Reference Books*. 10th ed. Chicago: American Library Association.

Shera, Jesse H. (1968). "An Epistemological Foundation for Library Science." In *The Foundations of Access to Knowledge; a Symposium*, Edward B. Montgomery, ed. Syracuse, NY: Syracuse University Press.

Simon, Herbert A. (1971). "Designing Organizations for an Information-Rich World." In *Computers, Communications, and the Public Interest*, Martin Greenberger, ed. Baltimore, MD: Johns Hopkins Press. 38-72 (includes remarks by discussants).

Simon, Herbert A. (1981). *The Sciences of the Artificial*. 2nd ed., rev. and enl. Cambridge, MA: MIT Press.

Slater, Margaret. (1981). *Ratio of Staff to Users; Implications for Library-Information Work and the Potential for Automation*. London: Aslib. (Aslib Occasional Publication 24; British Library Research and Development Report 5627).

Smith, David M. (1977). *Human Geography: a Welfare Approach.* London: Edward Arnold.

Standera, O. R. (1978). "Some Thoughts on Online Systems: the Searcher's Part and Plight." In *Proceedings,* American Society for Information Science, v. 15. White Plains, NY: Knowledge Industry Publications. 322-325.

Stiffler, Stuart A. (1972). "A Book Is a Book Is a Reference Book." *RQ* 11: 341-343.

Strong, William S. (1990). *The Copyright Book; a Practical Guide.* 3rd ed. Cambridge, MA: MIT Press.

Swanson, Don R. (1986). "Undiscovered Public Knowledge." *Library Quarterly* 56: 103-118.

Swanson, Don R. (1990). "The Absence of Co-Citation as a Clue to Undiscovered Causal Connections." In *Bibliometrics and Scholarly Communication,* Christine Borgman, ed. Newbury Park, CA: Sage. 129-137.

Tanselle, G. Thomas. (1977). "Descriptive Bibliography and Library Cataloguing." *Studies in Bibliography,* v. 30. Charlottesville: University of Virginia Press. 1-56.

Taylor, Margaret T., and Ronald R. Powell. (1985). *Basic Reference Sources.* 3rd ed. Metuchen, NJ: Scarecrow Press.

Tuchman, Barbara W. (1984). *The March of Folly: from Troy to Vietnam.* New York: Knopf.

U.S. National Science Board. (1969). Special Commission on the Social Sciences. *Knowledge into Action: Improving the Nation's Use of the Social Sciences.* Washington, D.C.: National Science Foundation.

Walford, Albert J. (1980-87). *Guide to Reference Material.* 4th ed. London: Library Association. 3 vols.

Weick, Karl E. (1970). "The Twigging of Overload." In *People and Information,* Harold B. Pepinsky, ed. New York: Pergamon. 67-129.

Wells, H. G. (1938). *World Brain.* Garden City, NY: Doubleday, Doran.

White, Howard D. (1977). "Numeric Data Files: an Introduction." *Drexel Library Quarterly* 13: 1-20.

White, Howard D. (1990). "Author Co-Citation Analysis: Overview and Defense." In *Scholarly Communication and Bibliometrics,* Christine Borgman, ed. Newbury Park, CA: Sage. 84-106.

White, Howard D., and Katherine W. McCain. (1989). "Bibliometrics." *Annual Review of Information Science and Technology,* v. 24. Amsterdam: Elsevier. 119-186.

White, Howard D, and Diana Woodward. (1990). "A Model of Reference Librarians' Expertise: Reviving Refsearch on a Microcomputer." In *Expert Systems in Libraries,* Rao Aluri and Donald E. Riggs, eds. Norwood, NJ: Ablex. 51-63.

Williams, William Proctor, and Craig S. Abbott. (1985). *An Introduction to Bibliographical and Textual Studies.* New York: Modern Language Association.

Wilson, Louis Round. (1938). *The Geography of Reading; a Study of the Distribution and Status of Libraries in the United States.* Chicago: American Library Association and University of Chicago Press.

Wilson, Patrick. (1968). *Two Kinds of Power; an Essay on Bibliographical Control.* Berkeley, CA: University of California Press. (University of California Publications in Librarianship: 5)

Wilson, Patrick. (1973). "Situational Relevance." *Information Storage and Retrieval* 9: 457-471.

Wilson, Patrick. (1977). *Public Knowlege, Private Ignorance; Toward a Library and Information Policy.* Westport, CT: Greenwood Press.

Wilson, Patrick. (1978). "Some Fundamental Concepts of Information Retrieval." *Drexel Library Quarterly* 14: 10-24.

Wilson, Patrick. (1983a). *Second-Hand Knowledge; an Inquiry into Cognitive Authority.* Westport, CT: Greenwood Press.

Wilson, Patrick. (1983b). "Pragmatic Bibliography." In *Back to the Books: Bibliographic Instruction and the Theory of Information Sources,* Ross Atkinson, ed. Papers of the Bibliographic Instruction Section, Association of College and Research Libraries, 101st annual conference. Chicago: American Library Association.

Wilson, Patrick. (1986). "The Face-Value Rule in Reference Work." *RQ* 25: 468-475.

Winchell, Constance M. (1967). *Guide to Reference Books.* 8th ed. Chicago: American Library Association.

Woodcock, George. (1962). *Anarchism; a History of Libertarian Ideas and Movements.* New York: Meridian Books (World Publishing Co.).

Yates, Francis A. (1966). *The Art of Memory.* Chicago: University of Chicago Press.

Young, Heartsill, ed. (1983). *ALA Glossary of Library and Information Science .* Chicago: American Library Association.

Young, J. Z. (1971). *An Introduction to the Study of Man.* New York: Oxford University Press.

Ziman, John. (1968). *Public Knowledge; an Essay Concerning the Social Dimension of Science.* Cambridge, UK: Cambridge University Press.

Author Index

Subject Index